Competition Law in China

Competition Law in China

Laws, Regulations, and Cases

Peter J. Wang, Sébastien J. Evrard,
Yizhe Zhang, and
Baohui Zhang

OXFORD
UNIVERSITY PRESS

OXFORD
UNIVERSITY PRESS

Great Clarendon Street, Oxford, OX2 6DP,
United Kingdom

Oxford University Press is a department of the University of Oxford.
It furthers the University's objective of excellence in research, scholarship,
and education by publishing worldwide. Oxford is a registered trade mark of
Oxford University Press in the UK and in certain other countries

© Oxford University Press, 2014

The moral rights of the authors have been asserted

First edition published in 2014

Impression: 1

Published in the United States of America by Oxford University Press
198 Madison Avenue, New York, NY 10016, United States of America

British Library Cataloguing in Publication Data
Data available

Library of Congress Control Number: 2013947173

ISBN 978-0-19-870382-2

Printed in Great Britain by
Lightning Source UK Ltd

Preface

China adopted its first comprehensive competition law, the Anti-Monopoly Law (AML) in 2008. Given the size of the Chinese economy, China has become one of the major competition law jurisdictions in the world.

Besides the AML itself, there are numerous rules or regulations that have been issued over the years by the three ministries that enforce the AML, the Ministry of Commerce, the State Administration for Industry and Commerce, and the National Development and Reform Commission. Other entities have also issued important rules such as the Anti-Monopoly Commission or the Supreme People's Court.

Over the years, we prepared unofficial translations of these documents to inform Jones Day's friends and clients about the development of competition law in China. Earlier translations of some of these texts were also included in the book we authored with our former Jones Day colleagues Steve Harris and Mark Cohen, *Anti-Monopoly Law and Practice in China*, published by Oxford University Press.

The purpose of this compilation is to offer a central repository of the most relevant texts applicable in this field, including all decisions issued by the Ministry of Commerce in merger cases. It also offers an unofficial English translation to enable foreign practitioners to better understand the regulatory framework.

Table of Contents

PART
A

LAWS
法律

A-1

Anti-Monopoly Law of the People's Republic of China

中华人民共和国反垄断法

(Adopted by the Standing Committee of the
10th National People's Congress on August 30, 2007,
effective as of August 1, 2008)

（第十届全国人民代表大会常务委员会于2007年8月30日审
议通过，自2008年8月1日起施行）

第一章 总则	Chapter I General Provisions
第一条 为了预防和制止垄断行为，保护市场公平竞争，提高经济运行效率，维护消费者利益和社会公共利益，促进社会主义市场经济健康发展，制定本法。	**Article 1** This law is enacted for the purposes of preventing and prohibiting monopoly conduct, safeguarding fair market competition, improving efficiency of economic operations, protecting consumers and the public interest, and promoting the healthy development of the socialist market economy.
第二条 中华人民共和国境内经济活动中的垄断行为，适用本法；中华人民共和国境外的垄断行为，对境内市场竞争产生排除、限制影响的，适用本法。	**Article 2** This law is applicable to monopoly conduct in economic activities within the territory of the People's Republic of China. This law is also applicable to monopoly conduct outside the territory of the People's Republic of China that has the effect of eliminating and/or restricting competition in the domestic market of the People's Republic of China.

(Continued)

第一章 总则	Chapter I General Provisions
第三条 本法规定的垄断行为包括: (一)　经营者达成垄断协议; (二)　经营者滥用市场支配地位; (三)　具有或者可能具有排除、限制 　　　竞争效果的经营者集中。	**Article 3** "Monopoly conduct" is defined in this law as the following conduct: (1)　monopoly agreements among undertakings; (2)　abuse of dominant market positions by undertakings; and (3)　concentrations of undertakings that have or may have the effect of eliminating and/or restricting competition.
第四条 国家制定和实施与社会主义市场经济相适应的竞争规则,完善宏观调控,健全统一、开放、竞争、有序的市场体系。	**Article 4** The State shall formulate and implement competition rules compatible with the socialist market economy, improve macroeconomic supervision and control, and develop a united, open, competitive, and orderly market system.
第五条 经营者可以通过公平竞争、自愿联合,依法实施集中,扩大经营规模,提高市场竞争能力。	**Article 5** Undertakings may, through fair competition and voluntary alliances, legally implement concentrations, to expand their business scale and improve their market competitiveness.
第六条 具有市场支配地位的经营者,不得滥用市场支配地位,排除、限制竞争。	**Article 6** Undertakings with a dominant market position shall not abuse their dominant position to eliminate and/or restrict competition.
第七条 国有经济占控制地位的关系国民经济命脉和国家安全的行业以及依法实行专营专卖的行业,国家对其经营者的合法经营活动予以保护,并对经营者的经营行为及其商品和服务的价格依法实施监管和调控,维护消费者利益,促进技术进步。 前款规定行业的经营者应当依法经营,诚实守信,严格自律,接受社会公众的监督,不得利用其控制地位或者专营专卖地位损害消费者利益。	**Article 7** In industries that have a vital bearing on the lifelines of the national economy and national security, which are controlled by state-owned enterprises, and in industries in which monopolies are granted by law, the State shall protect the lawful business activities of those enterprises, supervise and control their conduct and prices for the products and services in accordance with the law, protect the interests of consumers, and promote technological progress.

	The undertakings in the industries specified in the preceding paragraph shall conduct their business in accordance with the law, act in good faith, observe strict self-discipline, subject themselves to supervision from the public, and shall not impair the interests of consumers by exploitation of their control positions or granted monopolies.
第八条 行政机关和法律、法规授权的具有管理公共事务职能的组织不得滥用行政权力，排除、限制竞争。	**Article 8** Administrative agencies and organizations designated by laws and regulations to manage public affairs shall not abuse their administrative power to eliminate and/or restrict competition.
第九条 国务院设立反垄断委员会，负责组织、协调、指导反垄断工作，履行下列职责： （一）　研究拟订有关竞争政策； （二）　组织调查、评估市场总体竞争状况，发布评估报告； （三）　制定、发布反垄断指南； （四）　协调反垄断行政执法工作； （五）　国务院规定的其他职责。 国务院反垄断委员会的组成和工作规则由国务院规定。	**Article 9** The State Council will set up the Anti-Monopoly Commission ("AMC"), which is responsible for organizing, coordinating, and supervising anti-monopoly-related activities, and performs the following functions: (1)　researching and formulating competition policies; (2)　organizing investigations and evaluations of the overall market competitive conditions and publishing evaluation reports; (3)　formulating and publishing anti-monopoly guidelines; (4)　coordinating administrative enforcement of the Anti-Monopoly Law; and (5)　other functions specified by the State Council. The organization and working rules of the Anti-Monopoly Commission shall be formulated by the State Council.

(Continued)

第十条 国务院规定的承担反垄断执法职责的机构(以下统称国务院反垄断执法机构)依照本法规定，负责反垄断执法工作。 国务院反垄断执法机构根据工作需要，可以授权省、自治区、直辖市人民政府相应的机构，依照本法规定负责有关反垄断执法工作。	**Article 10** The Anti-Monopoly Enforcement Authority designated by the State Council to undertake the responsibilities of Anti-Monopoly Law enforcement (hereinafter referred to as Anti-Monopoly Enforcement Authority under the State Council, "AMEA") is responsible for the enforcement of the Anti-Monopoly Law. The AMEA, if necessary, may authorize corresponding organs of the People's Governments of provinces, autonomous regions, and provincial level municipalities to be responsible for relevant anti-monopoly enforcement activities in accordance with this law.
第十一条 行业协会应当加强行业自律，引导本行业的经营者依法竞争，维护市场竞争秩序。	**Article 11** Trade associations shall strengthen industry self-discipline, provide guidance for undertakings in relevant industries to compete lawfully, and maintain the order of market competition.
第十二条 本法所称经营者，是指从事商品生产、经营或者提供服务的自然人、法人和其他组织。 本法所称相关市场，是指经营者在一定时期内就特定商品或者服务(以下统称商品)进行竞争的商品范围和地域范围。	**Article 12** "Undertaking" in this law refers to a natural person, a legal person, or any other organization that engages in the production or operation of products or provision of services. "Relevant market" in this law refers to the products and geographic scope within which the undertakings compete against each other during a certain period of time with respect to specific products or services (hereinafter "products").
第二章 垄断协议	**Chapter II Monopoly Agreements**
第十三条 禁止具有竞争关系的经营者达成下列垄断协议： (一) 固定或者变更商品价格； (二) 限制商品的生产数量或者销售数量；	**Article 13** The following monopoly agreements among competing undertakings shall be prohibited: (1) fixing or changing prices of products;

（三） 分割销售市场或者原材料采购 市场； （四） 限制购买新技术、新设备或者 限制开发新技术、新产品； （五） 联合抵制交易； （六） 国务院反垄断执法机构认定的 其他垄断协议。 本法所称垄断协议，是指排除、限 制竞争的协议、决定或者其他协同 行为。	(2) restricting output or sales volume of products; (3) allocating sales market or raw material purchasing market; (4) restricting the purchase of new technology or new equipment, or restricting the development of new technologies or new products; (5) jointly boycotting; and (6) other monopoly agreements as determined by the AMEA. "Monopoly agreement" in this law refers to agreements, decisions, or other concerted conducts that eliminate and/or restrict competition.
第十四条 禁止经营者与交易相对人达成下列 垄断协议： （一） 固定向第三人转售商品的价 格； （二） 限定向第三人转售商品的最低 价格； （三） 国务院反垄断执法机构认定的 其他垄断协议。	**Article 14** The following monopoly agreements between undertakings and their trading partners shall be prohibited: (1) fixing the resale price to a third party; (2) restricting the minimum price for resale to a third party; or (3) other monopoly agreements determined by the AMEA.
第十五条 经营者能够证明所达成的协议属于下 列情形之一的，不适用本法第十三 条、第十四条的规定： （一） 为改进技术、研究开发新产品 的； （二） 为提高产品质量、降低成本、 增进效率，统一产品规格、标 准或者实行专业化分工的； （三） 为提高中小经营者经营效率， 增强中小经营者竞争力的； （四） 为实现节约能源、保护环境、 救灾救助等社会公共利益的； （五） 因经济不景气，为缓解销售量 严重下降或者生产明显过剩 的； （六） 为保障对外贸易和对外经济合 作中的正当利益的； （七） 法律和国务院规定的其他情 形。	**Article 15** An agreement shall be exempted from the application of Articles 13 and 14 if the undertakings prove that it was entered into for one of the following objectives: (1) improving techniques, or researching and developing new products; (2) upgrading product quality, reducing costs, improving efficiency, unifying product specifications and standards, or realizing job specialization; (3) improving operational efficiency and enhancing the competitiveness of small and medium-sized enterprises; (4) realizing public welfare such as conserving energy, protecting the environment, and providing disaster relief;

(Continued)

属于前款第一项至第五项情形，不适用本法第十三条、第十四条规定的，经营者还应当证明所达成的协议不会严重限制相关市场的竞争，并且能够使消费者分享由此产生的利益。	(5) mitigating the severe decrease of sales volume or excessive overstock during economic recessions; (6) protecting legitimate interests in foreign trade and economic cooperation; or (7) other circumstances stipulated by laws and regulations of the State Council. Where a monopoly agreement falls under items (1) to (5) in the preceding paragraph, the undertakings shall, in order to be exempted from application of Articles 13 and 14 of this law, also prove that the agreement will not substantially restrict competition in the relevant market and will enable the consumers to share the benefits derived from the agreement.
第十六条 行业协会不得组织本行业的经营者从事本章禁止的垄断行为。	**Article 16** Trade associations shall not organize industry undertakings to engage in any monopoly conduct prohibited under this Chapter.
第三章 滥用市场支配地位	**Chapter III Abuse of Dominant Market Position**
第十七条 禁止具有市场支配地位的经营者从事下列滥用市场支配地位的行为： （一） 以不公平的高价销售商品或者以不公平的低价购买商品； （二） 没有正当理由，以低于成本的价格销售商品； （三） 没有正当理由，拒绝与交易相对人进行交易； （四） 没有正当理由，限定交易相对人只能与其进行交易或者只能与其指定的经营者进行交易； （五） 没有正当理由搭售商品，或者在交易时附加其他不合理的交易条件；	**Article 17** Undertakings with a dominant market position are prohibited from engaging in any of the following conduct that abuses their dominant market position: (1) selling products at unfairly high prices or buying products at unfairly low prices; (2) without valid justification, selling products at prices below cost; (3) without valid justification, refusing to deal with trading partners; (4) without valid justification, restricting trading partners to deal exclusively with themselves or with undertakings designated by them;

（六） 没有正当理由，对条件相同的交易相对人在交易价格等交易条件上实行差别待遇； （七） 国务院反垄断执法机构认定的其他滥用市场支配地位的行为。 本法所称市场支配地位，是指经营者在相关市场内具有能够控制商品价格、数量或者其他交易条件，或者能够阻碍、影响其他经营者进入相关市场能力的市场地位。	(5) without valid justification, tying products or imposing other unreasonable trading conditions; (6) without valid justification, according differentiated treatment in regard to transaction conditions such as prices to equivalent trading partners; and (7) other activities determined by the AMEA as abuse of dominant market positions. "Dominant market position" in this law refers to a market position that enables an undertaking to control the price or quantity of products or other trading conditions in the relevant market or to impede or affect the entry of other undertakings into the relevant market.
第十八条 认定经营者具有市场支配地位，应当依据下列因素： （一） 该经营者在相关市场的市场份额，以及相关市场的竞争状况； （二） 该经营者控制销售市场或者原材料采购市场的能力； （三） 该经营者的财力和技术条件； （四） 其他经营者对该经营者在交易上的依赖程度； （五） 其他经营者进入相关市场的难易程度； （六） 与认定该经营者市场支配地位有关的其他因素。	**Article 18** A dominant market position shall be determined based on the following factors: (1) the market share of the undertaking and competitive conditions in the relevant market; (2) the ability of the undertaking to control the sales market or the raw material purchasing market; (3) the financial and technological capabilities of the undertaking; (4) the degree of reliance on the undertaking by other undertakings in transactions; (5) the difficulty for other undertakings to enter the relevant market; and (6) other factors relevant to the determination of the undertaking's dominant market position.
第十九条 有下列情形之一的，可以推定经营者具有市场支配地位： （一） 一个经营者在相关市场的市场份额达到二分之一的；	**Article 19** Undertakings can be presumed to have a dominant market position if any of the following conditions is fulfilled: (1) the market share of one undertaking accounts for more than half of the relevant market;

(Continued)

（二）　两个经营者在相关市场的市场份额合计达到三分之二的； （三）　三个经营者在相关市场的市场份额合计达到四分之三的。 有前款第二项、第三项规定的情形，其中有的经营者市场份额不足十分之一的，不应当推定该经营者具有市场支配地位。 被推定具有市场支配地位的经营者，有证据证明不具有市场支配地位的，不应当认定其具有市场支配地位。	(2)　the combined market share of two undertakings accounts for two-thirds of the relevant market; or (3)　the combined market share of three undertakings accounts for three-quarters of the relevant market. Among those undertakings that fall under item (2) or (3) of the preceding paragraph, an undertaking whose market share is less than 10% shall not be presumed to have a dominant market position. Where the undertaking presumed to have a dominant market position provides evidence of the absence of a dominant market position, such undertaking shall not be determined to hold a dominant market position.
第四章　经营者集中	**Chapter IV Concentrations of Undertakings**
第二十条 经营者集中是指下列情形: （一）　经营者合并； （二）　经营者通过取得股权或者资产的方式取得对其他经营者的控制权； （三）　经营者通过合同等方式取得对其他经营者的控制权或者能够对其他经营者施加决定性影响。	**Article 20** Concentrations of undertakings refer to the following situations: (1)　mergers; (2)　acquisition of control over other undertakings through the acquisition of equity or assets; or (3)　acquisition of control over other undertakings or the capacity to exercise decisive influence on other undertakings by contract or any other means.
第二十一条 经营者集中达到国务院规定的申报标准的，经营者应当事先向国务院反垄断执法机构申报，未申报的不得实施集中。	**Article 21** A prior notification shall be filed with the AMEA by the undertaking if the concentration exceeds the thresholds for notification stipulated by the State Council. The concentration transaction shall not be closed without prior notification.

第二十二条 经营者集中有下列情形之一的，可以不向国务院反垄断执法机构申报: (一)　参与集中的一个经营者拥有其他每个经营者百分之五十以上有表决权的股份或者资产的; (二)　参与集中的每个经营者百分之五十以上有表决权的股份或者资产被同一个未参与集中的经营者拥有的。	**Article 22** In any of the following situations, undertakings may choose not to file the notification with the AMEA: (1)　one undertaking involved in the concentration owns more than 50% of the voting shares or assets of every other undertaking; or (2)　an undertaking not involved in the concentration owns more than 50% of the voting shares or assets of each undertaking that is involved in the concentration.
第二十三条 经营者向国务院反垄断执法机构申报集中，应当提交下列文件、资料: (一)　申报书; (二)　集中对相关市场竞争状况影响的说明; (三)　集中协议; (四)　参与集中的经营者经会计师事务所审计的上一会计年度财务会计报告; (五)　国务院反垄断执法机构规定的其他文件、资料。 申报书应当载明参与集中的经营者的名称、住所、经营范围、预定实施集中的日期和国务院反垄断执法机构规定的其他事项。	**Article 23** Undertakings that make a notification of a concentration shall submit the following documents and information to the AMEA: (1)　a notification letter; (2)　an explanation regarding the effects that the concentration may have on competitive conditions in the relevant market; (3)　concentration agreement(s); (4)　financial reports, audited by a certified public accountant, of the undertakings concerned by the concentration in the previous fiscal year; and (5)　other information required by the AMEA. The notification letter shall contain the names of the undertakings concerned by the concentration, their domiciles, business scopes, the proposed date on which the concentration is to be implemented, and other information stipulated by the AMEA.
第二十四条 经营者提交的文件、资料不完备的，应当在国务院反垄断执法机构规定的期限内补交文件、资料。经营者逾期未补交文件、资料的，视为未申报。	**Article 24** Where the documents and materials submitted are not complete, the undertakings shall submit supplemental documents and materials within the time limit stipulated by the AMEA. If the undertakings fail to do so within the provided time limit, no notification shall be deemed made.

(Continued)

第二十五条	**Article 25**
国务院反垄断执法机构应当自收到经营者提交的符合本法第二十三条规定的文件、资料之日起三十日内，对申报的经营者集中进行初步审查，作出是否实施进一步审查的决定，并书面通知经营者。国务院反垄断执法机构作出决定前，经营者不得实施集中。	The AMEA shall conduct a preliminary review of the filed notification. It shall decide whether to initiate further review within 30 days from the date of receipt of the documents and materials as required by Article 23 of this law, and notify the undertakings of that decision in writing. Before the decision is made by the AMEA, the undertakings concerned shall be prohibited from implementing the concentration.
国务院反垄断执法机构作出不实施进一步审查的决定或者逾期未作出决定的，经营者可以实施集中。	Where the AMEA decides that no further review will be conducted or where the AMEA makes no decision at the expiry of the specified time limit, the undertakings may implement the concentration.
第二十六条	**Article 26**
国务院反垄断执法机构决定实施进一步审查的，应当自决定之日起九十日内审查完毕，作出是否禁止经营者集中的决定，并书面通知经营者。作出禁止经营者集中的决定，应当说明理由。审查期间，经营者不得实施集中。	If the AMEA decides to conduct a further review, it shall complete the review within 90 days from the date of its decision for further review, and decide whether to approve or prohibit the concentration, and notify the undertaking of its decision in writing. If the AMEA decides to prohibit the concentration, it shall explain the reasons thereof. The undertakings shall be prohibited from implementing the concentration during the review period.
有下列情形之一的，国务院反垄断执法机构经书面通知经营者，可以延长前款规定的审查期限，但最长不得超过六十日： （一）　经营者同意延长审查期限的； （二）　经营者提交的文件、资料不准确，需要进一步核实的； （三）　经营者申报后有关情况发生重大变化的。	Under any of the following circumstances, the AMEA may extend the time limit stipulated in the preceding paragraph, provided that the extension does not exceed 60 days at the maximum: (1)　the undertakings agree to extend the review period; (2)　the documents submitted by the notifying undertakings are inaccurate and need further verification; or (3)　the relevant circumstances have significantly changed after notification by the undertakings.
国务院反垄断执法机构逾期未作出决定的，经营者可以实施集中。	

	Where the AMEA fails to take a decision at the expiry of the specified period of time, the undertaking may implement the concentration.
第二十七条 审查经营者集中，应当考虑下列因素： （一） 参与集中的经营者在相关市场的市场份额及其对市场的控制力； （二） 相关市场的市场集中度； （三） 经营者集中对市场进入、技术进步的影响； （四） 经营者集中对消费者和其他有关经营者的影响； （五） 经营者集中对国民经济发展的影响； （六） 国务院反垄断执法机构认为应当考虑的影响市场竞争的其他因素。	**Article 27** The following factors shall be considered in the review of concentrations: (1) the market shares of the undertakings concerned by the concentration in the relevant market and their ability to control the market; (2) the level of concentration in the relevant market; (3) the effect of the concentration on the market entry and the progress of technologies; (4) the effect of the concentration on consumers and other undertakings; (5) the effect of the concentration on the development of the national economy; and (6) other factors affecting market competition as determined by the AMEA.
第二十八条 经营者集中具有或者可能具有排除、限制竞争效果的，国务院反垄断执法机构应当作出禁止经营者集中的决定。但是，经营者能够证明该集中对竞争产生的有利影响明显大于不利影响，或者符合社会公共利益的，国务院反垄断执法机构可以作出对经营者集中不予禁止的决定。	**Article 28** Where a concentration of undertakings results in or may result in the effect of eliminating and/or restricting market competition, the AMEA shall make a decision to prohibit the concentration. However, the AMEA may decide not to prohibit the concentration if the undertakings involved can prove either that the positive effects of the concentration exceed the adverse effects, or that the concentration is in the public interest.
第二十九条 对不予禁止的经营者集中，国务院反垄断执法机构可以决定附加减少集中对竞争产生不利影响的限制性条件。	**Article 29** Where a concentration is not prohibited, the AMEA may impose restrictive conditions to mitigate the adverse effects of the concentration on competition.

(Continued)

第三十条 国务院反垄断执法机构应当将禁止经营者集中的决定或者对经营者集中附加限制性条件的决定，及时向社会公布。	**Article 30** The AMEA shall publicize, in a timely manner, decisions to prohibit concentrations or decisions to impose restrictive conditions to concentrations.
第三十一条 对外资并购境内企业或者以其他方式参与经营者集中，涉及国家安全的，除依照本法规定进行经营者集中审查外，还应当按照国家有关规定进行国家安全审查。	**Article 31** In addition to reviews of concentrations stipulated by this law, mergers with or acquisitions of domestic companies by foreign investors or other forms of concentration involving foreign capital, which implicate national security, shall also undergo a national security review according to relevant laws and regulations.
第五章 滥用行政权力排除、限制竞争	**Chapter V Prohibition of Abuses of Administrative Powers to Restrict Competition**
第三十二条 行政机关和法律、法规授权的具有管理公共事务职能的组织不得滥用行政权力，限定或者变相限定单位或者个人经营、购买、使用其指定的经营者提供的商品。	**Article 32** Administrative agencies and organizations designated by laws and regulations to manage public affairs shall not abuse their administrative powers by requiring, or requiring in any disguised form, organizations or individuals to deal, purchase, or use products provided by designated undertakings.
第三十三条 行政机关和法律、法规授权的具有管理公共事务职能的组织不得滥用行政权力，实施下列行为，妨碍商品在地区之间的自由流通： （一）　对外地商品设定歧视性收费项目、实行歧视性收费标准，或者规定歧视性价格； （二）　对外地商品规定与本地同类商品不同的技术要求、检验标准，或者对外地商品采取重复检验、重复认证等歧视性技术措施，限制外地商品进入本地市场；	**Article 33** Administrative agencies and organizations designated by laws and regulations to manage public affairs shall not abuse their administrative powers to hamper the free movement of products among regions by employing one of the following behaviors: (1)　setting discriminatory fee items, implementing discriminatory fee standards, or setting discriminatory prices for products originating from other regions;

（三） 采取专门针对外地商品的行政许可，限制外地商品进入本地市场； （四） 设置关卡或者采取其他手段，阻碍外地商品进入或者本地商品运出； （五） 妨碍商品在地区之间自由流通的其他行为。	(2) imposing technical requirements or inspection standards on products originating from other regions that are different from those on similar local products, or taking discriminatory technical measures, such as repeated inspection or certification on products originating from other regions, so as to restrict the entry of products originating from other regions into the local market; (3) creating administrative licensing procedures targeting products from other regions to restrict the access of those products to the local market; (4) setting up checkpoints on roads to block either the entry of products originating from other regions or the exit of local products; or (5) other acts preventing the free flow of products among regions.
第三十四条 行政机关和法律、法规授权的具有管理公共事务职能的组织不得滥用行政权力，以设定歧视性资质要求、评审标准或者不依法发布信息等方式，排斥或者限制外地经营者参加本地的招标投标活动。	**Article 34** Administrative agencies and organizations designated by laws and regulations to manage public affairs shall not abuse their administrative powers to exclude or restrict the participation of undertakings from other regions in local bidding activities by imposing discriminatory qualification requirements or assessment standards or by failing to publish information in accordance with the law.
第三十五条 行政机关和法律、法规授权的具有管理公共事务职能的组织不得滥用行政权力，采取与本地经营者不平等待遇等方式，排斥或者限制外地经营者在本地投资或者设立分支机构。	**Article 35** Administrative agencies and organizations designated by laws and regulations to manage public affairs shall not abuse their administrative powers through the use of discriminatory treatment to exclude or restrict either investment in their region or the establishment of local branches by undertakings from other regions.

(Continued)

第三十六条 行政机关和法律、法规授权的具有管理公共事务职能的组织不得滥用行政权力，强制经营者从事本法规定的垄断行为。	**Article 36** Administrative agencies and organizations designated by laws and regulations to manage public affairs shall not abuse their administrative powers to compel undertakings to engage in monopoly conduct that is prohibited under this Law.
第三十七条 行政机关不得滥用行政权力，制定含有排除、限制竞争内容的规定。	**Article 37** Administrative agencies shall not abuse their administrative power to promulgate regulations containing provisions that eliminate and/or restrict competition.
第六章 对涉嫌垄断行为的调查	**Chapter VI The Investigation of Suspicious Monopoly Conduct**
第三十八条 反垄断执法机构依法对涉嫌垄断行为进行调查。 对涉嫌垄断行为，任何单位和个人有权向反垄断执法机构举报。反垄断执法机构应当为举报人保密。 举报采用书面形式并提供相关事实和证据的，反垄断执法机构应当进行必要的调查。	**Article 38** The AMEA shall investigate suspicious monopoly conduct in accordance with the law. Any entity or individual may report suspected monopoly conduct that is in violation of this law to the AMEA. The AMEA shall keep the name of the informer confidential. The AMEA shall conduct the necessary investigation for those reports that are in writing and contain related facts and evidence.
第三十九条 反垄断执法机构调查涉嫌垄断行为，可以采取下列措施： （一）　进入被调查的经营者的营业场所或者其他有关场所进行检查； （二）　询问被调查的经营者、利害关系人或者其他有关单位或者个人，要求其说明有关情况；	**Article 39** When investigating suspected monopoly conduct, the AMEA can take the following measures: (1)　conduct on-premise inspections of the place of business of the investigated undertaking or other relevant places; (2)　question the investigated undertaking, interested parties, and other relevant entities and individuals, requiring them to provide relevant information;

（三）　查阅、复制被调查的经营者、利害关系人或者其他有关单位或者个人的有关单证、协议、会计账簿、业务函电、电子数据等文件、资料； （四）　查封、扣押相关证据； （五）　查询经营者的银行账户。 采取前款规定的措施，应当向反垄断执法机构主要负责人书面报告，并经批准。	(3)　examine or copy relevant documents and information including related documentation, contracts, accounting books, business mails, and electronic data, etc. of the investigated undertaking, interested parties, and other relevant entities or individuals; (4)　seal up and detain relevant evidence; and (5)　inquire about the bank accounts of the undertakings. Before taking any of the measures stipulated in the preceding paragraph, the enforcement official shall report in writing to the principal of the AMEA and obtain approval.
第四十条 反垄断执法机构调查涉嫌垄断行为，执法人员不得少于二人，并应当出示执法证件。 执法人员进行询问和调查，应当制作笔录，并由被询问人或者被调查人签字。	**Article 40** When investigating suspected monopoly conduct, there shall be at least two law enforcement officials, and they shall present valid documents showing their authority to carry out the investigation. The law enforcement officials shall make a written record of the inquiry and investigation, and such report shall be signed by the inquired or investigated person.
第四十一条 反垄断执法机构及其工作人员对执法过程中知悉的商业秘密负有保密义务。	**Article 41** The AMEA and its officials shall keep confidential the business secrets obtained in the course of enforcement.
第四十二条 被调查的经营者、利害关系人或者其他有关单位或者个人应当配合反垄断执法机构依法履行职责，不得拒绝、阻碍反垄断执法机构的调查。	**Article 42** The investigated undertakings, interested parties, and other relevant entities and individuals shall cooperate with the AMEA, and shall not reject or obstruct the investigation conducted by the AMEA.

(Continued)

第四十三条 被调查的经营者、利害关系人有权陈述意见。反垄断执法机构应当对被调查的经营者、利害关系人提出的事实、理由和证据进行核实。	**Article 43** The investigated undertakings and interested parties have the right to submit statements. The AMEA shall hear the opinions of the investigated undertakings and interested parties and conduct necessary verification of the alleged facts, reasons, and evidence.
第四十四条 反垄断执法机构对涉嫌垄断行为调查核实后，认为构成垄断行为的，应当依法作出处理决定，并可以向社会公布。	**Article 44** Where the AMEA, after investigation and verification of the suspected monopoly conduct determines that such conduct constitutes a monopoly conduct, it shall make a decision in accordance with the law and may publicize the decision.
第四十五条 对反垄断执法机构调查的涉嫌垄断行为，被调查的经营者承诺在反垄断执法机构认可的期限内采取具体措施消除该行为后果的，反垄断执法机构可以决定中止调查。中止调查的决定应当载明被调查的经营者承诺的具体内容。 反垄断执法机构决定中止调查的，应当对经营者履行承诺的情况进行监督。经营者履行承诺的，反垄断执法机构可以决定终止调查。 有下列情形之一的，反垄断执法机构应当恢复调查： （一）　经营者未履行承诺的； （二）　作出中止调查决定所依据的事实发生重大变化的； （三）　中止调查的决定是基于经营者提供的不完整或者不真实的信息作出的。	**Article 45** During the investigation of the suspected monopoly conduct, the AMEA may suspend the investigation if the investigated undertakings commit to take concrete measures within the time limit as approved by the AMEA to eliminate the effects of such suspected conduct. The decision to suspend the investigation shall state the concrete commitments by the investigated undertakings. Where the AMEA has decided to suspend the investigation, the AMEA shall supervise the implementation of the commitments by the relevant undertakings. If the undertakings implement the commitments, the AMEA may terminate the investigation. However, the AMEA shall resume its investigation if any of the following occurs: (1)　the undertakings fail to implement the commitments; (2)　the facts on which the decision to suspend the investigation was based have undergone significant changes; or

	(3) the decision to suspend the investigation was based on incomplete or inaccurate information submitted by the undertakings.
第七章 法律责任	**Chapter VII Legal Liability**
第四十六条 经营者违反本法规定，达成并实施垄断协议的，由反垄断执法机构责令停止违法行为，没收违法所得，并处上一年度销售额百分之一以上百分之十以下的罚款；尚未实施所达成的垄断协议的，可以处五十万元以下的罚款。 经营者主动向反垄断执法机构报告达成垄断协议的有关情况并提供重要证据的，反垄断执法机构可以酌情减轻或者免除对该经营者的处罚。 行业协会违反本法规定，组织本行业的经营者达成垄断协议的，反垄断执法机构可以处五十万元以下的罚款；情节严重的，社会团体登记管理机关可以依法撤销登记。	**Article 46** Where undertakings reach and implement a monopoly agreement in violation of the relevant provisions of this law, the AMEA shall order the undertakings to cease and desist such acts, confiscate the illegal gains, and impose a fine of more than 1% but less than 10% of the total turnover of the undertaking in the previous year; if the monopoly agreement has not been implemented, a fine of less than RMB 500,000 may be imposed. If an undertaking involved in a monopoly agreement reports its monopoly conduct to the AMEA and provides material evidence, the AMEA may grant a reduced penalty or an exemption from penalty at the discretion of the AMEA. Where trade associations organize the undertakings in the relevant industry to conclude monopoly agreements in violation of this law, the AMEA may impose a fine of less than RMB 500,000; in serious circumstances, the Registration and Administration Authority for Social Organizations may cancel their registration in accordance with the law.
第四十七条 经营者违反本法规定，滥用市场支配地位的，由反垄断执法机构责令停止违法行为，没收违法所得，并处上一年度销售额百分之一以上百分之十以下的罚款。	**Article 47** Where an undertaking abuses its dominant market position in violation of the relevant provisions of this law, the AMEA shall order the undertaking to cease and desist such acts, confiscate the illegal gains, and impose a fine of more than 1% but less than 10% of the total turnover of the undertaking in the previous year.

(Continued)

第四十八条 经营者违反本法规定实施集中的，由国务院反垄断执法机构责令停止实施集中、限期处分股份或者资产、限期转让营业以及采取其他必要措施恢复到集中前的状态，可以处五十万元以下的罚款。	**Article 48** Where undertakings implement concentrations in violation of the relevant provisions of this law, the AMEA shall order the undertakings to stop implementing the concentration, to dispose of their stock or assets within a specified time limit, to sell their business within a specified time limit, to adopt other necessary measures to restore the market situation before the concentration, and a fine of less than RMB 500,000 may be imposed.
第四十九条 对本法第四十六条、第四十七条、第四十八条规定的罚款，反垄断执法机构确定具体罚款数额时，应当考虑违法行为的性质、程度和持续的时间等因素。	**Article 49** When determining the amount of fines pursuant to Article 46, Article 47, and Article 48, the AMEA shall consider factors such as the nature, seriousness, and duration of the illegal act.
第五十条 经营者实施垄断行为，给他人造成损失的，依法承担民事责任。	**Article 50** Undertakings that implement monopoly conduct and cause damages to others shall bear civil liability in accordance with the law.
第五十一条 行政机关和法律、法规授权的具有管理公共事务职能的组织滥用行政权力，实施排除、限制竞争行为的，由上级机关责令改正；对直接负责的主管人员和其他直接责任人员依法给予处分。反垄断执法机构可以向有关上级机关提出依法处理的建议。 法律、行政法规对行政机关和法律、法规授权的具有管理公共事务职能的组织滥用行政权力实施排除、限制竞争行为的处理另有规定的，依照其规定。	**Article 51** Administrative agencies and organizations designated by laws and regulations to manage public affairs shall be admonished by their superior agencies or departments if they abuse their administrative power to eliminate and/or restrict competition; the persons in charge and the individuals who are directly responsible shall be disciplined in accordance with the law. The AMEA may make a proposal on handling of the matter to the relevant superior authority. Where other laws or administrative regulations provide for the handling of abuses of administrative power by administrative agencies and organizations designated by laws and regulations to manage public affairs, those provisions shall apply.

第五十二条 对反垄断执法机构依法实施的审查和调查，拒绝提供有关材料、信息，或者提供虚假材料、信息，或者隐匿、销毁、转移证据，或者有其他拒绝、阻碍调查行为的，由反垄断执法机构责令改正，对个人可以处二万元以下的罚款，对单位可以处二十万元以下的罚款；情节严重的，对个人处二万元以上十万元以下的罚款，对单位处二十万元以上一百万元以下的罚款；构成犯罪的，依法追究刑事责任。	**Article 52** For those undertakings that refuse to submit related materials and information, submit fraudulent materials or information, conceal, destroy, or remove evidence, or refuse or obstruct investigations in any other way, the AMEA shall ask them to remedy the situation. A fine of less than RMB 20,000 may be imposed on individuals, and a fine of less than RMB 200,000 may be imposed on organizations; and in the case of a serious situation, the AMEA may impose fines from RMB 20,000 to RMB 100,000 against individuals or fines from RMB 200,000 to RMB 1 million against organizations; a criminal liability may be pursued if a violation of criminal law occurs.
第五十三条 对反垄断执法机构依据本法第二十八条、第二十九条作出的决定不服的，可以先依法申请行政复议；对行政复议决定不服的，可以依法提起行政诉讼。 对反垄断执法机构作出的前款规定以外的决定不服的，可以依法申请行政复议或者提起行政诉讼。	**Article 53** Where the undertakings are dissatisfied by the decisions made by the AMEA pursuant to Articles 28 and 29 of this law, they may first apply for administrative review; if they are still not satisfied with the decision of the administrative review, they may file an administrative lawsuit in accordance with the law. Where the undertakings are dissatisfied by any decision made by the AMEA other than the decisions specified in the preceding paragraph, the parties may apply for an administrative review or file an administrative lawsuit.
第五十四条 反垄断执法机构工作人员滥用职权、玩忽职守、徇私舞弊或者泄露执法过程中知悉的商业秘密，构成犯罪的，依法追究刑事责任；尚不构成犯罪的，依法给予处分。	**Article 54** Where the employees from the AMEA abuse their power, neglect their duties, receive bribes and cheat, or disclose business secrets obtained during their enforcement activities, which constitutes a crime, criminal liability shall be pursued according to the law; if their conduct does not constitute a crime, administrative penalties shall be given.

第八章 附则	**Chapter VIII Supplementary Provisions**
第五十五条 经营者依照有关知识产权的法律、行政法规规定行使知识产权的行为，不适用本法；但是，经营者滥用知识产权，排除、限制竞争的行为，适用本法。	**Article 55** This law is not applicable to the conduct of undertakings that exercise their intellectual property rights in accordance with the intellectual property laws and relevant administrative regulations; however, this law is applicable to the conduct of undertakings that abuse their intellectual property rights, eliminating and/or restricting competition.
第五十六条 农业生产者及农村经济组织在农产品生产、加工、销售、运输、储存等经营活动中实施的联合或者协同行为，不适用本法。	**Article 56** This law is not applicable to alliances or other concerted conduct by farmers and rural economic organizations in such operational activities as production, processing, sales, transportation, and storage of agricultural products.
第五十七条 本法自2008年8月1日起施行。	**Article 57** This law shall become effective as of August 1, 2008.

A-2

Criminal Law of the People's Republic of China (Articles 223, 225, and 226)

中华人民共和国刑法第二百二十三条、二百二十五条和二百二十六条

(Adopted by the 5th National People's Congress on July 1, 1979, last amended on February 25, 2011, effective as of May 1, 2011)

（第五届全国人民代表大会于1979年7月1日审议通过，2011年2月25日最新修订，自2011年5月1日起施行）

第二百二十三条 投标人相互串通投标报价，损害招标人或者其他投标人利益，情节严重的，处三年以下有期徒刑或者拘役，并处或者单处罚金。 投标人与招标人串通投标，损害国家、集体、公民的合法利益的，依照前款的规定处罚。	**Article 223** If a bidder colludes with other bidders in submitting their bid price quotations to harm the interests of the tendered or other tenders and if the circumstances are serious, the bidder shall be sentenced to a fixed-term imprisonment of not more than three years or criminal detention. It may be concurrently or independently subject to a fine. If a bidder colludes with the tendered in the tender to harm the legitimate interests of the State, collectives, or citizens, the bidder shall be sentenced in accordance with the preceding paragraph.
第二百二十五条 违反国家规定，有下列非法经营行为之一，扰乱市场秩序，情节严重的，处五年以下有期徒刑或者拘役，并处或者单处违法所得一倍以上五倍以下罚金；	**Article 225** If a person, in violation of the State's regulations, commits any of the following acts of illegal business operation, thus disturbing the market order, and if the circumstances are serious,

(Continued)

情节特别严重的，处五年以上有期徒刑，并处违法所得一倍以上五倍以下罚金或者没收财产： …… （四）　其他严重扰乱市场秩序的非法经营行为。	the person shall be sentenced to a fixed-term imprisonment of not more than five years or criminal detention and concurrently or independently subject to a fine of not less than one times and not more than five times the illegal gains therefrom. If the circumstance are especially serious, the person shall be subject to a fixed-term imprisonment of not less than five years and concurrently to a fine of not less than one times and not more than five times the illegal gains therefrom or confiscation of property: […] 4. to commit any other act of illegal business operation which seriously disturbs the market order.
第二百二十六条 以暴力、威胁手段，实施下列行为之一，情节严重的，处三年以下有期徒刑或者拘役，并处或者单处罚金；情节特别严重的，处三年以上七年以下有期徒刑，并处罚金： （一）　强买强卖商品的； （二）　强迫他人提供或者接受服务的； （三）　强迫他人参与或者退出投标、拍卖的； （四）　强迫他人转让或者收购公司、企业的股份、债券或者其他资产的； （五）　强迫他人参与或者退出特定的经营活动的。	**Article 226** If a person who, by means of violence or threat, commits any of the following acts and if the circumstances are serious, the person shall be sentenced to a fixed-term imprisonment of not more than three years or criminal detention and concurrently or independently subject to a fine. If the circumstances are especially serious, the person shall be sentenced to a fixed-term imprisonment of not less than three years and not more than seven years and concurrently subject to a fine: (1)　forcing others to purchase or sell products; (2)　forcing others to provide or accept services; (3)　forcing others to participate in or withdraw from a tender or auction; (4)　forcing others to transfer or acquire stocks, bonds, or other assets of a company; or (5)　forcing others to participate in or withdraw from certain business activities.

A-3

Patent Law of the People's Republic of China (Article 48)

中华人民共和国专利法第四十八条

(Adopted by the Standing Committee of the 6th National People's Congress on March 12, 1984, last amended on December 27, 2008, effective as of December 27, 2008)

（第六届全国人民代表大会常务委员会于1984年3月12日审议通过，2008年12月27日最新修订，自2008年12月27日起施行）

第四十八条 有下列情形之一的，国务院专利行政部门根据具备实施条件的单位或者个人的申请，可以给予实施发明专利或者实用新型专利的强制许可： （一）专利权人自专利权被授予之日起满三年，且自提出专利申请之日起满四年，无正当理由未实施或者未充分实施其专利的； （二）专利权人行使专利权的行为被依法认定为垄断行为，为消除或者减少该行为对竞争产生的不利影响的。	**Article 48** The relevant patent administrative authority under the State Council may grant a compulsory license to perform a patent for invention or utility model in the following cases upon an application from an entity or individual who fulfills the conditions for performing such patent: (a) where the patentee, after a lapse of three years from the grant of the patent right or four years from filing for the patent, has not performed the patent or has not sufficiently performed the patent without justification; (b) the patentee's performance of the patent right is determined as monopolistic according to law, and the grant of a compulsory license is for the purpose of eliminating or mitigating the adverse effect of such monopoly conduct on competition.

A-4

Anti-Unfair Competition Law of the People's Republic of China (Excerpts)

中华人民共和国反不正当竞争法（节选）

(Adopted by the Standing Committee of the
8th National People's Congress on September 2, 1993,
effective as of December 1, 1993)

（第八届全国人民代表大会常务委员会于1993年9月2日审议
通过，自1993年12月1日起施行）

第二条 经营者在市场交易中，应当遵循自愿、平等、公平、诚实信用的原则，遵守公认的商业道德。	**Article 2** In the course of market trading, undertakings shall observe the principles of voluntariness, equality, equitability, honesty, and trustworthiness and abide by generally accepted business ethics.
第六条 公用企业或者其他依法具有独占地位的经营者，不得限定他人购买其指定的经营者的商品，以排挤其他经营者的公平竞争。	**Article 6** Public utility enterprises or other undertakings that occupy a monopoly position according to law may not restrict other parties to purchasing the products of their designated undertakings in order to exclude fair competition by other undertakings.
第七条 政府及其所属部门不得滥用行政权力，限定他人购买其指定的经营者的商品，限制其他经营者正当的经营活动。	**Article 7** Governments and their subordinate departments may not abuse their administrative powers by restricting other parties to purchasing the products of their designated undertakings or by restricting the fair business activities of other undertakings.

政府及其所属部门不得滥用行政权力，限制外地商品进入本地市场，或者本地商品流向外地市场。	Governments and their subordinate departments may not abuse their administrative powers by restricting the entry of products from elsewhere into the local market or the outflow of local products to other markets.
第十一条 经营者不得以排挤竞争对手为目的，以低于成本的价格销售商品。 有下列情形之一的，不属于不正当竞争行为： （一）　销售鲜活商品； （二）　处理有效期限即将到期的商品或者其他积压的商品； （三）　季节性降价； （四）　因清偿债务、转产、歇业降价销售商品。	**Article 11** Undertakings may not sell products below cost for the purpose of forcing out competitors. Activities falling into any of the following circumstances are not regarded as unfair competition: (1)　sale of fresh or live products; (2)　disposal of products whose period of validity is due to expire soon or other overstocked products; (3)　seasonal price reductions; or (4)　sale of products at reduced prices in order to satisfy debts or due to a change in the line of production or closure of business.
第十二条 经营者销售商品，不得违背购买者的意愿搭售商品或者附加其他不合理的条件。	**Article 12** In selling products, undertakings may not tie the sale of one product to the sale of another against the purchaser's wishes, or attach other unreasonable conditions to the terms of a sale.
第十五条 投标者不得串通投标，抬高标价或者压低标价。 投标者和招标者不得相互勾结，以排挤竞争对手的公平竞争。	**Article 15** Bidders may not collude in the submission of tenders in order to force the tender price up or down. Bidders and the tenderee may not collude with each other in order to exclude fair competition by competitors.
第二十三条 公用企业或者其他依法具有独占地位的经营者，限定他人购买其指定的经营者的商品，以排挤其他经营者的公平竞争的，省级或者设区的市的监督检查部门应当责令停止违法行为，可以根据情节处以五万元以上二十万元以下的罚款。	**Article 23** If a utility enterprise or another undertaking that occupies a monopoly position according to law restricts other parties to purchasing the products of its designated undertaking in order to exclude fair competition by other undertakings, the supervision

(Continued)

被指定的经营者借此销售质次价高商品或者滥收费用的，监督检查部门应当没收违法所得，可以根据情节处以违法所得一倍以上三倍以下的罚款。	and examination authorities at the provincial level or of the municipality (if such municipality has established districts) shall order it to cease the illegal act and may, depending on the circumstances, impose a fine of not less than RMB 50,000 and not more than RMB 200,000. If a designated undertaking takes advantage of such restriction by selling substandard products at high prices or charging excessive fees, the supervision and examination authorities shall confiscate the illegal gains and may, depending on the circumstances, impose a fine of not less than one time and not more than three times the illegal gains.
第二十七条 投标者串通投标，抬高标价或者压低标价；投标者和招标者相互勾结，以排挤竞争对手的公平竞争的，其中标无效。监督检查部门可以根据情节处以一万元以上二十万元以下的罚款。	**Article 27** If bidders collude in the submission of tenders in order to force the tender price up or down, or if a bidder and the tenderee collude with each other in order to exclude fair competition by competitors, the successful bidder's winning of the tender shall be void. The supervision and examination authorities may, depending on the circumstances, impose a fine of not less than RMB 10,000 and not more than RMB 200,000.
第三十条 政府及其所属部门违反本法第七条规定，限定他人购买其指定的经营者的商品、限制其他经营者正当的经营活动，或者限制商品在地区之间正常流通的，由上级机关责令其改正；情节严重的，由同级或者上级机关对直接责任人员给予行政处分。被指定的经营者借此销售质次价高商品或者滥收费用的，监督检查部门应当没收违法所得，可以根据情节处以违法所得一倍以上三倍以下的罚款。	**Article 30** If a government or its subordinate department violates Article 7 hereof by restricting other parties to purchasing the products of its designated undertakings, by restricting the fair business activities of other undertakings, or by restricting the normal circulation of products between areas, its superior authorities shall order it to rectify the situation. In serious cases, its directly responsible personnel shall be subjected to administrative sanctions by authorities at the same or a higher level.

	If a designated undertaking takes advantage of such restriction by selling substandard products at high prices or charging excessive fees, the supervision and examination authorities shall confiscate the illegal gains and may, depending on the circumstances, impose a fine of not less than one time and not more than three times the illegal gains.

A-5

Foreign Trade Law of the People's Republic of China (Articles 2, 30, 32, and 33)

中华人民共和国对外贸易法第二条、三十条、三十二条和三十三条

(Adopted by the Standing Committee of the 8th National People's Congress on May 12, 1994, last amended on April 6, 2004, effective as of July 1, 2004)

（第八届全国人民代表大会常务委员会于1994年5月12日审议通过，2004年4月6日最新修订，自2004年7月1日起施行）

第二条 本法适用于对外贸易以及与对外贸易有关的知识产权保护。 本法所称对外贸易，是指货物进出口、技术进出口和国际服务贸易。	**Article 2** This law applies to foreign trade and foreign-trade-related intellectual property protection. The term "foreign trade" in this law refers to the import and export of goods and technologies as well as international trade of services.
第三十条 知识产权权利人有阻止被许可人对许可合同中的知识产权的有效性提出质疑、进行强制性一揽子许可、在许可合同中规定排他性返授条件等行为之一，并危害对外贸易公平竞争秩序的，国务院对外贸易主管部门可以采取必要的措施消除危害。	**Article 30** If any intellectual property right holder acts to, *inter alia*, prevent a licensee from challenging the validity of the intellectual property right in the license agreement, forces upon the licensee a license package, or specifies exclusive grant-back conditions in the license agreement, which, impairs the fair competition order of foreign trade, the competent foreign trade department of the State Council may take necessary measures to eliminate such impairment.

第三十二条 在对外贸易经营活动中，不得违反有关反垄断的法律、行政法规的规定实施垄断行为。 在对外贸易经营活动中实施垄断行为，危害市场公平竞争的，依照有关反垄断的法律、行政法规的规定处理。有前款违法行为，并危害对外贸易秩序的，国务院对外贸易主管部门可以采取必要的措施消除危害。	**Article 32** No monopoly conduct shall be made in the foreign trade business activities in violation of relevant anti-monopoly laws and administrative regulations. Anyone who carries out a monopoly conduct as part of its foreign trade business activities to the detriment of fair market competition shall be subject to the relevant anti-monopoly laws and administrative regulation. If any of the illegal activities as provided in the preceding paragraph occurs with the effect of impairing the foreign trade, the competent foreign trade department of the State Council may then take necessary measures to eliminate the impairment.
第三十三条 在对外贸易经营活动中，不得实施以不正当的低价销售商品、串通投标、发布虚假广告、进行商业贿赂等不正当竞争行为。 在对外贸易经营活动中实施不正当竞争行为的，依照有关反不正当竞争的法律、行政法规的规定处理。 有前款违法行为，并危害对外贸易秩序的，国务院对外贸易主管部门可以采取禁止该经营者有关货物、技术进出口等措施消除危害。	**Article 33** In foreign trade activities, such unfair competition activities as selling the products at unreasonable low prices, colluding with each other in a tender, producing and releasing false advertisements, and conducting commercial bribery are not allowed. Any unfair competition activities conducted in foreign trade activities shall be subject to relevant laws and administrative regulations against unfair competition. Where any illegal activities as provided in the preceding paragraph occur with the effect of impairing the foreign trade order, the competent foreign trade department of the State Council may take measures to eliminate the impairment, such as prohibiting the undertaking from importing or exporting the goods or technologies involved.

A-6

Price Law of the People's Republic of China (Articles 14, 40, and 41)

中华人民共和国价格法第十四条、四十条和四十一条

(Adopted by the Standing Committee of the 8th National People's Congress on December 29, 1997, effective as of May 1, 1998)

（第八届全国人民代表大会常务委员会于1997年12月29日审议通过，自1998年5月1日起施行）

第十四条 经营者不得有下列不正当价格行为： （一）　相互串通，操纵市场价格，损害其他经营者或者消费者的合法权益； （二）　在依法降价处理鲜活商品、季节性商品、积压商品等商品外，为了排挤竞争对手或者独占市场，以低于成本的价格倾销，扰乱正常的生产经营秩序，损害国家利益或者其他经营者的合法权益；	**Article 14** Undertakings must not engage in the following unfair pricing behavior: (1) colluding with others in manipulating market prices, thereby harming the lawful rights and interests of other undertakings or consumers; (2) dumping products below costs in order to force out competitors or to monopolize the market, thereby disturbing the normal order of production and business and harming the interests of the State or the lawful rights and interests of other undertakings, except for the lawful disposal at reduced prices of products such as fresh products, seasonal products, and overstocked products;

（三）捏造、散布涨价信息，哄抬价格，推动商品价格过高上涨的；	(3) fabricating and spreading rumors of price increases in order to drive up prices and cause product prices to increase excessively;
（四）利用虚假的或者使人误解的价格手段，诱骗消费者或者其他经营者与其进行交易；	(4) using false or misleading pricing practices in order to entice consumers or other undertakings into doing business with them;
（五）提供相同商品或者服务，对具有同等交易条件的其他经营者实行价格歧视；	(5) applying price discrimination when providing the same products or services to undertakings that have equal conditions for doing business;
（六）采取抬高等级或者压低等级等手段收购、销售商品或者提供服务，变相提高或者压低价格；	(6) purchasing or selling products or providing services by methods such as raising or reducing grade levels, thereby covertly forcing prices up or down;
（七）违反法律、法规的规定牟取暴利；	(7) seeking excessive profits in violation of laws and regulations; or
（八）法律、行政法规禁止的其他不正当价格行为。	(8) other unfair pricing acts prohibited by laws or administrative regulations.
第四十条 经营者有本法第十四条所列行为之一的，责令改正，没收违法所得，可以并处违法所得五倍以下的罚款；没有违法所得的，予以警告，可以并处罚款；情节严重的，责令停业整顿，或者由工商行政管理机关吊销营业执照。有关法律对本法第十四条所列行为的处罚及处罚机关另有规定的，可以依照有关法律的规定执行。	**Article 40** If an undertaking carries out any of the acts mentioned in Article 14, it shall be ordered to rectify the situation and its illegal gains shall be confiscated; and it may additionally be subjected to a fine of no more than five times the illegal gains. If there are no illegal gains, the undertaking shall be given a warning and, in addition, may be fined. If the circumstances are serious, the undertaking shall be ordered to suspend its business or the administration authority for industry and commerce shall revoke the undertaking's business license. If relevant laws contain different provisions in respect of the penalties and enforcing authorities for acts mentioned in Article 14, it may be handled in accordance with the provisions of the relevant laws.

第四十一条	**Article 41**
经营者因价格违法行为致使消费者或者其他经营者多付价款的，应当退还多付部分；造成损害的，应当依法承担赔偿责任。	An undertaking whose illegal pricing behavior results in overpayment by a consumer or another undertaking shall refund the overpaid portion of the price and, if damage is caused, assume liability for damages in accordance with the law.

A-7

Contract Law of the People's Republic of China (Articles 329 and 343)

中华人民共和国合同法第三百二十九条和三百四十三条

(Adopted by the 9th National People's Congress on March 15, 1999, effective as of October 1, 1999)

（第九届全国人民代表大会于1999年3月15日审议通过，自1999年10月1日起施行）

第三百二十九条 非法垄断技术、妨碍技术进步或者侵害他人技术成果的技术合同无效。	**Article 329** A technology contract that illegally monopolizes technology or impedes technological progress, or infringes upon the technological achievement of others shall be null and void.
第三百四十三条 技术转让合同可以约定让与人和受让人实施专利或者使用技术秘密的范围，但不得限制技术竞争和技术发展。	**Article 343** A technology transfer contract may specify the scope of the performing patent or use of know-how by the technology transferor and transferee, provided that no restriction be imposed on technological competition and technological development.

Interpretation of the Supreme People's Court Regarding Several Issues on the Application of Laws to Disputes over Technology Contracts (Article 10)

最高人民法院关于审理技术合同纠纷案件适用法律若干问题的解释第十条

(Adopted by the Supreme People's Court on November 30, 2004, effective as of January 1, 2005)

（2004年11月30日由最高人民法院审议通过，自2005年1月1日起施行）

第十条 下列情形，属于合同法第三百二十九条所称的"非法垄断技术、妨碍技术进步"： （一） 限制当事人一方在合同标的技术基础上进行新的研究开发或者限制其使用所改进的技术，或者双方交换改进技术的条件不对等，包括要求一方将其自行改进的技术无偿提供给对方、非互惠性转让给对方、无偿独占或者共享该改进技术的知识产权； （二） 限制当事人一方从其他来源获得与技术提供方类似技术或者与其竞争的技术； （三） 阻碍当事人一方根据市场需求，按照合理方式充分实施合同标的技术，包括明显不合理地限制技术接受方实施合同标的的技术生产产品或者提供服务的数量、品种、价格、销售渠道和出口市场；	Article 10 The following shall constitute "illegal monopolization of technology and impediment of technological progress" referred to in Article 329 of the Contract Law: (1) preventing a counter-party from conducting new R&D on the basis of the subject technology, restraining that party from using improvements to the technology, creating non-reciprocal conditions for the exchange of improvements, including requiring a party to share without compensation improvements that result solely from the efforts of that party, requiring the transfer of improvements to the other party on a non-reciprocal basis, or requiring the exclusive or joint holding of rights to improvements without compensation;

（四） 要求技术接受方接受并非实施技术必不可少的附带条件，包括购买非必需的技术、原材料、产品、设备、服务以及接收非必需的人员等； （五） 不合理地限制技术接受方购买原材料、零部件、产品或者设备等的渠道或者来源； （六） 禁止技术接受方对合同标的技术知识产权的有效性提出异议或者对提出异议附加条件。	(2) preventing a counter-party from acquiring from other sources technologies similar to, or in competition with, that provided by the transferor; (3) preventing a counter-party from fully employing the subject technology in a reasonable manner as required by the market, including unreasonably restricting quantity, variety, price, distribution channels, and export markets for products or services produced by the transferee using the contract technology; (4) imposing on the transferee additional conditions that are unnecessary for utilizing or employing the technology, including purchase of unnecessary technology, raw materials, products, equipment, or services, or acceptance of unnecessary personnel; (5) unreasonably restricting a transferee's channels or sources of procuring raw materials, parts, products, or equipment; and (6) prohibiting a technology transferee from challenging the validity of the intellectual property rights in the subject technology, or imposing additional conditions on making such challenges.

A-8

Bidding Law of the People's Republic of China (Excerpts)

中华人民共和国招标投标法（节选）

(Adopted by the Standing Committee of the
9th National People's Congress on August 30, 1999,
effective as of January 1, 2000)

（第九届全国人民代表大会常务委员会于1999年8月30日审
议通过，自2000年1月1日起施行）

第二十五条 投标人是响应招标、参加投标竞争的法人或者其他组织。 依法招标的科研项目允许个人参加投标的，投标的个人适用本法有关投标人的规定。	**Article 25** A bidder means a legal person or any other organization that responds to a tender and participates in a bid competition. If a scientific research project subject to tender according to law allows individual persons to participate in bidding, the provisions of this law on bidders shall apply to individual persons participating in bidding.
第三十二条 投标人不得相互串通投标报价，不得排挤其他投标人的公平竞争，损害招标人或者其他投标人的合法权益。 投标人不得与招标人串通投标，损害国家利益、社会公共利益或者他人的合法权益。 禁止投标人以向招标人或者评标委员会成员行贿的手段谋取中标。	**Article 32** A bidder may not collude with other bidders in submitting their bid price quotations or exclude fair competition by other bidders to prejudice the legitimate rights and interests of the tenderee or other bidders. A bidder may not collude with the bidder in submitting his bid to prejudice the State's interests, the social and public interests or the legitimate rights and interests of any other person.

	It is forbidden for bidders to offer bribes to the bidders or members of the bid assessment committees for winning.
第三十三条 投标人不得以低于成本的报价竞标，也不得以他人名义投标或者以其他方式弄虚作假，骗取中标。	**Article 33** A bidder may not submit his bid price quotation below cost for competition, and may not submit his bid in the name of another person or resort to any other false and deceptive method for winning.
第五十条 招标代理机构违反本法规定，泄露应当保密的与招标投标活动有关的情况和资料的，或者与招标人、投标人串通损害国家利益、社会公共利益或者他人合法权益的，处五万元以上二十五万元以下的罚款，对单位直接负责的主管人员和其他直接责任人员处单位罚款数额百分之五以上百分之十以下的罚款；有违法所得的，并处没收违法所得；情节严重的，暂停直至取消招标代理资格；构成犯罪的，依法追究刑事责任。给他人造成损失的，依法承担赔偿责任。 前款所列行为影响中标结果的，中标无效。	**Article 50** If a bidding agency violates this law by disclosing confidential information or materials relating to the bidding or conspiring with the tenderees or the bidders to prejudice the State's interests, the social and public interests or the legitimate rights and interests of any other person, it shall be subject to a fine of not less than RMB 50,000 and not more than RMB 250,000. The person-in-charge directly responsible for the entity or any other persons who are held directly responsible shall be subject to a fine of not less than 5% and not more than 10% of the total amount of fine imposed upon the entity. If there are illegal gains, such gains shall be confiscated. If the circumstances are serious, the agency's qualification may be suspended or even revoked. If the violation constitutes a crime, criminal liabilities shall be pursued in accordance with the law. If losses have resulted for others, the agency shall make compensations in accordance with the law. If the winning of the bid has been affected by any of the acts mentioned in the preceding paragraph, the bid shall be held invalid.

第五十三条 投标人相互串通投标或者与招标人串通投标的，投标人以向招标人或者评标委员会成员行贿的手段谋取中标的，中标无效，处中标项目金额千分之五以上千分之十以下的罚款，对单位直接负责的主管人员和其他直接责任人员处单位罚款数额百分之五以上百分之十以下的罚款；有违法所得的，并处没收违法所得；情节严重的，取消其一年至二年内参加依法必须进行招标的项目的投标资格并予以公告，直至由工商行政管理机关吊销营业执照；构成犯罪的，依法追究刑事责任。给他人造成损失的，依法承担赔偿责任。	**Article 53** If the bidder wins the bid by conspiring with the bidders or with the tenderee or paying bribes to the tenderee or members of the bid evaluation committee, the bid shall be invalid, and the bid winner shall be subject to a fine of not less than 0.5% and not more than 1% of the total value of the bidding project. The person-in-charge directly responsible for the entity or any other persons who are held directly responsible shall be subject to a fine of not less than 5% and not more than 10% of the total amount of the fine imposed upon the entity. If there are illegal gains, such gains shall be confiscated. If the circumstances are serious, the bidder shall be disqualified from participation in mandatory biddings for a term of one to two years and the penalties shall be published and the administration for industry and commerce may even revoke the bidder's business license. If the violation constitutes a crime, criminal liabilities shall be pursued in accordance with the law. If losses have resulted for others, the bidder shall make compensations in accordance with the law.
第五十四条 投标人以他人名义投标或者以其他方式弄虚作假，骗取中标的，中标无效，给招标人造成损失的，依法承担赔偿责任；构成犯罪的，依法追究刑事责任。 依法必须进行招标的项目的投标人有前款所列行为尚未构成犯罪的，处中标项目金额千分之五以上千分之十以下的罚款，对单位直接负责的主管人员和其他直接责任人员处单位罚款数额百分之五以上百分之十以下的罚款；有违法所得的，并处没收违法所得；情节严重的，取消其一年至三年内参加依法必须进行招标的项目的投标资格并予以公告，直至由工商行政管理机关吊销营业执照。	**Article 54** If the bidder wins the bid by using another person's name or through other fraudulent means, the bid shall be invalid. If losses have resulted for the tenderee, the bidder shall be responsible for compensation. If the bidder's act constitutes a crime, criminal liabilities shall be pursued in accordance with the law.

	If the bidder of a mandatory bidding commits any of the acts mentioned in the preceding paragraph, which does not constitute a crime, the bidder shall be subject to a fine of not less than 0.5% and not more than 1% of the total value of the bidding project. The person-in-charge directly responsible for the entity or any other persons who are held directly responsible shall be subject to a fine of not less than 5% and not more than 10% of the total amount of fine imposed upon the entity. If there are illegal gains, such gains shall be confiscated. If the circumstances are serious, the bidder shall be disqualified from participation in bidding for a term of one to three years from participation in mandatory biddings and the penalty shall be published and the administration for industry and commerce may even revoke the bidder's business license.

PART
B
REGULATIONS
法规

STATE COUNCIL

国务院法规

B-1

Regulation on Administrative Penalties for Pricing Violations (Excerpts)

价格违法行为行政处罚规定（节选）

(Adopted by the State Council on July 10, 1999, last amended on December 4, 2010, effective as of December 4, 2010)

（国务院于1999年7月10日审议通过，2010年12月4日最新修订，自2010年12月4日起施行）

第二条 县级以上各级人民政府价格主管部门依法对价格活动进行监督检查，并决定对价格违法行为的行政处罚。	**Article 2** The price authority of the people's governments at or above the county level shall supervise and inspect price-related activities in accordance with the law and determine the administrative penalties for pricing violations.
第三条 价格违法行为的行政处罚由价格违法行为发生地的地方人民政府价格主管部门决定；国务院价格主管部门规定由其上级价格主管部门决定的，从其规定。	**Article 3** The administrative penalties for pricing violations shall be determined by the price authority of the local people's government at the place where such violation occurs. If the price authority under the State Council provides that the administrative penalties shall be determined by the price authority at a higher level, such provisions shall prevail.
第四条 经营者违反价格法第十四条的规定，有下列行为之一的，责令改正，没收违法所得，并处违法所得5倍以下的罚款；没有违法所得的，	**Article 4** If an undertaking violates Article 14 of the Price Law by any of the following activities, it shall be ordered to take rectifying measures, have its illegal gains

(Continued)

处10万元以上100万元以下的罚款；情节严重的，责令停业整顿，或者由工商行政管理机关吊销营业执照： （一） 除依法降价处理鲜活商品、季节性商品、积压商品等商品外，为了排挤竞争对手或者独占市场，以低于成本的价格倾销，扰乱正常的生产经营秩序，损害国家利益或者其他经营者的合法权益的； （二） 提供相同商品或者服务，对具有同等交易条件的其他经营者实行价格歧视的。	confiscated and be imposed a fine of not more than five times the illegal gains. If there are no illegal gains, the undertaking shall be imposed a fine of not less than RMB 100,000 and not more than RMB 1 million. If the circumstances are serious, the undertaking shall be ordered to suspend its business or the administration authority for industry and commerce shall revoke the undertaking's business license: (1) dumping products below costs in order to force out competitors or to monopolize the market, thereby disturbing the normal order of production and business and harming the interests of the State or the lawful rights and interests of other undertakings, except for the lawful disposal at reduced prices of products such as fresh products, seasonal products, and overstocked products; (2) applying price discrimination when providing the same products or services to undertakings that have equal conditions for doing business.
第五条 经营者违反价格法第十四条的规定，相互串通，操纵市场价格，造成商品价格较大幅度上涨的，责令改正，没收违法所得，并处违法所得5倍以下的罚款；没有违法所得的，处10万元以上100万元以下的罚款，情节较重的处100万元以上500万元以下的罚款；情节严重的，责令停业整顿，或者由工商行政管理机关吊销营业执照。 除前款规定情形外，经营者相互串通，操纵市场价格，损害其他经营者或者消费者合法权益的，依照本规定第四条的规定处罚。	**Article 5** If an undertaking violates Article 14 of the Price Law by colluding with others to manipulate market prices, which has resulted in considerable increase of the product prices, it shall be ordered to take rectifying measures, have its illegal gains confiscated, and be imposed a fine of not more than five times the illegal gains. If there are no illegal gains, it shall be imposed a fine of not less than RMB 100,000 and not more than RMB 1 million, or a fine of not less than RMB 1 million and not more than RMB 5 million if the circumstances are relatively serious. If the circumstances are serious, the undertaking shall be ordered to suspend its business or the administration authority for industry and commerce shall revoke the undertaking's business license.

行业协会或者其他单位组织经营者相互串通，操纵市场价格的，对经营者依照前两款的规定处罚；对行业协会或者其他单位，可以处50万元以下的罚款，情节严重的，由登记管理机关依法撤销登记、吊销执照。	In addition to the circumstances provided in the preceding paragraph, if an undertaking colludes with others to manipulate market prices, thereby harming the lawful rights and interests of other undertakings or consumers, it shall be penalized in accordance with Article 4 of this regulation. If any trade association or other organization organizes undertakings to collude with others to manipulate market prices, the undertakings shall be penalized in accordance with the preceding two paragraphs and the trade association or other organization may be imposed a fine of not more than RMB 500,000 and, if the circumstances are serious, the registration administration can deregister them or revoke their licenses in accordance with the law.
第六条 经营者违反价格法第十四条的规定，有下列推动商品价格过快、过高上涨行为之一的，责令改正，没收违法所得，并处违法所得5倍以下的罚款；没有违法所得的，处5万元以上50万元以下的罚款，情节较重的处50万元以上300万元以下的罚款；情节严重的，责令停业整顿，或者由工商行政管理机关吊销营业执照： （一）　捏造、散布涨价信息，扰乱市场价格秩序的； （二）　除生产自用外，超出正常的存储数量或者存储周期，大量囤积市场供应紧张、价格发生异常波动的商品，经价格主管部门告诫仍继续囤积的； （三）　利用其他手段哄抬价格，推动商品价格过快、过高上涨的。 行业协会或者为商品交易提供服务的单位有前款规定的违法行为的，可以处50万元以下的罚款；情节严重的，由登记管理机关依法撤销登记、吊销执照。	**Article 6** If an undertaking violates Article 14 of the Price Law by any of the following activities that have pushed up the product prices too fast or to an excessive level, it shall be ordered to take rectifying measures, have its illegal gains confiscated, and be imposed a fine of not more than five times the illegal gains. If there are no illegal gains, it shall be imposed a fine of not less than RMB 50,000 and not more than RMB 500,000, or a fine of not less than RMB 500,000 and not more than RMB 3 million if the circumstances are relatively serious. If the circumstances are serious, the undertaking shall be ordered to suspend its business or the administration authority for industry and commerce shall revoke the undertaking's business license: (1)　fabricating and spreading rumors of price increases, thereby disrupting the market price order;

(*Continued*)

前两款规定以外的其他单位散布虚假涨价信息，扰乱市场价格秩序，依法应当由其他主管机关查处的，价格主管部门可以提出依法处罚的建议，有关主管机关应当依法处罚。	(2) except for the purpose of self-consumption in production, hoarding a large number of products that are in short supply or with abnormal price fluctuations beyond normal storage need or storage cycle and continuing to do so after being warned by the price authority; (3) taking other means to drive up product prices too fast or to an excessive level. If any trade association or any entity that provides product trading services engages in any of the violations provided in the preceding paragraph, it may be imposed a fine of not more than RMB 500,000 and, if the circumstances are serious, the registration administration can deregister them or revoke their licenses in accordance with the law. If any entity other than the ones provided in the preceding two paragraphs spreads false information of price increases, disrupting the market price order and shall be handled by other authorities, the price authorities can provide penalty suggestions and the relevant authorities shall issue penalties in accordance with the law.
第七条 经营者违反价格法第十四条的规定，利用虚假的或者使人误解的价格手段，诱骗消费者或者其他经营者与其进行交易的，责令改正，没收违法所得，并处违法所得5倍以下的罚款；没有违法所得的，处5万元以上50万元以下的罚款；情节严重的，责令停业整顿，或者由工商行政管理机关吊销营业执照。	**Article 7** If an undertaking violates Article 14 of the Price Law by using false or misleading pricing practices in order to entice consumers or other undertakings into doing business with it, the undertaking shall be ordered to take rectifying measures, have its illegal gains confiscated, and be imposed a fine of not more than five times the illegal gains. If there are no illegal gains, it shall be imposed a fine of not less than RMB 50,000 and not more than RMB 500,000. If the circumstances are serious, the undertaking shall be ordered to suspend its business or the administration authority for industry and commerce shall revoke the undertaking's business license.

第八条 经营者违反价格法第十四条的规定，采取抬高等级或者压低等级等手段销售、收购商品或者提供服务，变相提高或者压低价格的，责令改正，没收违法所得，并处违法所得5倍以下的罚款；没有违法所得的，处2万元以上20万元以下的罚款；情节严重的，责令停业整顿，或者由工商行政管理机关吊销营业执照。	**Article 8** If an undertaking violates Article 14 of the Price Law by purchasing or selling products or providing services by methods such as raising or reducing grade levels, thereby covertly forcing prices up or down, it shall be ordered to take rectifying measures, have its illegal gains confiscated, and be imposed a fine of not more than five times the illegal gains. If there are no illegal gains, it shall be imposed a fine of not less than RMB 20,000 and not more than RMB 200,000. If the circumstances are serious, the undertaking shall be ordered to suspend its business or the administration authority for industry and commerce shall revoke the undertaking's business license.

B-2

Regulation on the Administration of Import and Export of Technologies of the People's Republic of China (Articles 2, 27, and 29)

中华人民共和国技术进出口管理条例第二条、二十七条和二十九条

(Adopted by the State Council on October 31, 2001, last amended on January 8, 2011, effective as of January 8, 2011)

（国务院于2001年10月31日审议通过，2011年1月8日最新修订，自2011年1月8日起施行）

第二条 本条例所称技术进出口，是指从中华人民共和国境外向中华人民共和国境内，或者从中华人民共和国境内向中华人民共和国境外，通过贸易、投资或者经济技术合作的方式转移技术的行为。 前款规定的行为包括专利权转让、专利申请权转让、专利实施许可、技术秘密转让、技术服务和其他方式的技术转移。	**Article 2** Import and export of technologies in this regulation refer to the transfer of technologies from outside of the People's Republic of China into the People's Republic of China, or from inside of the People's Republic of China to outside of the People's Republic of China, by way of foreign trade, investment or economic or technological cooperation. Such transfer includes assignment of patent rights or rights to apply for patents, licensing of rights to implement patents, assignment of technical know-how, technical service and other means of technology transfer.

第二十七条 在技术进口合同有效期内，改进技术的成果属于改进方。	**Article 27** During the term of a contract of import of technologies, the ownership of improvements of the technologies shall be vested with the party making such improvements.
第二十九条 技术进口合同中，不得含有下列限制性条款: (一) 要求受让人接受并非技术进口必不可少的附带条件，包括购买非必需的技术、原材料、产品、设备或者服务; (二) 要求受让人为专利权有效期限届满或者专利权被宣布无效的技术支付使用费或者承担相关义务; (三) 限制受让人改进让与人提供的技术或者限制受让人使用所改进的技术; (四) 限制受让人从其他来源获得与让与人提供的技术类似的技术或者与其竞争的技术; (五) 不合理地限制受让人购买原材料、零部件、产品或者设备的渠道或者来源; (六) 不合理地限制受让人产品的生产数量、品种或者销售价格; (七) 不合理地限制受让人利用进口的技术生产产品的出口渠道。	**Article 29** A technology import contract shall not contain any of the following restrictive terms which require the transferee to: (1) accept conditions that are non-essential for the import of the technology, including the purchase of unnecessary technologies, raw materials, products, equipment or services; (2) pay license fees or assume relevant obligations for using technologies whose patent has expired or has been declared void; (3) refrain from making improvements to the technologies provided by the transferor or from using such improvements; (4) refrain from obtaining from other sources technologies similar to or competing with the technologies provided by transferor; (5) unreasonably limit the channels or sources from which the transferee may purchase raw materials, parts, products or equipment; (6) unreasonably limit the production quantity, type or sale price of the transferee's products; or (7) unreasonably limit the export channels for products produced by the transferee using the imported technologies.

B-3

Circular of the General Office of the State Council on the Main Functions and Constituent Members of the Anti-Monopoly Commission of the State Council

国务院办公厅关于国务院反垄断委员会主要职责和组成人员的通知

(Promulgated by the General Office of the State Council on July 28, 2008, effective as of July 28, 2008)

（国务院办公厅于2008年7月28日发布，
自2008年7月28日起施行）

各省、自治区、直辖市人民政府，国务院各部委、各直属机构： 根据《中华人民共和国反垄断法》的有关规定，成立国务院反垄断委员会。经国务院批准，现将有关事项通知如下：	The People's Government of each province, autonomous region, provincial level municipality, each ministry and commission under the State Council, and the Ministries, Commissions and other organizations directly under the State Council: Pursuant to the relevant provisions of the Anti-Monopoly Law of the People's Republic of China, the Anti-Monopoly Commission of the State Council is hereby established, and with the approval of the State Council, we hereby notify you of the following related issues:
一、主要职责 研究拟订有关竞争政策；组织调查、评估市场总体竞争状况，发布评估报告；制定、发布反垄断指南；协调反垄断行政执法工作；国务院规定的其他职责。	**1 Main Functions** Research and formulate related policies on competition; organize investigations and evaluations of the general competitive conditions on the market, and issue an evaluation report;

	formulate and release anti-monopoly guidelines, coordinate anti-monopoly administrative law enforcement work; other functions stipulated by the State Council.
二、组成人员 主任：　王岐山（国务院副总理） 副主任：陈德铭（商务部部长） 　　　　张平（发展改革委主任） 　　　　周伯华（工商总局局长） 　　　　毕井泉（国务院副秘书长） 委员：　张茅（发展改革委副主任） 　　　　欧新黔（工业和信息化部副部长） 　　　　姚增科（监察部副部长） 　　　　张少春（财政部副部长） 　　　　高宏峰（交通运输部副部长） 　　　　马秀红（商务部副部长） 　　　　黄淑和（国资委副主任） 　　　　钟攸平（工商总局副局长） 　　　　张勤（知识产权局副局长） 　　　　张穹（法制办副主任） 　　　　蔡鄂生（银监会副主席） 　　　　桂敏杰（证监会副主席） 　　　　魏迎宁（保监会副主席） 　　　　王禹民（电监会副主席）	**2 Constituent Members** **Chairman:** Wang Qishan, Vice-Premier of the State Council **Vice Chairmen:** Chen Deming, Minister of the Ministry of Commerce Zhang Ping, Chairman of the National Development and Reform Commission Zhou Bohua, Director of the State Administration for Industry and Commerce Bi Jingquan, Deputy Secretary-General of the State Council **Numbers of the Committee:** Zhang Mao, Vice Chairman of the National Development and Reform Commission Ou Xinqian, Vice Minister of the Ministry of Industry and Information Technology Yao Zengke, Vice Minister of the Ministry of Supervision Zhang Shaochun, Vice Minister of the Ministry of Finance Gao Hongfeng, Vice Minister of the Ministry of Communications Ma Xiuhong, Vice Minister of the Ministry of Commerce Huang Shuhe, Vice Chairman of the State-owned Assets Supervision and Administration Commission Zhong Youping, Vice Director of the State Administration for Industry and Commerce Zhang Qin, Vice Director of the State Intellectual Property Office

(Continued)

	Zhang Qiong, Deputy Director of the Legislative Affairs Office of the State Council
	Cai Esheng, Vice Chairman of the China Banking Regulatory Commission
	Gui Minjie, Vice Chairman of the China Securities Regulatory Commission
	Wei Yingning, Vice Chairman of the China Insurance Regulatory Commission
	Wang Yumin, Vice Chairman of the China Electricity Regulatory Commission
三、其他事项 国务院反垄断委员会的具体工作由商务部承担，马秀红同志兼任秘书长。委员会成员因工作变动需要调整的，由所在单位提出意见报委员会主任审批。	**3 Other Issues** The Ministry of Commerce shall handle the daily work of the Anti-Monopoly Commission of the State Council, and Vice Minister Ma Xiuhong shall concurrently serve as general secretary. In the event that a member of the Commission needs to be changed due to position change, the organization for which he/she works shall submit its opinion to the Chairman for approval.
中华人民共和国国务院办公厅 二〇〇八年七月二十八日	General Office of the State Council July 28, 2008

B-4

Regulation of the State Council on the Notification Thresholds for Concentrations of Undertakings

国务院关于经营者集中申报标准的规定

(Promulgated by the State Council on August 3, 2008, effective as of August 3, 2008)

（国务院于2008年8月3日发布，自2008年8月3日起施行）

第一条 为了明确经营者集中的申报标准，根据《中华人民共和国反垄断法》，制定本规定。	**Article 1** This Regulation is formulated in accordance with the Anti-Monopoly Law of the People's Republic of China for the purpose of defining the thresholds for prior notification of concentrations of undertakings.
第二条 经营者集中是指下列情形： （一）　经营者合并； （二）　经营者通过取得股权或者资产的方式取得对其他经营者的控制权； （三）　经营者通过合同等方式取得对其他经营者的控制权或者能够对其他经营者施加决定性影响。	**Article 2** A concentration of undertakings means any of the following: (1)　mergers; (2)　acquisition of control over other undertakings through the acquisition of equity or assets; or (3)　acquisition of control over other undertakings or the capacity to exercise decisive influence on other undertakings by contract or any other means.
第三条 经营者集中达到下列标准之一的，经营者应当事先向国务院商务主管部门申报，未申报的不得实施集中：	**Article 3** Where a concentration of undertakings reaches any of the following thresholds, the undertaking(s) concerned shall file a prior notification with the competent commerce department of the State Council,

(Continued)

（一）　参与集中的所有经营者上一会计年度在全球范围内的营业额合计超过100亿元人民币，并且其中至少两个经营者上一会计年度在中国境内的营业额均超过4亿元人民币；	and no such concentration may be implemented without the approval of prior notification:
（二）　参与集中的所有经营者上一会计年度在中国境内的营业额合计超过20亿元人民币，并且其中至少两个经营者上一会计年度在中国境内的营业额均超过4亿元人民币。	(1)　the combined worldwide turnover of all the undertakings concerned in the preceding financial year is more than RMB 10 billion yuan, and the nationwide turnover within China of each of at least two of the undertakings concerned in the preceding financial year is more than RMB 400 million yuan; or
营业额的计算，应当考虑银行、保险、证券、期货等特殊行业、领域的实际情况，具体办法由国务院商务主管部门会同国务院有关部门制定。	(2)　the combined nationwide turnover within China of all the undertakings concerned in the preceding financial year is more than RMB 2 billion yuan, and the nationwide turnover within China of each of at least two of the undertakings concerned in the preceding financial year is more than RMB 400 million yuan.
	For the calculation of turnover, the unique circumstances of such special industries or sectors as banking, insurance, securities, and futures shall be taken into account, and the specific measures therefore shall be formulated by the competent commerce department of the State Council in conjunction with other relevant departments of the State Council.
第四条 经营者集中未达到本规定第三条规定的申报标准，但按照规定程序收集的事实和证据表明该经营者集中具有或者可能具有排除、限制竞争效果的，国务院商务主管部门应当依法进行调查。	**Article 4** Where a concentration of undertakings does not reach any of the thresholds specified in Article 3 of this Regulation, but facts and evidence collected in accordance with the prescribed procedures establish that such concentration has the effect, or is likely to have the effect, of eliminating and/or restricting competition, the competent commerce department of the State Council shall initiate an investigation in accordance with the law.
第五条 本规定自公布之日起施行。	**Article 5** This Regulation shall become effective as of the date of promulgation.

B-5

Guidelines on the Definition of the Relevant Market by the Anti-Monopoly Commission of the State Council

国务院反垄断委员会关于相关市场界定的指南

(Promulgated by the Anti-Monopoly Commission of the State Council on May 24, 2009, effective as of May 24, 2009)

（国务院反垄断委员会于2009年5月24日发布，自2009年5月24日起施行）

第一章　总　则	Chapter 1　General
第一条　指南的目的和依据 为了给相关市场界定提供指导，提高国务院反垄断执法机构执法工作的透明度，根据《中华人民共和国反垄断法》（以下称《反垄断法》），制定本指南。	**Article 1　Purpose and Basis of the Guidelines** These guidelines are formulated in accordance with the Anti-Monopoly Law of the People's Republic of China ("AML") to provide guidance for the definition of the relevant markets and to improve transparency in the law enforcement actions by the anti-monopoly enforcement authorities under the State Council.
第二条　界定相关市场的作用 任何竞争行为（包括具有或可能具有排除、限制竞争效果的行为）均发生在一定的市场范围内。界定相关市场就是明确经营者竞争的市场范围。在禁止经营者达成垄断协议、禁止经营者滥用市场支配地位、控制具有或者可能具有排除、限制竞争效果的经营者集中等反垄断执法工作中，均可能涉及相关市场的界定问题。	**Article 2　The Significance of the Definition of the Relevant Market** All competitive conduct (including that which has or may have the effect of eliminating and/or restricting competition) takes place within a certain market. The definition of the relevant market aims at identifying the markets within which the undertakings compete. All anti-monopoly enforcement activities, such as the prohibition of monopoly

(Continued)

科学合理地界定相关市场，对识别竞争者和潜在竞争者、判定经营者市场份额和市场集中度、认定经营者的市场地位、分析经营者的行为对市场竞争的影响、判断经营者行为是否违法以及在违法情况下需承担的法律责任等关键问题，具有重要的作用。因此，相关市场的界定通常是对竞争行为进行分析的起点，是反垄断执法工作的重要步骤。	agreements between undertakings, the prohibition of any abuse of dominant market position, and the control of concentrations of undertakings that have or may have the effect of eliminating and/or restricting competition, may involve the issue of relevant market definition. Scientific and reasonable definition of the relevant market is of significant importance for key issues such as the identification of competitors and potential competitors, the determination of the market shares of undertakings and the level of market concentration, the determination of the market position of an undertaking, the analysis of the effect of an undertaking's conduct on market competition, and the determination of the legality of an undertaking's conduct and legal liabilities in case of a violation. Therefore, the definition of the relevant market is often the starting point for the analysis of a competitive conduct, and is an important step in anti-monopoly law enforcement actions.
第三条 相关市场的含义 相关市场是指经营者在一定时期内就特定商品或者服务(以下统称商品)进行竞争的商品范围和地域范围。在反垄断执法实践中，通常需要界定相关商品市场和相关地域市场。 相关商品市场，是根据商品的特性、用途及价格等因素，由需求者认为具有较为紧密替代关系的一组或一类商品所构成的市场。这些商品表现出较强的竞争关系，在反垄断执法中可以作为经营者进行竞争的商品范围。 相关地域市场，是指需求者获取具有较为紧密替代关系的商品的地理区域。这些地域表现出较强的竞争关系，在反垄断执法中可以作为经营者进行竞争的地域范围。	**Article 3 The Meaning of the Relevant Market** The relevant market refers to the product and geographic market within which the undertakings compete against each other during a certain period of time with respect to specific products or services (hereinafter "Product"). In anti-monopoly law enforcement practice, it is often required to define the relevant product and geographic market. The relevant product market comprises all those products of the same group or category which are regarded to be close substitutes by customers, by reason of the products' characteristics, their intended use, their prices, etc.

当生产周期、使用期限、季节性、流行时尚性或知识产权保护期限等已构成商品不可忽视的特征时，界定相关市场还应考虑时间性。 在技术贸易、许可协议等涉及知识产权的反垄断执法工作中，可能还需要界定相关技术市场，考虑知识产权、创新等因素的影响。	In anti-monopoly law enforcement actions, those products are in strong competition relationship and may be considered to constitute a product scope within which the undertakings compete. The relevant geographic market means the geographic area in which customers procure closely substitutable products. Such geographical areas are in strong competition relationship and in anti-monopoly law enforcement actions may be considered to constitute a geographical scope within which the undertakings compete. When the products are such that the relevant factors, such as the production cycle, service life, seasonal factors, fashion, or protection period of intellectual property rights, could not be ignored, the definition of the relevant market shall also consider the question of timeliness. In anti-monopoly enforcement involving IPRs, such as technology trade and licensing agreements, it also may be necessary to define the relevant technology market and to consider the effects of IPRs, innovation, and other factors.
第二章　界定相关市场的基本依据	**Chapter 2 Essential Basis for the Definition of the Relevant Market**
第四条　替代性分析 在反垄断执法实践中，相关市场范围的大小主要取决于商品（地域）的可替代程度。 在市场竞争中对经营者行为构成直接和有效竞争约束的，是市场里存在需求者认为具有较强替代关系的商品或能够提供这些商品的地域，因此，界定相关市场主要从需求者角度进行需求替代分析。当供给替代对经营者行为产生的竞争约束类似于需求替代时，也应考虑供给替代。	**Article 4 Analysis of Substitutability** In anti-monopoly law enforcement practice, the scope of the relevant market primarily depends on the level of substitutability of the products (geographic areas). The existence of products in the market deemed as close substitutes by customers or the existence of geographical areas offering such products constitute a direct and effective competitive constraint over the behavior of undertakings.

(Continued)

	Therefore, in defining the relevant market, the primary analysis is focused on demand substitution from the perspective of customers. When supply substitution places a similarly competitive constraint on the behavior of the undertakings as demand substitution does, supply substitution shall also be considered.
第五条　需求替代 需求替代是根据需求者对商品功能用途的需求、质量的认可、价格的接受以及获取的难易程度等因素，从需求者的角度确定不同商品之间的替代程度。 原则上，从需求者角度来看，商品之间的替代程度越高，竞争关系就越强，就越可能属于同一相关市场。	**Article 5 Demand Substitution** Demand substitution is analyzed from the perspective of the customer, in order to determine the level of substitutability among different products based on the customer's demand for the product's function and usage, quality, and price acceptance as well as accessibility to the products. In principle, from the perspective of the customer, the higher level of substitutability among products, the stronger the competition between them, and the more likely the products belong to the same relevant market.
第六条　供给替代 供给替代是根据其他经营者改造生产设施的投入、承担的风险、进入目标市场的时间等因素，从经营者的角度确定不同商品之间的替代程度。 原则上，其他经营者生产设施改造的投入越少，承担的额外风险越小，提供紧密替代商品越迅速，则供给替代程度就越高，界定相关市场尤其在识别相关市场参与者时就应考虑供给替代。	**Article 6 Supply Substitution** Supply substitution is analyzed from the perspective of undertakings, to determine the level of substitutability among different products based on such factors as the amount of investment required for other undertakings to retrofit production facilities, the risks thus undertaken, and the timeline for entry into the target market. In principle, the less investment required for other undertakings to retrofit production facilities, the lower the additional risks, the faster they can supply close substitutes of products, the higher level of supply substitutability, and supply substitution shall be considered when defining the relevant market, especially when identifying the participants in the relevant market.

第三章　界定相关市场的一般方法	**Chapter 3 General Methods for the Definition of Relevant Markets**
第七条　界定相关市场的方法概述 界定相关市场的方法不是唯一的。在反垄断执法实践中，根据实际情况，可能使用不同的方法。界定相关市场时，可以基于商品的特征、用途、价格等因素进行需求替代分析，必要时进行供给替代分析。在经营者竞争的市场范围不够清晰或不易确定时，可以按照"假定垄断者测试"的分析思路（具体见第十条）来界定相关市场。 反垄断执法机构鼓励经营者根据案件具体情况运用客观、真实的数据，借助经济学分析方法来界定相关市场。 无论采用何种方法界定相关市场，都要始终把握商品满足消费者需求的基本属性，并以此作为对相关市场界定中出现明显偏差时进行校正的依据。	**Article 7 Overview of the Methods Used in Defining the Relevant Market** There is more than one method for the definition of the relevant market. In anti-monopoly law enforcement practices, different methods may be employed depending on the actual circumstances. The relevant market may be defined by an analysis of the demand substitution based on such facts as the characteristics, usage, and price of the products, and, if necessary, by an analysis of the supply substitution. Where the scope of the market in which the undertakings compete is not clear enough, or is difficult to determine, the analytic methodology of the "Hypothetical Monopolist Test" (see Article 10 for details) may be employed to define the relevant market. The Anti-Monopoly Law Enforcement Authorities encourage undertakings to define the relevant market with the assistance of economic analysis on the basis of the specific circumstances as well as objective and genuine data. Regardless of the method used to define the relevant market, the fundamental attributes of the products which meet the demand of the customers shall not be overlooked, and such fundamental attributes shall be the basis for making corrections when there is any obvious deviation in definition of the relevant market.
第八条　界定相关商品市场考虑的主要因素 从需求替代角度界定相关商品市场，可以考虑的因素包括但不限于以下各方面： （一）　需求者因商品价格或其他竞争因素变化，转向或考虑转向购买其他商品的证据。	**Article 8 Primary Factors for Consideration in Defining the Relevant Product Market** When defining the relevant product market in terms of demand substitution, the following factors may be considered, including, without limitation:

(Continued)

（二） 商品的外形、特性、质量和技术特点等总体特征和用途。商品可能在特征上表现出某些差异，但需求者仍可以基于商品相同或相似的用途将其视为紧密替代品。 （三） 商品之间的价格差异。通常情况下，替代性较强的商品价格比较接近，而且在价格变化时表现出同向变化趋势。在分析价格时，应排除与竞争无关的因素引起价格变化的情况。 （四） 商品的销售渠道。销售渠道不同的商品面对的需求者可能不同，相互之间难以构成竞争关系，则成为相关商品的可能性较小。 （五） 其他重要因素。如，需求者偏好或需求者对商品的依赖程度；可能阻碍大量需求者转向某些紧密替代商品的障碍、风险和成本；是否存在区别定价等。 从供给角度界定相关商品市场，一般考虑的因素包括：其他经营者对商品价格等竞争因素的变化做出反应的证据；其他经营者的生产流程和工艺，转产的难易程度，转产需要的时间，转产的额外费用和风险，转产后所提供商品的市场竞争力，营销渠道等。 任何因素在界定相关商品市场时的作用都不是绝对的，可以根据案件的不同情况有所侧重。	(1) evidence that customers switch or consider switching to other products due to any change in the product price or any other competitive factors; (2) the overall characteristics and usage of the products, such as the products' appearance, property, quality, and technical features. Although there might be some differences in features among the products, the customers may still consider them as close substitutes based on identical or similar usage of the products; (3) price differences among products. Normally, prices of products with strong substitutable relationships are similar to each other and tend to move in the same direction in times of price change. In the process of price analysis, the circumstances where non-competition-related factors lead to price changes shall be ruled out; (4) the sales channel of the products. Products marketed through different sales channels will likely face different customers, and it would be difficult for competition to arise between those products, and thus it is less likely for them to constitute relevant products; and (5) other important factors, such as the customer's preference or reliance on certain products, any obstacle, risk, or costs that may impede mass switch to closely substitutable products, and existence of differentiated pricing, etc. When defining the relevant product market from the supply side, the following factors are generally considered: evidence of reactions

	of other undertakings to the change in competitive factors such as product price; the production process and techniques of other undertakings, the difficulties in shifting to production of products, the time required to make the shift, any extra expenses and risks incurred by the shift, the market competitiveness of the products manufactured after the shift, the marketing channels, etc. No factor plays an absolute role in defining relevant product markets, and more emphasis may be focused on some of the factors than on others on a case-by-case basis.
第九条　界定相关地域市场考虑的主要因素 从需求替代角度界定相关地域市场，可以考虑的因素包括但不限于以下各方面： （一）　需求者因商品价格或其他竞争因素变化，转向或考虑转向其他地域购买商品的证据。 （二）　商品的运输成本和运输特征。相对于商品价格来说，运输成本越高，相关地域市场的范围越小，如水泥等商品；商品的运输特征也决定了商品的销售地域，如需要管道运输的工业气体等商品。 （三）　多数需求者选择商品的实际区域和主要经营者商品的销售分布。 （四）　地域间的贸易壁垒，包括关税、地方性法规、环保因素、技术因素等。如关税相对商品的价格来说比较高时，则相关地域市场很可能是一个区域性市场。 （五）　其他重要因素。如，特定区域需求者偏好；商品运进和运出该地域的数量。 从供给角度界定相关地域市场时，一般考虑的因素包括：其他地域的经营者对商品价格等竞争因素的变化做出	**Article 9　Primary Factors for Consideration in Defining the Relevant Geographic Market** When defining the relevant geographic market from the demand side, the following factors may be considered, including, without limitation: (1)　evidence that customers switch or consider switching to other geographical areas for the product due to any change in the product price or any other competitive factors; (2)　the transportation costs and the characteristics of such transportation. The higher the transportation cost for a product, relative to the price of a product, the smaller the relevant geographic market, such as in the case of cement. The characteristics of transportation for a product will also determine the geographic area to which the product is marketed, such as in the case of industrial gas, which requires transportation by pipeline; (3)　the actual geographic areas from which the majority of customers select their products, and the geographic distribution of the major undertakings' products;

(Continued)

反应的证据；其他地域的经营者供应或销售相关商品的即时性和可行性，如将订单转向其他地域经营者的转换成本等。	(4) trade barriers between different geographic areas, such as tariffs, local rules, environmental protection, technical factors, etc. When customs duties are high relative to the price of the product, the relevant geographic market would likely be a regional market; and (5) other major factors such as the preference of customers within a certain region, and the quantity of inbound and outbound products for a certain geographic area. When defining the relevant geographic market from the supply side, the following factors are generally considered: evidence of the reactions of undertakings in other geographic areas to the change in competitive factors such as the product price; the promptness and feasibility for undertakings in other geographic areas to supply or market the relevant product, such as the switching costs associated with switching the orders to undertakings in other geographic areas.
第四章　关于假定垄断者测试分析思路的说明	**Chapter 4 Explanation of the Analytic Methodology of the Hypothetical Monopolist Test**
第十条　假定垄断者测试的基本思路 假定垄断者测试是界定相关市场的一种分析思路，可以帮助解决相关市场界定中可能出现的不确定性，目前为各国和地区制定反垄断指南时普遍采用。依据这种思路，人们可以借助经济学工具分析所获取的相关数据，确定假定垄断者可以将价格维持在高于竞争价格水平的最小商品集合和地域范围，从而界定相关市场。 假定垄断者测试一般先界定相关商品市场。首先从反垄断审查关注的经营者提供的商品（目标商品）开始考虑，	**Article 10 The Basic Idea of the Hypothetical Monopolist Test** The hypothetical monopolist test is an analytic methodology to define the relevant market, which can help overcome uncertainties which may arise in defining the relevant market and is currently widely adopted in formulating anti-monopoly guidelines by many countries and regions. Under this methodology, economic tools may be used to analyze the relevant data to determine the smallest product group and geographic scope within which the

假设该经营者是以利润最大化为经营目标的垄断者(假定垄断者)，那么要分析的问题是，在其他商品的销售条件保持不变的情况下，假定垄断者能否持久地(一般为1年)小幅(一般为5%－10%)提高目标商品的价格。目标商品涨价会导致需求者转向购买具有紧密替代关系的其他商品，从而引起假定垄断者销售量下降。如果目标商品涨价后，即使假定垄断者销售量下降，但其仍然有利可图，则目标商品就构成相关商品市场。

如果涨价引起需求者转向具有紧密替代关系的其他商品，使假定垄断者的涨价行为无利可图，则需要把该替代商品增加到相关商品市场中，该替代商品与目标商品形成商品集合。接下来分析如果该商品集合涨价，假定垄断者是否仍有利可图。如果答案是肯定的，那么该商品集合就构成相关商品市场；否则还需要继续进行上述分析过程。

随着商品集合越来越大，集合内商品与集合外商品的替代性越来越小，最终会出现某一商品集合，假定垄断者可以通过涨价实现盈利，由此便界定出相关商品市场。

界定相关地域市场与界定相关商品市场的思路相同。首先从反垄断审查关注的经营者经营活动的地域(目标地域)开始，要分析的问题是，在其他地域的销售条件不变的情况下，假定垄断者对目标地域内的相关商品进行持久(一般为1年)小幅涨价(一般为5%－10%)是否有利可图。如果答案是肯定的，目标地域就构成相关地域市场；如果其他地域市场的强烈替代使得涨价无利可图，就需要扩大地域范围，直到涨价最终有利可图，该地域就是相关地域市场。

hypothetical monopolist could maintain its prices above the competitive price level so as to define the relevant market.

Under the hypothetical monopolist test, the relevant product market is generally defined first. It will start with the product (target product) supplied by the undertaking which is in the focus of the anti-monopoly review. Let's assume that the undertaking is a monopolist (hypothetical monopolist) striving for maximization of profits; the question is, assuming the sales conditions remain unchanged for other products, whether the monopolist could increase the price of the target product by a modest percentage (normally 5–10%) for a non-transitory period (normally one year). The rise in price of the target product will cause customers to switch to other close substitutes, which will reduce the sales volume of the hypothetical monopolist. If upon the price increase of the target product, though the sales volume of the hypothetical monopolist drops but is still profitable for the hypothetical monopolist, the target product constitutes the relevant product market.

If customers switch to other close substitutes as a result of the price increase, which makes the price increase of the hypothetical monopolist unprofitable, such substitute should be included in the relevant product market, and such substitute and target product constitute a product group. The next step would be to analyze whether the hypothetical monopolist would be profitable upon increase in price of the said product group. If the answer is positive, the product group would constitute the relevant product market; otherwise, the above analytical process would be continued.

(Continued)

	As the product group expands, the substitutability between products within and outside the product groups will diminish, and a certain product group will finally emerge, in which, the hypothetical monopolist could profitably increase the price, and in this way, the relevant product market is defined.
	The methodology for defining the relevant geographic market is the same as that for the relevant product market. The starting point is the geographic area where the undertaking carries out activities (target geographic area). What we need to analyze is whether it would be profitable for the hypothetical monopolist to raise the price by a modest percentage (normally 5–10%) for the relevant products in the said geographic area for a non-transitory period (normally one year) when the sales conditions in the other geographic areas are kept constant. If the answer is positive, the target geographic area constitutes relevant geographic market; otherwise if the strong substitution from another geographic area makes the price increase unprofitable, the scope of the geographic area should be expanded, until the price increase finally becomes profitable for the hypothetical monopolist, at which point, such geographic area means the relevant geographic market.
第十一条　假定垄断者测试的几个实际问题 原则上，在使用假定垄断者测试界定相关市场时，选取的基准价格应为充分竞争的当前市场价格。但在滥用市场支配地位、共谋行为和已经存在共谋行为的经营者集中案件中，当前价格明显偏离竞争价格，	**Article 11 Several Practical Problems with the Hypothetical Monopolist Test** In principle, when defining the relevant market through the hypothetical monopolist test, the benchmark price used shall be the fully competitive and currently prevailing market price. However, in abuse of dominant market position,

选择当前价格作为基准价格会使相关市场界定的结果不合理。在此情况下，应该对当前价格进行调整，使用更具有竞争性的价格。 此外，一般情况下，价格上涨幅度为5%－10%，但在执法实践中，可以根据案件涉及行业的不同情况，对价格小幅上涨的幅度进行分析确定。 在经营者小幅提价时，并不是所有需求者(或地域)的替代反应都是相同的。在替代反应不同的情况下，可以对不同需求者群体(或地域)进行不同幅度的测试。此时，相关市场界定还需要考虑需求者群体和特定地域的情况。	collusion, or concentrations of undertakings where collusion already exists, the current price obviously deviates from the competitive price, and the application of current price as the benchmark price will result in an unreasonable definition of the relevant market. Under such a circumstance, the current price shall be adjusted so as to use a more competitive price. In addition, the range of price increase is normally 5–10%, while in law enforcement practices, the range of a small price increase can be analyzed and determined case by case based on the industries involved. When the undertakings increase the price by a small range, the substitute response of all customers (or geographical areas) is not identical. When the substitute responses are different, tests applying different ranges may be conducted to different groups of customers (or geographic areas), and in such case, the definition of the relevant market shall also consider the situation of a specific group of customers and specific geographic area.

B-6

Rules for the Calculation of Turnover for the Notification of Concentrations of Undertakings in the Financial Sector

金融业经营者集中申报营业额计算办法

(Adopted by the Anti-Monopoly Commission of the State Council and promulgated on July 15, 2009, effective as of August 15, 2009)

（国务院反垄断委员会审议通过，于2009年7月15日发布，自2009年8月15日起施行）

第一条 根据《反垄断法》及《国务院关于经营者集中申报标准的规定》（以下简称《规定》），为明确金融业经营者集中的申报标准，制定本办法。	**Article 1** In accordance with the Anti-Monopoly Law and the Regulation of the State Council on the Notification Thresholds for Concentrations of Undertakings (hereinafter the "Regulation"), these Rules are formulated for the purpose of clarifying the thresholds for the notification of concentrations of undertakings in the financial sector.
第二条 本办法适用于银行业金融机构、证券公司、期货公司、基金管理公司和保险公司等金融业经营者集中申报营业额的计算。	**Article 2** These Rules are applicable to the calculation of turnover for the notification of concentrations of undertakings in the financial sector, such as banking financial institutions, securities companies, futures companies, fund management companies, and insurance companies.

银行业金融机构包括商业银行、城市信用合作社、农村信用合作社等吸收公众存款的金融机构以及政策性银行。 对金融资产管理公司、信托公司、财务公司、金融租赁公司、汽车金融公司、货币经纪公司以及经银行业监督管理机构批准设立的其他金融机构的营业额计算办法，适用本办法对银行业金融机构的规定。	Banking financial institutions refer to financial institutions and policy banks which accept deposits from the public, including commercial banks, urban credit cooperations, rural credit cooperations, etc. The provisions of these Rules concerning banking financial institutions shall be applicable to the calculation of turnover of financial asset management companies, trust companies, financial companies, financial lease companies, automobile finance companies, money brokerage firms, as well as other financial institutions approved by the banking regulatory administrative authority.
第三条 银行业金融机构的营业额要素包括以下项目： 一、　利息净收入； 二、　手续费及佣金净收入； 三、　投资收益； 四、　公允价值变动收益； 五、　汇兑收益； 六、　其他业务收入。	**Article 3** The elements of the turnover of a banking financial institution shall include: (1)　net interest income; (2)　net income from commission fee and charges; (3)　investment income; (4)　income from changes in fair value; (5)　exchange gains; and (6)　other revenue.
第四条 证券公司的营业额要素包括以下项目： 一、　手续费及佣金净收入（包括经纪业务、资产管理业务、承销与保荐业务和财务顾问业务等）； 二、　利息净收入； 三、　投资收益； 四、　汇兑收益； 五、　其他业务收入。	**Article 4** The elements of the turnover of a securities company shall include: (1)　net income from commission fees and charges (including brokerage business, asset management business, underwriting and sponsorship business, and financial adviser business, etc.); (2)　net interest income; (3)　investment income; (4)　exchange gains; and (5)　other revenue.

(Continued)

第五条 期货公司的营业额要素包括以下项目： 一、 手续费及佣金净收入； 二、 银行存款利息净收入。	**Article 5** The elements of the turnover of a futures company shall include: (1) net income from commission fees and charges; and (2) net interest income from deposits.
第六条 基金管理公司的营业额要素包括以下项目： 一、 管理费收入； 二、 手续费收入。	**Article 6** The elements of the turnover of a fund management company shall include: (1) management fee income; and (2) commission income.
第七条 上述经营者集中申报营业额的计算公式为： 营业额＝(营业额要素累加－营业税金及附加)×10%	**Article 7** The formula for calculating the turnover for the notification of concentration of undertakings above shall be: Turnover ＝ (aggregate of all elements – business taxes and surcharges) × 10%
第八条 保险公司集中申报营业额的计算公式为： 营业额＝(保费收入－营业税金及附加)×10% 其中，保费收入＝原保险合同保费收入＋分入保费－分出保费	**Article 8** The formula for calculating the turnover for the notification of concentration of insurance companies shall be: Turnover ＝ (premium income – business taxes and surcharges) × 10% in which, the premium income ＝ premium income from the original insurance contracts ＋ reinsurance premium income – ceded-out premium.
第九条 以上营业额计算办法仅限于经营者集中申报。	**Article 9** These calculation Rules above shall only apply to the notification of concentration of undertakings.
第十条 本办法自发布之日起30日后生效。	**Article 10** These Rules shall take effect 30 days after the date of promulgation.

B-7

Circular of the General Office of the State Council Regarding the Institution of a Security Review System for Mergers and Acquisitions of Domestic Enterprises by Foreign Investors

国务院办公厅关于建立外国投资者并购境内企业安全审查制度的通知

(Promulgated by the General Office of the State Council on February 3, 2011, effective as of March 3, 2011)

（国务院办公厅于2011年2月3日发布，自2011年3月3日起施行）

各省、自治区、直辖市人民政府，国务院各部委、各直属机构：

近年来，随着经济全球化的深入发展和我国对外开放的进一步扩大，外国投资者以并购方式进行的投资逐步增多，促进了我国利用外资方式多样化，在优化资源配置、推动技术进步、提高企业管理水平等方面发挥了积极作用。为引导外国投资者并购境内企业有序发展，维护国家安全，经国务院同意，现就建立外国投资者并购境内企业安全审查（以下简称并购安全审查）制度有关事项通知如下：

The People's government of each province, autonomous region, and provincial level municipality, and the Ministries, Commissions, and other organizations directly under the State Council:

With the deepening of economic globalization and further opening of China to the world over recent years, investment by foreign investors in the form of mergers and acquisitions has become increasingly frequent, which has facilitated diversity in the ways foreign capital is utilized in China, and played a positive role in the optimal deployment of resources, advancement of technology, and improvement of corporate management. In order to guide the orderly development of mergers and acquisitions of domestic enterprises by foreign investors and safeguard national

(Continued)

	security, you are hereby notified of the Security Review System on Mergers and Acquisitions of Domestic Enterprises by Foreign Investors (hereinafter referred to as M&A Security Review) as follows as approved by the State Council:
一、并购安全审查范围	**I Scope of M&A Security Review**
（一） 并购安全审查的范围为：外国投资者并购境内军工及军工配套企业，重点、敏感军事设施周边企业，以及关系国防安全的其他单位；外国投资者并购境内关系国家安全的重要农产品、重要能源和资源、重要基础设施、重要运输服务、关键技术、重大装备制造等企业，且实际控制权可能被外国投资者取得。 （二） 外国投资者并购境内企业，是指下列情形： 　1　外国投资者购买境内非外商投资企业的股权或认购境内非外商投资企业增资，使该境内企业变更设立为外商投资企业。 　2　外国投资者购买境内外商投资企业中方股东的股权，或认购境内外商投资企业增资。 　3　外国投资者设立外商投资企业，并通过该外商投资企业协议购买境内企业资产并且运营该资产，或通过该外商投资企业购买境内企业股权。 　4　外国投资者直接购买境内企业资产，并以该资产投资设立外商投资企业运营该资产。 （三） 外国投资者取得实际控制权，是指外国投资者通过并购成为境内企业的控股股东或实际控制人。包括下列情形：	(1)　The scope of M&A Security Review is as follows: foreign investors' mergers and acquisitions of domestic military industrial enterprises and military-industry-associated enterprises, enterprises involving important or sensitive military facilities, and other enterprises that have a bearing on the security of the national defense; foreign investors' mergers and acquisitions of domestic enterprises that have a bearing on national security in areas such as important agricultural products, important energy and resources, important infrastructure, important transportation services, key technologies, key equipment manufacturing etc., with the possibility of foreign investors obtaining actual control. (2)　Merger and acquisition of a domestic enterprise by foreign investors refers to the following situations: 　a.　foreign investors purchase the equity of a domestic non-foreign-invested enterprise (non-FIE) or subscribe to a capital increase in a domestic non-FIE, and thus turn the domestic enterprise into an FIE; 　b.　foreign investors purchase equity held by Chinese shareholders in a domestic FIE, or subscribe to a capital increase in a domestic FIE;

1 外国投资者及其控股母公司、控股子公司在并购后持有的股份总额在50%以上。 2 数个外国投资者在并购后持有的股份总额合计在50%以上。 3 外国投资者在并购后所持有的股份总额不足50%，但依其持有的股份所享有的表决权已足以对股东会或股东大会、董事会的决议产生重大影响。 4 其他导致境内企业的经营决策、财务、人事、技术等实际控制权转移给外国投资者的情形。	c. foreign investors establish an FIE, purchase assets by agreement from a domestic enterprise through the FIE and operate such assets, or purchase equity of a domestic enterprise through the FIE; d. foreign investors purchase assets of a domestic enterprise directly, and take the assets as investment to establish an FIE to operate such assets. (3) Foreign investors' acquisition of actual control means that foreign investors become the controlling shareholder or actual controller of a domestic enterprise through M&A. It includes the following situations: a. after M&A, the foreign investor, its parent holding company, and its holding subsidiaries possess more than 50% of the total shares; b. after M&A, the shares held by several foreign investors exceed 50% of the total shares; c. after M&A, the total shares held by the foreign investor, albeit less than 50%, represent sufficient voting rights to exert material influence over the resolutions of the general meeting or shareholders' meeting and the board of directors; d. other situations that lead to the shift of actual control of a domestic enterprise, including operational decision making, finance, human resource management, technology etc., to foreign investors.

二、并购安全审查内容	**II Object of M&A Security Review**
（一） 并购交易对国防安全，包括对国防需要的国内产品生产能力、国内服务提供能力和有关设备设施的影响。 （二） 并购交易对国家经济稳定运行的影响。 （三） 并购交易对社会基本生活秩序的影响。 （四） 并购交易对涉及国家安全关键技术研发能力的影响。	(1) The impact of M&A transactions on national defense and security, including production capacity of domestic products, provision capacity of domestic services, and relevant equipment and facilities that are required by national defense. (2) The impact of M&A transactions on the stability of the national economy. (3) The impact of M&A transactions on basic social life order. (4) The impact of M&A transactions on the capacity of R&D of key technologies that have a bearing on national security.
三、并购安全审查工作机制	**III Working Mechanism of M&A Security Review**
（一） 建立外国投资者并购境内企业安全审查部际联席会议（以下简称联席会议）制度，具体承担并购安全审查工作。 （二） 联席会议在国务院领导下，由发展改革委、商务部牵头，根据外资并购所涉及的行业和领域，会同相关部门开展并购安全审查。 （三） 联席会议的主要职责是：分析外国投资者并购境内企业对国家安全的影响；研究、协调外国投资者并购境内企业安全审查工作中的重大问题；对需要进行安全审查的外国投资者并购境内企业交易进行安全审查并作出决定。	(1) An inter-ministerial panel on security review of M&A of domestic enterprises by foreign investors (the "Inter-Ministerial Panel") will be established to undertake the M&A Security Review. (2) The Inter-Ministerial Panel, led by the National Development and Reform Commission and the Ministry of Commerce under the leadership of the State Council, will work with relevant governmental departments to carry out the M&A Security Review, depending on the industries and sectors where the foreign investors' M&A take place. (3) The main responsibilities of the Inter-Ministerial Panel are as follows: analyzing the impact of foreign investors' M&A of domestic enterprises on national security; studying and coordinating key issues in the security review of foreign investors'

	M&A of domestic enterprises that are subject to security review; conducting security review of M&A covered by this Circular, and taking decisions.
四、并购安全审查程序	**IV Procedures of the M&A Security Review**
（一）　外国投资者并购境内企业，应按照本通知规定，由投资者向商务部提出申请。对属于安全审查范围内的并购交易，商务部应在5个工作日内提请联席会议进行审查。 （二）　外国投资者并购境内企业，国务院有关部门、全国性行业协会、同业企业及上下游企业认为需要进行并购安全审查的，可以通过商务部提出进行并购安全审查的建议。联席会议认为确有必要进行并购安全审查的，可以决定进行审查。 （三）　联席会议对商务部提请安全审查的并购交易，首先进行一般性审查，对未能通过一般性审查的，进行特别审查。并购交易当事人应配合联席会议的安全审查工作，提供安全审查需要的材料、信息，接受有关询问。 一般性审查采取书面征求意见的方式进行。联席会议收到商务部提请安全审查的并购交易申请后，在5个工作日内，书面征求有关部门的意见。有关部门在收到书面征求意见函后，应在20个工作日内提出书面意见。如有关部门均认为并购交易不影响国家安全，则不再进行特别审查，由联席会议在收到全部书面意见后5个工作日内提出审查意见，并书面通知商务部。	(1) The foreign investor shall make a filing with the Ministry of Commerce in accordance with this Circular with regard to its merger and acquisition of a domestic enterprise. If the M&A transaction falls into the scope of security review, the Ministry of Commerce shall submit it to the Inter-Ministerial Panel for review within five business days. (2) If governmental departments under the State Council, national trade associations, enterprises in the same industry, and upstream and downstream enterprises consider it necessary to conduct a security review of a merger and acquisition of a domestic enterprise by foreign investors, they may propose via the Ministry of Commerce that the M&A Security Review be conducted. If the Inter-Ministerial Panel considers it necessary to carry out the M&A Security Review, the Inter-Ministerial Panel may decide to carry out the review. (3) The Inter-Ministerial Panel will first carry out general review of M&A transactions submitted by the Ministry of Commerce for security review. If a case does not pass the general review, a special review will then be undertaken. Parties involved in the M&A transaction shall cooperate with the Inter-Ministerial Panel in the security review process, submit documents and information needed for the review, and take questions.

(Continued)

如有部门认为并购交易可能对国家安全造成影响，联席会议应在收到书面意见后5个工作日内启动特别审查程序。启动特别审查程序后，联席会议组织对并购交易的安全评估，并结合评估意见对并购交易进行审查，意见基本一致的，由联席会议提出审查意见；存在重大分歧的，由联席会议报请国务院决定。联席会议自启动特别审查程序之日起60个工作日内完成特别审查，或报请国务院决定。审查意见由联席会议书面通知商务部。 （四）　在并购安全审查过程中，申请人可向商务部申请修改交易方案或撤销并购交易。 （五）　并购安全审查意见由商务部书面通知申请人。 （六）　外国投资者并购境内企业行为对国家安全已经造成或可能造成重大影响的，联席会议应要求商务部会同有关部门终止当事人的交易，或采取转让相关股权、资产或其他有效措施，消除该并购行为对国家安全的影响。	General review is conducted through written inquiries. Within five (5) business days after receipt of the M&A filing submitted by the Ministry of Commerce for Security Review, the Inter-Ministerial Panel shall solicit the opinions of relevant agencies in writing, which shall respond with written comments within twenty (20) business days after receipt of the written request for comment. If all the relevant agencies believe that the M&A does not affect national security, no special review will be undertaken. The Inter-Ministerial Panel shall give its review findings and inform the Ministry of Commerce of the same in writing within five (5) business days after receipt of all written comments. If some agencies believe that the M&A may affect national security, the Inter-Ministerial Panel shall initiate the special review within five (5) business days after receipt of written comments. Upon initiation of the special review process, the Inter-Ministerial Panel shall organize security evaluation for the M&A, and review the M&A in connection with the evaluation results. If the Panel is in substantial agreement, the Inter-Ministerial Panel shall give its review decision, and if there is a major disagreement, the same shall be reported by the Inter-Ministerial Panel to the State Council for its decision. The Inter-Ministerial Panel shall complete the special review or report the same for decision by the State Council within sixty (60) business days from the date the special review is initiated. The review results will be notified by the Inter-Ministerial Panel to the Ministry of Commerce in writing. (4)　In the course of the M&A Security Review, the applicant may apply to the Ministry of Commerce to revise its transaction plans or cancel the M&A transaction.

	(5) The Ministry of Commerce is responsible for providing the applicant with a written notice of the result of an M&A Security Review.
	(6) If a case of foreign investors' M&A of domestic enterprises has impacted or may impact national security, the Inter-Ministerial Panel shall request the Ministry of Commerce, in collaboration with relevant departments, to terminate the transaction, or take other effective measures such as equity transfer, assets transfer etc., so as to eliminate the impact of the M&A on national security.
五、其他规定	**V Miscellaneous**
（一） 有关部门和单位要树立全局观念，增强责任意识，保守国家秘密和商业秘密，提高工作效率，在扩大对外开放和提高利用外资水平的同时，推动外资并购健康发展，切实维护国家安全。	(1) The relevant agencies and entities shall be aware of the overall situation, increase their awareness of their responsibilities, maintain in confidence state secrets and business secrets, improve work efficiency, and facilitate the sound growth of M&A activities by foreign investors and concretely safeguard national security while expanding China's opening-up and improving the use of foreign capital.
（二） 外国投资者并购境内企业涉及新增固定资产投资的，按国家固定资产投资管理规定办理项目核准。	(2) If a foreign investor's merger and acquisition of a domestic enterprise involves investment in new fixed assets, such M&A shall be subject to review and approval in accordance with the administrative rules of the government regarding fixed asset investment.
（三） 外国投资者并购境内企业涉及国有产权变更的，按国家国有资产管理的有关规定办理。	(3) If a foreign investor's merger and acquisition of a domestic enterprise involves a change in the ownership by the state, such M&A shall be processed in accordance with relevant regulations regarding administration of state-owned assets.
（四） 外国投资者并购境内金融机构的安全审查另行规定。	
（五） 香港特别行政区、澳门特别行政区、台湾地区的投资者进行并购，参照本通知的规定执行。	
（六） 并购安全审查制度自本通知发布之日起30日后实施.	

(Continued)

	(4) A separate rule will be formulated with regard to the security review of a foreign investor's merger and acquisition of a domestic financial institution. (5) Reference shall be made to this Circular for any merger and acquisition of a domestic enterprise by investors from Hong Kong Special Administrative Region, Macau Special Administrative Region, and Taiwan. (6) The Security Review System shall become effective 30 days from the date of release of this Circular.
国务院办公厅 二〇一一年二月三日	The General Office of the State Council February 3, 2011

MOFCOM

商务部法规

B-8

Rules for the Notification of Concentrations of Undertakings

经营者集中申报办法

(Promulgated by the Ministry of Commerce on November 21, 2009, effective as of January 1, 2010)

（商务部于2009年11月21日发布，自2010年1月1日起施行）

第一条 为规范经营者集中申报和反垄断执法机构受理申报，根据《中华人民共和国反垄断法》（以下简称《反垄断法》）和《国务院关于经营者集中申报标准的规定》（以下简称《规定》），制定本办法。	**Article 1** These Rules are formulated in accordance with the Anti-Monopoly Law of the People's Republic of China ("AML") and the Regulation of the State Council on the Notification Thresholds for Concentrations of Undertakings ("Regulation"), for the purpose of regulating the notification of concentrations by undertakings and the acceptance of notifications by the Anti-Monopoly Law enforcement authorities.
第二条 商务部是经营者集中反垄断审查执法机构，承担受理和审查经营者集中申报的具体执法工作。	**Article 2** The Ministry of Commerce of the People's Republic of China (hereinafter "MOFCOM") is the enforcement authority for the anti-monopoly review, and assumes the responsibility for the specific enforcement work in connection with the acceptance and review of notifications of concentrations of undertakings.

(Continued)

第三条 本办法所称经营者集中，系指《反垄断法》第二十条所规定的下列情形： （一）　经营者合并； （二）　经营者通过取得股权或者资产的方式取得对其他经营者的控制权； （三）　经营者通过合同等方式取得对其他经营者的控制权或者能够对其他经营者施加决定性影响。	**Article 3** A concentration of undertakings referred to herein means any of the following circumstances as set forth in Article 20 of the AML: (1)　mergers; (2)　acquisition of control over other undertakings through the acquisition of equity or assets; or (3)　acquisition of control over other undertakings or the capacity to exercise decisive influence on other undertakings by contract or any other means.
第四条 营业额包括相关经营者上一会计年度内销售产品和提供服务所获得的收入，扣除相关税金及其附加。 《规定》第三条所称"在中国境内"是指经营者提供产品或服务的买方所在地在中国境内。	**Article 4** Turnover includes the relevant undertakings' revenue from the sales of products and provision of services in the preceding fiscal year after deduction of taxes and associated charges. The term "within China" in Article 3 of the Regulation refers to the location of the buyer to which undertakings provide products or services in China.
第五条 参与集中的单个经营者的营业额应当为下述经营者的营业额总和： （一）　该单个经营者； （二）　第（一）项所指经营者直接或间接控制的其他经营者； （三）　直接或间接控制第（一）项所指经营者的其他经营者； （四）　第（三）项所指经营者直接或间接控制的其他经营者； （五）　第（一）至（四）项所指经营者中两个或两个以上经营者共同控制的其他经营者。 参与集中的单个经营者的营业额不包括上述（一）至（五）项所列经营者之间发生的营业额。	**Article 5** The turnover of an individual undertaking concerned by a concentration shall be the sum of the turnover of the following undertakings: (1)　the individual undertaking concerned; (2)　undertakings directly or indirectly controlled by the undertaking referred to in item (1); (3)　undertakings which directly or indirectly control the undertaking referred to in item (1); (4)　undertakings directly or indirectly controlled by the undertakings referred to in item (3); (5)　undertakings under common control by two or more undertakings referred to in items (1) to (4).

如果参与集中的单个经营者之间或者参与集中的单个经营者和未参与集中的经营者之间有共同控制的其他经营者，参与集中的单个经营者的营业额应当包括被共同控制的经营者与第三方经营者之间的营业额，且此营业额只计算一次。	The turnover of an individual undertaking concerned by the concentration shall not include the turnover derived from transactions between undertakings referred to in items (1) to (5). If there is any other undertaking under the common control of individual undertakings concerned by the concentration or of one individual undertaking concerned by the concentration and other undertakings not concerned by the concentration, the turnover of one individual undertaking concerned by the concentration shall include the turnover from the transactions between the undertaking under common control and third party undertakings, and such turnover shall be counted in only once.
第六条 如果参与集中的单个经营者之间有共同控制的其他经营者，则参与集中的所有经营者的合计营业额不应包括被共同控制的经营者与任何一个共同控制他的参与集中的经营者，或与后者有控制关系的经营者之间发生的营业额。	**Article 6** If the concentration involves any other undertaking under joint control of undertakings concerned by the concentration, then the aggregate turnover of all undertaking concerned by the concentration shall exclude the turnover from transactions between such undertakings under joint control and any undertakings concerned by the concentration who jointly control such undertakings, and any undertakings in a relationship of control with those who jointly control such undertakings.
第七条 在一项经营者集中包括收购一个或多个经营者的一部分时： （一）　对于卖方而言，只计算集中涉及部分的营业额；	**Article 7** When a concentration of undertakings involves parts of one or more undertakings: (1)　in respect of the seller, only the turnover from the part involved in the concentration shall be taken into account;

(*Continued*)

（二）相同经营者之间在两年内多次实施的未达到《规定》第三条规定的申报标准的经营者集中，应当视为一次集中交易，集中发生时间从最后一次交易算起，该经营者集中的营业额应当将多次交易合并计算。经营者通过与其有控制关系的其他经营者实施的上述行为，依照本项规定处理。 前款第（二）项所称"两年内"是指从第一次集中交易完成之日起至最后一次集中交易签订协议之日止的期间。	(2) various concentrations consecutively within two years by the same undertakings, each of which does not reach the notification thresholds stipulated in Article 3 of the Regulation, shall be deemed as a single concentration transaction. Such concentration shall be deemed to take place at the moment of the last transaction. The underlying turnover shall be the aggregate amount derived from the multiple transactions. This provision shall apply when the above transactions are implemented through other undertakings in a relationship of control with such undertakings. The term "within two years" in the preceding paragraph (2) refers to the two-year period starting on the date of closing of the first concentration transaction until the date of signing the transaction agreement for the last concentration.
第八条 在正式申报前，参与集中的经营者可以就集中申报的相关问题向商务部申请商谈。商谈申请应当以书面方式提出。	**Article 8** Prior to the submission of the formal notification, the parties to the transaction may request a consultation with MOFCOM regarding the relevant issues of the notification. The request for consultation shall be made in writing.
第九条 通过合并方式实施的经营者集中，由参与合并的各方经营者申报；其他方式的经营者集中，由取得控制权或能够施加决定性影响的经营者申报，其他经营者予以配合。 申报义务人未进行集中申报的，其他参与集中的经营者可以提出申报。 申报义务人可以自行申报，也可以依法委托他人代理申报。	**Article 9** Where a concentration of undertakings is achieved through a merger, the parties to the merger shall be responsible for the notification of the transaction, while for any other type of concentration of undertakings, the undertaking who gains the right of control or other decisive influence as a result of such transaction shall be responsible for the notification, and the other undertakings shall provide assistance.

	If the parties responsible for the notification fail to file the notification of a concentration, the other undertakings concerned by the concentration may file a notification of a concentration.
	The parties responsible for the notification may submit their notification on their own or through an authorized attorney in accordance with the law.
第十条 申报文件、材料应当包括如下内容: (一) 申报书。申报书应当载明参与集中的经营者的名称、住所、经营范围、预定实施集中的日期。申报人的身份证明或注册登记证明，境外申报人还须提交当地公证机关的公证文件和相关的认证文件。委托代理人申报的，应当提交经申报人签字的授权委托书。 (二) 集中对相关市场竞争状况影响的说明。具体包括：集中交易概况；相关市场界定；参与集中的经营者在相关市场的市场份额及其对市场的控制力；主要竞争者及其市场份额；市场集中度；市场进入；行业发展现状；集中对市场竞争结构、行业发展、技术进步、国民经济发展、消费者以及其他经营者的影响；集中对相关市场竞争影响的效果评估及依据。 (三) 集中协议及相关文件。具体包括：各种形式的集中协议文件，如协议书、合同以及相应的补充文件等。 (四) 参与集中的经营者经会计师事务所审计的上一会计年度财务会计报告。 (五) 商务部要求提交的其他文件、资料。	**Article 10** The documents and information required for a notification shall include: (1)　a notification letter. The notification letter shall include the name of the undertakings concerned by the concentration, their respective domicile address, scope of business, as well as the expected date of the transaction. The I.D. certificate or certificate of incorporation of the notifying parties are required. The foreign notifying party shall submit the documents notarized by the local notary public and certified by relevant authorities. If the notification is made by an authorized attorney, the power of attorney authorizing such notification signed by the notifying party shall be submitted. (2)　an explanation regarding the effects that the concentration may have on competitive conditions in the relevant market, which shall specifically include an overview of the transaction; a definition of the relevant market; the respective market shares held by the parties to the transaction in the relevant market as well as their respective power of control over the market; the main competitors and their respective market share; level of market concentration; market entry; the current development of the concerned industry;

(*Continued*)

	the effect of the concentration over market competition structure, industry development, technology advances, national economic growth, consumers, and other undertakings; an evaluation of the effect of the concentration over the competition in the relevant market and the basis of evaluation. (3) concentration agreement(s) and relevant documents, including in particular: concentration agreement(s) in various forms, such as agreements, contracts, and relevant supplementary documents, etc. (4) financial reports, audited by a certified public accountant, of the undertakings concerned by the concentration in the previous fiscal year; and (5) other documents or information as requested by MOFCOM.
第十一条 除本规定第十条要求提供的文件、资料外，申报人可以自愿提供有助于商务部对该集中进行审查和做出决定的其他文件、资料，如地方人民政府和主管部门等有关方面的意见，支持集中协议的各类报告等。	**Article 11** Aside from the documents and information as required under Article 10, the notifying parties may also voluntarily submit other documents or information which may help MOFCOM with its review of the concentration and its decision-making process; for example, the position of relevant authorities such as the position of the local government and the competent superior authorities, various reports underpinning the agreement, and so on.
第十二条 申报人提交纸质申报文件、资料的同时，应当提交内容相同的光盘电子文档。申报文件、资料应当合理编排以方便查阅。	**Article 12** When submitting hard copies of the notification documents, the notifying parties shall also submit their equivalent electronic version in CD-ROM format at the same time. The notification documents shall be reasonably ordered and binded for ease of reference.

申报人应当提交中文撰写的文件、资料。文件、资料的原件是外文书写的，应当提交中文翻译件并附外文原件。文件、资料为副本、复印件或传真件的，应当根据商务部的要求出示原件供验证。 申报人应当同时提交申报文件、资料的公开版本和保密版本。申报人应当对申报文件、资料中的商业秘密和其他需要保密的信息进行标注。	The notification documents shall be written in Chinese. Where the original is not written in Chinese, a Chinese translation shall be submitted together with the non-Chinese original. Where duplicates, photocopies, or facsimile copies of the notification documents are submitted, their originals shall be presented as required by MOFCOM for verification purposes. The notifying party shall submit the non-confidential version and confidential version of the notification documents at the same time, and shall also mark the business secrets and other information that shall be kept confidential in the notification documents.
第十三条 申报人应当提交完备的文件、资料，商务部应对申报人提交的文件、资料进行核查。商务部发现申报的文件、资料不完备的，可以要求申报人在规定期限内补交。申报人逾期未补交的，视为未申报。	**Article 13** The information contained in the notification documents submitted by the notifying party shall be accurate and complete. MOFCOM shall review the documents and information submitted by the notifying party. If the notification documents are found by MOFCOM to be incomplete, it may request the notifying parties to make supplemental submissions within a specified deadline. If the notifying parties fail to make such supplemental submissions in time, it shall be treated as if no notification has been made.
第十四条 商务部经核查认为申报文件、资料符合法定要求的，应当自收到完备的申报文件、资料之日予以立案并书面通知申报人。	**Article 14** If, after review, MOFCOM believes that the notification documents meet the relevant legal requirements, it shall decide to accept and file the transaction in its review docket as of the date when it receives such completed notification documents, and shall inform the notifying parties of the same in writing.

(Continued)

第十五条 申报人故意隐瞒重要情况或者提供虚假信息的，商务部不予立案。	**Article 15** Where important information is concealed or false information is submitted intentionally by the notifying parties, MOFCOM may refuse to accept the notification.
第十六条 经营者集中未达到《规定》第三条规定的申报标准，参与集中的经营者自愿提出经营者集中申报，商务部收到申报文件、资料后经审查认为有必要立案的，应当按照《反垄断法》的规定进行立案审查并作出决定。 在前款所述申报和立案审查期间，参与集中的经营者可以自行决定是否暂停实施其集中交易，并承担相应的后果。	**Article 16** Where the concentration of undertakings falls short of the notification thresholds as set forth in Article 3 of the Regulation, the parties to the concentration may make a voluntary notification, and if, after receipt of the notification documents, MOFCOM believes upon review that it is necessary to accept the notification, it may decide to accept the notification for review and make decisions in accordance with the AML. During the period of notification and review of the concentration mentioned in the preceding paragraph, the undertakings concerned by the concentration may decide at their own discretion whether to suspend the implementation of the concentration transaction and assume corresponding consequence by themselves.
第十七条 商务部和申报人对在经营者集中申报前商谈和申报审查工作中知悉的商业秘密和其他需要保密的信息承担保密义务。	**Article 17** MOFCOM and the notifying parties shall have a duty of confidentiality towards business secrets and other confidential information that come to their knowledge during the pre-notification consultation or the review of notification of a concentration.
第十八条 本办法自2010年1月1日起施行。	**Article 18** These Rules shall become effective as of January 1, 2010.

B-9

Rules for the Review of Concentrations of Undertakings

经营者集中审查办法

(Promulgated by the Ministry of Commerce on November 24, 2009, effective as of January 1, 2010)

（商务部于2009年11月24日发布，自2010年1月1日起施行）

第一条 为规范经营者集中反垄断审查工作，明确经营者集中反垄断审查程序，根据《中华人民共和国反垄断法》（以下简称《反垄断法》），制定本办法。	**Article 1** These Rules are made pursuant to the Anti-Monopoly Law of the People's Republic of China ("AML") to regulate the anti-monopoly review of concentrations of undertakings and set forth the applicable procedures for the anti-monopoly review of concentrations of undertakings.
第二条 商务部是经营者集中反垄断审查执法机构，承担受理和审查经营者集中申报的具体执法工作。	**Article 2** The Ministry of Commerce of the People's Republic of China ("MOFCOM") shall be the enforcement authority for the anti-monopoly review of concentrations of undertakings, and shall be responsible for daily law enforcement such as accepting and reviewing notifications of concentrations of undertakings.
第三条 在商务部立案之后、做出审查决定之前，申报人要求撤回经营者集中申报的，应当提交书面申请并说明理由。除放弃集中交易的情形外，申报的撤回应当经商务部同意。	**Article 3** Where a notifying party requests to withdraw the notification of a concentration of undertakings after the notification is accepted and before the review decision is made by MOFCOM,

(Continued)

撤回经营者集中申报的，审查程序终止。商务部同意撤回申报不视为对集中的批准。	the notifying party shall submit a written request and state the reason why a withdrawal is sought. The request of withdrawal is subject to MOFCOM's approval unless the concentration transaction is abandoned. The review procedure shall be terminated when the notification of a concentration of undertakings is withdrawn. MOFCOM's approval of a request of withdrawal shall in no case be regarded as an approval of the notification of a concentration.
第四条 在审查过程中，商务部鼓励申报人尽早主动提供有助于对经营者集中进行审查和做出决定的有关文件、资料。	**Article 4** During the review, MOFCOM encourages the notifying party to voluntarily provide as early as possible any additional information which may help MOFCOM to examine and make a decision on the notification of a concentration of undertakings.
第五条 在审查过程中，参与集中的经营者可以通过信函、传真等方式向商务部就有关申报事项进行书面陈述、申辩，商务部应当听取当事人的陈述和申辩。	**Article 5** During the review, undertakings involved in the concentration have the right to make written statements and defense concerning relevant issues in the notification of a concentration of undertakings to MOFCOM via mail or fax, and MOFCOM shall hear and consider such statements and defense.
第六条 在审查过程中，商务部可以根据需要征求有关政府部门、行业协会、经营者、消费者等单位或个人的意见。	**Article 6** During the review, MOFCOM may solicit comments, when necessary, from government departments, trade associations, undertakings, consumers, and any other entity or individual.
第七条 在审查过程中，商务部可以主动或应有关方面的请求决定召开听证会，调查取证，听取有关各方的意见。商务部召开听证会，应当提前书面通知听证会参加方。听证会参加方提出书面意见的，应当在听证会举办前向商务部提交。	**Article 7** During the review, MOFCOM may decide to hold hearings ex officio or at the request of the relevant parties to investigate, gather evidence, and hear opinions from various parties. When MOFCOM calls for a hearing, it shall deliver written notices for hearing to all attendants in advance.

商务部举行听证会，可以通知参与集中的经营者及其竞争者、上下游企业及其他相关企业的代表参加，并可以酌情邀请有关专家、行业协会代表、有关政府部门的代表以及消费者代表参加。 听证会参加方应当按时出席听证会，遵守听证会程序，服从听证会主持人安排。 听证会参加方出于商业秘密等保密因素考虑，希望单独陈述的，可以安排单独听证；安排单独听证的，听证内容应当按有关保密规定处理。	Attendants with written opinions shall submit the written opinions to MOFCOM before the hearing. MOFCOM may invite to the hearing the undertakings concerned by the concentration, their competitors, representatives of the undertakings in the upstream and downstream markets, or other relevant parties, and may also invite as necessary, the relevant experts, representatives of the trade associations concerned, relevant government authorities, and representatives of consumers. The parties to be heard shall attend the hearing on time, and conform to the procedures of the hearing and the arrangement of the chairman. Where an attendant wishes to state its opinion separately due to consideration of confidentiality of business secrets, etc., a separate hearing may be conducted. The contents of the separate hearing will be handled according to the relevant provisions on confidentiality.
第八条 听证会按照以下程序进行： （一） 听证会主持人宣布听证会开始，宣读听证会纪律； （二） 核对听证会参加方； （三） 参加方就听证内容进行陈述； （四） 听证会主持人就听证内容询问有关参加方； （五） 听证会主持人宣布听证会结束。	**Article 8** The hearing shall be conducted in the following sequence: (1) the chairman declares the commencement of the hearing and the rules that the parties shall follow; (2) the chairman checks and confirms the identities of the attendants; (3) attendants to the hearing express their opinions on the issues subject to the hearing; (4) the chairman makes inquiries to the attendants on the issues subject to the hearing; (5) the chairman declares that the hearing is over.

(*Continued*)

第九条 在初步审查阶段，商务部应当在《反垄断法》第二十五条规定的期限内做出是否实施进一步审查的决定。商务部做出不实施进一步审查决定的，应当书面通知申报人；认为有必要实施进一步审查的，应当做出实施进一步审查的决定，并书面通知申报人。 商务部做出不实施进一步审查的决定或者逾期未做出决定的，参与集中的经营者可以实施集中。	**Article 9** During the preliminary review, MOFCOM shall make a decision on whether further review is required pursuant to Article 25 of the AML. Where MOFCOM makes a decision that no further review is required, it shall inform the notifying party of its decision in writing; where MOFCOM finds that further review is necessary, it shall make a decision to such effect and inform the notifying party of its decision in writing. Where MOFCOM decides not to conduct further review or fails to make such a decision at the expiry of the prescribed time limit, the undertakings concerned may carry out the concentration.
第十条 在进一步审查阶段，商务部认为经营者集中具有或者可能具有排除、限制竞争效果的，应当将其反对意见告知参与集中的经营者，并设定一个允许参与集中的经营者提交书面抗辩意见的合理期限。 参与集中的经营者的书面抗辩意见应当包括相关的事实和理由，并提供相应的证据。参与集中的经营者逾期未提交书面抗辩意见的，视为对反对意见无异议。	**Article 10** During the further review, if MOFCOM finds that the concentration has or is likely to have the effect of eliminating and/or restricting competition, it shall inform the undertakings concerned by the concentration of its opposition and set a reasonable time limit by which the undertakings concerned by the concentration can submit a written defense. The written defense submitted by the undertakings concerned by the concentration shall include relevant facts and reasons, as well as corresponding evidence. Should the undertakings fail to submit a written defense within the time limit, it shall be deemed that the undertakings have no objection to MOFCOM's oppositions.
第十一条 在审查过程中，为消除或减少经营者集中具有或者可能具有的排除、限制竞争的效果，参与集中的经营者可以提出对集中交易方案进行调整的限制性条件。	**Article 11** During MOFCOM's review, the undertakings concerned by the concentration may propose restrictive conditions to adjust the proposed transaction in order to eliminate or mitigate the effect or likely effect of eliminating and/or restricting competition.

根据经营者集中交易具体情况，限制性条件可以包括如下种类： （一）　剥离参与集中的经营者的部分资产或业务等结构性条件； （二）　参与集中的经营者开放其网络或平台等基础设施、许可关键技术（包括专利、专有技术或其他知识产权）、终止排他性协议等行为性条件； （三）　结构性条件和行为性条件相结合的综合性条件。	The following types of restrictive conditions may be imposed according to the specific circumstances of the concentration: (1)　structural conditions such as the divestiture of certain assets or businesses of the undertakings concerned by the concentration; (2)　behavioral conditions such as granting access to the infrastructure including networks or platforms, etc., granting license of key technologies (including patents, know-how, and other intellectual property) or terminating exclusive contracts by the undertakings concerned by the concentration; and/or (3)　comprehensive conditions combining both structural and behavioral conditions.
第十二条 参与集中的经营者提出的限制性条件应当能够消除或减少经营者集中具有或者可能具有的排除、限制竞争效果，并具有现实的可操作性。限制性条件的书面文本应当清晰明确，以便于能够充分评价其有效性和可行性。	**Article 12** The restrictive conditions proposed by the undertakings concerned by the concentration shall be sufficient to eliminate or mitigate the effect or likely effect of eliminating and/or restricting competition and be feasible in practice. The written restrictive conditions shall be clear and unambiguous so as to allow a comprehensive evaluation of their effectiveness and feasibility.
第十三条 在审查过程中，为消除或减少经营者集中具有或者可能具有的排除、限制竞争效果，商务部和参与集中的经营者均可以提出对限制性条件进行修改的意见和建议。	**Article 13** During the review, both the undertakings concerned by the concentration and MOFCOM may propose opinions and suggestions to modify the proposed restrictive conditions to eliminate or mitigate the effect or likely effect of eliminating and/or restricting competition.

(Continued)

第十四条	**Article 14**
商务部应当在《反垄断法》第二十六条规定的期限内做出禁止或不予禁止经营者集中的决定，并书面通知申报人。对不予禁止的经营者集中，商务部可以决定附加减少集中对竞争产生不利影响的限制性条件。商务部做出进一步审查决定前，参与集中的经营者不得实施集中。 商务部做出对经营者集中不予禁止的决定或逾期未做出决定的，参与集中的经营者可以实施集中。	MOFCOM shall make a decision on whether to prohibit the proposed concentration within the time limits prescribed by Article 26 of the AML and notify such decision to the notifying party in writing. When MOFCOM decides not to prohibit the concentration, it may decide to impose restrictive conditions which will mitigate the adverse effect of the concentration on competition. The undertakings concerned by the concentration shall not implement the concentration before MOFCOM makes its decision on further review. Where MOFCOM decides not to prohibit the concentration or fails to take a decision within the prescribed time limit, the undertakings concerned by the concentration may implement the concentration.
第十五条	**Article 15**
对于附加限制性条件批准的经营者集中，商务部应当对参与集中的经营者履行限制性条件的行为进行监督检查，参与集中的经营者应当按指定期限向商务部报告限制性条件的执行情况。 参与集中的经营者未依限制性条件履行规定义务的，商务部可以责令其限期改正；参与集中的经营者在规定期限内未改正的，商务部可以依照《反垄断法》相关规定予以处理。	With regard to a concentration approved with restrictive conditions, MOFCOM shall supervise and inspect the implementation of restrictive conditions by the undertakings concerned by the concentration. Undertakings concerned by the concentration shall submit periodic reports to MOFCOM on their implementation of the restrictive conditions according to the timeline specified by MOFCOM. Where the undertakings concerned by the concentration fail to perform the obligations imposed under the restrictive conditions, MOFCOM may order the undertakings to take rectifying measures within a certain time limit. Where the undertakings fail to make such rectification within the prescribed time limit, MOFCOM may deal with the non-compliance pursuant to the relevant provisions of the AML.

第十六条 商务部、申报人以及其他单位和个人对于在经营者集中审查中知悉的商业秘密和其他需要保密的信息承担保密义务。	**Article 16** MOFCOM, the notifying party, and other entities or individuals have a duty of confidentiality toward business secrets and other confidential information learned through the review process of the concentration.
第十七条 本办法自2010年1月1日起施行。	**Article 17** These Rules shall become effective as of January 1, 2010.

B-10

Interim Provisions on Asset or Business Divestiture during the Implementation of Concentrations of Undertakings

关于实施经营者集中资产或业务剥离的暂行规定

(Promulgated by the Ministry of Commerce on July 5, 2010, effective as of July 5, 2010)

（商务部于2010年7月5日发布，自2010年7月5日生效）

第一条 为规范经营者集中附加资产或业务剥离限制性条件决定的实施，确保资产或业务剥离的顺利完成，根据《经营者集中审查办法》，制定本规定。	**Article 1** These Provisions are formulated in accordance with the Rules for the Review of Concentrations of Undertakings, for the purpose of regulating the implementation of review decisions that provide asset or business divestiture as a restrictive condition for a concentration of undertakings to ensure the orderly completion of asset or business divestiture.
第二条 本规定所称资产或业务剥离是指根据商务部经营者集中审查决定(下称审查决定)，负有资产或业务剥离义务的参与集中的经营者(下称剥离义务人)剥离其部分资产或业务及与之有关的行为(下称剥离)。 剥离义务人被剥离的部分资产或业务称为剥离业务。	**Article 2** For the purpose of these Provisions, asset or business divestiture refers to the divestiture of part of the assets or businesses or related conduct of an undertaking (the "Divesting Undertaking") concerned by a concentration, which is obligated to divest such assets or business pursuant to MOFCOM's review decision ("Review Decision"). The assets or businesses to be divested by the Divesting Undertaking is referred to as the To-Be-Divested Business.

第三条	**Article 3**
剥离义务人应当在审查决定规定的期限内，找到适当的买方并签订出售协议及其他相关协议（下称自行剥离）；如果剥离义务人未能如期完成自行剥离，则由剥离受托人按照审查决定规定的期限和方式找到适当的买方，并达成出售协议及其他相关协议（下称受托剥离）。	Within the time limit set forth in the Review Decision, the Divesting Undertaking shall search for, and enter into a purchase agreement and other related agreements with an appropriate buyer ("Self Divestiture"). In case the Divesting Undertaking fails to complete Self Divestiture as scheduled, then the divestiture trustee shall search for, and enter into a purchase agreement and other related agreements with an appropriate buyer within such time limit and by such manner as set forth in the Review Decision ("Trustee Divestiture").
剥离义务人应当在出售协议及其他相关协议签订之日起3个月内将剥离业务转移给买方，并完成所有权转移等相关法律程序。根据案件具体情况，经剥离义务人申请并说明理由，商务部可酌情延长业务转移的期限。	The Divesting Undertaking shall transfer the To-Be-Divested Business to the buyer and finish all relevant legal procedures for the transfer of ownership thereof within three months after the purchase agreement and other related agreements have been entered into. Upon application from the Divesting Undertaking and the provision of a statement of reasons, MOFCOM may grant an extension of the time limit for the business transfer at its own discretion depending on the merits of each case.
第四条	**Article 4**
剥离义务人应当根据审查决定的要求委托监督受托人，并在受托剥离阶段委托剥离受托人。	The Divesting Undertaking shall designate a supervision trustee and a divestiture trustee in the Trustee Divestiture stage pursuant to the requirement of the Review Decision.
监督受托人是指受剥离义务人委托，负责对业务剥离进行全程监督的自然人、法人或其他组织。	A supervision trustee is a natural person, legal entity, or organization of other kinds entrusted by the Divesting Undertaking to be responsible for supervising the whole course of the business divestiture.
剥离受托人是指在受托剥离阶段，受剥离义务人委托，负责找到适当的买方并达成出售协议及其他相关协议的自然人、法人或其他组织。	A divestiture trustee is a natural person, legal entity, or organization of other kinds entrusted by the Divesting Undertaking to be responsible for searching for, and entering into a
剥离义务人应当在商务部做出审查决定之日起15日内向商务部提交监督受托人人选，在进入受托剥离阶段30日前向商务部提交剥离受托人人选。	

(Continued)

	purchase agreement and other related agreements with an appropriate buyer during the Trustee Divestiture stage.

The Divesting Undertaking shall notify MOFCOM of the suggested supervision trustee within 15 days after MOFCOM makes its review decision, and of the suggested Divestiture Trustee at least 30 days before the Trustee Divestiture stage. |
| 第五条

监督受托人和剥离受托人必须是具有从事受托业务的必要资源和能力的自然人、法人或其他组织，并且应独立于参与集中的经营者和剥离业务的买方，与其不存在实质性利害关系。监督受托人和剥离受托人可以是相同的自然人、法人或其他组织。

监督受托人和剥离受托人应当向商务部负责并报告工作。非经商务部同意，剥离义务人不得对监督受托人和剥离受托人发出指示。 | **Article 5**

The supervision and divestiture trustees shall be natural persons, legal entities, or organizations of other kinds that have the resources and capability to fulfill the entrusted task, and shall be substantially a non-interested third party that is independent from the undertaking to the concentration and the buyer of the To-Be-Divested Business. The supervision and divestiture trustees may be the same natural person, legal entity, or organization of another kind.

The supervision and divestiture trustees shall answer and report to MOFCOM. Without MOFCOM's consent, the Divesting Undertaking shall not give any instruction to the supervision and divestiture trustees. |
| 第六条

剥离义务人应当与监督受托人和剥离受托人签订书面委托协议，明确双方的职责和义务。

监督受托人应当在自委托协议生效之日起，至业务剥离完成之日止的期间内履行职责；剥离受托人应当在自委托协议生效之日起，至受托剥离阶段结束之日止的期间内履行职责。非经商务部同意，剥离义务人不得解除、变更与监督受托人和剥离受托人的委托协议。

监督受托人和剥离受托人的报酬由剥离义务人支付，报酬数量及其支付方式不得损害监督受托人和剥离受托人履行受托职责的独立性及工作效率。 | **Article 6**

The Divesting Undertaking shall enter into trust agreements in writing with the supervision trustee and the divestiture trustee, clarifying responsibilities and obligations of parties.

The supervision trustee shall fulfill its responsibility from the date on which the trust agreement comes into effect to the date when the business divestiture is completed. The Divestiture Trustee shall fulfill its responsibilities from the date on which the trust agreement comes into effect to the ending of the Trustee Divestiture stage. Without MOFCOM's consent, the Divesting Undertaking shall not cancel or alter |

	the trust agreement with the supervision or divestiture trustee. The Divesting Undertaking shall pay a remuneration to the supervision and divestiture trustees. The amount of remuneration and payment method shall not have the effect of affecting the independence or the working efficiency of the supervision and divestiture trustees.
第七条 监督受托人应当在商务部监督下，本着勤勉、尽职的原则，独立于剥离义务人履行下列职责： （一）监督剥离义务人履行本规定第十二条规定的义务，并定期向商务部提交监督报告； （二）对剥离义务人推荐的买方人选、拟签订的出售协议及其他相关协议等进行评估，并向商务部提交评估报告； （三）监督出售协议及其他相关协议的执行，并定期向商务部提交监督报告； （四）负责协调剥离义务人与潜在买方就剥离事项产生的争议，并向商务部报告； （五）应商务部要求提交其他与业务剥离有关的报告。 监督受托人委托协议中应当明确规定监督受托人的上述职责。 剥离义务人应当对监督受托人履行上述职责提供必要的支持和便利，包括向监督受托人提供剥离业务相关当事方的信息，剥离业务的账簿和记录，剥离义务人提供给潜在买方的信息，潜在买方的信息，剥离过程的进展以及监督受托人为履行职责需要的其他信息和支持等。 潜在买方是指符合本规定第九条所规定的标准，并向剥离义务人提出购买剥离业务意愿的经营者。 未经商务部同意，监督受托人不得向剥离义务人披露其在履行职责过程中向商务部提交的各种报告。	**Article 7** The supervision trustee shall, under the supervision of MOFCOM, fulfill the responsibilities as below in accordance with the principle of diligence and independence from the Divesting Undertaking: (1) supervising fulfillment of the obligations of the Divesting Undertaking that are provided in Article 12 of these Provisions, and periodically providing reports to MOFCOM; (2) evaluating the potential buyers recommended by the Divesting Undertaking, and draft purchase agreements and other related agreements, and reporting on the evaluation to MOFCOM; (3) supervising the enforcement of the purchase agreement and other related agreements, and periodically reporting to MOFCOM; (4) coordinating disputes on divestiture matters between the Divesting Undertaking and the potential buyer, and reporting to MOFCOM; (5) upon request, providing MOFCOM with other reports concerning the business divestiture. The trust agreement with the supervision trustee shall expressly specify the above responsibilities of the supervision trustee.

(Continued)

监督受托人应当保守在履行职责过程中获悉的商业秘密和其他保密信息。	The Divesting Undertaking shall provide the necessary support and convenience to the supervision trustee for the fulfillment of the above responsibilities, including providing information of the parties relating to the To-Be-Divested Business, books and records of the To-Be-Divested Business, information communicated to the potential buyers, information of the potential buyers, and the progress of the business divestiture, as well as other information and support necessary for the supervision trustee to fulfill its responsibilities. A potential buyer means an undertaking which conforms to the standard set forth in Article 9 and proposes to the Divesting Undertaking to purchase the To-Be-Divested Business. Without MOFCOM's consent, the supervision trustee shall not disclose to the Divesting Undertaking various reports submitted to MOFCOM during its performance of responsibilities. The supervision trustee shall keep confidential business secrets and other confidential information obtained during the fulfillment of its responsibilities.
第八条 剥离受托人应当在商务部监督下，按照审查决定规定的期限和方式，找到适当的买方并达成出售协议和其他相关协议。 剥离义务人在委托协议中应当给予剥离受托人独立处理剥离业务的书面授权，并应当为剥离受托人履行职责提供必要的支持和便利。 未经商务部同意，剥离受托人不得向剥离义务人披露其履行职责过程中的信息；剥离受托人应当向商务部定期报告其履行职责的进展情况，并保守在履行职责过程中获悉的商业秘密和其他保密信息。	**Article 8** The divestiture trustee shall, under the supervision of MOFCOM, search for and enter into a purchase agreement and other related agreements with an appropriate buyer within such time limit and in such manner as set forth in the Review Decision. The Divesting Undertaking shall give the divestiture trustee written authorization to deal with the To-Be-Divested Business independently, and provide support and convenience necessary for the divestiture trustee's fulfillment of responsibilities.

	Without MOFCOM's consent, the divestiture trustee shall not disclose to the Divesting Undertaking information during its performance of responsibilities. The divestiture trustee shall report the progress of fulfillment of its responsibilities periodically to MOFCOM, and keep confidential business secrets and other confidential information obtained during fulfillment of its responsibilities.
第九条 剥离业务的买方应当符合下列要求: (一) 独立于参与集中的经营者，与其不存在实质性利害关系; (二) 拥有必要的资源、能力并有意愿维护和发展被剥离业务; (三) 购买剥离业务不会产生排除、限制竞争的问题; (四) 如果购买剥离业务需要其他有关部门的批准，买方应当具备取得其他监管机构批准的必要条件。	**Article 9** The buyer of the To-Be-Divested Business shall satisfy the following conditions: (1) it is independent from and is not a substantively interested party to the undertakings concerned by the concentration; (2) it has necessary resources, capacity, and intention to maintain and develop the To-Be-Divested Business; (3) its acquisition of the To-Be-Divested Business will not lead to concerns of elimination or restriction of competition; (4) it is expected to get approval of all other supervision authorities if the same is necessary for its purchase of the To-Be-Divested Business.
第十条 剥离义务人与买方之间签署的任何协议，包括剥离业务出售协议、过渡期协议等，不得含有与审查决定相违背的条款。	**Article 10** Any agreement between the Divesting Undertaking and the buyer, including the purchase agreement, transition agreement, etc., shall not contradict the Review Decision of MOFCOM.
第十一条 商务部将根据本规定第五条、第九条、第十条的规定，对剥离义务人提交的监督受托人、剥离受托人、剥离业务买方人选、委托协议和拟签订的剥离业务出售协议及相关协议等进行评估，以确保其符合审查决定的要求。商务部在上述评估过程中所用时间不计入剥离期限之内。	**Article 11** MOFCOM will, in accordance with Articles 5, 9, and 10 of these Provisions, evaluate the suggested supervision trustee, divestiture trustee, buyer of the To-Be-Divested Business, trust agreement, and the draft purchase agreement for the To-Be-Divested Business, and other related agreements

(Continued)

商务部应当对监督受托人和剥离受托人履行职责的情况进行监督和评估。	to be executed to make certain that they meet the requirements of the Review Decision. Any time spent on the above evaluation by MOFCOM shall not be counted into the time limit for divestiture. MOFCOM shall supervise and evaluate the supervision trustee and divestiture trustee's fulfillment of their responsibilities.
第十二条 在剥离完成之前，参与集中的经营者应当履行下列义务，以确保剥离业务的价值： （一）保持剥离业务与其他业务之间相互独立，并以最符合剥离业务利益的方式进行管理； （二）不得实施任何可能对剥离业务有不利影响的行为，包括聘用被剥离业务的员工，获得剥离业务的商业秘密和其他保密信息等； （三）指定专门的管理人，负责管理剥离业务并履行第（一）、（二）项规定的义务。管理人在监督受托人的监督下履行职责，其任命和更换应得到监督受托人的同意； （四）确保潜在买方能够以公平合理的方式获得有关剥离业务的充分信息，使得潜在买方能够评估剥离业务的价值、范围和商业潜力； （五）根据买方的要求向其提供必要的支持和帮助，确保剥离业务的顺利交接和稳定经营； （六）向买方及时移交剥离业务并履行相关法律程序。	**Article 12** To guarantee the value of the To-Be-Divested Business, prior to the completion of the divestiture, undertakings concerned by the concentration shall fulfill the following obligations: (1)　keep the To-Be-Divested Business independent from other businesses and manage it in a way that will bring the maximum benefits to it; (2)　refrainin from any activity that will adversely affect the To-Be-Divested Business, including hiring employees of the To-Be-Divested Business and obtaining business secrets or any other secret information of the To-Be-Divested Business; (3)　designate a special administrator to administrate the To-Be-Divested Business and fulfill the obligations listed in (1) and (2) above. The administrator shall fulfill its responsibilities under the supervision of the supervision trustee. Designation and re-designation of the administrator is subject to approval of the supervision trustee; (4)　make sure that the buyer is able to have access to sufficient information of the To-Be-Divested Business in a fair and legitimate way, so that the potential buyer is able to value the To-Be-Divested

	Business, and evaluate the scope and the potential of the To-Be-Divested Business; (5) provide necessary support and assistance as per the buyer's request, to ensure the orderly handover and stable operation of the To-Be-Divested Business; and (6) hand over the To-Be-Divested Business to the buyer in a timely manner and go through the relevant legal procedures.
第十三条 《经营者集中审查办法》第十一条规定的其他限制性条件的实施，可以参照适用本规定中的有关规定。	**Article 13** The implementation of other restrictive conditions prescribed in Article 11 of the Rules for the Review of Concentrations of Undertakings may refer to relevant stipulations in these Provisions.

B-11

Provisions of the Ministry of Commerce on the Implementation of the Security Review System for Mergers and Acquisitions of Domestic Enterprises by Foreign Investors

商务部实施外国投资者并购境内企业安全审查制度的规定

(Promulgated by the Ministry of Commerce on August 25, 2011, effective as of September 1, 2011)

（商务部于2011年8月25日发布，自2011年9月1日起施行）

根据《国务院办公厅关于建立外国投资者并购境内企业安全审查制度的通知》（国办发［2011］6号）以及外商投资相关法律法规，在广泛征求公众意见的基础上，我部对《商务部实施外国投资者并购境内企业安全审查制度有关事项的暂行规定》（商务部公告2011年第8号）进行了完善，形成了《商务部实施外国投资者并购境内企业安全审查制度的规定》。现予以公布，自2011年9月1日起实施。

Pursuant to the Circular by the General Office of the State Council Regarding the Institution of a Security Review System for Mergers and Acquisitions of Domestic Enterprises by Foreign Investors (Guo Ban Fa [2011] No. 6) and the relevant laws and regulations of foreign investments, and based on extensive canvassed public opinions, the Ministry of Commerce perfected the Interim Provisions of the Ministry of Commerce on Issues Related to the Implementation of the Security Review System for Mergers and Acquisitions of Domestic Enterprises by Foreign Investors (Announcement [2011] No. 8 of the Ministry of Commerce) and enacted the Provisions of the Ministry of Commerce on the Implementation of the Security Review System for Mergers and Acquisitions of Domestic Enterprises by Foreign Investors which is hereby promulgated and shall come into force on September 1, 2011.

第一条 外国投资者并购境内企业，属于《国务院办公厅关于建立外国投资者并购境内企业安全审查制度的通知》明确的并购安全审查范围的，外国投资者应向商务部提出并购安全审查申请。 两个或者两个以上外国投资者共同并购的，可以共同或确定一个外国投资者(以下简称申请人)向商务部提出并购安全审查申请。	**Article 1** With regard to mergers and acquisitions (M&A) of domestic enterprises by foreign investors that fall under the scope of the M&A security review specified in the Circular by the General Office of the State Council Regarding the Institution of a Security Review System for Mergers and Acquisitions of Domestic Enterprises by Foreign Investors, the investors shall file an application with the Ministry of Commerce for M&A security review. If an M&A is carried out by two or more foreign investors, they may jointly file an application with the Ministry of Commerce for M&A security review or designate one of the investors (hereinafter referred to as the "applicant") to do so.
第二条 地方商务主管部门在按照《关于外国投资者并购境内企业的规定》、《外商投资企业投资者股权变更的若干规定》、《关于外商投资企业境内投资的暂行规定》等有关规定受理并购交易申请时，对于属于并购安全审查范围，但申请人未向商务部提出并购安全审查申请的，应暂停办理，并在5个工作日内书面要求申请人向商务部提交并购安全审查申请，同时将有关情况报商务部。	**Article 2** Where local competent commerce authorities handle an application for an M&A transaction in accordance with the Provisions on Merger and Acquisitions of Domestic Enterprises by Foreign Investors, Certain Provisions on Change of the Equity Interests of the Investors of a Foreign-Invested Enterprise, the Interim Provisions on Investment Made by Foreign-Invested Enterprises in China, and other relevant provisions, if the concerned M&A transaction falls under the scope of security review while the applicants fail to file an application with the Ministry of Commerce for M&A security review, the competent local commerce authorities shall suspend the acceptance of the application, and shall, within five (5) working days, require the applicants to file an application for M&A security review with the Ministry of Commerce, and in the meantime, report the relevant information to the Ministry of Commerce.

(Continued)

第三条	**Article 3**
外国投资者并购境内企业，国务院有关部门、全国性行业协会、同业企业及上下游企业认为需要进行并购安全审查的，可向商务部提出进行并购安全审查的建议，并提交有关情况的说明（包括并购交易基本情况、对国家安全的具体影响等），商务部可要求利益相关方提交有关说明。属于并购安全审查范围的，商务部应在5个工作日内将建议提交联席会议。联席会议认为确有必要进行并购安全审查的，商务部根据联席会议决定，要求外国投资者按本规定提交并购安全审查申请。	With regard to M&A of domestic enterprises by foreign investors, if government agencies under the State Council, national trade associations, enterprises in the same industry, and upstream and downstream enterprises consider it necessary to conduct the M&A security review, they may make proposals to the Ministry of Commerce on conducting M&A security review, and submit a statement with the relevant information (including the basic information of the M&A transaction, the specific influence on the national security, etc.); the Ministry of Commerce may require the interested parties to submit the relevant statements. If the Inter-Ministerial Panel views it indeed necessary to carry out the M&A security review, the Ministry of Commerce shall, according to the decision of the Inter-Ministerial Panel, require the foreign investor to file an application for M&A security review in accordance with these Provisions.
第四条	**Article 4**
在向商务部提出并购安全审查正式申请前，申请人可就其并购境内企业的程序性问题向商务部提出商谈申请，提前沟通有关情况。该预约商谈不是提交正式申请的必经程序，商谈情况不具有约束力和法律效力，不作为提交正式申请的依据。	Before filing an official application with the Ministry of Commerce for the M&A security review, an applicant may request a discussion with the Ministry of Commerce on procedural issues concerning its M&A of a domestic enterprise, and to communicate the relevant information in advance. Such discussion is not a required procedure prior to the official application; the discussion is not binding and shall not have legal effect, and shall not be deemed as the basis for the official application.

第五条	**Article 5**
在向商务部提出并购安全审查正式申请时，申请人应提交下列文件：	An applicant shall submit the following documents when filing an official application with the Ministry of Commerce for the M&A security review:
（一） 经申请人的法定代表人或其授权代表签署的并购安全审查申请书和交易情况说明；	(1) a written application for M&A security review and a statement describing the concerned M&A transaction, which shall be signed by the legal representative of the applicant or the representative authorized by the legal representative;
（二） 经公证和依法认证的外国投资者身份证明或注册登记证明及资信证明文件；法定代表人身份证明或外国投资者的授权代表委托书、授权代表身份证明；	(2) the identity certification or certificate of incorporation, and creditworthiness certification documents of the foreign investor, which shall be notarized and legalized in accordance with the law; an identity certification of the legal representative, or a power of attorney issued by the foreign investor and identity certification document of the authorized representative thereof;
（三） 外国投资者及关联企业（包括其实际控制人、一致行动人）的情况说明，与相关国家政府的关系说明；	(3) information of the foreign investor and its affiliated enterprises (including its actual controller or parties acting in concert), and its relationship with the government of relevant countries;
（四） 被并购境内企业的情况说明、章程、营业执照（复印件）、上一年度经审计的财务报表、并购前后组织架构图、所投资企业的情况说明和营业执照（复印件）；	(4) information of the acquired domestic enterprise, its articles of association, business license (photocopy), audited financial statements for the previous year, and organization charts of the acquired domestic enterprise prior to and after the M&A, and information of enterprises invested by the acquired domestic enterprise, and business licenses (photocopy) of such enterprises;
（五） 并购后拟设立的外商投资企业的合同、章程或合伙协议以及拟由股东各方委任的董事会成员、聘用的总经理或合伙人等高级管理人员名单；	
（六） 为股权并购交易的，应提交股权转让协议或者外国投资者认购境内企业增资的协议、被并购境内企业股东决议、股东大会决议，以及相应资产评估报告；	
（七） 为资产并购交易的，应提交境内企业的权力机构或产权持有人同意出售资产的决议、资产购买协议（包括拟购买资产的清单、状况）、协议各方情况，以及相应资产评估报告；	
（八） 关于外国投资者在并购后所享有的表决权对股东会或股东大会、董事会决议、合伙事务执行的影响说明，其他导致境内企业的经营决策、财务、人事、技术等实际控制权转移给	

(Continued)

外国投资者或其境内外关联企业的情况说明，以及与上述情况相关的协议或文件； （九）　商务部要求的其他文件。	(5) the joint venture contract, articles of association, or partnership agreement of the foreign-invested enterprise to be established after the M&A, and the name list of the members of the board of directors thereof appointed by the shareholders, and the name list of the general manager, partners, or other senior management; (6) in the case of M&A involving equity transfer, the equity transfer agreement or the agreement on subscription for capital increase of the domestic enterprise by the foreign investor, shareholder resolutions or resolutions of the general meeting of the shareholders, and the relevant asset evaluation report shall be submitted; (7) in the case of M&A involving the transfer of assets, the resolution of the decision-making body of the domestic enterprise or property right holder approving the sale of the assets, the asset purchase agreement (including a list of the assets purchased and the status of such assets), information of the parties to the agreement, and the relevant asset evaluation report shall be submitted; (8) impact of the voting rights enjoyed by the foreign investor after the M&A on the resolutions of the shareholders' meeting or the general meeting of shareholders, or the board of directors, or on the execution of partnership businesses, a statement on other situations that may result in the transfer of actual controlling rights related to business decision-making, financial matters, human resources, technologies, etc.,

	to the foreign investor or its domestic or overseas affiliated enterprises, and the agreement or documents relevant to the aforementioned situations; and (9) other documents required by the Ministry of Commerce.
第六条 申请人所提交的并购安全审查申请文件完备且符合法定要求的，商务部应书面通知申请人受理申请。 属于并购安全审查范围的，商务部在15个工作日内书面告知申请人，并在其后5个工作日内提请外国投资者并购境内企业安全审查部际联席会议（以下简称联席会议）进行审查。 自书面通知申请人受理申请之日起的15个工作日内，申请人不得实施并购交易，地方商务主管部门不得审批并购交易。15个工作日后，商务部未书面告知申请人的，申请人可按照国家有关法律法规办理相关手续。	**Article 6** Where the application documents for M&A security review submitted by an applicant are complete and meet the statutory requirements, the Ministry of Commerce shall notify the applicant in writing of the acceptance of the application. Where the M&A transaction falls under the scope of M&A security review, the Ministry of Commerce shall notify the applicant in writing within fifteen (15) working days and, within the following five (5) working days, file a request with the inter-ministerial panel for the security review of M&A of domestic enterprises by foreign investors (hereinafter referred to as the "Inter-Ministerial Panel") for its review. Within fifteen (15) working days after the applicant is notified of the acceptance of the application, the applicant shall not proceed with the M&A transaction, and the local competent commerce authority shall not approve the M&A transaction. If the Ministry of Commerce has not given a written notice to the applicant after fifteen (15) working days, the applicant may proceed with the relevant formalities in accordance with the relevant laws and regulations of the State.
第七条 商务部收到联席会议书面审查意见后，在5个工作日内将审查意见书面通知申请人（或当事人），以及负责并购交易管理的地方商务主管部门。	**Article 7** The Ministry of Commerce shall, within five (5) working days upon the receipt of the written review results of the Inter-Ministerial Panel, notify the same to the applicant (or the parties)

(Continued)

（一） 对不影响国家安全的，申请人可按照《关于外国投资者并购境内企业的规定》、《外商投资企业投资者股权变更的若干规定》、《关于外商投资企业境内投资的暂行规定》等有关规定，到具有相应管理权限的相关主管部门办理并购交易手续。 （二） 对可能影响国家安全且并购交易尚未实施的，当事人应当终止交易。申请人未经调整并购交易、修改申报文件并经重新审查，不得申请并实施并购交易。 （三） 外国投资者并购境内企业行为对国家安全已经造成或可能造成重大影响的，根据联席会议审查意见，商务部会同有关部门终止当事人的交易，或采取转让相关股权、资产或其他有效措施，以消除该并购行为对国家安全的影响。	and the local competent commerce authority responsible for the administration of M&A transactions. (1) Where the M&A will have no impact on national security, the applicant may proceed with the M&A formalities with the relevant authorities with the corresponding administration authority in accordance with the Provisions on Merger and Acquisitions of Domestic Enterprises by Foreign Investors, Certain Provisions on Change of the Equity Interests of the Investors of a Foreign-Invested Enterprise, the Interim Provisions on Investment Made by Foreign-Invested Enterprises in China, and other relevant provisions. (2) Where the M&A is likely to have an impact on the national security and the M&A transaction has not been implemented, the parties shall terminate the transaction. The applicant shall not apply for and proceed with the M&A transaction before the M&A transaction has been adjusted and the notification documents have been modified and re-reviewed. (3) Where the M&A of a domestic enterprise by a foreign investor has already caused, or is likely to cause, serious impact on national security, according to the review results of the Inter-Ministerial Panel, the Ministry of Commerce shall, in collaboration with relevant authorities, terminate the transaction, or take other effective measures such as equity transfer and assets transfer, so as to eliminate the impact of the M&A on national security.

第八条 在商务部向联席会议提交审查后，申请人修改申报文件、撤销并购交易或应联席会议要求补交、修改材料的，应向商务部提交相关文件。商务部在收到申请报告及有关文件后，于5个工作日内提交联席会议。	**Article 8** After the Ministry of Commerce files a request with the Inter-Ministerial Panel for its review, if the applicant modifies the notification documents, cancels the M&A transaction, or supplements or modifies the filing documents per request of the Inter-Ministerial Panel, the applicant shall submit the relevant documents to the Ministry of Commerce. The Ministry of Commerce shall submit the filing report and the relevant documents within five (5) working days to the Inter-Ministerial Panel.
第九条 对于外国投资者并购境内企业，应从交易的实质内容和实际影响来判断并购交易是否属于并购安全审查的范围；外国投资者不得以任何方式实质规避并购安全审查，包括但不限于代持、信托、多层次再投资、租赁、贷款、协议控制、境外交易等方式。	**Article 9** Whether an M&A of domestic enterprises by foreign investors falls under the scope of M&A security review shall be decided based on the substance and the actual impact of the M&A transaction; foreign investors shall not evade the security review by any means, including without limitation, holding shares by nominees, entrustment, phased-investment, leasing, loans, control agreements, and overseas transactions.
第十条 外国投资者并购境内企业未被提交联席会议审查，或联席会议经审查认为不影响国家安全的，若此后发生调整并购交易、修改有关协议文件、改变经营活动以及其他变化（包括境外实际控制人的变化等），导致该并购交易属于《国务院办公厅关于建立外国投资者并购境内企业安全审查制度的通知》明确的并购安全审查范围的，当事人应当停止有关交易和活动，由外国投资者按照本规定向商务部提交并购安全审查申请。	**Article 10** Where an M&A of a domestic enterprise by a foreign investor is not submitted to the Inter-Ministerial Panel for its review or the Inter-Ministerial Panel considers the M&A transaction would not have any impact on the national security after review, if, thereafter, the M&A transaction is adjusted, the relevant transactional documents are modified, the business activities are changed, or other changes occur (including the change of the overseas actual controller), resulting in the M&A transaction falling under the scope of M&A security review stipulated in the Circular by the General Office of the State Council

(Continued)

	Regarding the Institution of a Security Review System for Mergers and Acquisitions of Domestic Enterprises by Foreign Investors, the concerned parties shall suspend the relevant transaction and activities, and the foreign investor shall file an application with the Ministry of Commerce for M&A security review in accordance with these Provisions.
第十一条 参与并购安全审查的商务主管部门、相关单位和人员应对并购安全审查中的国家秘密、商业秘密及其他需要保密的信息承担保密义务。	**Article 11** The competent commerce authorities, the relevant entities and personnel who take part in the M&A security review shall be responsible for keeping confidential the state secrets, business secrets, and other confidential information disclosed during the M&A security review.
第十二条 本规定自2011年9月1日起实施。	**Article 12** These Provisions shall come into force on September 1, 2011.

B-12

Interim Provisions for the Assessment of the Effects of Concentrations of Undertakings on Competition

关于评估经营者集中竞争影响的暂行规定

(Promulgated by the Ministry of Commerce on August 29, 2011, effective as of September 5, 2011)

（商务部于2011年8月29日发布，自2011年9月5日起施行）

为规范经营者集中反垄断审查的竞争影响评估，指导经营者做好经营者集中申报工作，根据《中华人民共和国反垄断法》、《经营者集中申报办法》和《经营者集中审查办法》，商务部制定了《关于评估经营者集中竞争影响的暂行规定》。现予公布，自2011年9月5日起施行。	To standardize the assessment of the effect of the concentration of undertakings on competition, and guide undertakings in their notification of concentration of undertakings, in accordance with the Anti-Monopoly Law of the People's Republic of China, the Rules for the Notification of Concentrations of Undertakings, and the Rules for the Review of Concentrations of Undertakings, the Ministry of Commerce formulated the Interim Provisions for the Assessment of the Effects of Concentrations of Undertakings on Competition which are hereby promulgated and shall become effective as of September 5, 2011.
第一条 为规范经营者集中反垄断审查工作，评估经营者集中的竞争影响，指导经营者做好经营者集中申报工作，根据《中华人民共和国反垄断法》，制定本规定。	**Article 1** These Provisions are formulated in accordance with the Anti-Monopoly Law of the People's Republic of China to standardize the assessment of the effect of the concentration of undertakings on competition,

(Continued)

	to assess the effect of the concentration of undertakings on competition, and to guide undertakings in their notification of concentration of undertakings.
第二条 商务部依法对经营者集中行为进行反垄断审查。	**Article 2** The Ministry of Commerce conducts an anti-monopoly review of concentrations of undertakings in accordance with the law.
第三条 审查经营者集中，根据个案具体情况和特点，综合考虑下列因素： （一）　参与集中的经营者在相关市场的市场份额及其对市场的控制力； （二）　相关市场的市场集中度； （三）　经营者集中对市场进入、技术进步的影响； （四）　经营者集中对消费者和其他相关经营者的影响； （五）　经营者集中对国民经济发展的影响； （六）　应当考虑的影响市场竞争的其他因素。	**Article 3** Depending on the specific circumstances and characteristics of a concentration of undertakings, the following factors shall be comprehensively taken into consideration when reviewing the concentration: (1)　the market shares of the undertakings concerned by the concentration in the relevant market and their ability to control the market; (2)　the level of concentration in the relevant market; (3)　the effect of the concentration on the market entry and the progress of technologies; (4)　the effect of the concentration on consumers and other undertakings; (5)　the effect of the concentration on the development of the national economy; and (6)　other factors affecting market competition that shall be considered.
第四条 评估经营者集中对竞争产生不利影响的可能性时，首先考察集中是否产生或加强了某一经营者单独排除、限制竞争的能力、动机及其可能性。 当集中所涉及的相关市场中有少数几家经营者时，还应考察集中是否产生或加强了相关经营者共同排除、限制竞争的能力、动机及其可能性。	**Article 4** When assessing the possibility of an adverse effect on competition caused by a concentration of undertakings, the initial factor to be considered is whether the concentration would generate or reinforce a single undertaking's ability, incentive, or possibility to eliminate and/or restrict competition by itself.

当参与集中的经营者不属于同一相关市场的实际或潜在竞争者时，重点考察集中在上下游市场或关联市场是否具有或可能具有排除、限制竞争效果。	Where the relevant market is controlled by a small number of undertakings, it shall also be considered whether the concentration would generate or reinforce the relevant undertakings' ability, incentive, or ability to jointly eliminate and/or restrict competition. Where the undertakings concerned by a concentration are not actual or potential competitors in the same relevant market, the review shall focus on whether the concentration has or may have the effect of eliminating and/or restricting competition in the upstream and downstream markets or associated markets.
第五条 市场份额是分析相关市场结构、经营者及其竞争者在相关市场中地位的重要因素。市场份额直接反映了相关市场结构、经营者及其竞争者在相关市场中的地位。 判断参与集中的经营者是否取得或增加市场控制力时，综合考虑下列因素： （一） 参与集中的经营者在相关市场的市场份额，以及相关市场的竞争状况； （二） 参与集中的经营者产品或服务的替代程度； （三） 集中所涉相关市场内未参与集中的经营者的生产能力，以及其产品或服务与参与集中经营者产品或服务的替代程度； （四） 参与集中的经营者控制销售市场或者原材料采购市场的能力； （五） 参与集中的经营者商品购买方转换供应商的能力； （六） 参与集中的经营者的财力和技术条件； （七） 参与集中的经营者的下游客户的购买能力； （八） 应当考虑的其他因素。	**Article 5** Market share is a major factor in analyzing the market structure and the market status of a undertaking and its competitors in the relevant market. Market share directly reflects the market structure of the relevant market, and market status of the undertaking and its competitors in the relevant market. The following factors shall be comprehensively taken into consideration when assessing whether the undertakings concerned by the concentration will obtain or reinforce its market power: (1) the market share of undertakings concerned by the concentration in the relevant market and the competitive conditions of the related market; (2) the level of substitutability between the products or services of the undertakings concerned by the concentration; (3) the production capacity of the undertakings in the relevant market that are not concerned by the concentration, and the level of substitutability between the products or services of the

(*Continued*)

	non-participating undertakings and those of the undertakings concerned; (4) the ability of the undertakings concerned by the concentration to control the sales market or the raw material procurement market; (5) the ability of the customers of the undertakings concerned by the concentration to switch suppliers; (6) the financial strength and technical capabilities of the undertakings concerned by the concentration; (7) the purchasing power of downstream customers of undertakings concerned by the concentration; and (8) other factors that shall be taken into consideration.
第六条 市场集中度是对相关市场的结构所作的一种描述，体现相关市场内经营者的集中程度，通常可用赫芬达尔-赫希曼指数（HHI指数，以下简称赫氏指数）和行业前N家企业联合市场份额（CRn指数，以下简称行业集中度指数）来衡量。赫氏指数等于集中所涉相关市场中每个经营者市场份额的平方之和。行业集中度指数等于集中所涉相关市场中前N家经营者市场份额之和。 市场集中度是评估经营者集中竞争影响时应考虑的重要因素之一。通常情况下，相关市场的市场集中度越高，集中后市场集中度的增量越大，集中产生排除、限制竞争效果的可能性越大。	**Article 6** The level of market concentration is a description of the structure of the relevant market, reflecting the level of concentration of undertakings in the relevant market. It can generally be measured with the Herfindahl-Hirschman Index (hereinafter referred to as "HHI") and the combined market share of N-largest companies in the industry (CRn Ratio, hereinafter referred to as "Industry Concentration Ratio"). The HHI is equal to the sum of the squared market shares of each individual undertaking in the relevant market concerning the concentration. The Industry Concentration Ratio is equal to the combined market share of the N-largest undertakings in the relevant market concerning the concentration. The level of market concentration shall be one of the major factors when assessing the effect of the concentration of undertakings on competition. Generally, the higher the concentration of the relevant market, the greater the increment of the market

	concentration after the concentration will be and the more likely the concentration will have the effect of eliminating and/or restricting competition.
第七条 经营者集中可能提高相关市场的进入壁垒，集中后经营者可行使其通过集中而取得或增强的市场控制力，通过控制生产要素、销售渠道、技术优势、关键设施等方式，使其他经营者进入相关市场更加困难。 评估经营者集中竞争影响时，可考察潜在竞争者进入的抵消效果。 如果集中所涉及的相关市场进入非常容易，未参与集中的经营者能够对集中交易方的排除、限制竞争行为作出反应，并发挥遏制作用。 判断市场进入的难易程度，需全面考虑进入的可能性、及时性和充分性。	**Article 7** Concentration of undertakings may increase barriers to entry into the relevant market. After the concentration, an undertaking may exercise its market power obtained or reinforced through the concentration, and make it harder for other undertakings to enter the market by controlling production factors, sales channels, superior technologies, key facilities, and other factors. The offsetting effect created by potential competitors entering the market may be taken into consideration when assessing the effect of the concentration of undertakings on competition. If it is quite easy to enter the relevant market involved in the concentration, then non-participating undertakings are able to react to the conduct of the undertakings concerned by the concentration that eliminates or restricts competition, and to limit such effect. The possibility, timeliness, and adequacy of the entry shall be considered comprehensively when assessing the difficulty of market entry.
第八条 经营者通过集中，可更好地整合技术研发的资源和力量，对技术进步产生积极影响，抵消集中对竞争产生的不利影响，并且技术进步所产生的积极影响有助于增进消费者利益。 集中也可能通过以下方式对技术进步产生消极影响：减弱参与集中的经营者的竞争压力，降低其科技创新的动力和投入；参与集中的经营者也可通过集中提高其市场控制力，阻碍其他经营者对相关技术的投入、研发和利用。	**Article 8** Through concentrations, an undertaking may better integrate the resources and capabilities of technology research and development, have a positive impact on technological progress, and offset the adverse effect caused by the concentration on competition. The positive impact of technological progress also helps to enhance consumer welfare. A concentration may also have an adverse effect on technology advancement through the following

(*Continued*)

	ways: it may lower the competition pressure of the participating undertakings and reduce their motive and investment in technology innovation; a participating undertaking may also enhance its market power through the concentration, thereby hindering the investment, research and development, and utilization of the relevant technology by other undertakings.
第九条 经营者集中可提高经济效率、实现规模经济效应和范围经济效应、降低产品成本和提高产品多样化，从而对消费者利益产生积极影响。 集中也可能提高参与集中经营者的市场控制力，增强其采取排除、限制竞争行为的能力，使其更有可能通过提高价格、降低质量、限制产销量、减少科技研发投资等方式损害消费者利益。	**Article 9** A concentration of undertakings may increase economic efficiency, achieve economies of scale and economies of scope, reduce product costs and enhance product diversification, and therefore have a positive effect on consumer welfare. A concentration may also enhance the market power of the participating undertakings, strengthening their ability to commit acts eliminating and/or restricting competition, enabling them to harm consumer welfare by raising prices, lowering quality, restricting production or sales quantity, reducing investment in technology research and development or other means.
第十条 经营者集中可能提高相关市场经营者的竞争压力，有利于促使其他经营者提高产品质量，降低产品价格，增进消费者利益。 凭借通过集中而取得或增强的市场控制力，参与集中经营者可能通过实施某些经营策略或手段，限制未参与集中经营者扩大经营规模或削弱其竞争能力，从而减少相关市场的竞争，也可能对其上下游市场或关联市场竞争产生排除、限制竞争效果。	**Article 10** A concentration of undertakings may increase the competitive pressure of the undertakings in the relevant market, help to promote other undertakings to improve product quality, reduce product prices, and enhance consumer welfare. With the market power obtained or reinforced through the concentration, the participating undertakings may exercise certain business strategies or measures to restrict the ability of the non-participating undertakings to expand their operation scale, or to weaken their competiveness, thereby reducing competition in the relevant market; such business strategies or measures may also have the effect of

	eliminating and/or restricting competition in upstream and downstream markets or in associated markets.
第十一条 经营者集中有助于扩大经营规模，增强市场竞争力，从而提高经济效率，促进国民经济发展。 在特定情况下，经营者集中也可能破坏相关市场的有效竞争和相关行业的健康发展，对国民经济造成不利影响。	**Article 11** A concentration of undertakings helps to expand business scale, strengthen market competitiveness, thereby improving economic efficiency and promoting the development of the national economy. Under certain circumstances, a concentration of undertakings may also damage effective competition in the relevant market and the sound development of the relevant industry, and cause an adverse effect on the national economy.
第十二条 评估经营者集中时，除考虑上述因素，还需综合考虑集中对公共利益的影响、集中对经济效率的影响、参与集中的经营者是否为濒临破产的企业、是否存在抵消性买方力量等因素。	**Article 12** When assessing a concentration of undertakings, in addition to the above factors, consideration shall also be given to the impact of the concentration on the public interest and economic efficiency, and to whether the participating undertakings are on the verge of bankruptcy, whether countervailing buyer power exists, and to other factors.
第十三条 经营者集中具有或者可能具有排除、限制竞争效果的，商务部应当作出禁止经营者集中的决定。但是，经营者能够证明该集中对竞争产生的有利影响明显大于不利影响，或者符合社会公共利益的，商务部可以作出对经营者集中不予禁止的决定。 对于不予禁止的经营者集中，商务部可以决定附加减少集中对竞争产生不利影响的限制性条件。	**Article 13** Where the concentration of undertakings have or may have the effect of eliminating and/or restricting competition, the Ministry of Commerce shall make a decision to prohibit the concentration. However, if the undertakings are able to prove that the positive effect of the concentration obviously outweighs its adverse effect, or the concentration is in accordance with social and public interests, the Ministry of Commerce may make a decision not to prohibit the concentration. For a concentration of undertakings that is not prohibited, the Ministry

(Continued)

	of Commerce may decide to impose restrictive conditions to mitigate the adverse effect of the concentration on competition.
第十四条 本暂行规定自2011年9月5日起施行。	**Article 14** These interim provisions shall become effective as of September 5, 2011.

B-13

Interim Rules on the Investigation and Handling of Concentrations of Undertakings not Notified in Accordance with the Law

未依法申报经营者集中调查处理暂行办法

(Promulgated by the Ministry of Commerce on December 30, 2011, effective as of February 1, 2012)

（商务部于2011年12月30日发布，自2012年2月1日起施行）

《未依法申报经营者集中调查处理暂行办法》已经2011年12月7日商务部第57次部务会议审议通过，现予公布，自2012年2月1日起施行。	The Interim Rules on the Investigation and Handling of Concentrations of Undertakings not Notified in Accordance with the Law (the "Rules") have been reviewed and adopted by the Ministry of Commerce's 57th ministry affairs meeting of December 7, 2011, and are released hereby. The Rules shall become effective as of February 1, 2012.
第一条 为规范达到申报标准但未依法申报经营者集中的调查处理，根据《中华人民共和国反垄断法》（以下简称《反垄断法》）和《国务院关于经营者集中申报标准的规定》（以下简称《规定》）的有关规定，制定本办法。	**Article 1** In accordance with the Anti-Monopoly Law of the People's Republic of China (hereinafter "AML") and the Regulation of the State Council on the Thresholds for Notification of Concentrations of Undertakings (hereinafter the "Regulation"), these Rules are enacted for the purposes of regulating the investigation and handling of concentrations of undertakings that have reached the notification thresholds but were not notified in accordance with the law.

(Continued)

第二条	**Article 2**
本办法所称未依法申报经营者集中，是指经营者集中达到《规定》设定的申报标准，经营者未依照《反垄断法》的规定事先向商务部申报而实施的集中。	The concentrations of undertakings that were not duly notified, as mentioned in these Rules, refer to the concentrations of undertakings that have reached the notification thresholds set by the Regulation but were implemented without a prior notification filed with the Ministry of Commerce ("MOFCOM") in accordance with the AML.
银行业金融机构、证券公司、期货公司、基金管理公司和保险公司营业额的计算，适用《金融业经营者集中申报营业额计算办法》。	The calculation of the turnover for the notification of concentrations involving banking financial institutions, securities companies, futures companies, fund management companies, and insurance companies is regulated by the Rules for the Calculation of Turnover for the Notification of Concentrations of Undertakings in the Financial Sector.
第三条	**Article 3**
商务部负责未依法申报经营者集中的调查处理工作。	MOFCOM is responsible for the investigation and handling of concentrations of undertakings that were not duly notified.
商务部根据工作需要，可以委托省级商务主管部门协助调查本地区内的未依法申报经营者集中。	MOFCOM, when necessary, may authorize competent commerce departments at the provincial level to assist in investigating the concentrations of undertakings in those provinces that were not duly notified.
第四条	**Article 4**
对涉嫌未依法申报经营者集中，任何单位和个人有权向商务部举报。商务部应当为举报人保密。	Any entity or person is entitled to report to MOFCOM any suspected concentration of undertakings that was not duly notified. MOFCOM shall keep the informer confidential.
举报采用书面形式，并提供举报人和被举报人基本情况、涉嫌未依法申报经营者集中的相关事实和证据等内容的，商务部应当进行必要的核实。	In relation to any report that is made in writing and provides information such as basic information of the informer and suspected infringers and relevant facts and evidence in relation to the reported concentration of undertakings, MOFCOM shall carry out necessary review and verification.
对于从其他途径获悉的涉嫌未依法申报经营者集中的相关事实和证据，商务部可以进行必要的核实。	

	In relation to the facts and evidence obtained in other ways in relation to any concentration of undertakings that was not duly notified, MOFCOM may carry out necessary review and verification.
第五条 对有初步事实和证据表明存在未依法申报嫌疑的经营者集中，商务部应当立案，并书面通知被调查的经营者。 本办法所称被调查的经营者，是指《经营者集中申报办法》第九条规定的申报义务人。	**Article 5** For any concentration of undertakings that was not duly notified, as suspected by preliminary facts and evidence, MOFCOM shall initiate the investigation and notify in writing the investigated undertakings. The investigated undertakings, as mentioned in these Rules, refer to the parties responsible for the notification, as provided for in Article 9 of the Rules for the Notification of Concentrations of Undertakings.
第六条 被调查的经营者应当在立案通知送达之日起30日内，向商务部提交与被调查交易是否属于经营者集中、是否达到申报标准、是否已实施且未申报等有关的文件、资料。	**Article 6** The investigated undertakings shall, within 30 days of receiving the notice of case initiation, submit to MOFCOM documents and materials regarding whether the transaction under investigation is a concentration of undertakings, whether it has reached the notification thresholds, and whether it has been implemented.
第七条 商务部应当自收到被调查的经营者依据本办法第六条提交的文件、资料之日起60日内，对被调查的交易是否属于未依法申报经营者集中完成初步调查。 属于未依法申报经营者集中的，商务部应进行进一步调查，并书面通知被调查的经营者。经营者应暂停实施集中。 不属于未依法申报经营者集中的，商务部应当作出不实施进一步调查的决定，并书面通知被调查的经营者。	**Article 7** MOFCOM shall complete the preliminary investigation of the transaction regarding whether the transaction is a concentration of undertakings that was not duly notified, within 60 days of receiving the documents and materials submitted by the investigated undertakings in accordance with Article 6 of these Rules. For any transaction that is considered as a concentration of undertakings that was not duly notified, MOFCOM shall conduct a further investigation and notify the investigated undertakings in writing. The undertakings shall suspend the implementation of the concentration.

(Continued)

	For any transaction that is not considered as a concentration of undertakings that was not duly notified, MOFCOM shall decide not to conduct a further investigation and notify the investigated undertakings in writing.
第八条 商务部决定实施进一步调查的，被调查的经营者应当自收到商务部书面通知之日起30日内，按照《经营者集中申报办法》的规定向商务部提交相关文件、资料。 商务部应当自收到被调查的经营者提交的符合前款规定的文件、资料之日起180日内，完成进一步调查。 在进一步调查阶段，商务部应按照《反垄断法》及《经营者集中审查办法》等的相关规定，对被调查的交易是否具有或者可能具有排除、限制竞争效果进行评估。	**Article 8** Where MOFCOM has decided to conduct a further review, the investigated undertakings shall submit to MOFCOM relevant documents and materials in accordance with the Rules for the Notification of Concentrations of Undertakings within 30 days of receiving the written notice from MOFCOM. MOFCOM shall complete the further investigation within 180 days of receiving the documents and materials submitted by the investigated undertakings in accordance with the preceding paragraph. During such further investigation, MOFCOM shall assess whether the transaction under investigation has or may have the effect of eliminating and/or restricting competition according to the relevant provisions such as the AML and the Rules for the Review of Concentrations of Undertakings.
第九条 商务部进行调查，可以采取《反垄断法》第三十九条规定的措施。	**Article 9** MOFCOM may use the measures prescribed in Article 39 of the AML in its investigation.
第十条 商务部调查未依法申报经营者集中，调查人员不得少于2人，并应当出示合法证件。 调查人员进行询问和调查，应当制作笔录，并由被询问人或者被调查人签字。	**Article 10** MOFCOM shall investigate concentrations of undertakings that were not duly notified with at least two investigation officers who shall present identification documents. The investigation officers shall make a written record of the inquiry and investigation, which shall be signed by the inquired or investigated person.

第十一条 在调查过程中，被调查的经营者、利害关系人有权陈述意见。商务部应当对被调查的经营者、利害关系人提出的事实、理由和证据进行核实。	**Article 11** During the investigation, the investigated undertakings and interested parties have the right to submit statements. MOFCOM shall verify the facts, reasons, and evidence submitted by the investigated undertakings and the interested parties.
第十二条 被调查的经营者、利害关系人或者其他有关单位或者个人应当配合商务部依法履行职责，不得拒绝、阻碍商务部的调查。	**Article 12** The investigated undertakings, the interested parties, and other relevant entities and persons shall cooperate with MOFCOM in the performance of its obligations, and shall not refuse or obstruct MOFCOM's investigation.
第十三条 经调查认定被调查的经营者未依法申报而实施集中的，商务部可以对被调查的经营者处50万元以下的罚款，并可责令被调查的经营者采取以下措施恢复到集中前的状态： （一）　停止实施集中； （二）　限期处分股份或者资产； （三）　限期转让营业； （四）　其他必要措施。 商务部依据前款进行处理时，应当考虑未依法申报行为的性质、程度、持续的时间，以及依据本办法第八条第三款做出的竞争效果评估结果等因素。	**Article 13** Where, after investigation, it is determined that the investigated undertakings have implemented the concentration but failed to duly file a notification, MOFCOM may impose a fine of no more than RMB 500,000 and, in addition, may order the investigated undertakings to take the following measures to restore the market situation before the concentration: (1)　to stop implementing the concentration; (2)　to dispose of their stock or assets within a specified time limit; (3)　to divest their business within a specified time limit; and/or (4)　to take other necessary measures. When handling the case according to the preceding paragraph, MOFCOM shall consider factors such as the nature, seriousness, and duration of the failure to duly notify the concentration, as well as the concentration's effect on competition assessed according to the third paragraph of Article 8 of these Rules.

(Continued)

第十四条 商务部在依据本办法第十三条作出处理决定前，应当将调查结论及所依据的事实和证据告知被调查的经营者。 被调查的经营者应当在商务部设定的期限内提交书面意见。书面意见应当包括相关事实和证据。	**Article 14** Before making a decision according to Article 13 of these Rules, MOFCOM shall inform the investigated undertakings of the conclusion of the investigation and the facts and evidence on which such a conclusion is based. The investigated undertakings shall submit opinions in writing within the time limit prescribed by MOFCOM. Such written opinions shall include the relevant facts and evidence.
第十五条 商务部应当将依据本办法第十三条作出的处理决定书面通知被调查的经营者。对未依法申报经营者集中的处理决定可以向社会公布。	**Article 15** MOFCOM shall inform in writing the investigated undertakings of the decision MOFCOM has made according to Article 13 of these Rules. MOFCOM may publish its decision in respect of any concentration of undertakings that was not duly notified.
第十六条 对商务部依法实施的调查，拒绝提供有关材料、信息，或者提供虚假信息，或者隐匿、销毁、转移证据，或者有其他拒绝、阻碍调查行为的，商务部依据《反垄断法》第五十二条的规定给予处罚。	**Article 16** With respect to investigations duly carried out by MOFCOM, MOFCOM shall impose penalties according to Article 52 of the AML on any refusal to provide the relevant materials or information, or provision of false information, or concealing, destroying, or transferring evidence, or any other act of refusing to cooperate, or impeding the investigation.
第十七条 对于需送达被调查的经营者的书面文件，送达方式参照《中华人民共和国民事诉讼法》的有关规定执行。 商务部以公告送达方式送达的，应在商务部官方网站上公布需送达的文件。	**Article 17** The service of written documents which need to be delivered to the investigated undertakings shall be made in accordance with the relevant provisions in the Civil Procedure Law of the People's Republic of China. If MOFCOM effects service by way of a public notice, it shall publish the documents which need to be delivered on its official website.

第十八条 经营者对商务部依据本办法做出的决定不服的，可以先依法申请行政复议；对行政复议决定不服的，可以依法提起行政诉讼。	**Article 18** Undertakings that are not satisfied with the decisions MOFCOM makes according to these Rules may apply for an administrative review according to the law. If they are still not satisfied with the decision of the administrative review, they may file an administrative lawsuit in accordance with the law.
第十九条 商务部、被调查的经营者以及其他单位和个人应当对调查过程中知悉的商业秘密和其他需要保密的信息保密，但根据法律法规规定应当披露的或者事先取得商业秘密权利人同意的除外。	**Article 19** MOFCOM, the investigated undertakings, and other entities and persons shall keep confidential the business secrets and other confidential information obtained during the investigation process, except where disclosure is required by laws and regulations or the prior approval from the owner of the business secrets is obtained.
第二十条 商务部工作人员滥用职权、玩忽职守、徇私舞弊或者泄露执法过程中知悉的商业秘密，构成犯罪的，依法追究刑事责任；尚不构成犯罪的，依法给予处分。	**Article 20** Where employees from MOFCOM abuse their power, neglect their duties, receive bribes and cheat, or disclose business secrets obtained during their enforcement activities, which constitutes a crime, criminal liability shall be pursued according to the law; if their conduct does not constitute a crime, penalties shall be given in accordance with the law.
第二十一条 本办法自2012年2月1日起施行。	**Article 21** These Rules shall become effective as of February 1, 2012.

B-14

Anti-Monopoly Notification Form for Concentrations of Undertakings

经营者集中反垄断审查申报表

(Promulgated by the Ministry of Commerce on June 6, 2012, effective as of July 7, 2012)

（商务部于2012年6月6日发布，自2012年7月7日起施行）

申报编号：

经营者集中反垄断审查申报表

填报时间：年月日

□ 保密版　□ 非保密版¹　（选择请用þ替换 □）

本申报表标明*的项目为非必填项目。申报人可以根据申报案件的具体情况自行判断是否有必要提供选填项中的全部或部分内容，如申报人认为不必填写，应详细说明理由。

申报人应确保申报书、申报书的附件以及申报人在申报过程中提供的所有信息在其所知范围内是真实、完整和准确的，复印件与原件完全一致，不得提供任何虚假材料和误导性信息。申报人隐瞒重要情况、提供虚假材料或误导性信息的，应当承担相应的法律责任。
1. 交易名称
2. 交易性质（可多选）
□ 新设合并 □ 吸收合并

□ 股权收购
  □ 现金收购
  □ 公开要约收购
    □ 未获目标公司董事会或管理层支持的要约收购
  □ 换股
  □ 其他（具体说明：＿＿＿＿＿＿＿＿）□ 资产收购
□ 合营企业
□ 通过合同等方式取得控制权或者能够施加决定性影响
  （具体说明：＿＿＿＿＿＿＿＿＿＿＿＿＿＿＿）

---

3. 申报依据

□ 达到《国务院关于经营者集中申报标准的规定》规定的申报标准
  □ 参与集中的所有经营者上一会计年度在全球范围内营业额合计超过100亿元人民币，并且其中至少两个经营者上一会计年度在中国境内的营业额均超过4亿元人民币
  □ 参与集中的所有经营者上一会计年度在中国境内的营业额合计超过20亿元人民币，并且其中至少两个经营者上一会计年度在中国境内的营业额均超过4亿元人民币
□未达申报标准自愿申报

---

4. 参与集中的经营者[2]

包括：1、 2、 （3、......）[请列举，详细情况在下栏填写]

4.1 [请填写参与集中的经营者名称/姓名]

4.1.1 是否是申报人[3]	□ 是（身份证明或注册登记证明、公证认证文件等，见附件[ ]） □ 否		
4.1.2 联系地址	地 址		
	邮 编	网 址	
4.1.3 经营者内部的联系人	姓 名	部 门	
	职 务	电子邮件	
	手机及固定电话号码	传真号码	

	□ 有 □ 无			
4.1.4 代理人 （或代理律师）	姓 名		单 位	
	职 务		联系地址	
	手机及固定 电话号码		电子邮件	
	传真号码		授权委托书原件	见附件［ ］。
4.1.5 在交易中的 地位（可多选）	□ 合并方 □ 收购方 □ 被收购方 □ 股权出让方 □ 被收购方的原有股东（股权出让方除外） □ 合营方 □ 其他（具体说明：＿＿＿＿＿＿＿）			
4.1.6 设立时间				
4.1.7 注册地/ 住所	注册地/国籍 （自然人）		住 所	
4.1.8 组织形式	□ 有限责任公司 □ 股份有限公司（非上市公司） □ 上市公司（上市时间、交易所、 股票代码：＿＿＿＿＿＿＿＿＿＿＿＿） 　□ 股份有限公司 　□ 其他（具体说明：＿＿＿＿＿＿） □ 合伙企业 □ 自然人[4] □ 其他（具体说明：＿＿＿＿＿＿）			
4.1.9 上一会计 年度营业额[5]	年 度	［ ］年度 □ 日历年度 □ 财务年度 （起止日期：＿＿＿＿＿＿＿＿＿＿）		
	中国境内	人民币［ ］亿元 （原计价币种及金额： ［ ］亿元[币种]） （汇率[6]：＿＿＿＿＿＿＿＿＿＿）		
	全 球	人民币［ ］亿元 （原计价币种及金额： ［ ］亿元[币种]） （汇率：＿＿＿＿＿＿＿＿＿＿）		

4.1.10 设立和重要变更的历史情况		
4.1.11 主要业务[7]	全球范围	
	中国境内	
4.1.12 股权结构	股东名称及持股比例[8]	
	股权结构图	见附件［ ］。
	是否有最终控制人	□ 有 □ 无[9]
4.1.13 最终控制人（如有）	名称/姓名	
	成立时间[10]	
	注册地/国籍（自然人）	住 所
	组织形式	□ 有限责任公司 □ 股份有限公司（非上市公司） □ 上市公司（上市时间、交易所、股票代码：＿＿＿＿＿＿＿） □ 股份有限公司 □ 其他（具体说明：＿＿＿＿＿） □ 合伙企业 □ 自然人 □ 其他（具体说明：＿＿＿＿＿）
	主要业务（包括整个集团）	
	与参与集中的经营者之间的关系	
	股权结构图	见附件［ ］。

4.1.14 关联实体[11]	境外关联实体[12]	名称及股权结构见附件［ ］[13]。		
		从事与本项集中相关业务的关联企业详细介绍[14]		
	中国境内关联实体	基本信息（名称、注册地、主要业务、股权结构）见附件［ ］[15]。营业执照、外商投资企业批准证书复印件见附件［ ］。		
		从事与本项集中相关业务的关联企业详细介绍[16]		
4.1.15 经营者及关联实体过去三年在相关市场的经营者集中情况				
4.1.16 相关文件	上一会计年度经审计的财务报表	见附件［ ］。		
	上一会计年度年报[17]	□ 有（见附件［ ］） □ 无		
	*研究、分析和报告	交易方内部编制的研究、分析和报告[18]	□ 有（见附件［ ］） □ 无	
		第三方编制的研究、分析和报告	专为本交易[19]	□ 有（见附件［ ］） □ 无
			非专为本交易[20]	□ 有（见附件［ ］） □ 无
5. 参与交易的其他经营者[21]				
包括：1、 （2、……）［请列举，详细情况在下栏填写］				

5.1 ［请填写参与交易的其他经营者的名称/姓名］				
5.1.1 联系地址	地 址			
	邮 编		网 址	
5.1.2 联系人	姓 名		单 位	
	职 务		电子邮件	
	电 话		传 真	
5.1.3 在交易中的地位	□ 股权出让方 □ 资产出让方 □ 被收购方 □ 无控制权或决定性影响的合营方 □ 其他（具体说明：＿＿＿＿＿＿＿＿）			
5.1.4 基本信息	成立时间[22]			
	注册地/国籍 （自然人）		住 所	
	组织形式	□ 有限责任公司 □ 股份有限公司（非上市公司） □ 上市公司（上市时间、交易所、股票代码：＿＿＿＿＿＿＿＿＿＿＿） 　□ 股份有限公司 　□ 其他（具体说明：＿＿＿＿＿＿） □ 合伙企业 □ 自然人 □ 其他（具体说明：＿＿＿＿＿＿）		
5.1.5 主要业务				
6. 集中交易概况				
6.1 集中协议	形 式[23]	□ 正式协议/合同/公司章程 □ 公开要约 □ 非正式或初步协议（如正式协议、合同或公司章程的草案/框架协议/备忘录/意向书等，在下栏说明不能提供正式协议的理由） □ 无交易文件（在下栏说明不能提供集中协议的理由）		

	理 由				
	名 称[24]		签署时间[25]		
	协议方[26]		文 本[27]	见附件〔 〕。	
6.2 交易金额[28]	现金		折合人民币		
	股份数目及估值				
	资产类别及估值				
	其他权益及估值				
	汇率			合计	
6.3 交易的描述[29]	交易前后的股权结构图见附件〔 〕。				
6.4 交易前后股权和控制权结构[30]	交易前后的股权结构图见附件〔 〕。				
6.5 预计交割时间及特殊时限要求（如有，并解释）					
6.6 交易的背景、动机、经济合理性					
6.7 市场发展计划					
6.8 合营企业[31]	名 称[32]				
	注册地 ／ 住所	☐ 境内 ☐ 境外（具体： _____）			
	合营各方拟/已投入的资金、资产和业务等资源[33]				
	合营各方持有合营企业的主要权利和权益				
	合营企业主营业务、运作方式、经营区域、与合营各方及其关联方的业务关系				
	合营各方及关联方之间的其他协议或安排				

7. 集中对相关市场竞争状况的影响					
7.1 集中各方的业务关系	横向重叠	□ 有 □ 无			
		中国国家统计局代码[34]	产品或服务描述[35]		经营者[36]
	纵向关系	□ 有 □ 无			
		中国国家统计局代码	产品或服务描述		经营者
	相邻市场[37]	□ 有 □ 无			
		中国国家统计局代码	产品或服务描述		经营者
7.2 相关市场界定及理由[38]	产品市场	理由	地域市场	理由	
	1、				
7.3 集中对市场竞争的影响[39]	集中各方及主要竞争者市场份额				
	具体分析	市场评估的依据及相关文件见附件［ ］。			
7.4 主要竞争者相关信息[40]	见附件［ ］。				

8. 相关市场的供应和需求结构										

*8.1 供应 结构	集中各方在每一相关市场的主要供应商[41]	[　]市场								
		[参与集中的经营者名称]的主要供应商：								
		排名	供应商名称	采购的产品名称	采购数量	采购数量占比	采购金额	采购金额占比	联系人	联系方式
	相关市场的供应结构									

8.2 需求 结构	集中各方在每一相关市场的主要客户[42]	[　]市场								
		[参与集中的经营者名称]的主要客户：								
		排名	客户名称	*销量	*销量占比	*销售金额	*销售金额占比	联系人	联系方式	
	相关市场的需求结构									

*9. 市场进入					

*9.1 过去五年的市场进入情况[43]	□ 有 □ 无				
	详细信息：				
	名称	进入时间	市场份额	联系人	联系方式
	1、				

*9.2 潜在的进入者[44]	□ 有 □ 无				
	详细信息：				
	名称	联系人	联系方式	可能的进入时间	理由

*9.3 进入市场的难易程度	进入的总成本[45]	
	法律或政策上的限制	
	因知识产权而产生的限制	
	产品生产和经销的规模经济的重要性	
	原材料和基础设施等可用性	

*10. 横向或纵向合作协议[46]

□ 有 □ 无
详细信息：

*11. 集中可能产生的效率

*12. 集中是否涉及破产企业或濒临破产企业

□ 是（详细说明：_____）
□ 否

13. 相关市场行业协会信息

编号	名称	地址	联系人	电话号码	传真号码	网址

14. 交易是否需要中国政府其他部门（包括商务部其他司局）审批

□ 是（详细说明[47]：_____）
□ 否

*15. 有关方面对本次集中的意见[48]
□ 有 □ 无 □ 不了解 详细信息： 有关方面的意见见附件［ ］。

16. 本项交易的合规性及集中各方在中国境内的合规性[49]	
16.1 本项交易的 合规性	
16.2 集中各方主 体资格及业务的 合规性	

17. 交易是否需要在其他国家/地区申报
□ 是（说明需要申报的司法辖区、已申报/拟申报时间及审查进度等：＿＿ ＿＿＿＿＿＿＿＿＿＿＿＿＿＿＿＿＿＿） □ 否

18. 其他需要说明的情况
□ 有 □ 无 详细信息：

19. 申报人承诺[50]
申报人在此承诺，就其所知，本申报书、申报书的附件以及申报人在申报过程中提供的任何文件和信息都是真实、完整和准确的，复印件与原件一致，不存在任何虚假陈述或误导性信息。申报人承担违反上述承诺的相关法律责任。 　　　　　　　　　　　　　　申报人（盖章）： 　　　　　　　　　　　　　　姓名（签字）： 　　　　　　　　　　　　　　职位：

附件目录

编号	附件名称	所属条目

1 非保密版应当提供的信息包括但不限于：参与集中经营者的中文名称、注册地/自然人国籍、成立时间、上市情况（包括是否上市及上市时间和地点）、主要业务、全球及中国境内营业额、在中国境内的关联实体情况；参与集中经营者的最终控制人的上述信息；交易概况，包括交易名称、交易类型、交易过程、交易金额、交易所涉及的行业、产品和地域等；本项交易在其他司法辖区的申报情况、进展情况；交易动机和经济合理性；相关产品和地域市场界定的原因及结论；相关市场竞争情况说明、参与集中的经营者及主要竞争者在相关市场内的市场份额；市场进入情况。上述信息中，营业额、交易金额和市场份额等数据可以区间形式提供，其中营业额和交易金额的区间幅度不应超过10%，市场份额的区间幅度不应超过5%。
2 需根据经营者集中的具体情形界定参与集中的经营者。
一般而言，在经营者合并的情况下，无论是吸收合并还是新设合并，合并各方均为参与集中的经营者；在经营者通过取得股权或者资产的方式取得对其他经营者的控制权的情况下，取得控制权的经营者和目标经营者为参与集中的经营者；在经营者通过合同等方式取得对其他经营者的控制权或者能够对其他经营者施加决定性影响的情况下，取得控制权或能够施加决定性影响的经营者和目标经营者为参与集中的经营者。如集中后两个以上经营者对目标经营者有控制权或者能够施加决定性影响，则上述两个以上经营者均为参与集中的经营者。
尽管有上述说明，在新设合营企业的情况下，合营企业的共同控制方均为参与集中的经营者，合营企业本身不是参与集中的经营者。在既存企业的基础上通过交易形成合营企业的，如既存企业本身为合营企业，既存企业和交易后所有对其有控制权或者能够施加决定性影响的经营者均为参与集中的经营者。如既存企业在交易前由一个经营者单独控制，交易后所有有控制权或者能够施加决定性影响的经营者为参与集中的经营者；如交易前的单独控制方交易后仍拥有控制权或者能够施加决定性影响，既存企业不是参与集中的经营者；交易前单独控制方交易后不再拥有控制权或者能够施加决定性影响的，既存企业是参与集中的经营者。
3 通过合并方式实施的经营者集中，由参与合并的各方经营者申报；其他方式的经营者集中，由取得控制权或能够施加决定性影响的经营者申报，其他经营者予以配合。申报义务人未进行集中申报的，其他参与集中的经营者可以提出申报。直接参与交易的经营者是收购或投资工具的，不宜作为申报人。
4 如选择本项，则不填写第4.1.6、4.1.10、4.1.12、4.1.13项。
5 如申报时上一会计年度的财务报表尚未完成审计，请提供上一会计年度未经审计的营业额、最近会计年度经审计的营业额及经审计的财务报表，并请在申报后及时提供上一会计年度经审计的财务报表。
6 请注明适用的汇率及汇率的来源和计算方法。通常情况下，将以外币计算的营业额换算为人民币时宜适用中国人民银行公布的相应会计年度的汇率中间价平均值。下同。
7 请详细介绍参与集中的经营者与本项集中相关的业务，并概要介绍该经营者的其他主要业务。
8 如经营者股权结构非常分散，请提供主要股东及持股比例，并说明选择理由。非有限责任公司或股份有限公司的，提供经营者权益持有者名称及持有权益的比例、安排或约定。
9 若答案为否，则不填写第4.1.13项。
10 最终控制人属于自然人的，不填此项。

11 一个经营者的关联实体包括该经营者直接或间接控制的所有经营者、该经营者的最终控制人以及最终控制人直接或间接控制的所有经营者等。

12 对于境外关联实体，请至少提供以下两种实体的名称和基本信息：一是与参与集中的经营者有共同或单独控制关系的实体，包括直接和间接的；二是在本项集中的相关市场从事经营的实体。

13 请以表格形式提供。

14 对于关联企业中从事与本项交易相同或相关业务的企业，请着重对其产品和服务进行详细描述。

15 请以表格形式提供。

16 对于关联企业中从事与本项交易相关业务的企业，请着重对其产品和服务进行详细描述。

17 如年度报告为外文，请同时报送中文译本或主要部分中文摘要（如无现成的中文译本）。

18 请提供由交易方及其最终控制人的董事、监事和高管（或行使类似职能的机构或个人）提供或为其提供的，评估或者分析本次集中的所有研究、分析或报告，包括市场份额、竞争条件、实际或潜在的竞争对手、集中的合理性、销售增长或者扩展进入其他产品或地域市场的潜力、总体市场状况、集中带来的协同效应和效率等。此类文件包括但不限于董事会会议记录、公司发展战略等。请注明此类文件的制作时间、制作人姓名、单位、职务及联系方式（原文件中如没有注明）。

19 请提供第三方为评估或分析本次集中而制作的相关文件。

20 请提供第三方并非为本次集中专门制作但与本次集中所涉及行业或市场相关的文件，如行业发展研究报告等。

21 本项填写参与交易但不属于参与集中经营者的相关方信息。

22 参与交易的其他经营者是自然人的，可不填写此项。

23 经营者申报时应提供经正式签署的集中协议；经营者能够提供充分证据证明因交易的特殊安排、其他法律法规章或政策的强制性要求、其他司法辖区的强制性规定或其他合理的理由，申报时无法提供经正式签署的集中协议，或者在集中协议签署后申报将无法遵守《反垄断法》第二十五条、二十六条关于审查期限的规定的，可以在集中协议签署前向商务部申报，但应当提供相关材料如备忘录或框架协议、集中协议草稿、公开要约等，同时提供交易的主要条款和条件，以确保交易的确定性。上述材料应包括经营者集中审查所需的信息。无论审查是否结束，一旦签署集中协议，申报方都应不加拖延向商务部提供集中协议，并说明集中协议与原申报材料的异同；如果申报后经营者集中的内容发生足以影响商务部审查和决定的重大变化的，申报人应及时通知商务部，并更新申报内容或重新申报。

24 如有多份文件，请分别填写。

25 如为要约收购，则填写发出正式要约的时间。

26 如为要约收购，则填写要约方的名称。

27 请同时提供目标公司/合营企业经签署的股东协议、章程（如有），以及交易各方之间及与目标公司/合营企业间的非竞争协议或条款等（如有）。如为要约收购，则提供要约文件。

28 请提供交易总价值，包括现金、股权、资产和其他对价。以非现金作为对价的，请提供其评估价值。以其他币种计价的，请说明币种、汇率并转换为人民币。

29 请描述交易，包括交易架构、交易各方的名称、交易标的和交易各方的对价、交易各关键步骤及时间点、交易进展情况和预计完成时间等。

30 请对交易前后的股权结构进行描述，并对交易前后的控制权结构、控制权变化进行说明并分析。并请以附件的形式提供交易前后的股权结构图。

31 如果交易导致形成合营企业（包括新设合营企业及在既存企业基础上通过交易形成合营企业），请填写此项。

32 如为新设合营企业，在此填写拟使用的名称。

33 请详细说明各合营方投入或承诺的投资资本。如涉及投入资产和业务，请说明其具体范围、内容、价值和上一会计年度的营业额，并说明集中后合营各方是否将继续从事上述业务。涉及不同合营方的，请分别列明。

34 请填写中国国家统计局公布的产品所属最细分类的代码。网址：www.stats.gov.cn/tjbz/tjycpflml。

35 请描述相关产品或服务并简介经营者从事相关业务情况，包括具体经营主体、客户范围和业务模式等。请按中国国家统计局产品分类代码逐项填写，不同经营者分别填写。

36 请注明从事相关业务的参与集中的经营者。

37 指具有互补性，或者具有相同客户群和相同最终用途的一系列产品。

38 请按照《国务院反垄断委员会关于相关市场界定的指南》的规定，从需求替代和供给替代两个方面界定相关产品市场和地域市场，并说明详细理由（请尽量以数据和事实作为支持，并注明所引用数据和事实的来源，如数据系申报人估算，请注明计算的方法和依据）。

39 包括但不限于：根据销售量和销售额计算的市场总体规模，市场发展现状，集中各方及主要竞争对手的销售额、销售量、市场份额，交易前后的HHI/CRn指数及二者的差额（即交易后HHI/CRn指数的增量）。并请说明集中对市场结构、行业发展、竞争者、上下游经营者、消费者、技术进步、经济发展和公共利益的影响。如申报人无法提供HHI指数，请说明理由。请注明每一项数据的来源、计算方法和依据，以附件形式提供能够证明数据来源的文件，并在本栏中注明附件的编号。

40 请以表格形式提供。包括名称、联系人、联系方式（地址、电话、传真），如主要竞争者为外国企业，请同时提供其中国分支机构的联系方式（如有）。

41 请就本交易涉及的每一相关市场，以表格的形式分别提供集中各方主要供应商（通常指前五家主要供应商）的信息，包括排名、供应商名称、采购的产品种类和名称、采购数量、采购数量占比、采购金额、采购金额占比、联系人、联系方式等。请提供独立供应商（即与该经营者没有关联关系的供应商）的上述信息。

42 请就本交易涉及的每一相关市场，以表格的形式分别提供集中各方主要客户（通常指前五家主要客户）的信息，包括排名、客户名称、销售数量、销售数量占比、销售金额、销售金额占比、联系人、联系方式等。请提供独立客户（即与该经营者没有关联关系的客户）的上述信息。

43 请说明过去五年中是否有经营者明显已经进入了相关市场。如有，请提供在此期间内进入市场的经营者名称、进入时间、市场份额、联系人及联系方式。如没有，请分析原因。如集中的任何一方在此期间内进入相关市场，请分析其遇到的市场壁垒。如五年以上或不到五年为更有意义的时间区间，可采用并说明理由。

44 请说明是否存在可能进入相关市场的潜在进入者。如有，请提供潜在进入者的名称、联系人、联系方式，并分析可能的进入时间，说明可能发生此种进入的理由。

45 包括但不限于研发、生产、建立经销系统、推销、广告宣传、服务等所需的时间和费用成本。

46 请提供参与集中的经营者在相关市场内参与的主要横向或纵向合作协议，例如研发、许可协议、联合生产、分销、长期供应以及信息交换等方面的协议。并请说明上述协议在全球范围内被调查的情况。并可以以附件形式提供相关的协议文本或证明材料等。

47 请说明需要经过哪些审批、目前的报批/审批进度，并以附件形式提供相关部门的审批意见（如有）。

48 请介绍有关方面（包括但不限于主管部门、地方政府、行业协会、竞争者、上游企业、客户、媒体、公众等）对本项交易的意见。

49 请说明本项交易是否符合中国法律、法规、规章及相关规定、政策。并请确认集中各方及其关联企业在中国是否存在既往的涉及实体设立、经营管理、外资审批和行业准入监管等方面的未决问题和合规性问题。

50 另有承诺或声明的，可以附件形式提供。如申报人以附件形式另行提供承诺函，其承诺的范围和强度实质上不应弱于第19项的申报人承诺格式文本。

Anti-Monopoly Notification Form for Concentrations of Undertakings

Date of Notification: (Year) (Month) (Day)

☐ Confidential Version ☐ Non-Confidential Version[1] (Please use ☑ to choose)

Items with * are optional, only if the notifying parties explain why such information is not necessary.

The notifying parties shall ensure that the information contained in this notification, its annexes, and all the information provided by the notifying parties during the notification process is true, complete, and accurate to the best of their knowledge, copies of documents are exactly consistent with the originals, and the notifying parties did not provide any false materials or misleading information. The notifying parties shall bear the relevant legal liabilities if they conceal important information or provide false materials or misleading information.

1. Name of the Transaction

2. Nature of the Transaction (multiple)

☐ Merger into a new company
☐ Merger into an existing company
☐ Equity acquisition
    ☐ Cash offer
    ☐ Public tender offer
        ☐ Tender offer without support from the board of directors or management of the target company
    ☐ Share exchange
    ☐ Others (specifically: _____)
☐ Asset acquisition
☐ Joint venture
☐ Acquisition of control or the capacity to exercise decisive influence by contract or any other means (specifically: _____)

3. Basis of Notification

☐ Concentration reaching the notification thresholds specified by the Regulation of the State Council on the Notification Thresholds for Concentrations of Undertakings

☐ The combined worldwide turnover of all the undertakings concerned in the preceding financial year is more than RMB 10 billion yuan, and the turnover within China of each of at least two of the undertakings concerned in the preceding financial year is more than RMB 400 million yuan
☐ The combined turnover within China of all the undertakings concerned in the preceding financial year is more than RMB 2 billion yuan, and the turnover within China of each of at least two of the undertakings concerned in the preceding financial year is more than RMB 400 million yuan
☐ Voluntary notification for a transaction below the notification thresholds

4. Undertakings Concerned[2]

Including: 1. 2. (3.… …) [Please list and fill in details below]

4.1 [Please fill in names of the undertakings concerned]

4.1.1 Is it a notifying party[3]	☐ Yes (Identification or Certificate of Incorporation, and legalized/notarized documents attached as Annex [ ]) ☐ No		
4.1.2 Contact address	Address		
	Zip Code		Website
4.1.3 Internal contact person	Name		Department
	Position		E-mail
	Mobile and tel.		Fax
4.1.4 Appointed agent or attorney	☐ Yes ☐ No		
	Name		Firm
	Position		Address
	Mobile and tel.		E-mail
	Fax		POA (original)	Attached as Annex [ ]

4.1.5 **Position(s) in** **the transaction** **(multiple)**	☐ Merging party ☐ Acquiror ☐ Acquiree ☐ Equity transferor ☐ Original shareholders of the acquiree (other than the equity transferor) ☐ Joint venture party ☐ Others (specifically: _____)
4.1.6 Date of **incorporation**	

4.1.7 Place of incorporation/ domicile	**Place of incorporation/ nationality (natural person)**		**Registered office/ domicile (natural person)**	

4.1.8
Corporate
form
	☐ Limited liability company
	☐ Company limited by shares (non-public)
	☐ Public company (date of listing, stock exchange, stock code: _____)
	   ☐ Company limited by shares
	   ☐ Others (specifically: _____)
	☐ Partnership
	☐ Natural person[4]
	☐ Others (specifically: _____)

4.1.9 Turnover in preceding fiscal year[5]	Fiscal year	**Year [ ]** ☐ Calendar year ☐ Fiscal year (beginning and ending dates: _____)
	Mainland China	**RMB [ ]** (Original denominated currency and amount: [Currency] [ ] (Exchange rate[6]: _____)
	Worldwide	**RMB [ ]** (Original denominated currency and amount: [Currency] [ ] (Exchange rate: _____)

4.1.10 **Establishment** **and major** **changes in** **history**	

4.1.11 Main businesses[7]	Worldwide	
	Mainland China	
4.1.12 Equity structure	Shareholders and shareholdings[8]	
	Corporate organization chart	Attached as Annex [ ]
	Any ultimate controlling person	□Yes □ No[9]
4.1.13 Ultimate controlling person (if any)	Name	
	Date of incorporation[10]	
	Place of incorporation/ nationality (natural person)	Registered office/ domicile (natural person)
	Corporate form	□ Limited liability company □ Company limited by shares (non-public) □ Public company (date of listing, stock exchange, stock code: _____) □ Company limited by shares □ Others (specifically: _____) □ Partnership □ Natural person □ Others (specifically: _____)
	Main businesses (group-wide)	
	Relationship with the undertakings concerned	
	Corporate organization chart	Attached as Annex [ ]

4.1.14 Affiliates[11]	Affiliates outside Mainland China[12]	Name and corporate organization chart attached as Annex [ ][13]			
		Detailed description of affiliates engaging in businesses relevant to the transaction[14]			
	Affiliates in Mainland China	Basic information (name, place of incorporation, main businesses, corporate organization structure) attached as Annex [ ][15] Photocopies of business licenses and certificates of approval for foreign invested enterprises attached as Annex [ ]			
		Detailed description of affiliates engaging in the businesses relevant to the transaction[16]			
4.1.15 Description of concentrations of undertakings involving any of the undertakings concerned and their affiliates in the relevant markets in the past three years					
4.1.16 Relevant documents	Audited financial statements of preceding fiscal year	Attached as Annex [ ]			
	Annual report of preceding fiscal year[17]	☐ Yes (attached as Annex [ ]) ☐ No			
	* Studies, analyses, and reports	Prepared by transaction parties[18]	☐ Yes (attached as Annex [ ]) ☐ No		
		Prepared by third parties	Exclusively for the transaction[19]	☐ Yes (attached as Annex [ ]) ☐ No	
			Not exclusively for the transaction[20]	☐ Yes (attached as Annex [ ]) ☐ No	

5. Other Undertakings Involved in the Concentration[21]					
Including: 1. (2........) [Please list and fill in details below]					
5.1 [Please fill in names of other undertakings involved in the transaction]					
5.1.1 Contact address	**Address**				
	Zip Code		**Website**		
5.1.2 Contact person	**Name**		**Company**		
	Position		**E-mail**		
	Phone		**Fax**		
5.1.3 Position in the transaction	☐ Equity transferor ☐ Asset transferor ☐ Acquiree ☐ Joint venture party without control or capacity of exercising decisive influence ☐ Others (specifically: _____)				
5.1.4 Basic information	**Date of incorporation**[22]				
	Place of incorporation/ nationality (natural person)		**Registered office/ domicile (natural person)**		
	Corporate form	☐ Limited liability company ☐ Company limited by shares (non-public) ☐ Public company (date of listing, stock exchange, stock code: _____ _____) ☐ Company limited by shares ☐ Others (specifically: _____) ☐ Partnership ☐ Natural person ☐ Others (specifically: _____)			
5.1.5 Main businesses					

6. Overview of the Transaction				
6.1 Concentration agreements	**Form**[23]	☐ Formal agreement/contract/articles of association ☐ Public offer ☐ Informal or preliminary agreement (e.g. draft of formal agreement, contract or articles of association/ framework agreement/memorandum of understanding/letter of intent. Explain below why the formal agreements are not available) ☐ No transaction documents (Explain below why the concentration agreements are not available)		
	Reason of unavailability			
	Name[24]		**Date of execution**[25]	
	Parties[26]		**Copy**[27]	Attached as Annex [ ]
6.2 Transaction amount[28]	**Cash**			
	Number of shares and estimated value		**Converted into RMB**	
	Asset category and estimated value			
	Other interests and estimated value			
	Exchange rate		**Total**	
6.3 Description of transaction[29]				
6.4 Equity and control structures pre- and post-transaction[30]	Corporate organization charts pre- and post-transaction attached as Annex [ ]			

6.5 Anticipated date of closing and special time limit (explain if any)		
6.6 Background, motive, and economic rationale of the transaction		
6.7 Market development plan		
6.8 Joint ventures[31]	**Name**[32]	
	Place of incorporation/ domicile	☐ **Domestic** ☐ **Overseas (specifically: _____)**
	Resources (to be) contributed by each JV party to the JV such as capital, assets, and businesses[33]	
	Main rights and interests enjoyed by each JV party in the JV	
	Main businesses, operation model, and business regions of the JV, and its business relationship with each JV party and with the party's affiliates	
	Other agreements or arrangements among the JV parties and their affiliates	

7. Effects of the Concentration on Competition in the Relevant Markets

7.1 Business relationships among the parties to the concentration	**Horizontal overlap**	☐ Yes ☐ No		
		Codes by the National Bureau of Statistics of China[34]	**Description of products or services**[35]	**Undertakings**[36]

	Vertical relationship	☐ Yes ☐ No			
		Codes by the National Bureau of Statistics of China	Description of product or service	Undertakings	
	Adjacent markets[37]	☐ Yes ☐ No			
		Codes by the National Bureau of Statistics of China	Description of product or service	Undertakings	
7.2 Definition of the relevant markets and reasons[38]	Product market	Reasons	Geographic market	Reasons	
	1.				
7.3 Effects of the concentration on market competition[39]	Market shares of the parties and their main competitors				
	Detailed analysis	Basis and relevant documents for market assessment attached as Annex [ ]			
7.4 Information related to main competitors[40]	Attached as Annex [ ]				

8. Supply and Demand Structures in the Relevant Markets

*8.1 Supply structure	Main suppliers of each party in each relevant market[41]	Market for [ ] Main suppliers of [name of the undertaking concerned]:				
		Ranking	Supplier	Product purchased	Purchase quantity	Percentage by quantity

	Supply structure in each relevant market	Purchase amount	Percentage by amount	Contact person	Contact information

8.2 Demand structure	Main customers of each party in each relevant market[42]	Market for [ ] Main customers of [name of the undertaking concerned]:			

Ranking	Customer		*Sales quantity	*Percentage by quantity

*Sales amount	*Percentage by amount	Contact person	Contact information	

Demand structure in each relevant market	

*9. Market Entries

*9.1 Market entries in the past five years[43]	☐ Yes ☐ No
	Details:

Name	Time of entry	Market share	Contact person	Contact information
1.				

*9.2 Potential entrants[44]	☐ Yes ☐ No
	Details:

Name	Contact person	Contact information	Possible time of entry	Reasons

*9.3 Difficulties of market entries in each relevant market	Total entry costs[45]	
	Legal or policy barriers	
	Limitation due to IP issues	
	Importance of economy of scale for manufacture and sales	
	Access to raw materials and infrastructure	

*10. Horizontal or Vertical Cooperation Agreements[46]

☐ Yes ☐ No
Details:

*11. Possible Efficiency that May Be Generated by the Concentration

*12. Any (To Be) Bankrupt Enterprises Involved in the Concentration

☐ Yes (details: _____)
☐ No

13. Information of Trade Associations in the Relevant Markets

No.	Name	Address	Contact person	Tel.	Fax	Website

14. Transaction Subject to Approvals by Other Chinese Government Agencies (including Other Departments of the Ministry of Commerce)

☐ Yes (details[47]: _____)
☐ No

*15. Opinion from Other Parties on the Concentration[48]

☐ Yes ☐ No ☐ Unclear
Details:

Opinions from other parties attached as Annex [ ]

16. Compliance of the Transaction and of the Parties in China[49]	
16.1 **Compliance of the transaction**	
16.2 **Compliance of the incorporation of the parties and their businesses**	

17. Transaction Subject to Filings in Other Jurisdictions

☐ Yes (jurisdiction, actual or intended filing date, review status, etc.: _____
_____)
☐ No

18. Other Issues to Clarify

☐ Yes   ☐ No
Details:

19. Representation by the Notifying Party[50]

The notifying party represents that, to the best of its knowledge, information contained in this notification, its annexes, and any documents and information provided by the notifying party during the notification process are true, complete, and accurate, the photocopies are consistent with the originals, and there is no false statement or misleading information. The notifying party undertakes the legal liabilities in respect of any breach of the above representations.

Notifying party (corporate seal):
Name (signature):
Position:

List of Annexes

No.	Name of Annex	Item Reference

1 The information provided in the non-confidential version shall include, but is not limited to: Chinese name of each undertaking concerned by the concentration, place of incorporation/nationality for natural persons, date of incorporation, information about stock exchange listing (including whether it is listed, and if so date and location of stock exchange), main businesses, turnovers worldwide and in China, and information about its affiliates in China; all the above information about its ultimate controlling person(s); overview of the transaction, including name, type, process, transaction amount, and industries, products, and regions involved in the transaction; status of the notifications of the transaction in other jurisdictions; motive and economic rationale of the transaction; definition of the relevant product and geographic markets along with the basis for such definition; competitive conditions in the relevant markets, market shares of the undertakings concerned and their main competitors in the relevant markets; market entries. In respect of the above information, turnover, transaction amount, and market share data can be presented using ranges, within a total range of 10% for turnover and transaction amount data and 5% for market shares.

2 The "undertakings concerned" shall be determined based on the specifics of the concentration. Generally speaking, in respect of a merger, either by absorption or by formation of a new company, the undertakings concerned are all the parties to the merger; in respect of an acquisition of control over other undertakings by equity or asset acquisition, the undertakings concerned are the undertakings acquiring control and the target undertaking; in respect of an acquisition of control over or the capacity of exercising decisive influence on other undertakings by contract or by any other means, the undertakings concerned are the undertakings acquiring control or capacity of exercising decisive influence and the target undertaking. If post-concentration more than two undertakings will have control over or capacity of exercising decisive influence on the target undertakings, they are all the undertakings concerned.

Notwithstanding the above, in respect of the new establishment of a joint venture, the undertakings concerned are the jointly controlling parties to the joint venture and do not include the joint venture itself. When a joint venture will be formed by the transaction based on an existing enterprise, if the existing enterprise itself is a joint venture, the undertakings concerned are the existing enterprise and all the undertakings that after the transaction will have control over or capacity of exercising decisive influence on the joint venture. Where an existing enterprise is solely controlled by a single undertaking before the transaction, the undertakings concerned include the undertakings that will have control over or capacity of exercising decisive influence after the transaction; if the single controlling person before the transaction will still have control or capacity of exercising decisive influence after the transaction, the undertakings concerned do not include the existing enterprise; if the single controlling person before the transaction will no longer have control or capacity of exercising decisive influence after the transaction, the undertakings concerned also include the existing enterprise.

3 In respect of a concentration by merger, the notifying parties are all the parties to the merger; in respect of concentrations by other means, the notifying parties are the undertakings that will have control over or capacity of exercising decisive influence, while other undertakings involved shall cooperate in the notification. If the notifying parties fail to notify the concentration, other undertakings involved may do so. Where the undertakings directly involved in the transaction

serve as acquisition or investment vehicles, it is not appropriate for them to act as notifying parties.

4 If this item is selected, skip items 4.1.6, 4.1.10, 4.1.12, and 4.1.13.

5 If the financial statements of the preceding fiscal year have not been audited upon notification, please provide the unaudited turnovers of the preceding fiscal year and the latest audited fiscal year-end turnovers and financial statements. Please promptly provide the audited financial statements of the preceding fiscal year when they are available after the notification.

6 Please indicate the exchange rate used, and the source and calculation method of the exchange rate. Normally, when converting the turnover denominated in a foreign currency into Renminbi, it is recommended to use the average central parity rate of the corresponding fiscal year published by the People's Bank of China. The same below.

7 Please describe in detail the undertaking's main businesses relevant to the concentration, and briefly describe its other businesses.

8 If the shareholders of the undertaking are widely dispersed, please provide the major shareholders and their respective shareholdings, and explain why such shareholders are selected as the major shareholders. For undertakings that are not limited liability companies or companies limited by shares, provide the equity holders of the undertaking and their respective equity holdings, arrangements, or agreements.

9 If the answer is no, skip item 4.1.13.

10 Skip this item if the ultimate controlling person is a natural person.

11 The affiliates of an undertaking include all the undertakings directly or indirectly controlled by such undertaking, the ultimate controlling person(s) of such undertaking, and all the undertakings directly or indirectly controlled by such ultimate controlling person(s).

12 For affiliates outside Mainland China, please provide the name and basic information (including name, place of incorporation, main businesses, corporate organization structure) for at least the following two kinds of entities: 1) entities that are jointly or solely controlled by or controlling the undertakings concerned, whether directly or indirectly; and 2) entities that engage in the businesses relevant to the concentration.

13 Please submit in the form of tables.

14 In respect of affiliates that engage in the businesses relevant to the concentration, the detailed description shall focus on their products and services.

15 Please submit in the form of tables.

16 In respect of affiliates that engage in the businesses relevant to the concentration, the detailed description shall focus on their products and services.

17 If the annual report is not in Chinese, please provide a Chinese translation or Chinese abstract of the report (if no Chinese version is readily available).

18 Any studies, analyses, and reports prepared by or for any officer, director, or senior management (or institutions or individuals exercising similar functions) of the parties or of their ultimate controlling person(s) for the purpose of evaluating or analyzing the transaction with respect to, for example, market shares, competition, actual or potential competitors, rationale of the transaction, potential for sales growth or expansion into other product or geographic markets, overall market condition, and synergies and efficiencies that can be created by the transaction. These documents include but are not limited to minutes of board meetings and company development strategies. Please indicate the date of production as well as the name, company, title, and contact information of the producers of such documents (if such information is not available in the original documents).

19 Please provide the relevant documents prepared by third parties for the purpose of evaluating or analyzing the transaction.

20 Please provide the documents relevant to the industries or markets involved in the transaction, which are prepared non-exclusively for this transaction by third parties, such as industry reports.

21 Please fill in information of the undertakings that are involved in the transaction but are not included in the undertakings concerned.

22 Skip this item if the undertaking is a natural person.

23 Upon notification, a copy of the formally executed concentration agreements shall be submitted. If the undertakings can provide sufficient evidence that due to special deal arrangements, compulsory requirements by other laws, regulations or policies, compulsory provisions of other jurisdictions, or other reasonable excuses, the formally executed version of any concentration agreement is not available upon notification or after execution of the concentration agreement the notification is unable to follow the review period provisions of Articles 25 and 26 of the *Anti-Monopoly Law*, they may file the concentration with the Ministry of Commerce before execution of the concentration agreements. However, in this case, the undertakings shall submit other relevant documents such as memorandums of understanding or framework agreements, draft concentration agreements and tender offer documentation, along with the key transaction terms and conditions to show the certainty of the transaction. The materials required above shall include information needed for the review of the transaction. No matter whether the review is complete, once the concentration agreements are executed, the notifying parties shall promptly submit to the Ministry of Commerce the executed version, along with an explanation on the similarities and differences from the materials previously provided. If after notification, the concentration is altered so significantly that the review and decision of the Ministry of Commerce may be affected, the notifying parties shall promptly notify the Ministry of Commerce and amend or re-file the notification.

24 Please provide the names separately for multiple documents.

25 In respect of tender offers, please fill in the time when the offer is made.

26 In respect of tender offers, please fill in the name of the offeror.

27 Please also provide the executed version of the shareholders agreements and articles of association (if any) of the target company/joint venture and non-complete agreements or terms (if any) among the joint venture parties or with the target company/joint venture. In respect of tender offers, please provide the tender offer documentation.

28 Please provide the total value of the transaction, including cash, equity shares, assets, and other considerations. In case of non-cash considerations, please provide the evaluated value. In case of considerations denominated in foreign currencies, please specify the currency, exchange rate, and amount converted into Renminbi.

29 Please describe the transaction, including the deal structure, names of the parties, object of the transaction and consideration from each party, key steps and timeline, progress and anticipated date of closing.

30 Please describe the equity structures pre- and post-transaction, along with an explanation and analysis of the control structures pre- and post-transaction, and changes of control post-transaction. Please also attach the equity structure charts pre- and post-transaction as an annex to the notification.

31 Fill in this part if the transaction leads to formation of a joint venture (including new establishment of a joint venture or formation of a joint venture based on an existing enterprise through the transaction).

32 In respect of joint ventures to be newly established, please fill in the proposed name.

33 For each joint venture party, please specify the investment capital it has contributed or undertakes to contribute to the joint venture, and in respect of any assets and businesses contributed or to be contributed, please specify the scope, substance, and value of such assets and businesses and the turnover generated by such assets and businesses in the preceding fiscal year. Please also explain whether any of the joint venture parties will continue to engage in such businesses after the transaction.

34 Please fill in the lowest-level product code provided by the National Bureau of Statistics of China, available at: <www.stats.gov.cn/tjbz/tjycpflml>.

35 Please describe the relevant products or services, and briefly introduce the undertakings' businesses in relation to the products or services, including the specific operation entities, customer scope, and business model. Please provide such information by product (as classified by the codes provided by the National Bureau of Statistics of China) for each undertaking separately.

36 Please specify the undertakings concerned by the concentration that engage in the relevant businesses.

37 It refers to a series of products that are complimentary to each other or are for the same group of customers with the same ultimate use.

38 With the guidance from the *Guidelines on the Definition of the Relevant Market by the Anti-Monopoly Commission of the State Council,* please define the relevant product markets and geographic markets from the perspectives of demand substitutability and supply substitutability. Please also specify the detailed reasons for such definition (to the extent possible, please use data and facts as support, and specify the source of the data and facts as well as the method and basis for estimations if the data are estimated by the notifying parties).

39 Including but not limited to: market sizes by quantity and amount, respectively, current status of the market development, sales amount, sales quantity and market shares of the undertakings concerned by the concentration and of their main competitors, the HHI/CRn pre- and post-transaction, and the difference (i.e. increase of the HHI/CRn post-transaction). Explain the competitive effects of the transaction on the market structure, industry development, competitors, upstream and downstream undertakings, consumers, technology development, economic development, and public welfare. If the notifying parties are unable to provide the HHI, please explain why not. Please specify the source, calculation method, and basis of each data, attach documents which can evidence the source of the data, and provide the serial numbers of such attachments in this column.

40 Please submit in the form of tables, including name, contact person, and contact information (address, telephone, and fax). If any of the competitors is a foreign entity, please also provide the contact information of its Chinese branch (if any).

41 In respect of each relevant market, please submit in the form of tables, information of each party's main suppliers (normally the top five), including ranking, name, products purchased, purchase quantity, percentage by quantity, purchase amount, percentage by amount, contact person, and contact information. Please also provide such information of the independent suppliers (i.e., suppliers that are not affiliates of the party).

42 In respect of each relevant market, please submit in the form of tables, information of each party's main customers (normally the top five), including ranking, name, sales quantity, percentage by quantity, sales amount, percentage by amount, contact person, and contact information. Please also provide such information of the independent customers (i.e., customers that are not affiliates of the party).

43 Please explain whether any undertakings have apparently entered any relevant market in the past five years. If yes, please provide the name, time of entry, market share, contact person, and contact information of such undertakings. If no, please analyze why not. If any party to the transaction entered any relevant market in the past five years, please analyze the market barriers it encountered. If any time period other than five years is more sensible for such analysis, the notifying parties can use such other period and explain the reason.

44 Please explain if there are any potential entrants in any relevant market. If yes, please provide the name, contact person, and contact information of such potential entrants, along with an analysis of the possible time and reason of such entry.

45 Including but not limited to the time and costs needed for research and development, manufacturing, establishment of sales network, marketing, advertising, and services.

46 Please provide the main horizontal or vertical cooperation agreements that involve the undertakings concerned in the relevant markets, such as agreements in respect of research

and development, licensing, joint production, distribution, long-term supply, or information exchange. Also explain whether any of those agreements is under investigation by any authority in the world. The notifying parties may attach copies of those agreements or evidences.

47 Please specify what approvals are required, and the current status of the applications/approvals. Please also attach the review opinions from the relevant authorities (if any).

48 Please provide opinions from other parties on the transaction, including but not limited to opinions from the responsible government agencies, local governments, trade associations, competitors, suppliers, customers, media, and the general public.

49 Please explain whether the transaction is in compliance with Chinese laws, regulations, rules, and policies. Please also confirm whether the parties to the transaction and their affiliates have any pending or compliance issue in China in terms of incorporation or establishment, operation and management, foreign investment approval, and industry access regulation.

50 The notifying parties can attach separate representations or undertakings, which in substance shall be at least as wide in scope and strong as those in the template provided in item 19.

B-15

Provisions on Regulating Competition Activities in Foreign Investment and Cooperation

规范对外投资合作领域竞争行为的规定

(Published by the Ministry of Commerce on March 18, 2013, effective as of April 18, 2013)

（商务部于2013年3月18日发布，自2013年4月18日施行）

第一条 为促进对外投资合作业务健康和可持续发展，规范对外投资合作企业（以下简称企业）海外经营行为，鼓励和保护公平竞争，打击不正当竞争行为，根据《中华人民共和国对外贸易法》、《中华人民共和国反不正当竞争法》、《对外承包工程管理条例》、《对外劳务合作管理条例》和《境外投资管理办法》等有关法律法规，制定本规定。	**Article 1** In order to promote the healthy and sustainable development of the foreign investment and cooperation business, regulate the companies (hereinafter referred to as "Companies") that engage in foreign investment and cooperation, encourage and protect fair competition, and prevent unfair competition acts, these provisions are promulgated in accordance with the Foreign Trade Law of the People's Republic of China, the Anti-Unfair Competition Law of the People's Republic of China, the Administrative Regulation on Contracting Foreign Projects, the Administrative Regulation on Foreign Labor Cooperation, the Measures for Overseas Investment Management, and other relevant laws and regulations.
第三条 企业在经营中应当遵循平等、公平、诚实守信的原则，遵守公认的商业道德。企业不应采取不正当竞争行为损害其他企业的合法权益，扰乱对外投资合作经营秩序。	**Article 3** In the course of their business activities, the Companies shall observe the principles of equality, equitability, honesty, and trustworthiness, and abide by generally accepted business ethics.

(Continued)

	The Companies shall not harm the lawful rights and interests of other companies or disrupt the business order in foreign investment and cooperation.
第五条 对外投资合作领域不正当竞争行为包括: (一) 以商业贿赂争取市场交易机会; (二) 以排挤竞争对手为目的的不正当价格竞争行为; (三) 串通投标; (四) 诋毁竞争对手商誉; (五) 虚假宣传业绩; (六) 其他依法被认定为不正当竞争的行为。	**Article 5** Unfair competition acts in foreign investment and cooperation include: (1)　seeking trading opportunities by commercial bribery; (2)　unfair price-related competition acts with the purpose of excluding competitors; (3)　colluding in bidding submissions; (4)　denigrating competitors' business reputation; (5)　publishing false performances; and (6)　other behaviors that are determined as unfair competition acts in accordance with the law.
第九条 举报有关企业存在不正当竞争行为的, 举报人应以实名向商务部提出, 举报内容必须详实、准确, 同时提交相应证据。	**Article 9** In reporting Companies' unfair competition acts, the informer shall report to MOFCOM with the informer's real name, detailed and accurate information of the reported acts as well as relevant evidence.
第十条 商务部履行监督检查职能。可以委托地方商务主管部门、驻外使领馆经商机构或其他有关单位, 依照法律、行政法规的规定对对外投资合作领域不正当竞争行为进行调查和认定。涉及单位和个人应当对调查给予配合、协助。	**Article 10** MOFCOM shall be in charge of supervision and inspection. It may authorize local commerce authorities, economic and commercial offices of the Chinese embassies, or other competent organizations to investigate and find unfair competition acts in foreign investment and cooperation. The entities and individuals involved shall offer cooperation and assistance in the investigations.

第十一条	**Article 11**
商务部将会同有关部门建立对外投资合作不良信用记录制度，对违反本规定构成不正当竞争的对外投资合作经营行为将记录在案，并通报有关部门和机构。涉及企业3年内不得享受国家有关支持政策。	MOFCOM will, together with other relevant authorities, establish a system for poor credit records in foreign investment and cooperation to record the business activities in foreign investment and cooperation that constitute unfair competition acts in violation of these provisions and will notify such violations to the relevant authorities and organizations. The Companies involved shall not benefit from the relevant national supporting policies in the following three years.

B-16

Interim Rules on the Gathering of Evidence for Suspected Monopolistic Concentrations of Undertakings not Reaching the Notification Thresholds (Draft for Public Comment)

关于对未达申报标准涉嫌垄断的经营者集中证据收集的暂行办法（草案）

(Published by the Ministry of Commerce on January 19, 2009)

（商务部于2009年1月19日发布）

第一条 【立法目的】 为了规范对未达申报标准但涉嫌具有或者可能具有排除、限制竞争效果的经营者集中立案调查前的证据收集行为，根据《中华人民共和国反垄断法》（以下简称《反垄断法》）和《国务院关于经营者集中申报标准的规定》（以下简称《规定》），制定本办法。	**Article 1 Legislative Purpose** In accordance with the Anti-Monopoly Law of the People's Republic of China (hereinafter referred to as "AML") and the Regulation of the State Council on the Notification Thresholds for Concentrations of Undertakings (the "Regulation"), these Rules are formulated for the purpose of regulating evidence gathering before initiating investigations into concentrations which do not meet any of the notification thresholds but are suspected to have or may have the effect of eliminating and/or restricting competition.
第二条 【适用范围】 中华人民共和国商务部（以下简称"商务部"）依据《规定》第四条，对未达申报标准但涉嫌具有或者可能具有排除、限制竞争效果的经营者集中进行证据收集，适用本办法。	**Article 2 Applicable Scope** These Rules shall apply to the evidence gathering by the Ministry of Commerce (hereinafter referred to as "MOFCOM") according to Article 4 of the Regulation, regarding concentrations of undertakings

本办法中的申报标准，是指《规定》第三条所规定的申报标准。	which do not reach the notification thresholds but are suspected to have or may have the effect of eliminating and/or restricting competition. The notification thresholds mentioned in these Rules refer to the notification thresholds provided in Article 3 of the Regulation.
第三条 【启动证据收集程序前的初步分析】 商务部可以根据举报、媒体信息、相关部门的意见等合法渠道获取的信息，对未达申报标准的经营者集中是否涉嫌具有或者可能具有排除、限制竞争效果进行初步分析。 举报采用书面形式并提供相关事实和证据的，商务部应当进行初步分析。	**Article 3 Preliminary Analysis before Initiating the Evidence-Gathering Procedure** MOFCOM may, based on information obtained through legitimate channels such as reports, media information, opinions of relevant departments, etc., make a preliminary analysis as to whether a concentration of undertakings which does not meet the notification thresholds is suspected to have or may have the effect of eliminating and/or restricting competition. For any report made in writing and providing relevant facts and evidence, MOFCOM shall make a preliminary analysis.
第四条 【启动证据收集程序的考虑因素】 商务部在进行初步分析时，可以考虑以下因素：参与集中的经营者的市场份额、集中涉及的地域范围、同行业竞争者、上下游企业、消费者和社会舆论反响的强烈程度等。	**Article 4 Factors to Be Taken into Account to Initiate the Evidence-Gathering Procedure** MOFCOM may consider the following factors when making a preliminary analysis: market share of the undertakings concerned by the concentration, geographical scope of the concentration, competitors in the industry, upstream and downstream undertakings, consumers, reaction from the general public, etc.
第五条 【启动证据收集程序的条件】 经过初步分析，有充分理由怀疑未达申报标准的经营者集中具有或者可能具有排除、限制竞争效果的，商务部应当启动本办法规定的证据收集程序。	**Article 5 Conditions for the Initiation of the Evidence-Gathering Procedure** If, after the preliminary analysis, there are sufficient reasons to suspect that a concentration of undertakings which does not reach the notification thresholds has or is likely to have the effect of eliminating and/or restricting competition, MOFCOM shall initiate

(Continued)

	the evidence-gathering procedure set out in these Rules.
第六条 【证据收集途径】 商务部可以通过下列途径进行证据收集： （一） 从公开渠道获取相关信息； （二） 询问参与集中的经营者，要求参与集中的经营者提供与集中有关的信息和文件资料； （三） 在必要的情况下，向相关行业协会、行业主管部门和地方政府部门、参与集中的经营者的供应商、客户、竞争者及其他有关单位和个人核实相关数据和情况，请其协助提供有关信息和文件资料； （四） 商务部认为有必要采取的其他合法措施。	**Article 6 Evidence-Gathering Methods** MOFCOM may use the following methods to gather evidence: (1) obtain relevant information from publicly available sources; (2) inquire undertakings of the concentration and request the undertakings concerned to provide relevant information and documentation related to the concentration; (3) when necessary, check relevant data and information with relevant trade associations, governmental departments in charge of the industry, local government, suppliers, customers, and competitors of the undertakings concerned, and other relevant entities and individuals, and request their assistance in providing relevant information and documentation; and/or? (4) other necessary legitimate measures as deemed necessary by MOFCOM to obtain relevant evidence.
第七条 【证据收集程序】 商务部根据本办法第六条进行证据收集，执法人员不得少于二人，并应当表明身份。 执法人员进行询问，应当制作笔录，并由被询问人签字确认。执法人员要求有关单位和个人提供信息和文件资料，应当要求提供信息和文件资料的单位和个人在提供的材料上签字盖章。被询问人或者其他提供证据的单位或个人拒绝签字盖章的，执法人员应当注明情况。	**Article 7 Evidence-Gathering Procedure** MOFCOM shall conduct the gathering of evidence in accordance with Article 6 of these Rules, with at least two law enforcement officials who shall present identification documents for enforcement. During the inquiring, the law enforcement officials shall keep a written record which shall be signed and confirmed by the inquired person. When requiring relevant entities and individuals to provide information, documents, and materials, the enforcement officers shall require

	the relevant entities and individuals to sign such materials provided and affix seals. If the inquired person or other entities or individuals providing evidence refuse to sign and affix seals, the enforcement officers shall clearly indicate such situation in the relevant documents.
第八条 【证据收集的范围】 在证据收集阶段，商务部判断未达申报标准的经营者集中是否涉嫌具有或者可能具有排除、限制竞争效果，可以收集以下方面的证据： （一） 参与集中的经营者在相关市场的市场份额； （二） 相关市场的规模、市场集中度及市场竞争状况； （三） 相关市场的进入难易程度； （四） 消费者和其他经营者对经营者集中的反应； （五） 相关行业协会、行业主管部门和地方政府部门的意见； （六） 参与集中的经营者在集中前实施经查实的垄断行为的记录； （七） 经营者集中的目的； （八） 商务部认为需要收集的其他证据。	**Article 8 Scope of the Evidence Gathering** During the evidence-gathering phase, in assessing whether a concentration of undertakings below the notification thresholds has or may have the effect of eliminating and/or restricting competition, MOFCOM may gather the following evidence regarding: (1) market share of the undertakings concerned in the relevant market; (2) scale, level of market concentration, and competitive conditions in the relevant market; (3) degree of difficulty of entry into the relevant market; (4) reaction of consumers and other undertakings to the concentration; (5) opinions of trade associations, governmental departments in charge of the industry, and departments of local government; (6) verified record of monopoly conduct by the undertakings concerned prior to the concentration; (7) the purpose of the concentration; and/or (8) other evidence which MOFCOM deems necessary to gather.
第九条 【完成证据收集后的处理方式】 有充分证据表明经营者集中涉嫌具有或者可能具有排除、限制竞争效果，需要立案调查的，商务部应当立案调查。调查程序另行规定。 不需要立案调查的，商务部应当终止证据收集。	**Article 9 Handling after the Completion of the Gathering of Evidence** If there is sufficient evidence indicating that a concentration of undertakings is suspected to have or likely to have the effect of eliminating and/or restricting competition, and it is necessary to initiate an investigation, MOFCOM

(*Continued*)

	shall initiate an investigation. The investigation procedure shall be set forth in separate regulations. If it is not necessary to initiate an investigation, MOFCOM shall cease to collect evidence.
第十条 【参与集中的经营者在立案调查前的陈述权】 在作出立案调查的决定前，商务部应当给予参与集中的经营者陈述意见和提出申辩的机会。	**Article 10 Right of the Undertakings Concerned by the Concentration to Make Statements before the Initiation of the Investigation** Prior to the decision to initiate an investigation, MOFCOM shall give the undertakings concerned by the concentration the opportunity to make statements and present its defense.
第十一条 【证据的审查】 商务部应当依法对证据的真实性、合法性进行审核。	**Article 11 Review of Evidence** MOFCOM shall review and verify the authenticity and legality of the evidence in accordance with the law.
第十二条 【保密义务】 商务部应当对证据收集程序的启动、过程和内容保密，但法律法规规定应当披露，或者为根据本办法的规定收集证据而有必要向有关单位或个人披露的除外。 根据前款规定有必要披露获知的商业秘密的，商务部应当在披露前取得商业秘密权利人的书面同意。 因商务部根据本办法收集证据而知悉证据收集程序的启动、过程、内容及有关商业秘密的单位和个人应当对其知悉的情况保密。	**Article 12 Confidentiality Obligation** MOFCOM shall keep the initiation, evolution, and content of the evidence-gathering procedure confidential, except where the relevant laws and regulations provide otherwise or where disclosure to relevant entities or individuals is necessary to gather evidence in accordance with the provisions of these Rules. Where it is necessary, in accordance with the preceding paragraph, to disclose business secrets obtained, MOFCOM shall obtain the written approval from the owner of the business secrets before disclosure. Entities and individuals who, as a result of the collection of evidence by MOFCOM in accordance with these Rules, become aware of the initiation, process, and of the content of the evidence collection procedure and related business secrets shall keep such information confidential.

第十三条 【法律责任】 参与集中的经营者对依据本办法进行的证据收集不予配合的，商务部可以依据可获得的最优证据确定是否立案调查。对提供虚假材料、信息的，商务部可以根据《反垄断法》第五十二条的规定进行处罚。	**Article 13 Legal Liabilities** If the undertakings concerned by the concentration refuse to cooperate in the evidence-gathering conducted in accordance with these Rules, MOFCOM may decide to initiate an investigation based on the best evidence available. MOFCOM may punish the provision of false materials and information in accordance with Article 52 of the AML.
第十四条 【执行部门】 商务部反垄断局负责本办法的具体实施。	**Article 14 Enforcement Authority** The Anti-Monopoly Bureau of MOFCOM is responsible for the specific implementation of these Rules.
第十五条 【解释权】 本办法由商务部负责解释。	**Article 15 Interpretation** These Rules shall be subject to interpretation by MOFCOM.
第十六条 【生效时间】 本办法自 年 月 日起施行。	**Article 16 Effective Date** These Rules shall become effective as of [ ].

Interim Rules on the Investigation and Handling of Suspected Monopolistic Concentrations of Undertakings not Reaching the Notification Thresholds (Draft for Public Comment)

关于对未达申报标准涉嫌垄断的经营者集中调查处理的暂行办法（草案）

(Published by the Ministry of Commerce on February 6, 2009)

（商务部于2009年2月6日发布）

第一条 【立法目的】 为规范对未达申报标准但涉嫌具有或者可能具有排除、限制竞争效果的经营者集中的调查处理，根据《中华人民共和国反垄断法》（以下简称《反垄断法》）和《国务院关于经营者集中申报标准的规定》（以下简称《规定》），制定本办法。	**Article 1 Legislative Purpose** In accordance with the Anti-Monopoly Law of the People's Republic of China (hereinafter "AML") and the Regulation of the State Council on the Notification Thresholds for Concentrations of Undertakings (hereinafter "Regulation"), these Rules are enacted for the purposes of investigating and handling concentrations of undertakings which are suspected to have the effect of eliminating and/or restricting competition, but do not reach the notification thresholds.
第二条 【启动调查的通知】 中华人民共和国商务部(以下简称"商务部")依据《规定》和《关于对未达申报标准涉嫌垄断的经营者集中证据收集的暂行办法》，	**Article 2 Notice of the Initiation of an Investigation** When the Ministry of Commerce of the People's Republic of China (hereinafter "MOFCOM") decides to investigate a concentration of undertakings which does not reach

决定对未达申报标准但涉嫌具有或者可能具有排除、限制竞争效果的经营者集中进行调查的，应当书面通知被调查的经营者，告知启动调查的决定以及被调查的经营者应当提交的文件、资料等。	the notification thresholds but is suspected to have or may have the effect of eliminating and/or restricting competition in accordance with the Regulation and the Interim Rules on the Evidence Gathering of Suspected Monopolistic Concentrations of Undertakings not Reaching the Notification Thresholds, a written notice shall be provided to the investigated undertakings, informing them of the decision to initiate an investigation and the documentation and materials that the investigated undertakings shall provide.
第三条 【调查措施】 商务部依法调查，可以采取包括《反垄断法》第三十九条在内的有关措施，并可以根据需要征求其他政府部门、行业协会、经营者、消费者等单位或者个人的意见。	**Article 3 Investigation Measures** MOFCOM shall conduct investigations lawfully and may take measures including those provided in Article 39 of the AML, as well as soliciting the opinions of other governmental departments, trade associations, undertakings, customers, or individuals.
第四条 【相关各方的配合义务】 被调查的经营者、利害关系人以及其他有关单位和个人应当按照《反垄断法》第四十二条的规定配合调查。	**Article 4 The Obligation to Cooperate for the Relevant Parties** The investigated undertakings, the interested parties, and other relevant entities and individuals shall cooperate with the investigation under Article 42 of the AML.
第五条 【调查期限】 商务部进行调查，调查期限参照《反垄断法》关于经营者集中审查期限的规定执行。	**Article 5 Investigation Period** For the investigation by MOFCOM, the investigation period shall be determined with reference to the provisions on the review period for concentrations of undertakings under the AML.
第六条 【商谈】 经营者集中尚未完成的，被调查的经营者可以申请与商务部进行商谈。 被调查的经营者可以书面承诺在商务部认可的期限内中止集中。被调查的经营者作出书面承诺的，商务部将尽最大努力在上述期限内完成调查。	**Article 6 Consultation** If the concentration has not been completed, the investigated undertakings may apply for consultation with MOFCOM. The investigated undertakings may commit in writing to suspend the concentration within the period approved by MOFCOM. Where

(Continued)

	the investigated undertakings offer written commitments, MOFCOM shall make every effort to complete the investigation within the above-mentioned period.
第七条 【继续实施集中的风险】 经营者集中尚未完成，且被调查的经营者在商务部依据本办法作出调查处理决定前继续实施集中的，应当承担商务部依据《反垄断法》第四十八条作出调查处理决定而给经营者带来的全部风险。	**Article 7 The Risk of Proceeding with a Concentration** If the concentration has not been completed, and the investigated undertakings proceed with the concentration before MOFCOM makes a decision after the investigation in accordance with these Rules, the investigated undertakings shall bear all the risks of any decision made by MOFCOM according to Article 48 of the AML.
第八条 【考虑因素】 商务部依据《反垄断法》第二十七条规定的因素判断未达申报标准的经营者集中是否具有或者可能具有排除、限制竞争效果。	**Article 8 Factors to Be Considered** MOFCOM determines whether the concentration of the undertakings below the notification threshold has or may have the effect of eliminating and/or restricting competition according to the factors set forth in Article 27 of the AML.
第九条 【听证程序】 在调查过程中，商务部可以主动或应被调查的经营者或者利害关系人的申请组织听证。听证程序参照《经营者集中审查暂行办法》的相关规定执行。	**Article 9 Hearing Procedure** During the investigation, MOFCOM may organize the hearing ex officio or upon the request of the investigated undertakings or the interested parties. Regarding the hearing procedure, reference shall be made to the relevant provisions of the Interim Rules for the Review of Concentrations of Undertakings.
第十条 【调查的中止】 被调查的经营者承诺在商务部认可的期限内采取具体措施消除集中具有或者可能具有的排除、限制竞争效果的，商务部可以依据《反垄断法》第四十五条的规定处理。 经营者承诺的具体程序和要求参照《经营者集中审查暂行办法》的相关规定执行。	**Article 10 Suspension of the Investigation** If the investigated undertakings commit to adopt specific measures within the period approved by MOFCOM to eliminate the effect or likely effect of eliminating and/or restricting competition brought by the concentration, MOFCOM may handle the case according to Article 45 of the AML.

	The specific procedure and requirement of commitments by the undertakings shall be in accordance with the relevant provisions of the Interim Rules for the Review of Concentration of Undertakings.
第十一条 【调查后的处理】 经过调查，商务部应当按照下列规定作出处理决定: (一) 经营者集中尚未实施，且具有或者可能具有排除、限制竞争效果的，商务部可以依据《反垄断法》第二十八条、第二十九条的规定作出处理决定。 (二) 经营者集中已经实施，且具有或者可能具有排除、限制竞争效果的，商务部可以依据《反垄断法》第四十八条的规定作出处理决定。 (三) 经营者集中不具有排除、限制竞争效果的，或者被调查的经营者履行根据本办法第十条作出的承诺，消除集中具有或者可能具有的排除、限制竞争效果的，终止调查。	**Article 11 The Handling after the Investigation** After the investigation, MOFCOM shall make a decision in accordance with the following provisions: (1) if the concentration of undertakings has not been implemented, and has or may have the effect of eliminating and/or restricting competition, MOFCOM may make a decision according to Article 28 and Article 29 of the AML. (2) if the concentration of undertakings has been implemented, and has or may have the effect of eliminating and/or restricting competition, MOFCOM may make a decision according to Article 48 of the AML. (3) if the concentration of undertakings does not have the effect of eliminating and/or restricting competition, or the investigated undertakings implement the commitments made in accordance with Article 10 of these Rules so as to eliminate the effect of eliminating and/or restricting competition which the concentration has or may have, the investigation shall be terminated.
第十二条 【被调查经营者的申辩权】 商务部应当给予被调查的经营者陈述意见和提出申辩的机会。	**Article 12 The Right of Defense of the Investigated Undertakings** MOFCOM shall give the investigated undertakings the opportunity to make statements and present their defense.

(Continued)

第十三条 【调查决定的公开】

商务部应当将依据本办法作出的决定书面通知被调查的经营者。

商务部应当将禁止经营者集中的决定或者对经营者集中附加限制性条件的决定，及时向社会公布。

Article 13 Publication of the Investigation Decision

MOFCOM shall notify the investigated undertakings of the decision made in accordance with these Rules.

MOFCOM shall publish in time the decision prohibiting a concentration or imposing restrictive conditions on a concentration of undertakings.

第十四条 【送达】

对于必须送达被调查的经营者的书面文件，送达方式参照《中华人民共和国民事诉讼法》的有关规定执行。

商务部以公告送达方式送达的，应在商务部官方网站上公布须送达的文件。公告送达自发出公告之日起，经过两个星期，即视为送达。需送达到境外的公告送达，自公告之日起，经过六个星期，即视为送达。

对台湾、香港、澳门地区受送达人的公告送达，准用前款境外公告送达的规定。

Article 14 Service

The service of written documents which must be delivered to the investigated undertakings shall be made in accordance with the relevant provisions in the Civil Procedure Law of the People's Republic of China.

If MOFCOM effects service by way of public notice, it shall publish the documents which need to be delivered on the official website of MOFCOM. Service made through public notice shall be deemed as effected two weeks after the date of issuance of the public notice. Service through public notice which needs to be delivered beyond the territory of the People's Republic of China shall be deemed as effected six weeks after the date of issuance of the public notice.

The stipulations in the preceding paragraph on service through public notice to be delivered beyond the territory of the People's Republic of China shall apply to service through public notice to recipients in the regions of Taiwan, Hong Kong, and Macau.

第十五条 【保密义务】

商务部、被调查的经营者以及其他单位和个人应当对在调查过程中知悉的商业秘密保密，但根据法律法规规定应当披露的或者取得商业秘密权利人事先同意的除外。

Article 15 Confidentiality Obligation

MOFCOM, the investigated undertakings, as well as other entities and individuals shall keep confidential the business secrets obtained during the investigation process, except where disclosure is required by laws and regulations or the prior approval from the owner of the business secrets is obtained.

第十六条 【执行部门】 商务部反垄断局负责本办法的具体实施。	**Article 16 Enforcement Authority** The Anti-Monopoly Bureau of MOFCOM is responsible for the specific implementation of these Rules.
第十七条 【解释权】 本办法由商务部负责解释。	**Article 17 Interpretation** These Rules are subject to interpretation by MOFCOM.
第十八条 【生效时间】 本办法自 年 月 日起施行。	**Article 18 Effective Date** These Rules shall become effective as of [ ].

B-18

Provisions on the Imposition of Restrictive Conditions on Concentrations of Undertakings (Draft for Public Comment)

关于经营者集中附加限制性条件的规定 （征求意见稿）

(Published by the Ministry of Commerce on March 27, 2013)

（商务部于2013年3月27日发布）

第一章 总则	Chapter 1 General Provisions
第二章 限制性条件的确定	Chapter 2 Determination of Restrictive Conditions
第三章 限制性条件的实施	Chapter 3 Implementation of Restrictive Conditions
第四章 限制性条件的监督	Chapter 4 Supervision of Restrictive Conditions
第五章 限制性条件的变更和解除	Chapter 5 Modification and Termination of Restrictive Conditions
第六章 法律责任	Chapter 6 Legal Liabilities
第七章 附则	Chapter 7 Supplementary Provisions
第一章 总则	**Chapter 1 General Provisions**
第一条 为规范经营者集中附加限制性条件的确定、实施及监督，减少集中对竞争产生的不利影响，根据《中华人民共和国反垄断法》，制定本规定。	**Article 1** These provisions are formulated in accordance with the Anti-Monopoly Law of the People's Republic of China for the purpose of regulating the determination, implementation, and supervision of restrictive conditions imposed on concentrations of undertakings, in order to mitigate the adverse effect of the concentration on competition.

第二条　对不予禁止的经营者集中，商务部可以附加减少集中对竞争产生不利影响的限制性条件。	**Article 2**　The Ministry of Commerce ("MOFCOM") may impose restrictive conditions on a concentration of undertakings that is not prohibited, in order to mitigate the adverse effects of a concentration on competition.
第三条　本规定所称限制性条件，是指商务部批准集中时，申报方提出并经商务部认可的减少集中对竞争产生的不利影响的解决方案。	**Article 3**　The term "restrictive conditions" in these provisions refers to the solutions proposed by the notifying parties and accepted by MOFCOM to mitigate the adverse effects of a concentration on competition, when MOFCOM approves the concentration.
第四条　本规定所称剥离义务人，是指负有资产或业务剥离义务的参与集中的经营者。 监督受托人，是指受申报方委托，负责对业务剥离或行为性条件进行全程监督的自然人、法人或其他组织。 剥离受托人，是指在受托剥离阶段，受剥离义务人委托，负责找到适当的买方并达成出售协议及其他相关协议的自然人、法人或其他组织。	**Article 4**　The term "divesting party" in these provisions refers to the undertaking concerned by the concentration, which is obligated to divest its assets or business. The term "supervision trustee" refers to the natural person, legal entity, or organization of other kinds entrusted by the notifying parties to be responsible for supervising the whole process of the business divestiture or the behavioral conditions. The term "divestiture trustee" refers to the natural person, legal entity, or organization of other kinds entrusted by the divesting party to be responsible for finding a buyer and entering into a sales agreement and other related agreements during the trustee divestiture period.
第二章　限制性条件的确定	**Chapter 2　Determination of Restrictive Conditions**
第五条　根据经营者集中交易具体情况，限制性条件可以包括如下种类： （一）　剥离参与集中的经营者的有形资产、知识产权或相关权益等结构性条件； （二）　参与集中的经营者开放其网络或平台等基础设施、许可关键技术（包括专利、专有技术或其他知识产权）、终止排他性协议等行为性条件；	**Article 5**　Depending on the specifics of the concentration of undertakings, the restrictive conditions may be categorized as follows: (1)　structural conditions such as the divestiture of tangible assets, intellectual property rights, or other relevant rights and interests of the undertakings concerned by the concentration;

(*Continued*)

（三）　结构性条件和行为性条件相结合的综合性条件。	(2)　behavioral conditions such as granting access to infrastructure including networks or platforms, etc., granting license of key technologies (including patents, know-how, and other intellectual property), and terminating exclusive contracts by the undertakings concerned by the concentration; (3)　comprehensive conditions combining both structural and behavioral conditions.
第六条　剥离是指剥离义务人将剥离业务出售给其他经营者的行为。 剥离业务是指经营者在相关市场开展有效竞争所需要的所有要素，包括剥离义务人的有形资产、无形资产、股权、关键人员以及客户协议或供应协议等权益。 剥离业务可以是参与集中经营者的子公司、分支机构或者业务部门。	**Article 6**　The term "divestiture" refers to the conduct of the divesting party to sell the divested business to other undertakings. The term "divested business" refers to all the elements necessary for an undertakings to compete effectively in the relevant market, including the divesting party's tangible assets, intangible assets, equity interests, key personnel, customer agreements or supply agreements, and other rights and interests. The divested business may be a subsidiary, branch, or business division of the undertakings concerned by the concentration.
第七条　为便于申报方提出限制性条件建议（以下简称附条件建议），商务部应适时提出集中具有或可能具有的排除、限制竞争效果及并说明理由，并要求申报方提出附条件建议。	**Article 7**　In order to facilitate the notifying parties in the proposal of restrictive conditions (a "condition proposal"), MOFCOM shall raise in due time the existence of the effect of eliminating and/or restricting competition the concentration of undertakings has or may have and specify the reasons, and request the notifying parties to submit a condition proposal.
第八条　针对商务部提出的集中具有或可能具有的排除、限制竞争效果，申报方可以在商务部规定的期限内提出附条件建议。	**Article 8**　In response to the existence of the effect of eliminating and/or restricting competition the concentration of

申报方在规定期限内未提出附条件建议的，或者所提出的附条件建议不足以减少集中对竞争产生的不利影响的，商务部应当禁止该项集中。 特定情况下，商务部提出集中具有或可能具有排除、限制竞争效果之前，申报方也可以提出附条件建议。	undertakings has or may have as raised by MOFCOM, the notifying parties may submit a condition proposal within the time limit prescribed by MOFCOM. Where the notifying parties fail to submit a condition proposal within the prescribed time limit or the condition proposal is insufficient to mitigate the adverse effects of the concentration on competition, MOFCOM shall decide to prohibit the concentration. Under special circumstances, the notifying parties may submit a condition proposal before MOFCOM raises that the concentration of undertakings has or may have the effect of eliminating and/or restricting competition.
第九条 附条件建议提出后，商务部应对该建议的有效性、可行性和及时性进行评估，并将评估结果通知申报方。	**Article 9**　After a condition proposal is submitted, MOFCOM shall assess whether the proposal is efficient, feasible, and timely, and shall inform the notifying parties of the result of the assessment.
第十条 评估附条件建议时，商务部可以采用以下方式: (一)　征求相关政府部门、行业协会、经营者、消费者的意见; (二)　发放调查问卷; (三)　召开听证会; (四)　其他方式。	**Article 10**　MOFCOM may assess the condition proposal through the following means: (1)　seeking opinions from the relevant government authorities, trade associations, undertakings, and consumers; (2)　issuing questionnaires; (3)　holding hearings; and (4)　other means.
第十一条 申报方在规定期限内提出附条件建议的，商务部应与申报方进行协商。 申报方提出附条件建议最终修改方案的时间不得晚于审查期限截止日之前第二十日。	**Article 11**　If the notifying parties submit the condition proposal within the prescribed time limit, MOFCOM shall negotiate with the notifying parties. The notifying parties shall submit the final revised condition proposal no later than the twentieth day before the review deadline.

(Continued)

第十二条 商务部应当将对经营者集中附加限制性条件的审查决定及时向社会公布。 审查决定是限制性条件实施的依据，具有法律约束力。 商务部应在审查决定中明确，是否要求申报方委托受托人及适用的剥离程序。	**Article 12** MOFCOM publish its review decision on imposing restrictive conditions to a concentration of undertakings in a timely manner. The review decision serves as the basis for implementing the restrictive conditions and is legally binding. MOFCOM shall specify in its review decision whether the notifying parties are requested to entrust trustees and the applicable divestiture procedure.
第十三条 商务部做出审查决定时应规定行为性条件的实施期限。审查决定未规定的，实施期限为十年。	**Article 13** When issuing its review decision, MOFCOM shall specify the implementation time period of the behavioral conditions. If it is not specified in the review decision, the implementation time period shall be ten years.
第三章 限制性条件的实施	**Chapter 3 Implementation of Restrictive Conditions**
第十四条 剥离可采取自行剥离或者受托剥离的方式。 剥离义务人应当在审查决定规定的期限内，找到适当的买方、签订出售协议并经商务部审核批准（以下简称为自行剥离）。 如果剥离义务人未能如期完成自行剥离，则出剥离受托人在审查决定规定的期限内找到买方并签订出售协议并经商务部审核批准（以下简称为受托剥离）。	**Article 14** Divestiture may be conducted by way of voluntary divestiture or trustee divestiture. The divesting party shall, within the time limit prescribed in the review decision, find a proper buyer, enter into a sales agreement, and obtain MOFCOM's approval (a "voluntary divestiture"). If the divesting party fails to complete the voluntary divestiture within such time limit, the divestiture trustee shall find a proper buyer, enter into a sales agreement, and obtain MOFCOM's approval within the time limit prescribed in the review decision (a "trustee divestiture").
第十五条 剥离义务人应在审查决定规定的期限内找到买方。剥离业务的买方应当符合下列要求：	**Article 15** The divesting party shall find a buyer within the time limit prescribed in the review decision. The buyer of the divested business shall meet the following requirements:

（一） 独立于参与集中的经营者； （二） 拥有必要的资源、能力并有意愿使用剥离业务参与市场竞争； （三） 取得其他监管机构的批准； （四） 不得向参与集中的经营者融资购买剥离业务； （五） 商务部根据具体案件情况提出的其他要求。	(1) it shall be independent from the undertakings concerned by the concentration; (2) it shall have necessary resources, capability, and incentives to use the divested business to participate in market competition; (3) it has obtained approvals from other regulatory authorities; (4) it shall not obtain finance from the undertakings concerned by the concentration to acquire the divested business; and (5) other requirements made by MOFCOM depending on the specifics of the case.
第十六条 剥离义务人应在审查决定规定的期限内向商务部提交买方人选及其与买方签署的出售协议。 商务部对买方人选及其与买方签署的出售协议进行审查。 商务部审查买方人选及其与买方签署的出售协议的时间，不计入剥离期限。	**Article 16** The divesting party shall submit to MOFCOM, within the time limit prescribed in the review decision, the candidate buyer and the sales agreement entered into with the buyer. MOFCOM shall review the candidate buyer and the sales agreement executed with the buyer. The time used by MOFCOM in reviewing the candidate buyer and the sales agreement executed with the buyer shall not be counted into the time limit for divestiture.
第十七条 剥离义务人应当在审查决定规定期限内找到买方并签订出售协议。审查决定未规定期限的，剥离义务人应在审查决定之日起六个月内找到买方并签订出售协议。 根据案件具体情况，经剥离义务人说明理由，商务部可以酌情延长期限，但延期最长不得超过三个月。	**Article 17** The divesting party shall find a proper buyer and enter into a sales agreement within the time limit prescribed in the review decision. If the review decision is silent about such time limit, the divesting party shall find a proper buyer and enter into a sales agreement with the buyer within six months of the date of the review decision. After the divesting party submits explanations and depending on the specifics of the case, MOFCOM may extend the time limit at its discretion, but such extension shall be no more than three months.

(Continued)

第十八条 在下列情况下，商务部可以要求剥离义务人在集中实施之前找到买方并签订出售协议： （一） 剥离之前维持剥离业务的竞争性和可销售性存在较大风险； （二） 买方的身份对剥离业务能否恢复市场竞争具有决定性影响； （三） 剥离义务人无法在规定时间内找到剥离业务的合格买方； （四） 第三方对剥离业务主张权利； （五） 商务部认定的其他情形。	**Article 18** Under the following circumstances, MOFCOM may request the divesting party to find a buyer and enter into a sales agreement before the implementation of the concentration: (1) there is a significant risk in maintaining the competitiveness and marketability of the divested business before the divestiture; (2) the identity of the buyer has a decisive influence over the ability of the divested business to restore market competition; (3) the divesting party is unable to find a qualified buyer for the divested business within the prescribed time limit; (4) there is a third party claiming rights over the divested business; and/or (5) other circumstances determined by MOFCOM.
第十九条 集中实施之前难以确定买方的，商务部可以在审查决定中要求剥离义务人在首选方案基础上提出备选方案。 备选方案应比首选方案的条件更为严格，可以包括有形资产、知识产权或相关权益。	**Article 19** If it is difficult to determine the buyer before the implementation of the concentration, in the review decision, MOFCOM may request the divesting party to submit an alternative plan to the preferred plan. The conditions in the alternative proposal shall be more stringent than in the preferred plan. They may include tangible assets, intellectual property rights, or relevant rights and interests.
第二十条 剥离义务人应当在出售协议签订之日起三个月内将剥离业务转移给买方，并完成所有权转移等相关法律程序。 根据案件具体情况，经剥离义务人申请并说明理由，商务部可酌情延长业务转移的期限，但所延期限最长不得超过一个月。	**Article 20** The divesting party shall, within three months of the execution date of the sales agreement, transfer the divested business to the buyer and finish the legal procedures for transfer of ownership. After the divesting party submits an application and explanation and depending on the specifics of the case, MOFCOM may extend at its discretion the time limit for business transfer, but

	such extension shall be no more than one month.
第二十一条 经商务部批准的买方购买剥离业务达到《国务院关于经营者集中申报标准的规定》经营者集中申报标准的，应向商务部申报。 商务部做出审查决定之前，申报方不得将剥离业务出售给买方。	**Article 21** If the purchase of the divested business by the buyer(s) as approved by MOFCOM reaches the notification thresholds for concentrations of undertakings under the Regulation of the State Council on the Notification Thresholds for Concentrations of Undertakings, the buyer shall notify the transaction to MOFCOM. The notifying parties shall not sell the divested business to the buyer before MOFCOM issues the review decision.
第二十二条 其他限制性条件的实施，可以参照适用有关结构性条件的规定。	**Article 22** The implementation of other restrictive conditions may refer to the provisions concerning structural conditions.
第四章 限制性条件的监督	**Chapter 4 Supervision of Restrictive Conditions**
第二十三条 剥离义务人应在商务部做出审查决定之日起十五日内向商务部提交监督受托人人选，在进入受托剥离阶段三十日前向商务部提交剥离受托人人选。申报方认为不需要监督受托人的，应当说明理由。 剥离义务人应与监督受托人或者剥离受托人签订书面协议，明确各自的权利和义务。 剥离义务人应负责支付监督受托人或者剥离受托人的报酬。 剥离义务人应对监督受托人或者剥离受托人和剥离业务买方提供必要的支持和便利。	**Article 23** The divesting party shall, within 15 days after MOFCOM issues the review decision, submit the candidate supervision trustee to MOFCOM and, within 30 days before entering the trustee divestiture period, submit the candidate divestiture trustee to MOFCOM. If the notifying parties believe it unnecessary to have a supervision trustee, they shall specify the reasons. The divesting party shall sign a written agreement with the supervision trustee or the divestiture trustee, specifying the rights and obligations of each party. The divesting party shall be responsible for paying a remuneration to the supervision trustee or the divestiture trustee. The divesting party shall provide necessary support and convenience to the supervision trustee or the divestiture trustee and the buyer of the divested business.

(*Continued*)

第二十四条 在剥离完成之前，为确保剥离业务的存活性、竞争性和可销售性，参与集中的经营者应当履行下列义务： （一） 保持剥离业务与其保留的业务之间相互独立，并采取一切必要措施以最符合剥离业务发展的方式进行维护； （二） 不得实施任何可能对剥离业务有不利影响的行为，包括聘用被剥离业务的关键员工，获得剥离业务的商业秘密或其他保密信息等； （三） 指定专门的管理人，负责管理剥离业务。管理人在监督受托人的监督下履行职责，其任命和更换应得到监督受托人的同意； （四） 确保潜在买方能够以公平合理的方式获得有关剥离业务的充分信息，评估剥离业务的商业价值和发展潜力； （五） 根据买方的要求向其提供必要的支持和帮助，确保剥离业务的顺利交接和稳定经营； （六） 向买方及时移交剥离业务并履行相关法律程序； 剥离义务人应当及时履行向商务部报告的义务，报告其遵守审查决定、实施剥离和执行相关协议等情况，监督受托人负责对剥离义务人的报告事项进行监督。	**Article 24** Before the completion of the divestiture, the undertakings concerned by the concentration shall perform the following obligations to ensure the survival, competitiveness, and marketability of the divested business: (1) keep the divested business independent of the remaining businesses and take all necessary measures to manage the divested business in the best way of developing the divested business; (2) refrain from any conduct that may have an adverse impact on the divested business, including employing key employees of the divested business and obtaining the business secrets or other confidential information of the divested business; (3) designate a person to be responsible for managing the divested business. Such person shall perform its duties and responsibilities under the supervision of the supervision trustee, and the appointment and replacement of such person requires consent of the supervision trustee; (4) ensure that the potential buyer is able to obtain sufficient information of the divested business through fair and reasonable means so as to evaluate the business value and development potential of the divested business; (5) provide necessary support and assistance to the buyer upon its request so as to ensure the smooth transition and stable operation of the divested business; (6) transfer the divested business to the buyer in a timely manner and undergo the relevant legal procedures.

	The diverting party shall perform its obligations of reporting to MOFCOM in a timely manner, including reporting its compliance with the review decision, implementation of the divestiture, and performance of the relevant agreements. The supervision trustee shall be responsible for supervising the divesting party's reporting matters.
第二十五条 受托人包括监督受托人和剥离受托人。 监督受托人负责监督自行剥离；剥离受托人负责监督受托剥离。 受托人应当符合下列要求： （一） 独立于剥离义务人和剥离业务的买方； （二） 具有履行受托人职责的专业团队，团队成员应当具有对限制性条件进行监督所需的专业知识、技能及相关经验； （三） 受托人提出可行的工作方案； （四） 商务部考虑的其他因素。	**Article 25** The trustees include the supervision trustee and the divestiture trustee. The supervision trustee shall be responsible for supervising voluntary divestiture; the divestiture trustee shall be responsible for supervising trustee divestiture. The trustees shall satisfy the following requirements: (1) be independent from the divesting party and the buyer of the divested business; (2) have a professional team to perform the duties and responsibilities of the trustees. The team members shall have the professional knowledge, skills, and relevant experience necessary for supervising the restrictive conditions; (3) have put forward a feasible working plan; (4) other factors taken into account by MOFCOM.
第二十六条 监督受托人应当在商务部的监督下，本着勤勉、尽职的原则履行下列职责： （一） 监督剥离义务人履行本规定、审查决定及相关协议规定的义务；	**Article 26** A supervision trustee shall, under the supervision of MOFCOM, perform the following duties and responsibilities conscientiously and diligently: (1) supervise the divesting party's performance of the obligations prescribed in these provisions, in the review decision and in the relevant agreements; (2) evaluate the candidate buyer recommended by the divesting

(Continued)

（二） 对剥离义务人推荐的买方人选、拟签订的出售协议进行评估，并向商务部提交评估报告； （三） 监督出售协议的执行，并定期向商务部提交监督报告； （四） 协调剥离义务人与潜在买方就剥离事项产生的争议； （五） 应商务部的要求提交其他与剥离有关的报告； （六） 不得披露其在履行职责过程中向商务部提交的各种报告及相关信息。	party and the sales agreement to be signed, and submit an evaluation report to MOFCOM; (3) supervise the implementation of the sales agreement, and submit supervision reports to MOFCOM on a regular basis; (4) mediate disputes arising between the divesting party and the potential buyer; (5) submit other reports relating to the business divestiture when requested by MOFCOM; (6) refrain from disclosing the various reports and relevant information it has submitted to MOFCOM during its performance of the duties and responsibilities.
第二十七条 在受托剥离阶段，剥离受托人负责为剥离业务找到买方并达成出售协议。 剥离受托人有权以无底价方式出售剥离业务。	**Article 27** During the trustee divestiture period, the divestiture trustee shall find a proper buyer for the divested business and enter into a sales agreement. The divestiture trustee shall have the right to sell the divested business without a reserve price.
第二十八条 如果参与集中的经营者违反审查决定，未能及时、有效地履行剥离义务，相关的政府部门、行业协会、经营者、消费者等单位或个人可以向商务部举报。商务部应当为举报人保密。	**Article 28** Where the undertakings concerned by the concentration violate the review decision, and fail to perform the divestiture obligations in a timely and effective manner, any organization or individual such as the relevant government authorities, trade associations, undertakings, and consumers may report it to MOFCOM. MOFCOM shall keep the informers confidential.
第二十九条 商务部可以要求申报方委托受托人对其他限制性条件履行情况进行监督。其他限制性条件义务人的职责、义务、受托人的选择及其职责，可以参照适用有关结构性条件的规定。	**Article 29** MOFCOM may request the notifying party to entrust a trustee to supervise the implementation of other restrictive conditions. The duties and responsibilities of the obligors of other restrictive conditions, the selection of the trustees and the duties and obligations of the trustees may refer to the provisions on the structural conditions.

第五章　限制性条件的变更和解除	**Chapter 5　Modification and Termination of Restrictive Conditions**
第三十条　审查决定生效后，实施限制性条件不可能或无必要的，或因市场竞争环境变化致使限制性条件无法减少不利竞争影响的，商务部可以对限制性条件进行重新审查，变更或者解除限制性条件。	**Article 30**　After the review decision comes into effect, in the event that it is impossible or unnecessary to implement the restrictive conditions or the anti-competitive effect could not be mitigated due to changes to the market competition environment, MOFCOM may re-examine the restrictive conditions and modify or terminate the restrictive conditions.
第三十一条　集中后经营者申请变更或解除限制性条件的，应向商务部提出书面申请，并说明理由。	**Article 31**　After the concentration, if an undertaking intends to apply to modify or terminate the restrictive conditions, it shall submit a written application to MOFCOM and specify the reasons.
第三十二条　商务部评估变更或解除限制性条件请求时，应考虑如下因素： （一）　审查决定所依据的基础交易是否发生重大变化； （二）　相关市场竞争状况是否发生了实质性变化； （三）　变更或解除限制性条件是否符合社会公共利益。 （四）　其他因素。	**Article 32**　When assessing the application to modify or terminate the restrictive conditions, MOFCOM shall consider the following factors: (1)　whether major changes have occurred to the underlying transaction based on which the review decision was made; (2)　whether any material changes have occurred to the competitive conditions in the relevant market; (3)　whether it is in line with the public interests to modify or terminate the restrictive conditions; and/or (4)　other factors.
第三十三条　商务部决定变更或解除限制性条件的，应当及时向社会公布。	**Article 33**　MOFCOM shall publish its decision to modify or terminate the restrictive conditions in a timely manner.
第六章　法律责任	**Chapter 6　Legal Liabilities**
第三十四条　参与集中的经营者违反审查决定，商务部应责令限期改正。情节严重的，商务部应责令停止实施集中、限期处分股份或者资产、限期转让营业以及采取其他必要措施恢复到集中前的状态，	**Article 34**　Where undertakings concerned by the concentration violate the review decision, MOFCOM shall order them to take rectifying measures within a prescribed time limit. In serious circumstances, MOFCOM

(*Continued*)

可以处五十万元以下的罚款。商务部应当撤销审查决定，要求参与集中的经营者重新申报。 商务部做出审查决定后，发现剥离义务人在审查决定之前从事影响剥离业务竞争性的行为的，商务部应责令剥离义务人提出新的附条件建议。情节严重的，商务部应当撤销审查决定，要求参与集中的经营者重新申报。	shall order them to stop implementing the concentration, dispose of their stock or assets within a specified time limit, divest their business within a specified time limit, and take other necessary measures to restore the market situation before the concentration. MOFCOM may also impose a fine of no more than RMB 500,000. MOFCOM shall withdraw the review decision and request the undertakings concerned by the concentration to re-notify the concentration. Where MOFCOM, after issuing the review decision, finds that the divesting party has engaged in any conduct that has affected the competitiveness of the divested business before the review decision was made, it shall order the divesting party to submit a new condition proposal. In serious circumstances, MOFCOM shall withdraw the review decision and request the undertakings concerned by the concentration to re-notify the concentration.
第三十五条 受托人提供虚假信息，未能勤勉、尽职地履行本规定第二十七条的职责，商务部可以责令改正、责令返还或者没收受托人取得的报酬、取消本次受托人资格。情节严重的，商务部可以取消其未来担任受托人的资格。	**Article 35** Where a trustee provides false information and fails to conscientiously and diligently perform the duties and responsibilities prescribed in Article 27 of these provisions, MOFCOM may order the trustee to take rectifying measures and to return or confiscate the remuneration earned by the trustee, and disqualify the trustee. In serious circumstances, MOFCOM may disqualify the trustee from being selected as a trustee in the future.
第三十六条 剥离业务的买方违反本规定的，商务部责令改正；情节严重的，取消买方资格。	**Article 36** Where the buyer of the divested business violates these provisions, MOFCOM shall order it to take rectifying measures. In serious circumstances, MOFCOM may disqualify the buyer.

第三十七条 商务部工作人员滥用职权、玩忽职守、徇私舞弊或者泄露执法过程中知悉的商业秘密，构成犯罪的，依法追究刑事责任；尚不构成犯罪的，依法给予处分。	**Article 37**　Where the employees of MOFCOM abuse their power, neglect their duties, receive bribes and cheat, or disclose business secrets obtained during their enforcement activities, which constitutes a crime, criminal liability shall be pursued according to the law; if their conduct does not constitute a crime, administrative penalty shall be given.
第七章 附则	**Chapter 7　Supplementary Provisions**
第三十八条 本规定自2013年 月 日起施行，《关于实施经营者集中资产或业务剥离的暂行规定》（商务部公告2010年第41号）同时废止。	**Article 38**　These provisions shall come into effect as of [ ] 2013. The Interim Provisions on Asset or Business Divestiture during the Implementation of Concentrations of Undertakings (Ministry of Commerce Announcement [2010] No. 41) shall be abolished at the same time.

Procedural Rules of the Administration for Industry and Commerce Regarding the Investigation and Handling of Cases Relating to Monopoly Agreements and Abuses of Dominant Market Positions

工商行政管理机关查处垄断协议、滥用市场支配地位案件程序规定

(Promulgated by the State Administration for Industry and Commerce on May 26, 2009, effective as of July 1, 2009)

（国家工商行政管理总局于2009年5月26日发布，自2009年7月1日起施行）

第一条 为规范和保障工商行政管理机关依法查处垄断行为，依据《中华人民共和国反垄断法》制定本规定。	**Article 1** These Rules are promulgated in accordance with the Anti-Monopoly Law of the People's Republic of China for the purpose of regulating and safeguarding enforcement activities by the Administration for Industry and Commerce ("AIC") in investigations and handling of monopoly conduct in accordance with the law.
第二条 国家工商行政管理总局统一负责垄断协议、滥用市场支配地位方面的反垄断执法工作。	**Article 2** The State Administration for Industry and Commerce ("SAIC") is, in general, responsible for anti-monopoly law enforcement activities with regard to monopoly agreements and abuses of dominant market position.

国家工商行政管理总局根据工作需要，可以授权有关省、自治区、直辖市工商行政管理局(以下简称省级工商行政管理局)负责垄断协议、滥用市场支配地位方面的反垄断执法工作。	Where necessary, the SAIC may delegate to the relevant AIC of a province, an autonomous region, or a provincial level municipality ("Provincial AIC") the authority of anti-monopoly law enforcement with regard to monopoly agreements and abuses of dominant market position.
第三条 下列垄断行为应当由国家工商行政管理总局负责查处： （一）　全国范围内有重大影响的； （二）　国家工商行政管理总局认为应当由其管辖的。 下列垄断行为可以授权省级工商行政管理局负责查处： （一）　该行政区域内发生的； （二）　跨省、自治区、直辖市发生，但主要行为地在该行政区域内的； （三）　国家工商行政管理总局认为可以授权省级工商行政管理局管辖的。 授权以个案的形式进行。被授权的省级工商行政管理局不得再次向下级工商行政管理局授权。	**Article 3** The SAIC shall be responsible for investigating and handling the following monopoly conduct: (1)　conduct that has significant impact throughout the country; (2)　conduct that the SAIC finds within its jurisdiction. Provincial AICs may be authorized to investigate and handle the following monopoly conduct: (1)　conduct that occurs within that administrative region; (2)　conduct that involves several provinces, autonomous regions, or provincial level municipalities, but that principally occurs in that administrative region; (3)　other conduct that the SAIC may deem advisable to be authorized for jurisdiction by a Provincial AIC. Delegation of authority will be decided on a case-by-case basis. The delegated Provincial AICs must not re-delegate that authority to a lower AIC.
第四条 工商行政管理机关依据职权，或者通过举报、其他机关移送、上级机关交办等途径，发现垄断行为并依法查处。	**Article 4** The AIC may, ex officio or by way of reporting, transfer from another AIC or delegation from a higher AIC or other means, discover, investigate, and handle monopoly conduct in accordance with the law.
第五条 任何单位和个人有权向工商行政管理机关举报涉嫌垄断行为，工商行政管理机关应当为举报人保密。	**Article 5** Any entity or person is entitled to report suspected monopoly conduct to the AIC, and the AIC shall keep the informer confidential.

(Continued)

举报采取书面形式的，应当包括以下内容： （一）　举报人的基本情况。举报人为个人的，应当提供姓名、住址、联系方式等。举报人为经营者的，应当提供名称、地址、联系方式、主要从事的行业、生产的产品或者提供的服务等； （二）　被举报人的基本情况。包括经营者名称、地址、主要从事的行业、生产的产品或者提供的服务等； （三）　涉嫌垄断的相关事实。包括被举报人违反法律、法规和规章实施垄断行为的事实以及有关行为的时间、地点等； （四）　相关证据。包括书证、物证、证人证言、视听资料、计算机数据、鉴定结论等，有关证据应当有证据提供人的签名并注明获得证据的来源； （五）　是否就同一事实已向其他行政机关举报或者向人民法院提起诉讼。	The report of suspected monopoly conduct shall include the following materials if it is made in writing: (1)　basic information of the informer, including name, address, and contact information in the case of a natural person, and including name, address, contact information, and industries mainly engaged in and major products or services provided in the case of an undertaking; (2)　basic information of the suspected infringer, including name, address, and industries mainly engaged in and major products or services provided; (3)　relevant facts of the suspected monopoly conduct, including facts relating to monopoly conduct in violation of relevant laws, regulations, or rules, and the time and place of the suspected monopoly conduct; (4)　relevant evidence, including documentary evidence, physical exhibits, testimonies, visual and audio materials, electronic data, certification of examination, etc. Evidence shall bear the signature of the evidence provider the source of the evidence shall be identified; (5)　information on whether the same fact has been reported to any other administrative authority or filed with the People's Court.
第六条 国家工商行政管理总局和省级工商行政管理局负责举报材料的受理。省级以下工商行政管理机关收到举报材料的，应当在5个工作日内将有关举报材料报送省级工商行政管理局。 受理机关收到举报材料后，应当进行登记并对举报内容进行核查。	**Article 6** The SAIC and Provincial AICs shall be responsible for the acceptance of reporting materials. AICs below provincial level that have received reporting materials shall, within five working days, transfer the relevant reporting materials to the Provincial AIC.

举报材料不齐全的，应当通知举报人及时补齐。 对于匿名的书面举报，如果有具体的违法事实并提供相关证据的，受理机关应当进行登记并对举报内容进行核查。	The authority for acceptance of the reporting materials shall record the report and examine and verify the content of the reporting materials. If the reporting materials are not complete, the informer shall be notified to supplement the materials in time. In case of anonymous written reporting, if specific facts of suspected violations are substantiated by evidence, the authority for acceptance of the reporting materials shall make record of the report and examine and verify the content of the reporting materials.
第七条 省级工商行政管理局应当对主要发生在本行政区域内涉嫌垄断行为的举报进行核查，并将核查的情况以及是否立案的意见报国家工商行政管理总局。 省级工商行政管理局对举报材料齐全、涉及两个以上省级行政区域的涉嫌垄断行为的举报，应当及时将举报材料报送国家工商行政管理总局。	**Article 7** Provincial AICs shall examine and verify a report of suspected monopoly conduct that principally occurs within their administrative region and submit to the SAIC the findings of their examination and verification and opinions on whether to the initiate the case. For reporting materials which are complete and refer to suspected monopoly conduct that involves two or more provincial administrative regions, a Provincial AIC shall transfer them to the SAIC in a timely manner.
第八条 国家工商行政管理总局根据对举报内容核查的情况，决定立案查处工作。国家工商行政管理总局可以自己立案查处，也可以根据本规定第三条的规定授权有关省级工商行政管理局立案查处。	**Article 8** The SAIC shall decide whether to initiate the case according to the findings of examination and verification of the reporting materials. The SAIC may initiate an investigation and decide a case on its own or delegate the authority to a Provincial AIC to investigate and decide a case pursuant to Article 3 of these Rules.
第九条 国家工商行政管理总局对自己立案查处的案件，可以自行开展调查，也可以委托有关省级、计划单列市、副省级市工商行政管理局开展案件调查工作。	**Article 9** For cases filed by the SAIC for investigation and handling, the SAIC may investigate by itself or authorize relevant AICs of the corresponding province, autonomous region, or

(*Continued*)

省级工商行政管理局对经授权由其立案查处的案件，应当依据本规定组织案件调查等相关工作。	municipality, a city specifically designated in the state plan, or sub-provincial city to carry out the investigation. As to the case authorized by the SAIC, the Provincial AIC shall organize investigation and relevant work for such case in accordance with these Rules.
第十条 工商行政管理机关调查涉嫌垄断行为，经向有权查处垄断案件机关的主要负责人书面报告并经批准，可以采取下列调查措施： （一）进入被调查的经营者的营业场所或者其他有关场所进行检查； （二）询问被调查的经营者、利害关系人或者其他有关单位或者个人，要求其说明有关情况； （三）查阅、复制被调查的经营者、利害关系人或者其他有关单位或者个人的有关单证、协议、会计账簿、业务函电、电子数据等文件、资料； （四）查封、扣押相关证据； （五）查询经营者的银行账户。	**Article 10** The AIC may, subject to a written report to and approval by the principal of the AIC who has the authority to handle the case, take the following measures to investigate suspected monopoly conduct: (1) enter the place of business of the investigated undertakings or other relevant places to conduct investigation; (2) inquire about the investigated undertakings, interested parties, or any other relevant entities or natural person for relevant information; (3) inspect and copy relevant documents and materials such as certificates, agreements, accounting books, business correspondence, and electronic data of the aforementioned persons; (4) seal up and detain relevant evidence; (5) inspect the bank account of the undertakings.
第十一条 工商行政管理机关执法人员调查案件，不得少于两人，并应当出示执法证件。	**Article 11** When conducting an investigation, at least two law enforcement officials of an AIC must be present, and they shall present valid documents showing their authority to carry out the investigation.
第十二条 工商行政管理机关调查涉嫌垄断行为时，可以要求被调查的经营者、利害关系人或者其他有关单位或者个人（以下简称被调查人）在规定时限内提供以下书面材料：	**Article 12** When conducting an investigation into suspected monopoly conduct, the AIC may ask the investigated undertakings, interested parties, or any other relevant entities or natural persons

（一） 被调查人的基本情况，包括组织形式、名称、联系人及联系方式、营业执照或者社会团体法人登记证书、法人组织代码副本复印件。经营者为个人的，提供身份证复印件及联系方式； （二） 被调查人为经营者的，还应提供近三年的生产经营状况、年销售额情况、缴税情况、与交易相对人业务往来及合作协议、境外投资情况等，上市公司还要提供股票收益情况； （三） 被调查人为行业协会的，还应提供行业组织章程、相关产业政策依据、本行业生产经营规划以及执行情况、与涉嫌垄断行为有关的会议、活动情况及文件等； （四） 就工商行政管理机关提出的相关问题所作的说明； （五） 工商行政管理机关认为需要提供的其他书面材料。 工商行政管理机关及其工作人员对执法过程中知悉的商业秘密负有保密义务。	(hereinafter referred to as the "Investigated Person") to submit the following materials in writing within the prescribed time: (1) basic information of the Investigated Person, including its legal form, name, contacts, business license or registration certificate for social organization, and a copy of the organization code of the legal person. If the Person under Investigation is an individual, a photocopy of his/her ID card and contacts shall be provided; (2) where the Investigated Person is an undertaking, additional information such as its business operation in the most recent three years, annual turnover, taxes paid, business correspondence, and agreements with its trading counterparties and overseas investment shall be provided. Where the Person under Investigation is a listed company, the information of earnings of the shares shall also be provided; (3) where the Investigated Person is a trade association, additional information such as the articles of association, the basis of relevant industry policies, the production and operation plan for the industry and its implementation status, and meetings, activities, or documents relating to the suspected monopoly conduct shall be provided; (4) explanation in response to questions raised by the AIC; and (5) any other written materials that the AIC may deem necessary. The AIC and its employees shall keep confidential business secrets which become known to them during law enforcement.

(Continued)

第十三条 被调查的经营者、利害关系人有权陈述意见。工商行政管理机关应当对被调查的经营者、利害关系人提出的事实、理由和证据进行核实。	**Article 13** The investigated undertakings and the interested parties are entitled to state their opinions. The AIC shall make verification of the facts, reasons, and evidence provided by the investigated undertakings and the interested parties.
第十四条 对工商行政管理机关依法实施的调查，拒绝提供、不完全提供或者超过规定时限提供有关材料、信息，或者提供虚假材料、信息，或者隐匿、销毁、转移证据，或者有拒绝、阻碍调查行为的，依照《反垄断法》第五十二条的规定处理。	**Article 14** During an investigation carried out by the AIC in accordance with the law, those who refuse to provide, provide incomplete relevant materials or information, or fail to provide within the prescribed time limit, or provide false materials or information, or conceal, destroy, or transfer evidence, or refuse or obstruct the investigation, shall be punished in accordance with Article 52 of the Anti-Monopoly Law.
第十五条 涉嫌垄断行为的经营者在被调查期间，可以提出中止调查的申请，承诺在工商行政管理机关认可的期限内采取具体措施消除行为影响。	**Article 15** During the investigation of the suspected monopoly conduct, the investigated undertakings may apply for a suspension of the investigation and commit to take specific measures within a specified time approved by the AIC to eliminate the effects of the suspected violations.
第十六条 中止调查申请应当以书面形式提出，并由法定代表人、其他组织负责人或者个人签字并盖章。申请书应当载明以下事项： （一）　涉嫌违法的事实及可能造成的影响； （二）　消除行为影响拟采取的具体措施； （三）　实现承诺的日程安排和保证声明。	**Article 16** An application for suspension of an investigation shall be in writing, shall be signed by the legal representative, other principals of the entity, or private person, and shall be sealed. The application shall include the following items: (1)　a statement of the facts relating to the suspected violation and its potential effects; (2)　the measures to be taken to eliminate the effects; and (3)　a time schedule for fulfilling the commitments and a representation of guarantee.

第十七条 工商行政管理机关根据被调查经营者的申请，在考虑行为的性质、持续时间、后果及社会影响等具体情况后，可以决定中止调查，并作出中止调查决定书。中止调查决定书应当载明被调查经营者涉嫌违法的事实、承诺的具体内容、消除影响的具体措施、时限以及不履行或者部分履行承诺的法律后果等内容。	**Article 17** The AIC may, upon application, decide to suspend the investigation taking into consideration the nature of the conduct, duration, effect, and social impact, etc., and make a written decision to suspend the investigation. The written decision shall indicate the facts of the suspected violation, the content of the commitments, the specific measures to be taken to eliminate the effects, the time limit, and the legal consequences for failing to fulfill or partly fulfilling the commitments, etc.
第十八条 决定中止调查的，经营者应当在规定的时限内向工商行政管理机关提交履行承诺进展情况的书面报告。	**Article 18** If a suspension of the investigation is decided, the undertaking concerned shall submit to the AIC, within a prescribed time limit, a written report regarding the progress in implementing the commitments.
第十九条 工商行政管理机关对经营者履行承诺的情况进行监督。确定经营者已经履行承诺的，可以决定终止调查，并作出终止调查决定书。终止调查决定书应当载明被调查经营者涉嫌违法的事实、承诺的具体内容、消除影响的具体措施、履行承诺的具体步骤和时间等内容。 有下列情形之一的，应当恢复调查： （一） 经营者未履行承诺的； （二） 作出中止调查所依据的事实发生重大变化的； （三） 中止调查的决定是基于经营者提供的不完整、不正确或者误导性的信息作出的。	**Article 19** The AIC shall supervise the implementation of the commitments by the undertakings. If the commitments are fulfilled, the AIC may decide to terminate the investigation and make a written decision to terminate the investigation. The written decision shall indicate the facts of the suspected violation, the content of the commitment, the specific measures to be taken to eliminate the effects, and the steps and schedule in implementing the commitments, etc. The investigation may be resumed under any of the following circumstances: (1) the undertaking fails to implement the commitment; (2) the facts on which the decision to suspend the investigation was based have major changes; (3) the decision to suspend the investigation was based on incomplete, inaccurate, or misleading information provided by the undertaking.

(Continued)

第二十条 工商行政管理机关对主动报告达成垄断协议有关情况并提供重要证据的经营者，可以酌情减轻或者免除处罚。 对垄断协议的组织者，不适用前款规定。 重要证据应当是能够启动调查或者对认定垄断协议行为起到关键性作用的证据。	**Article 20** The AIC may, at its discretion, mitigate or exempt the undertaking from punishment for undertakings that voluntarily report monopoly agreement reached and provide material evidence. The preceding paragraph shall not be applicable to the organizing undertakings that arranged the monopoly agreement. Material evidence means evidence that plays a key role in the decision to initiate an investigation or in a finding of monopoly agreements.
第二十一条 经营者能够证明所达成的协议符合《反垄断法》第十五条规定情形的，工商行政管理机关可以对有关行为予以豁免。	**Article 21** If the undertaking can demonstrate that the agreement satisfies the conditions under Article 15 of the Anti-Monopoly Law, the AIC may exempt the relevant conduct.
第二十二条 工商行政管理机关对涉嫌垄断行为调查核实后，认定构成垄断行为的，应当依法作出行政处罚决定。	**Article 22** After investigation and verification of the suspected monopoly conduct, if the monopoly conduct is found, the AIC shall render a decision to impose an administrative penalty in accordance with the law.
第二十三条 国家工商行政管理总局对重大垄断案件，在作出行政处罚决定前应当向国务院反垄断委员会报告。 经授权的省级工商行政管理局应当依法作出中止调查、终止调查或者行政处罚决定，但在作出决定前应当向国家工商行政管理总局报告。省级工商行政管理局应当在作出决定后10个工作日内，将有关情况、相关决定书及案件调查终结报告报国家工商行政管理总局备案。	**Article 23** Regarding anti-monopoly cases with great significance, the SAIC shall report the case to the Anti-Monopoly Commission of the State Council before making decisions to impose administrative penalties. The authorized Provincial AIC shall make decisions to suspend an investigation, terminate an investigation, or administrative penalty in accordance with the law, but it shall report to the SAIC before making the above decisions. Provincial AICs shall file with the SAIC for record the relevant information, decisions, and concluding report of the case within ten working days after the issuance of the decision.

第二十四条 国家工商行政管理总局研究决定不适用《反垄断法》，但可以转致适用其他工商行政管理法律、法规处理的举报，应当及时转送有关工商行政管理机关依法处理。属于其他行政机关管辖的，应当依法移送其他有权机关。 省级以下工商行政管理机关可以依照其他法律、法规的规定，对发生在本行政区域内的公用企业或者其他依法具有独占地位经营者的限制竞争行为进行监督检查。	**Article 24** Where the SAIC decides, after deliberation, that other laws and regulations within the jurisdiction of industry and commerce administration rather than the Anti-Monopoly Law are applicable, such reporting materials shall be transferred to the relevant AIC for disposition according to law. If the reported matter is within the jurisdiction of other administrative authorities, it shall be transferred to such competent authorities according to law. The AIC below provincial level may, in accordance with provisions of other laws and regulations, supervise and investigate conduct that was taken by public utilities or other undertakings with a dominant position according to law to restrict competition and that occurred within its own administrative region.
第二十五条 工商行政管理机关对依法查处的垄断案件，可以向社会公布。	**Article 25** For anti-monopoly cases investigated and penalized according to law, the AIC may publish to the general public.
第二十六条 本规定对垄断行为调查、听证和处罚程序未做规定的，依照《中华人民共和国行政处罚法》、《工商行政管理机关行政处罚程序规定》、《工商行政管理机关行政处罚案件听证规则》的有关规定执行，但有关时限的规定不适用《工商行政管理机关行政处罚程序规定》、《工商行政管理机关行政处罚案件听证规则》。	**Article 26** Where there is no provision in these Rules with respect to the procedure for investigation, hearing, and penalties of monopoly conduct, relevant provisions under the PRC Law of Administrative Penalties, the SAIC Rules on the Procedures for Imposition of Administrative Penalties, and the SAIC Rules on Hearings for the Imposition of Administrative Penalties shall be applied with the exception of the provisions of the two SAIC Rules with regard to time limit.
第二十七条 对工商行政管理机关依照本规定作出的行政处罚等决定不服的，可以依法申请行政复议或者提起行政诉讼。	**Article 27** Undertakings that are not satisfied with the administrative penalty or any other decisions by the AIC may apply for an administrative review or file an administrative lawsuit in accordance with the law.

(Continued)

第二十八条 工商行政管理机关在反垄断执法工作中，要加强与其他反垄断执法机构和有关部门的信息沟通和执法协作。	**Article 28** During the enforcement of the Anti-Monopoly Law, the AIC shall strengthen the information exchange and enforcement cooperation with other antitrust authorities and relevant ministries.
第二十九条 工商行政管理机关工作人员违反本规定，滥用职权、玩忽职守、徇私舞弊或者泄露执法过程中知悉的商业秘密，尚不构成犯罪的，依法给予行政处分；涉嫌犯罪的，移送司法机关处理。	**Article 29** Where employees from the AIC abuse their power, neglect their duties, receive bribes and cheat, or disclose business secrets obtained during their enforcement activities in violation of these Rules, they shall be subject to administrative sanctions if the violation does not constitute a crime, and shall be transferred to judicial authorities if the violation may constitute a crime.
第三十条 本规定不适用于查处垄断协议、滥用市场支配地位方面的价格垄断行为。	**Article 30** These Rules are not applicable to the investigation and punishment for price monopoly conduct with regards to monopoly agreements and abuses of dominant market position.
第三十一条 本规定由国家工商行政管理总局负责解释。	**Article 31** The SAIC is responsible for the interpretation of these Rules.
第三十二条 本规定自2009年7月1日起施行。	**Article 32** These Rules shall become effective as of July 1, 2009.

B-20

Procedural Rules of the Administration for Industry and Commerce Regarding the Prohibition of Abuses of Administrative Power that Eliminate and/or Restrict Competition

工商行政管理机关制止滥用行政权力排除、限制竞争行为程序规定

(Promulgated by the State Administration for Industry and Commerce on May 26, 2009, effective as of July 1, 2009)

（国家工商行政管理总局于2009年5月26日发布，自2009年7月1日起施行）

第一条 为制止滥用行政权力排除、限制竞争行为，依据《中华人民共和国反垄断法》制定本规定。	**Article 1** These rules are promulgated in accordance with the Anti-Monopoly Law of the People's Republic of China in order to prevent abuse of administrative power for the purpose of eliminating and/or restricting competition.
第二条 行政机关和法律、法规授权的具有管理公共事务职能的组织滥用行政权力，实施排除、限制竞争行为的，由上级机关责令改正；对直接负责的主管人员和其他直接责任人员依法给予处分。国家工商行政管理总局和省、自治区、直辖市工商行政管理局（以下简称省级工商行政管理局）可以向有关上级机关提出依法处理的建议。	**Article 2** Where an administrative agency or organization designated by laws and regulations to manage public affairs abuses its administrative power to eliminate and/or restrict competition, the department at a higher level shall instruct it to rectify; the leading person directly in charge and the other persons directly responsible shall be given administrative penalties in accordance with the law.

(Continued)

	The State Administration for Industry and Commerce ("SAIC"), and the relevant Administration for Industry and Commerce of the province, autonomous region, or provincial level municipality ("Provincial AIC") may submit a proposal to the relevant department at a higher level for handling the matter according to the law.
第三条 国家工商行政管理总局对国务院所属部门、省级人民政府滥用行政权力排除、限制竞争的，可以向国务院提出依法处理的建议。 对法律、法规授权的具有管理全国公共事务职能的组织滥用行政权力排除、限制竞争的，国家工商行政管理总局可以向管理该组织的机关提出依法处理的建议。	**Article 3** In case of an abuse of administrative power to eliminate and/or restrict competition committed by any authority under the State Council or by a provincial People's government, the SAIC may make a proposal for duly handling the offense to the State Council. In case of any abuse of administrative power to eliminate and/or restrict competition committed by an organization authorized by laws or regulations to manage national public affairs, the SAIC may make a proposal for duly handling the offense to the authority governing the abusing authority.
第四条 省级工商行政管理局对省级人民政府所属部门、省以下地方人民政府及其所属部门滥用行政权力排除、限制竞争的，可以向有关上级机关提出依法处理的建议。 对法律、法规授权的具有管理地方公共事务职能的组织滥用行政权力排除、限制竞争的，省级工商行政管理局可以向管理该组织的机关提出依法处理的建议。	**Article 4** In case of an abuse of administrative power to eliminate and/or restrict competition committed by any department of the provincial People's government, or by a People's government below the provincial level and its relevant departments, the Provincial AIC may make a proposal for duly handling the offense to the relevant superior authority. In case of an abuse of administrative power to eliminate and/or restrict competition committed by an organization designated by laws and regulations to manage public affairs, the Provincial AIC may make a proposal for duly handling the offense to the authority governing the abusing authority.

第五条 经营者不得以行政机关和法律、法规授权的具有管理公共事务职能的组织强制、指定、授权等为由，从事垄断行为。 经营者从事垄断协议和滥用市场支配地位行为的，适用《工商行政管理机关查处垄断协议、滥用市场支配地位案件程序规定》。	**Article 5** No undertaking shall engage in any monopoly conduct on the ground that it is forced, designated, or authorized by any administrative agency or organization designated by laws and regulations to manage public affairs. Any monopoly agreement entered into or any abuse of dominant market position by an undertaking shall be subject to and governed by the Procedural Rules of the Administration for Industry and Commerce Regarding the Investigation and Handling of Cases Relating to Monopoly Agreements and Abuses of Dominant Market Positions.
第六条 法律、行政法规对行政机关和法律、法规授权的具有管理公共事务职能的组织滥用行政权力排除、限制竞争行为的处理另有规定的，依照其规定。	**Article 6** Where a law or administrative regulation provides otherwise regarding the handling of an abuse of administrative power to eliminate and/or restrict competition by an administrative authority or an organization designated by laws and regulations to manage public affairs, such laws and administrative regulations shall govern.
第七条 省级工商行政管理局依据本规定第四条提出依法处理的建议后，应当于十个工作日内报国家工商行政管理总局备案。	**Article 7** Within ten business days after making a proposal according to Article 4 hereof by the Provincial AIC for handling the offenses in accordance with law, the Provincial AIC shall file with the SAIC for record.
第八条 工商行政管理机关工作人员违反本规定，滥用职权、玩忽职守、徇私舞弊，尚不构成犯罪的，依法给予行政处分；构成犯罪的，依法追究刑事责任。	**Article 8** Where the employees from the AIC abuse their power, neglect their duties, receive bribes, and cheat in violation of these rules, which does not constitute a crime, administrative penalties shall be given; if their conduct constitutes a crime, criminal liability shall be pursued according to the law.

(Continued)

第九条 本规定不适用于制止行政机关和法律、法规授权的具有管理公共事务职能的组织滥用行政权力排除、限制竞争涉及的价格方面的行为。	**Article 9** These rules shall not be applicable to the prevention of any price-related conduct by any administrative authority or any organization designated by laws and regulations to manage public affairs by abusing administrative power to eliminate and/or restrict competition.
第十条 本规定由国家工商行政管理总局负责解释。	**Article 10** The SAIC is responsible for the interpretation of these rules.
第十一条 本规定自2009年7月1日起施行。	**Article 11** These rules shall become effective as of July 1, 2009.

B-21

Rules of the Administration for Industry and Commerce on the Prohibition of Monopoly Agreements

工商行政管理机关禁止垄断协议行为的规定

(Promulgated by the State Administration for Industry and Commerce on December 31, 2010, effective as of February 1, 2011)

（国家工商行政管理总局于2010年12月31日发布，自2011年2月1日起施行）

第一条 为了制止经济活动中的垄断协议行为，根据《中华人民共和国反垄断法》（以下简称《反垄断法》），制定本规定。	**Article 1** These Rules are formulated in accordance with the Anti-Monopoly Law of the People's Republic of China (hereinafter referred to as "AML") for the purpose of preventing monopoly agreements in economic activities.
第二条 禁止经营者在经济活动中达成垄断协议。 垄断协议是指违反《反垄断法》第十三条、第十四条、第十六条的规定，经营者之间达成的或者行业协会组织本行业经营者达成的排除、限制竞争的协议、决定或者其他协同行为。 协议或者决定包括书面形式和口头形式。 其他协同行为是指经营者虽未明确订立书面或者口头形式的协议或者决定，但实质上存在协调一致的行为。	**Article 2** Undertakings are prohibited from reaching any monopoly agreement in economic activities. Monopoly agreements shall mean any agreement, decision, and other concerted conducts reached among undertakings or organized by a trade association that eliminate and/or restrict competition in violation of Articles 13, 14, and 16 of the AML. An agreement or decision may take written and oral forms.

(Continued)

	Other concerted conducts shall mean colluded coordination in substance between undertakings without express oral or written agreements or decisions.
第三条 认定其他协同行为，应当考虑下列因素： （一）　经营者的市场行为是否具有一致性； （二）　经营者之间是否进行过意思联络或者信息交流； （三）　经营者能否对一致行为作出合理的解释。 认定其他协同行为，还应当考虑相关市场的结构情况、竞争状况、市场变化情况、行业情况等。	**Article 3** To determine other concerted conducts, the following factors shall be considered: (1)　whether the market conduct of undertakings is uniform; (2)　whether there is any communication on intentions or exchange of information between the undertakings; (3)　whether the undertakings can provide a reasonable justification for the uniformity of conduct. The market structure, competitive conditions, changes in the market, industry conditions, etc. shall also be considered in the determination of other concerted conduct.
第四条 禁止具有竞争关系的经营者就限制商品的生产数量或者销售数量达成下列垄断协议： （一）　以限制产量、固定产量、停止生产等方式限制商品的生产数量或者限制商品特定品种、型号的生产数量； （二）　以拒绝供货、限制商品投放量等方式限制商品的销售数量或者限制商品特定品种、型号的销售数量。	**Article 4** Competing undertakings shall be prohibited from entering into the following monopoly agreements that restrict output or sales volume of products: (1)　agreements that restrict output volume of products or certain types or models of a product by curtailing production, fixed production, stop production, or otherwise; (2)　agreements that restrict sales volume of products, or certain types or models of a product by refusing to supply, restricting the products supply, or otherwise.
第五条 禁止具有竞争关系的经营者就分割销售市场或者原材料采购市场达成下列垄断协议： （一）　划分商品销售地域、销售对象或者销售商品的种类、数量；	**Article 5** Competing undertakings shall be prohibited from entering into the following monopoly agreements that split sales market or raw material purchasing market：

（二） 划分原料、半成品、零部件、相关设备等原材料的采购区域、种类、数量； （三） 划分原料、半成品、零部件、相关设备等原材料的供应商。	(1) agreements that split market by territory, customer, or product type and volume; (2) agreements that split purchasing market of raw material, semi-finished products, parts and components, relevant equipments, and other raw materials by territory, type, and volume; (3) agreements that split suppliers of raw material, semi-finished products, parts and components, relevant equipment, and other raw materials.
第六条 禁止具有竞争关系的经营者就限制购买新技术、新设备或者限制开发新技术、新产品达成下列垄断协议： （一） 限制购买、使用新技术、新工艺； （二） 限制购买、租赁、使用新设备； （三） 限制投资、研发新技术、新工艺、新产品； （四） 拒绝使用新技术、新工艺、新设备； （五） 拒绝采用新的技术标准。	**Article 6** Competing undertakings shall be prohibited from entering into the following monopoly agreements that restrict purchasing new technologies, new equipments, or restrict developing new technologies, or new products: (1) agreements that restrict purchasing and using new technologies, or new processes; (2) agreements that restrict purchasing, leasing, or using new equipment; (3) agreements that restrict investing in and developing new technologies, new processes, or new products; (4) agreements that refuse to use new technologies, new processes, or new equipment; and/or (5) agreements that refuse to adopt new technical standards.
第七条 禁止具有竞争关系的经营者就联合抵制交易达成以下垄断协议： （一） 联合拒绝向特定经营者供货或者销售商品； （二） 联合拒绝采购或者销售特定经营者的商品； （三） 联合限定特定经营者不得与其具有竞争关系的经营者进行交易。	**Article 7** Competing undertakings shall be prohibited from entering into the following monopoly agreements to jointly boycott: (1) concerted refusal to supply or sell products to a specific undertaking; (2) concerted refusal to purchase or sell products of a specific undertaking;

(Continued)

	(3) concerted restraint on a specific undertaking from dealing with a competing undertaking.
第八条 本规定未明确规定的其他垄断协议，除价格垄断协议外，由国家工商行政管理总局依法认定。	**Article 8** With the exception of price monopoly agreements, the State Administration for Industry and Commerce shall be responsible for finding other monopoly agreements according to the law that are not expressly provided for in these Rules.
第九条 禁止行业协会以下列方式组织本行业的经营者从事本规定禁止的垄断协议行为： （一） 制定、发布含有排除、限制竞争内容的行业协会章程、规则、决定、通知、标准等； （二） 召集、组织或者推动本行业的经营者达成含有排除、限制竞争内容的协议、决议、纪要、备忘录等。	**Article 9** Trade associations shall be prohibited from organizing their members to engage in any monopoly agreement as prohibited hereunder by means set forth below: (1) formulating and issuing articles of association, rules, decisions, notices, or standards containing provisions eliminating and/or restricting competition by the trade association; (2) convening, organizing, or promoting undertakings in the relevant industry to reach agreements, decisions, minutes, and/or memorandums containing provisions eliminating and/or restricting competition.
第十条 经营者违反本规定第四条至第八条规定，达成并实施垄断协议的，由工商行政管理机关责令停止违法行为，没收违法所得，并处上一年度销售额百分之一以上百分之十以下的罚款；尚未实施所达成的垄断协议的，可以处五十万元以下的罚款。 行业协会违反本规定第九条规定，组织本行业的经营者达成垄断协议的，工商行政管理机关可以对其处五十万元以下的罚款；情节严重的，工商行政管理机关可以提请社会团体登记管理机关依法撤销登记。	**Article 10** Where undertakings have entered into and implemented a monopoly agreement in violation of provisions from Article 4 to Article 8 of these Rules, the AIC shall order them to cease the violation, confiscate the illegal gains, and impose a fine of 1–10% of the turnover in the previous fiscal year; where the monopoly agreement has not been implemented, the infringer may be imposed a fine of no more than RMB 500,000.

工商行政管理机关确定具体罚款数额时，应当考虑违法行为的性质、情节、程度、持续的时间等因素。 经营者之间串通或者行业协会组织经营者串通，尚未达成垄断协议的，工商行政管理机关应当及时予以制止。 经营者主动停止垄断协议行为的，工商行政管理机关可以酌情减轻或者免除对该经营者的处罚。	The AIC shall impose a fine of no more than RMB 500,000 on any trade association that organizes its members to enter into monopoly agreements in violation of Article 9 of these Rules. In serious cases, the AIC may request the relevant social organization registration administration to duly deregister such trade association. When determining the specific magnitude of the fine, the AIC shall consider the nature, circumstances, seriousness, and duration of the violation, and other relevant factors. Where undertakings collude or trade associations organize undertakings in the relevant industry to collude and a monopoly agreement has not yet been concluded, the AIC shall prevent it in time. Where the undertakings voluntarily cease a monopoly agreement, they may, at the discretion of the AIC, be given a mitigated penalty or be exempted from penalty.
第十一条 经营者主动向工商行政管理机关报告所达成垄断协议的有关情况并提供重要证据的，工商行政管理机关可以酌情减轻或者免除对该经营者的处罚。 工商行政管理机关决定减轻或者免除处罚，应当根据经营者主动报告的时间顺序、提供证据的重要程度、达成、实施垄断协议的有关情况以及配合调查的情况确定。 重要证据是指能够对工商行政管理机关启动调查或者对认定垄断协议行为起到关键性作用的证据，包括参与垄断协议的经营者、涉及的产品范围、达成协议的内容和方式、协议的具体实施情况等。	**Article 11** Undertakings that report a monopoly agreement to the AIC and provide material evidence on their own initiative may be granted a mitigated penalty by the AIC or be exempted from penalty. Exemption or mitigation of the penalty by the AIC shall be determined in accordance with the time sequence of the voluntary self-reports by the undertakings, the importance of the evidence provided, relevant information about concluding or implementing the monopoly agreement, and its cooperation with the investigation. Material evidence refers to evidence that is sufficient to initiate an investigation or that plays a critical role in finding a monopoly agreement by the AIC,

(Continued)

	including information on the parties to the agreement, the products involved, the form and content of the agreement, and specific details regarding the implementation of the agreement.
第十二条 对第一个主动报告所达成垄断协议的有关情况、提供重要证据并全面主动配合调查的经营者，免除处罚。对主动向工商行政管理机关报告所达成垄断协议的有关情况并提供重要证据的其他经营者，酌情减轻处罚。	**Article 12** For the first undertaking that voluntarily self-reports the monopoly agreement to the AIC, provides material evidence, and cooperates with the investigation comprehensively and voluntarily, it shall be exempted from the penalty. For other undertakings that voluntarily self-report the monopoly agreement, and provide material evidence, the penalty shall be mitigated discretionally.
第十三条 本规定第十一条、第十二条所称的减轻或者免除处罚，主要是指对《反垄断法》第四十六条规定的罚款的减轻或者免除。	**Article 13** Exemption or mitigation of penalty referred to in Articles 11 and 12 primarily refer to exemption or mitigation of fines that are specified in Article 46 of the AML.
第十四条 经营者能够提供材料，证明所达成的协议符合《反垄断法》第十五条规定的，经工商行政管理机关认定，不适用本规定。	**Article 14** Where undertakings can provide materials to prove that the agreement concluded falls under Article 15 of the AML, and the AIC finds so, these Rules shall not be applicable to such agreement.
第十五条 对工商行政管理机关依照本规定作出的行政处罚等决定不服的，可以依法申请行政复议或者提起行政诉讼。	**Article 15** Undertakings that are not satisfied with the administrative penalty or any other rulings rendered by the AIC according to these Rules may apply for an administrative review or file an administrative lawsuit in accordance with law.
第十六条 工商行政管理机关反垄断执法人员应当按照《工商行政管理机关查处垄断协议、滥用市场支配地位案件程序规定》的规定，严格依法办案。	**Article 16** Anti-monopoly law enforcement officials with the AIC shall handle cases strictly in accordance with the Procedural Rules of the Administration for Industry and Commerce Regarding

工商行政管理机关反垄断执法人员滥用职权、玩忽职守、徇私舞弊或者泄露执法过程中知悉的商业秘密的，依照有关规定处理。	the Investigation and Handling of Cases Relating to Monopoly Agreements and Abuses of Dominant Market Positions. Anti-monopoly law enforcement officials from the AIC who abuse their power, neglect their duties, receive bribes and cheat, or disclose business secrets obtained during their enforcement activities, shall be punished according to relevant rules and regulations.
第十七条 农业生产者及农村经济组织在农产品生产、加工、销售、运输、储存等经营活动中实施的联合或者协同行为，不适用本规定。	**Article 17** These Rules are not applicable to alliances or other concerted conduct by farmers and rural economic organizations in such operational activities as production, processing, sales, transportation, and storage of agricultural products.
第十八条 本规定所称商品包括服务。	**Article 18** For the purpose of these Rules, products shall include services.
第十九条 本规定由国家工商行政管理总局负责解释。	**Article 19** These Rules are subject to interpretation by the State Administration for Industry and Commerce.
第二十条 本规定自2011年2月1日起施行。	**Article 20** These Rules shall become effective as of February 1, 2011.

B-22

Rules of the Administration for Industry and Commerce on the Prohibition of Abuses of Dominant Market Position

工商行政管理机关禁止滥用市场支配地位行为的规定

(Promulgated by the State Administration for Industry and Commerce on December 31, 2010, effective as of February 1, 2011)

（国家工商行政管理总局于2010年12月31日发布，自2011年2月1日起实施）

第一条 为了制止经济活动中的滥用市场支配地位行为，根据《中华人民共和国反垄断法》（以下简称《反垄断法》），制定本规定。	**Article 1** These Rules are formulated in accordance with the Anti-Monopoly Law of the People's Republic of China ("AML") for the purpose of prohibiting abuses of dominant market position in economic activities.
第二条 禁止具有市场支配地位的经营者在经济活动中滥用市场支配地位，排除、限制竞争。	**Article 2** An undertaking with a dominant market position is prohibited from abusing its dominant market position to eliminate and/or restrict competition in economic activities.
第三条 市场支配地位是指经营者在相关市场内具有能够控制商品价格、数量或者其他交易条件，或者能够阻碍、影响其他经营者进入相关市场能力的市场地位。	**Article 3** "A dominant market position" refers to a market position which enables an undertaking to control price, output, or other transaction conditions of a product in the relevant market, or to impede or prevent entry into the relevant market by other undertakings.

本条所称其他交易条件是指除商品价格、数量之外能够对市场交易产生实质影响的其他因素，包括商品品质、付款条件、交付方式、售后服务等。 本条所称能够阻碍、影响其他经营者进入相关市场，是指排除其他经营者进入相关市场，或者延缓其他经营者在合理时间内进入相关市场，或者其他经营者虽能够进入该相关市场，但进入成本提高难以在市场中开展有效竞争等。	For the purpose of this article, "other transaction conditions" refers to elements other than price and volume that may substantially affect market transactions, including product quality, payment conditions, delivery methods, and after-sale service of the product, etc. For the purpose of this Article, "impeding or preventing entry into the relevant market by other undertakings" refers to preventing other undertakings from entering the relevant market, or deferring other undertakings' entry into the relevant market within a reasonable time, or increasing the market entry cost, thus making it difficult for the new entrant to compete effectively on the market, although entry into the relevant market is possible.
第四条 禁止具有市场支配地位的经营者没有正当理由，通过下列方式拒绝与交易相对人进行交易： （一）削减与交易相对人的现有交易数量； （二）拖延、中断与交易相对人的现有交易； （三）拒绝与交易相对人进行新的交易； （四）设置限制性条件，使交易相对人难以继续与其进行交易； （五）拒绝交易相对人在生产经营活动中以合理条件使用其必需设施。 在认定前款第（五）项时，应当综合考虑另行投资建设、另行开发建造该设施的可行性、交易相对人有效开展生产经营活动对该设施的依赖程度、该经营者提供该设施的可能性以及对自身生产经营活动造成的影响等因素。	**Article 4** An undertaking with a dominant market position is prohibited from refusing to deal with a counterparty by means of the following, without valid justification: (1) reducing its current trade volume with the counterparty; (2) delaying, terminating its current transaction with the counterparty; (3) refusing to have any new transaction with the counterparty; (4) imposing restrictive conditions which makes it difficult for the counterparty to continue its dealings with the said undertaking; and/or (5) refusing to allow the counterparty to use its necessary facilities under reasonable conditions in the course of production and operations. For a finding of violation under item (5), factors such as the following shall be considered on a comprehensive basis: feasibility to separately invest and build, or develop such facility, degree

(*Continued*)

	of reliance of the counterparty on such facility in effectively running its production and operations, possibilities of the undertaking in question making available such facility, and its impact over the production and operations of the undertaking in question.
第五条 禁止具有市场支配地位的经营者没有正当理由，实施下列限定交易行为： （一）限定交易相对人只能与其进行交易； （二）限定交易相对人只能与其指定的经营者进行交易； （三）限定交易相对人不得与其竞争对手进行交易。	**Article 5** An undertaking with a dominant market position is prohibited from engaging in any of the following restrictive trading conduct, without valid justification: (1) restricting the counterparty to trade exclusively with itself; (2) restricting the counterparty to trade exclusively with a designated undertaking; or (3) restricting the counterparty from trading with any of its competitors.
第六条 禁止具有市场支配地位的经营者没有正当理由搭售商品，或者在交易时附加其他不合理的交易条件： （一）违背交易惯例、消费习惯等或者无视商品的功能，将不同商品强制捆绑销售或者组合销售； （二）对合同期限、支付方式、商品的运输及交付方式或者服务的提供方式等附加不合理的限制； （三）对商品的销售地域、销售对象、售后服务等附加不合理的限制； （四）附加与交易标的无关的交易条件。	**Article 6** An undertaking with a dominant market position is prohibited from tying products or imposing any other unreasonable trading condition at the time of the transaction: (1) forcibly tying different products or bundling different products in violation of the trade practices or consumer habits, or in disregard of the functions of the product; (2) imposing unreasonable restrictions regarding contract term, payment method, product transport, product or service delivery methods, etc. (3) imposing unreasonable restrictions regarding sales territory, target customers, and after-sales services, etc. for the products; (4) imposing trading conditions irrelevant to the subject matter of the transaction.

第七条 禁止具有市场支配地位的经营者没有正当理由，对条件相同的交易相对人在交易条件上实行下列差别待遇： （一）实行不同的交易数量、品种、品质等级； （二）实行不同的数量折扣等优惠条件； （三）实行不同的付款条件、交付方式； （四）实行不同的保修内容和期限、维修内容和时间、零配件供应、技术指导等售后服务条件。	**Article 7** An undertaking with a dominant market position is prohibited from according differential treatment to similarly situated counterparties in respect of conditions of the transaction without valid justification: (1) offering different trade volumes, grades, qualities; (2) offering differential preferential conditions, such as differential quantity-based discounts; (3) applying differential terms of payment conditions and delivery methods; (4) applying differential after-sales services conditions, such as different warranty services and warranty period, different maintenance items and maintenance period, different spare parts supply, and technical instructions.
第八条 工商行政管理机关认定本规定第四条至第七条所称的正当理由，应当综合考虑下列因素： （一）有关行为是否为经营者基于自身正常经营活动及正常效益而采取； （二）有关行为对经济运行效率、社会公共利益及经济发展的影响。	**Article 8** The relevant Administration for Industry and Commerce shall consider the following factors on a comprehensive basis when determining the valid justification in Articles 4 to 7: (1) whether the conduct is based on normal operations and for normal benefits of the undertaking; (2) the effect of the relevant conduct on economic efficiency, public interest, and economic growth.
第九条 本规定未明确规定的其他滥用市场支配地位行为，除价格垄断行为外，由国家工商行政管理总局依法认定。	**Article 9** Except for price monopoly conduct, the State Administration for Industry and Commerce shall determine, according to law, any other abuse of dominant market position not expressly covered in these Rules.

(Continued)

第十条	**Article 10**
认定经营者具有市场支配地位，应当依据下列因素：	In finding of a dominant market position, the following factors shall be taken into consideration:
（一）该经营者在相关市场的市场份额，以及相关市场的竞争状况。	(1) The market share of the undertaking and competitive conditions in the relevant market.
市场份额是指一定时期内经营者的特定商品销售额、销售数量等指标在相关市场所占的比重。	Market share refers to the turnover, sales volume, and other measurements of an undertaking expressed as a percentage in the relevant market over a given period of time.
分析相关市场竞争状况应当考虑相关市场的发展状况、现有竞争者的数量和市场份额、商品差异程度以及潜在竞争者的情况等。	When analyzing the competitive conditions in the relevant market, consideration shall be given to the development of the relevant market, the number of existing competitors, market shares, the differentiation of products, and the situation of potential competitors, etc.
（二）该经营者控制销售市场或者原材料采购市场的能力。	(2) The ability of the undertaking to control the sales market or the raw material purchasing market.
认定经营者控制销售市场或者原材料采购市场的能力，应当考虑该经营者控制销售渠道或者采购渠道的能力、影响或者决定价格、数量、合同期限或者其它交易条件的能力以及优先获得企业生产经营所必需的原料、半成品、零部件及相关设备等原材料的能力。	When determining the ability of an undertaking to control the sales market or the raw materials purchasing market, consideration shall be given to its ability to control the sales channels or the purchase channels, the ability to impact or determine the price, the output, term, or other contract conditions, and to have priority access to raw materials, such as raw material supplies, semi-products, parts and components, as well as relevant equipment necessary for the production and operation of an undertaking.
（三）该经营者的财力和技术条件。	(3) The financial and technological capabilities of the undertaking.
认定经营者的财力和技术条件，应当考虑该经营者的资产规模、财务能力、盈利能力、融资能力、研发能力、技术装备、技术创新和应用能力、拥有的知识产权等。	When determining the financial and technological conditions of the undertaking, consideration shall be given to the capital scale, the financial position, the profitability, the financing capability, the R&D capability, technical equipment, technology
对于经营者的财力和技术条件的分析认定，应当同时考虑其关联方的财力和技术条件。	
（四）其他经营者对该经营者在交易上的依赖程度。	
认定其他经营者对该经营者在交易上的依赖程度，应当考虑其他经营者与该经营者之间的交易量、交易关系的持续时间、转向其他交易相对人的难易程度等。	
（五）其他经营者进入相关市场的难易程度。	

认定其他经营者进入相关市场的难易程度，应当考虑市场准入制度、拥有必需设施的情况、销售渠道、资金和技术要求以及成本等。 （六）与认定该经营者市场支配地位有关的其他因素。	innovation, application ability, and the intellectual property owned by such undertaking. The analysis of the financial and technological condition of the undertaking shall also take into consideration those of its affiliates. (4) The degree of reliance on the undertaking by other undertakings in transactions. When determining the degree of reliance of other undertakings on the undertaking in question, consideration shall be given to the transaction volume, the duration of the trading relationship with the undertaking in question, and the degree of difficulty to switch to other counterparties. (5) The difficulty for other undertakings to enter the relevant market. When determining the degree of difficulty for other undertakings to enter the relevant market, consideration shall be given to regulations on market entry, possession of necessary facilities, sales channels, financial and technological requirements, and costs, etc. (6) Other factors relevant to the determination of the undertaking's dominant market position.
第十一条 有下列情形之一的，可以推定经营者具有市场支配地位： （一）一个经营者在相关市场的市场份额达到二分之一的； （二）两个经营者在相关市场的市场份额合计达到三分之二的； （三）三个经营者在相关市场的市场份额合计达到四分之三的。 有前款第二项、第三项规定的情形，其中有的经营者市场份额不足十分之一的，不应当推定该经营者具有市场支配地位。	**Article 11** Undertakings may be considered to have a dominant market position in one of the following events: (1) the market share of one undertaking in the relevant market reaches or exceeds one half; (2) the combined market share of two undertakings in the relevant market reaches or exceeds two-thirds; or (3) the combined market share of three undertakings in the relevant market reaches or exceeds three-quarters.

(Continued)

	Among those undertakings falling under item (2) or (3) of the preceding paragraph, an undertaking shall not be considered to have a dominant market position if the market share of such undertaking is less than one-tenth.
第十二条 被推定具有市场支配地位的经营者，能够根据本规定第十条所列因素，证明其在相关市场内不具有控制商品价格、数量或者其他交易条件，或者不具有能够阻碍、影响其他经营者进入相关市场的能力，则不应当认定其具有市场支配地位。	**Article 12** Where an undertaking that is presumed to hold a dominant market position proves that, based on the elements set forth in Article 10, it has no ability to control the price, the output of the product, or other transaction conditions in the relevant market, or the ability to prevent or affect entry into the relevant market by other undertakings, it shall not be considered to hold a dominant market position.
第十三条 涉嫌滥用市场支配地位行为的经营者，在工商行政管理机关规定的期限内，可以陈述其行为合理性的理由并提供有关证据。	**Article 13** An undertaking that is suspected of having abused its dominant market position may provide reasons of legitimacy and supporting evidence to prove the justification for the challenged conduct within the time limit stipulated by the Administration for Industry and Commerce.
第十四条 经营者违反本规定第四条至第七条、第九条规定，滥用市场支配地位的，由工商行政管理机关责令停止违法行为，没收违法所得，并处上一年度销售额百分之一以上百分之十以下的罚款。 工商行政管理机关确定具体罚款数额时，应当考虑违法行为的性质、情节、程度、持续的时间等因素。 经营者主动停止滥用市场支配地位行为的，工商行政管理机关可以酌情减轻或者免除对该经营者的处罚。	**Article 14** Where an undertaking abuses a dominant market position, violating Articles 4 to 7 and 9 of these Rules, the Administration for Industry and Commerce shall order the undertaking to cease the violation, confiscate its illegal gains, and impose a fine of 1–10% of the turnover in the previous fiscal year. The Administration for Industry and Commerce shall consider the nature, circumstances, seriousness, and duration of the violation, and other relevant factors, when determining the specific magnitude of the fine. Where the undertakings voluntarily cease their abuse of a dominant

	market position, the Administration for Industry and Commerce, at its discretion, may grant a mitigated penalty or exemption from the penalty to the undertakings.
第十五条 对工商行政管理机关依照本规定作出的行政处罚等决定不服的，可以依法申请行政复议或者提起行政诉讼。	**Article 15** Undertakings that are not satisfied with the administrative penalty or any other ruling by the Administration for Industry and Commerce may apply for an administrative review or file an administrative lawsuit according to law.
第十六条 工商行政管理机关反垄断执法人员应当按照《工商行政管理机关查处垄断协议、滥用市场支配地位案件程序规定》的规定，严格依法办案。 工商行政管理机关反垄断执法人员滥用职权、玩忽职守、徇私舞弊或者泄露执法过程中知悉的商业秘密的，依照有关规定处理。	**Article 16** Anti-monopoly law enforcement officials of the Administration for Industry and Commerce shall handle cases strictly in accordance with the Procedural Rules of the Administration for Industry and Commerce Regarding the Investigation and Handling of Cases Relating to Monopoly Agreements and Abuses of Dominant Market Positions. Anti-monopoly law enforcement officials from the AIC who abuse their power, neglect their duties, receive bribes and cheat, or disclose business secrets obtained during their enforcement activities, shall be punished according to relevant rules and regulations.
第十七条 本规定所称商品包括服务。	**Article 17** For the purpose of these Rules, a "product" referred to herein shall include services.
第十八条 本规定由国家工商行政管理总局负责解释。	**Article 18** The State Administration for Industry and Commerce is responsible for interpreting these Rules.
第十九条 本规定自2011年2月1日起施行。	**Article 19** These Rules shall become effective as of February 1, 2011.

B-23

Rules of the Administration for Industry and Commerce on the Prohibition of Abuses of Administrative Power that Eliminate and/or Restrict Competition

工商行政管理机关制止滥用行政权力排除、限制竞争行为的规定

(Promulgated by the State Administration for Industry and Commerce on December 31, 2010, effective as of February 1, 2011)

（国家工商行政管理总局于2010年12月31日发布，自2011年2月1日起施行）

第一条 为了制止滥用行政权力排除、限制竞争行为，根据《中华人民共和国反垄断法》（以下简称《反垄断法》），制定本规定。	**Article 1** These Rules are promulgated in accordance with the Anti-Monopoly Law of the People's Republic of China (hereinafter "Anti-Monopoly Law") in order to prevent abuses of administrative power for the purpose of eliminating and/or restricting competition.
第二条 行政机关和法律、法规授权的具有管理公共事务职能的组织不得滥用行政权力，排除、限制竞争。	**Article 2** Administrative agencies and organizations designated by laws and regulations to manage public affairs shall not abuse their administrative power, eliminating and/or restricting competition.

第三条	**Article 3**
行政机关和法律、法规授权的具有管理公共事务职能的组织不得滥用行政权力，从事下列行为：	Administrative agencies and organizations designated by laws and regulations to manage public affairs shall not abuse their administrative power by engaging in any of the following conduct:
（一） 以明确要求、暗示或者拒绝、拖延行政许可以及重复检查等方式限定或者变相限定单位或者个人经营、购买、使用其指定的经营者提供的商品或者限定他人正常的经营活动；	(1) restricting or disguisedly restricting organizations or individuals to deal, purchase, or use products provided by designated undertakings or restricting the normal operation activities of others by expressly requiring, implying, rejecting, or postponing administrative licensing, repeatedly inspecting, or any other forms;
（二） 对外地商品执行与本地同类商品不同的技术要求、检验标准，或者采取重复检验、重复认证等歧视性技术措施，阻碍、限制外地商品进入本地市场；	(2) blocking or restricting the entry of products originating from other regions into the local market by imposing different technical requirements or inspection standards on products originating from other regions than those on similar local products, or taking discriminatory technical measures, such as repeated inspection or certification on products originating from other regions;
（三） 采取专门针对外地商品的行政许可，或者对外地商品实施行政许可时采取不同的许可条件、程序、期限等，阻碍、限制外地商品进入本地市场；	(3) blocking or restricting the entry of products originating from other regions into the local market by creating administrative licensing for particular products from other regions, or adopting different conditions, procedures, or time limit when implementing administrative licensing on products originating from other regions;
（四） 设置关卡或者采取其他手段，阻碍、限制外地商品进入本地市场或者本地商品运往外地市场；	(4) blocking or restricting either the entry of products originating from other regions into the local market or the exit of local products to the market of other regions by setting up checkpoints or other measures;
（五） 以设定歧视性资质要求、评审标准或者不依法发布信息等方式，排斥或者限制外地经营者参加本地的招标投标活动；	
（六） 采取不平等待遇等方式，排斥或者限制外地经营者在本地投资或者设立分支机构或者妨碍外地经营者在本地的正常经营活动；	
（七） 强制经营者之间达成、实施排除、限制竞争的垄断协议，强制具有市场支配地位的经营者从事滥用市场支配地位行为。	

(Continued)

	(5) precluding or restricting participation of undertakings from other regions in local bidding activities by imposing discriminatory qualification requirements or assessment standards or by failing to publish information in accordance with the law; (6) precluding or restricting either investment or the establishment of local branches in their region by undertakings from other regions by adopting discriminatory treatment, etc. or interfering with their normal business operation in the region; (7) compelling undertakings to conclude and implement monopoly agreement for the purpose of eliminating and/or restricting competition, or compelling undertakings to abuse their dominant market position.
第四条 行政机关不得滥用行政权力，以决定、公告、通告、通知、意见、会议纪要等形式，制定、发布含有排除、限制竞争内容的规定。 前款规定适用于法律、法规授权的具有管理公共事务职能的组织。	**Article 4** Administrative agencies shall not abuse their administrative power by promulgating or issuing any regulation containing provisions eliminating and/or restricting competition by forms of decision, public notice, announcement, notification, opinion, meeting minutes, or any other forms. The preceding paragraph applies to organizations designated by laws and regulations to manage public affairs.
第五条 经营者不得从事下列行为： （一） 以行政机关和法律、法规授权的具有管理公共事务职能的组织的行政限定为由，达成、实施垄断协议和滥用市场支配地位； （二） 以行政机关和法律、法规授权的具有管理公共事务职能的组织的行政授权为由，达成、实施垄断协议和滥用市场支配地位；	**Article 5** Undertakings shall not engage in any of the following conduct: (1) conclude, implement a monopoly agreement, or abuse a dominant market position on the basis of the administrative restriction by administrative agencies and organizations designated by laws and regulations to manage public affairs;

(三) 以依据行政机关和法律、法规授权的具有管理公共事务职能的组织制定、发布的行政规定为由，达成、实施垄断协议和滥用市场支配地位。	(2) conclude, implement a monopoly agreement, or abuse a dominant market position on the grounds of the administrative authorization by administrative agencies and organizations designated by laws and regulations to manage public affairs; or (3) conclude, implement a monopoly agreement, or abuse a dominant market position on the basis of the administrative regulation promulgated or issued by administrative agencies and organizations designated by laws and regulations to manage public affairs.
第六条 行政机关和法律、法规授权的具有管理公共事务职能的组织违反本规定第三条、第四条规定的，国家工商行政管理总局和省、自治区、直辖市工商行政管理局依照《反垄断法》第五十一条的规定，可以就行政机关和法律、法规授权的具有管理公共事务职能的组织滥用行政权力排除、限制竞争的行为表现及其后果，向其有关上级机关提出依法处理的建议。	**Article 6** When an administrative agency or an organization designated by laws and regulations to manage public affairs administration violates Articles 3 or 4 of these Rules, the SAIC and Provincial AICs may, in accordance with Article 51 of the Anti-Monopoly Law, make a proposal for handling the matter to the relevant superior authority in connection with any abuse of administrative power, and effects thereof, by administrative agencies and organizations designated by laws and regulations to manage public affairs for the purpose of eliminating and/or restricting competition.
第七条 经营者违反本规定第五条规定从事垄断行为的，依照《工商行政管理机关禁止垄断协议行为的规定》、《工商行政管理机关禁止滥用市场支配地位行为的规定》处理。	**Article 7** An undertaking which engages in monopoly conduct in violation of Article 5 shall be dealt with in accordance with the SAIC Rules on the Prohibition of Monopoly Agreements and the SAIC Rules on the Prohibition of a Dominant Market Position.

(Continued)

第八条	**Article 8**
经营者达成并实施垄断协议的，由工商行政管理机关责令停止违法行为，没收违法所得，并处上一年度销售额百分之一以上百分之十以下的罚款；尚未实施所达成的垄断协议的，可以处五十万元以下的罚款。经营者滥用市场支配地位的，由工商行政管理机关责令停止违法行为，没收违法所得，并处上一年度销售额百分之一以上百分之十以下的罚款。	Where an undertaking has entered into and implemented a monopoly agreement, the AIC shall order the undertaking to cease the violation, confiscate the illegal gains, and impose a fine of 1–10% of the turnover in the previous fiscal year; where the monopoly agreement has not been implemented, the undertaking may be imposed a fine of no more than RMB 500,000. Where an undertaking abuses its dominant market position, the AIC shall order the undertaking to cease the violation, confiscate the illegal gains, and impose a fine of 1–10% of the turnover in the previous fiscal year.
第九条	**Article 9**
法律、行政法规对行政机关和法律、法规授权的具有管理公共事务职能的组织滥用行政权力实施排除、限制竞争行为的处理另有规定的，依照其规定。	Where other laws or administrative regulations provide for the handling of abuses by administrative agencies and organizations designated by laws and regulations to manage public affairs of their administrative power to engage in conduct that eliminates or restricts competition, those provisions shall apply.
第十条	**Article 10**
工商行政管理机关反垄断执法人员应当按照《工商行政管理机关制止滥用行政权力排除、限制竞争行为程序规定》的规定，严格依法办案。 工商行政管理机关反垄断执法人员滥用职权、玩忽职守、徇私舞弊或者泄露执法过程中知悉的商业秘密的，依照有关规定处理。	AIC anti-monopoly law enforcement officials shall handle cases strictly in accordance with the Procedural Rules of the Administration for Industry and Commerce Regarding the Prohibition of Abuses of Administrative Power that Eliminate and/or Restrict Competition. Anti-monopoly law enforcement officials from the AIC who abuse their power, neglect their duties, receive bribes and cheat, or disclose business secrets obtained during their enforcement activities, shall be punished according to relevant rules and regulations.

第十一条	**Article 11**
本规定所称商品包括服务。	For the purpose of these Rules, products shall include services.
第十二条	**Article 12**
本规定由国家工商行政管理总局负责解释。	These Rules are subject to interpretation by the State Administration for Industry and Commerce.
第十三条	**Article 13**
本规定自2011年2月1日起施行。	These Rules shall become effective as of February 1, 2011.

NDRC
国家发展和改革委员会法规

B-24

Anti-Price Monopoly Rules
反价格垄断规定

(Promulgated by the National Development and
Reform Commission on December 29, 2010,
effective as of February 1, 2011)

（国家发展和改革委员会于2010年12月29日发布，
自2011年2月1日起施行）

第一条 为了预防和制止价格垄断行为，保护市场公平竞争，维护消费者利益和社会公共利益，根据《中华人民共和国反垄断法》（以下简称反垄断法），制定本规定。	**Article 1** These Rules are promulgated in accordance with the Anti-Monopoly Law of the People's Republic of China (hereinafter referred to as "AML") for the purpose of preventing and prohibiting price monopoly conduct, protecting fair market competition, and safeguarding consumer interests and the public interest.
第二条 中华人民共和国境内经济活动中的价格垄断行为，适用本规定；中华人民共和国境外的价格垄断行为，对境内市场竞争产生排除、限制影响的，适用本规定。	**Article 2** These Rules are applicable to price monopoly conduct in economic activities within the territory of the People's Republic of China. These Rules are also applicable to price monopoly conduct outside the territory of the People's Republic of China that has the effect of eliminating and/or restricting competition in the domestic market of the People's Republic of China.

第三条 本规定所称价格垄断行为包括: (一) 经营者达成价格垄断协议; (二) 具有市场支配地位的经营者使用价格手段,排除、限制竞争。 行政机关和法律、法规授权的具有管理公共事务职能的组织滥用行政权力,在价格方面排除、限制竞争的行为,适用本规定。	**Article 3** "Price monopoly conduct" is defined in these Rules as the following conduct: (1) price monopoly agreements between undertakings; (2) any use of price-related means by an undertaking with a dominant market position to eliminate and/or restrict competition. These Rules are also applicable to abuses of administrative power to eliminate and/or restrict price competition by administrative authorities and organizations designated by laws and regulations to manage public affairs.
第四条 国有经济占控制地位的关系国民经济命脉和国家安全的行业以及依法实行专营专卖的行业,国家对其经营者的合法经营活动予以保护,并对经营者的经营行为及其商品和服务的价格依法实施监管和调控,维护消费者利益,促进技术进步。 前款规定行业的经营者应当依法经营,诚实守信,严格自律,接受社会公众的监督,不得利用其控制地位或者专营专卖地位损害消费者利益。	**Article 4** In industries that have a vital bearing on the national economic and national security, which are controlled by state-owned enterprises, and in industries in which monopolies are granted by law, the State shall protect the lawful business activities of undertakings in these industries, supervise and control their conduct and prices for the products and services pursuant to law, protect the interests of consumers, and promote technological progress. The undertakings in the industries specified in the preceding paragraph shall conduct their business in accordance with the law, act in good faith, observe strict self-discipline, subject themselves to the supervision from the public, and shall not damage the interests of consumers by exploitation of their controlling or exclusive and monopoly positions.
第五条 本规定所称价格垄断协议,是指在价格方面排除、限制竞争的协议、决定或者其他协同行为。	**Article 5** "Price monopoly agreements" in these Rules refer to agreements, decisions, or other concerted conducts, which have the effect of eliminating and/or restricting competition with regard to price.

(Continued)

第六条 认定其他协同行为，应当依据下列因素： （一）　经营者的价格行为具有一致性； （二）　经营者进行过意思联络； 认定协同行为还应考虑市场结构和市场变化等情况。	**Article 6** A finding of other concerted conducts shall be based upon the following factors: (1)　uniformity between the pricing conduct of undertakings; (2)　there has been a communication of intentions between the undertakings. For finding of a concerted conduct, the market structure, market change, and other conditions shall also be taken into consideration.
第七条 禁止具有竞争关系的经营者达成下列价格垄断协议： （一）　固定或者变更商品和服务（以下统称商品）的价格水平； （二）　固定或者变更价格变动幅度； （三）　固定或者变更对价格有影响的手续费、折扣或者其他费用； （四）　使用约定的价格作为与第三方交易的基础； （五）　约定采用据以计算价格的标准公式； （六）　约定未经参加协议的其他经营者同意不得变更价格； （七）　通过其他方式变相固定或者变更价格； （八）　国务院价格主管部门认定的其他价格垄断协议。	**Article 7** The following price monopoly agreements among competing undertakings shall be prohibited: (1)　fixing or changing the price level of products and services (collectively "products"); (2)　fixing or changing the range of price change; (3)　fixing or changing fees, discounts, or other charges that affect prices; (4)　setting an agreed price as the basis for transacting with third parties; (5)　agreeing to adopt a formula for calculating price; (6)　agreeing not to change prices without the consent of other undertakings to the agreement; (7)　fixing or changing prices in a disguised form by other means; and/or (8)　other price monopoly agreements as determined by the Price Authority under the State Council.
第八条 禁止经营者与交易相对人达成下列价格垄断协议： （一）　固定向第三人转售商品的价格； （二）　限定向第三人转售商品的最低价格； （三）　国务院价格主管部门认定的其他价格垄断协议。	**Article 8** The following price monopoly agreements between undertakings and their trading counterparties shall be prohibited: (1)　fixing the resale price to a third party; (2)　restricting the minimum price for resale to a third party; and/or

	(3) other price monopoly agreements as determined by the Price Authority under the State Council.
第九条 禁止行业协会从事下列行为： （一）　制定排除、限制价格竞争的规则、决定、通知等； （二）　组织经营者达成本规定所禁止的价格垄断协议； （三）　组织经营者达成或者实施价格垄断协议的其他行为。	**Article 9** Trade associations shall be prohibited from engaging in the following conduct: (1) formulating any industry regulation, decision, or notice that eliminates or restricts price competition; (2) organizing undertakings to reach prohibited price monopoly agreements; (3) other conduct of such associations to organize undertakings to reach or implement price monopoly agreements.
第十条 经营者能够证明所达成的协议符合反垄断法第十五条规定的，不适用本规定第七条、第八条的规定。	**Article 10** If undertakings can prove that an agreement satisfies the conditions stipulated in Article 15 of the AML, Articles 7 and 8 of these Rules shall not apply.
第十一条 具有市场支配地位的经营者不得以不公平的高价销售商品或者以不公平的低价购买商品。 认定"不公平的高价"和"不公平的低价"，应当考虑下列因素： （一）　销售价格或者购买价格是否明显高于或者低于其他经营者销售或者购买同种商品的价格； （二）　在成本基本稳定的情况下，是否超过正常幅度提高销售价格或者降低购买价格； （三）　销售商品的提价幅度是否明显高于成本增长幅度，或者购买商品的降价幅度是否明显高于交易相对人成本降低幅度； （四）　需要考虑的其他相关因素。	**Article 11** Undertakings with a dominant market position shall be prohibited from selling products at unfairly high prices or buying products at unfairly low prices. Finding of "unfairly high prices" or "unfairly low prices" shall be based on the following factors: (1) whether the selling price is obviously higher, or the buying price is obviously lower than that charged or paid by other undertakings to sell or purchase the same type of products; (2) whether the selling price or the buying price is increased or decreased by a percentage above the normal level, where costs are basically stable; (3) whether the selling price of the product is increased with a

(Continued)

	percentage obviously larger than the increase of the cost or the buying price is decreased with a percentage obviously larger than the decrease of the cost of the trading counterparty; and/or (4) other relevant factors that need to be considered.
第十二条 具有市场支配地位的经营者没有正当理由，不得以低于成本的价格销售商品。 本条所称"正当理由"包括: （一） 降价处理鲜活商品、季节性商品、有效期限即将到期的商品和积压商品的; （二） 因清偿债务、转产、歇业降价销售商品的; （三） 为推广新产品进行促销的; （四） 能够证明行为具有正当性的其他理由。	**Article 12** Without valid justification, undertakings with a dominant market position shall be prohibited from selling products at prices below cost. Valid justifications include: (1) disposing of fresh and live products, seasonal products, products with a coming expiry date, or overstocked products, at a reduced price; (2) selling at a reduced price for the repayment of debts, change of business, or closing down; (3) sales promotions in order to disseminate new products; (4) other grounds that can justify the conduct.
第十三条 具有市场支配地位的经营者没有正当理由，不得通过设定过高的销售价格或者过低的购买价格，变相拒绝与交易相对人进行交易。 本条所称"正当理由"包括: （一） 交易相对人有严重的不良信用记录，或者出现经营状况持续恶化等情况，可能会给交易安全造成较大风险的; （二） 交易相对人能够以合理的价格向其他经营者购买同种商品、替代商品，或者能够以合理的价格向其他经营者出售商品的; （三） 能够证明行为具有正当性的其他理由。	**Article 13** Without valid justification, an undertaking with a dominant market position shall be prohibited from refusing to deal with a trading counterparty in a disguised form by setting excessively high selling prices or excessively low buying prices. Valid justifications include: (1) the trading counterparty has a seriously bad credit standing, or is beset with continually worsening operating conditions, which may pose significant risks for the transaction; (2) the trading counterparty could purchase the same type of products or substitute products from other undertakings at a reasonable

	price, or sell products to other undertakings at a reasonable price; (3) other grounds that can justify the conduct.
第十四条 具有市场支配地位的经营者没有正当理由，不得通过价格折扣等手段限定交易相对人只能与其进行交易或者只能与其指定的经营者进行交易。 本条所称"正当理由"包括： （一） 为了保证产品质量和安全的； （二） 为了维护品牌形象或者提高服务水平的； （三） 能够显著降低成本、提高效率，并且能够使消费者分享由此产生的利益的； （四） 能够证明行为具有正当性的其他理由。	**Article 14** Without valid justification, an undertaking with a dominant market position shall not restrict, by means of price discounts or otherwise, the trading counterparty to trade exclusively with it or another undertaking designated by it. Valid justifications include: (1) the conduct is undertaken for the purpose of guaranteeing product quality and safety; (2) the conduct is undertaken for the purpose of maintaining the image of the brand or to improve service; (3) the conduct could significantly lower costs or improve efficiency, the benefits of which could be shared by consumers; (4) other grounds that can justify the conduct.
第十五条 具有市场支配地位的经营者不得在交易时在价格之外附加不合理的费用。	**Article 15** An undertaking with a dominant market position shall not impose any additional unreasonable charges, in addition to the price, at the time of transaction.
第十六条 具有市场支配地位的经营者没有正当理由，不得对条件相同的交易相对人在交易价格上实行差别待遇。	**Article 16** Without valid justification, an undertaking with a dominant market position shall not make any price discrimination against trading counterparties under the same conditions.
第十七条 本规定所称市场支配地位，是指经营者在相关市场内具有能够控制商品价格、数量或者其他交易条件，或者能够阻碍、影响其他经营者进入相关市场能力的市场地位。	**Article 17** For the purpose of these Rules, "a dominant market position" refers to a market position enabling an undertaking to control the price, output, or other transaction conditions of a product in the relevant market, or to impede or prevent entry into the relevant market by other undertakings.

(Continued)

其他交易条件,是指除商品价格、数量之外能够对市场交易产生实质影响的其他因素,包括商品等级、付款条件、交付方式、售后服务、交易选择权和技术约束条件等。 阻碍、影响其他经营者进入相关市场,是指排除、延缓其他经营者进入相关市场,或者导致其他经营者虽能够进入该相关市场但进入成本大幅度提高,无法与现有经营者开展有效竞争等。	Other transaction conditions means elements other than price and output that may substantially affect market transactions, including product grade, payment conditions, delivery methods, and after-sale service of the product, transaction options, and technical constraints. Impeding or preventing entry into the relevant market by other undertakings means preventing or deferring other undertakings' entry into the relevant market, or significantly increasing the market entry costs, thus making it impossible for the new entrant to compete effectively with the incumbent undertakings though entry into the relevant market is possible.
第十八条 认定经营者具有市场支配地位,应当在界定相关市场的基础上,依据下列因素: (一) 该经营者在相关市场的市场份额,以及相关市场的竞争状况; (二) 该经营者控制销售市场或者原材料采购市场的能力; (三) 该经营者的财力和技术条件; (四) 其他经营者对该经营者在交易上的依赖程度; (五) 其他经营者进入相关市场的难易程度; (六) 与认定该经营者市场支配地位有关的其他因素。	**Article 18** Finding a dominant market position shall be based on the definition of the relevant market and take the following factors into consideration: (1) the market share of the undertaking and competitive conditions in the relevant market; (2) the ability of the undertaking to control the sales market or the raw material purchasing market; (3) the financial and technological capabilities of the undertaking; (4) the degree of reliance on the undertaking by other undertakings in transactions; (5) the difficulty for other undertakings to enter the relevant market; and (6) other factors relevant to the determination of the undertaking's dominant market position.
第十九条 有下列情形之一的,可以推定经营者具有市场支配地位: (一) 一个经营者在相关市场的市场份额达到二分之一的;	**Article 19** An undertaking can be presumed to have a dominant market position if any of the following conditions is fulfilled:

（二） 两个经营者在相关市场的市场份额合计达到三分之二的； （三） 三个经营者在相关市场的市场份额合计达到四分之三的。 有前款第二项、第三项规定的情形，其中有的经营者市场份额不足十分之一的，不应当推定该经营者具有市场支配地位。 被推定具有市场支配地位的经营者，有证据证明不具有市场支配地位的，不应当认定其具有市场支配地位。	(1) the market share of one undertaking accounts for half of the relevant market; (2) the combined market share of two undertakings accounts for two-thirds of the relevant market; or (3) the combined market share of three undertakings accounts for three-quarters of the relevant market. Among those undertakings that fall under item (2) or (3) of the preceding paragraph, an undertaking whose market share is less than 10% shall not be presumed to have a dominant market position. Where the undertaking presumed to have a dominant market position provides evidence of the absence of a dominant market position, such undertaking shall not be found to hold a dominant market position.
第二十条 行政机关和法律、法规授权的具有管理公共事务职能的组织不得滥用行政权力，实施下列行为，妨碍商品的自由流通： （一） 对外地商品设定歧视性收费项目； （二） 对外地商品实行歧视性收费标准； （三） 对外地商品规定歧视性价格； （四） 妨碍商品自由流通的其他规定价格或者收费的行为。	**Article 20** Administrative authorities and organizations designated by laws and regulations to manage public affairs shall not abuse their administrative powers to hamper the free movement of products by one of the following conduct: (1) setting discriminatory charges for non-local products; (2) setting discriminatory standards for charges against non-local products; (3) setting discriminatory prices for non-local products; or (4) other pricing or charging conduct that hampers the free movement of products.
第二十一条 行政机关和法律、法规授权的具有管理公共事务职能的组织不得滥用行政权力，强制经营者从事本规定禁止的各类价格垄断行为。	**Article 21** Administrative authorities and organizations designated by laws and regulations to manage public affairs shall not abuse their administrative

(*Continued*)

	powers to compel undertakings to engage in price monopoly conduct that is prohibited under these Rules.
第二十二条 行政机关不得滥用行政权力，制定含有排除、限制价格竞争内容的规定。	**Article 22** Administrative authorities shall not abuse their administrative power to promulgate regulations that eliminate and/or restrict price competition.
第二十三条 经营者有本规定所列价格垄断行为的，由国务院价格主管部门和经授权的省、自治区、直辖市人民政府价格主管部门依据反垄断法第四十六条、第四十七条和第四十九条的规定予以处罚。 行业协会违反本规定，组织本行业的经营者达成价格垄断协议的，依照反垄断法第四十六条和第四十九条的规定予以处罚。	**Article 23** The Price Authority under the State Council or authorized price authorities of a province, an autonomous region, or a provincial level municipality shall impose penalties according to Articles 46, 47, and 49 of the AML for price monopoly conduct prohibited by these Rules. Trade associations that organize undertakings in their industry to enter into price monopoly agreements shall be punished in accordance with Articles 46 and 49 of the AML.
第二十四条 行政机关和法律、法规授权的具有管理公共事务职能的组织有本规定所列滥用行政权力，实施排除、限制竞争行为的，依照反垄断法第五十一条的规定处理。	**Article 24** Administrative authorities and organizations designated by laws and regulations to manage public affairs who engage in conduct prohibited by these Rules by abusing their administrative power to eliminate and/or restrict competition shall be punished in accordance with Article 51 of the AML.
第二十五条 对政府价格主管部门依法实施的调查，拒绝提供有关材料、信息，或者提供虚假材料、信息，或者隐匿、销毁、转移证据，或者有其他拒绝、阻碍调查行为的，依照反垄断法第五十二条的规定予以处罚。	**Article 25** Any refusal to provide relevant information or material, or provision of false information or material, or concealment, destruction, or removal of evidence in connection with or any refusal or obstruction of the Price Authority's investigation shall be punished in accordance with Article 52 of the AML.

第二十六条 经营者依照有关知识产权的法律、行政法规规定行使知识产权的行为，不适用本规定；但是，经营者滥用知识产权，排除、限制竞争的价格垄断行为，适用本规定。	**Article 26** These Rules are not applicable to the conduct of undertakings that exercise their intellectual property rights in accordance with the intellectual property laws and relevant administrative regulations; however, these Rules are applicable to the conduct of undertakings that abuse their intellectual property rights, eliminating and/or restricting competition.
第二十七条 农业生产者及农村经济组织在农产品生产、加工、销售、运输、储存等经营活动中实施的联合或者协同行为，不适用本规定。	**Article 27** These Rules are not applicable to alliances or other concerted conduct by farmers and rural economic organizations in such operational activities as production, processing, sales, transportation, and storage of agricultural products.
第二十八条 本规定由国家发展和改革委员会负责解释。	**Article 28** These Rules are subject to interpretation by the National Development and Reform Commission.
第二十九条 本规定自2011年2月1日起施行。2003年6月18日国家发展和改革委员会发布的《制止价格垄断行为暂行规定》同时废止。	**Article 29** These Rules shall become effective as of February 1, 2011, and the Interim Rules for Prohibiting Price Monopolies issued by the National Development and Reform Commission on June 18, 2003 shall be rescinded simultaneously.

B-25

Procedural Rules on Administrative Enforcement against Price Monopoly

反价格垄断行政执法程序规定

(Promulgated by the National Development and Reform Commission on December 29, 2010, effective as of February 1, 2011)

（国家发展和改革委员会于2010年12月29日发布，自2011年2月1日起施行）

第一条 为规范和保障政府价格主管部门依法履行反价格垄断职责，保护公民、法人和其他组织的合法权益，根据《中华人民共和国反垄断法》（以下简称反垄断法），制定本规定。	**Article 1** These Rules are promulgated in accordance with the Anti-Monopoly Law of the People's Republic of China (hereinafter referred to as "AML") for the purpose of regulating and safeguarding the anti-price monopoly functions of the Price Authority of the government in accordance with the law and protecting the legitimate rights and interests of citizens, legal persons, and other organizations.
第二条 政府价格主管部门实施反价格垄断执法，适用本规定。	**Article 2** These Rules are applicable to anti-price monopoly law enforcement performed by the government's Price Authority.
第三条 国务院价格主管部门负责全国反价格垄断执法工作。 国务院价格主管部门授权的省、自治区、直辖市人民政府价格主管部门，负责本行政区域内的反价格垄断执法工作。	**Article 3** The Price Authority under the State Council shall be in charge of anti-price monopoly law enforcement throughout the country.

对跨省、自治区、直辖市发生的价格垄断案件，由国务院价格主管部门指定有关省、自治区、直辖市人民政府价格主管部门进行查处，重大案件由国务院价格主管部门直接组织查处。	The price authorities of a province, an autonomous region, or a provincial level municipality authorized by the Price Authority under the State Council shall be in charge of anti-price monopoly law enforcement within their respective administrative regions.
	Price monopoly cases involving several provinces, autonomous regions, or provincial level municipalities shall be investigated and handled by the Price Authority of the concerned province, autonomous region, and provincial level municipality which is designated by the Price Authority under the State Council, and major cases shall be investigated and handled directly by the Price Authority under the State Council.
第四条 对涉嫌价格垄断行为，国务院和省、自治区、 直辖市人民政府价格主管部门可以在其法定权限内委托下一级政府价格主管部门实施调查。 受委托的政府价格主管部门在委托范围内，以委托机关的名义实施调查，不得再委托其他行政机关、组织或者个人实施调查。	**Article 4** As for any suspected price monopoly conduct, the Price Authority under the State Council or the Price Authority of a province, an autonomous region, or a provincial level municipality may grant a delegation, within the scope of its legal authority, to a Price Authority at a lower level to carry out an investigation. The delegated Price Authority shall, within the scope of the delegated authority, carry out the investigation in the name of the delegating entity, and shall not grant a sub-delegation to any other administrative agency, organization, or individual to carry out the investigation.
第五条 对涉嫌价格垄断行为，任何单位和个人有权向政府价格主管部门举报。政府价格主管部门应当为举报人保密。 举报采用书面形式并提供相关事实和证据的，政府价格主管部门应当进行必要的调查。调查事项包括：	**Article 5** Any entity or individual may report any suspected monopoly conduct to the Price Authority, and the Price Authority shall maintain the confidentiality of the informer. Where any report is in writing and contains relevant facts and evidence, the

(*Continued*)

（一） 举报人是否就同一事项已向其他行政机关举报或者向人民法院提起诉讼； （二） 被举报人的基本情况； （三） 举报人提供的相关事实和证据； （四） 需要调查的其他事项。	Price Authority shall conduct the necessary investigation. Matters to be investigated include: (1) whether the informer has reported the same matter to other administrative agencies or has brought an action before the People's court; (2) basic information about the suspected infringer; (3) relevant facts and evidence provided by the informer; and (4) other matters that need to be investigated.
第六条 政府价格主管部门调查涉嫌价格垄断行为，可以采取下列措施： （一） 进入被调查的经营者的营业场所或者其他有关场所进行检查； （二） 询问被调查的经营者、利害关系人或者其他有关单位或者个人（以下统称被调查人），要求其说明有关情况； （三） 查阅、复制被调查人的有关单证、协议、会计账簿、业务函电、电子数据等文件、资料； （四） 查封、扣押相关证据； （五） 查询经营者的银行账户。 采取前款规定的措施，应当向政府价格主管部门主要负责人书面报告，并经批准。	**Article 6** When conducting investigations on a suspected price monopoly conduct, the Price Authority may take the following measures: (1) conduct inspections of business premises or other relevant places of the investigated undertakings; (2) inquire the investigated undertakings, interested parties, and other relevant entities or individuals (the "Investigated Person") and request them to provide relevant information; (3) inspect or copy the relevant documents and information including related certificates, agreements, accounting books, business correspondence, electronic data, etc of the Persons under Investigation; (4) seal up or detain relevant evidence; and/or (5) inspect the bank account of the undertakings. Before taking the measures as specified in the preceding paragraph, the enforcing official shall report in writing to the principal of the Price Authority and obtain approval.

第七条 执法人员询问被调查人，可以采取面谈、电话或者书面等方式。 面谈或者电话询问的，应当制作调查询问笔录。调查询问笔录应当交被询问人核对后，由被询问人签字；对没有阅读能力的，应当向其宣读。 书面询问的，应当向被调查人送达调查问卷或者调查提纲，载明调查事项。 被询问人应当按照价格主管部门的要求，说明有关情况。	**Article 7** Law enforcement officials may inquire the Investigated Person through interview, telephone, or in writing. When making the inquiries through interview or telephone, an inquiry record shall be made. The inquiry record shall be signed by the inquired person after verification by that person; in case of illiterates, the record shall be read out to the inquired person. When making the inquiry in writing, the investigation questionnaire or investigation outline shall be served to the Investigated Person, stating the investigated matters. The inquired person shall provide relevant information according to the requirement of the Price Authority.
第八条 政府价格主管部门调查涉嫌价格垄断行为，执法人员不得少于二人，并应当出示中华人民共和国价格行政执法证件。	**Article 8** At least two law enforcement officials from the Price Authority shall participate in any investigation of suspected price monopoly conduct, and they shall present valid documents showing their authority ID of administrative enforcement to carry out the investigation.
第九条 政府价格主管部门及其工作人员对执法过程中知悉的商业秘密负有保密义务。	**Article 9** The Price Authority and its employees shall keep confidential the business secrets obtained during the enforcement of the law.
第十条 被调查人应当配合政府价格主管部门依法履行职责，不得拒绝、阻碍政府价格主管部门的调查。	**Article 10** The Investigated Person shall cooperate with the Price Authority in the Authority's performance of their functions according to law, and shall not refuse or hinder the investigation of the Price Authority.
第十一条 被调查的经营者、利害关系人有权陈述意见。 政府价格主管部门应当对被调查的经营者、	**Article 11** The investigated undertakings and the interested parties shall have the right to state their opinions.

(*Continued*)

利害关系人提出的事实、理由和证据进行核实。	The Price Authority shall verify the facts, reasons, and evidence produced by the investigated undertakings and interested parties.
第十二条 政府价格主管部门对涉嫌价格垄断行为调查核实后，认为构成价格垄断行为的，应当依法作出处理决定，并可以向社会公布。	**Article 12** Where the Price Authority after investigating and verifying the suspected price monopoly conduct determines that the conduct constitutes a price monopoly conduct, it shall make a decision in accordance with the law, and may publish the decision.
第十三条 经营者认为其所达成的协议属于反垄断法第十五条规定的情形的，应当提供有关证据材料，由政府价格主管部门审查核实。	**Article 13** Where the undertakings believe that the agreement reached falls under the conditions specified in Article 15 of the AML, they shall provide relevant evidence and information for review and verification by the Price Authority.
第十四条 经营者主动向政府价格主管部门报告达成价格垄断协议的有关情况并提供重要证据的，政府价格主管部门可以酌情减轻或者免除对该经营者的处罚。 第一个主动报告达成价格垄断协议的有关情况并提供重要证据的，可以免除处罚；第二个主动报告达成价格垄断协议的有关情况并提供重要证据的，可以按照不低于50%的幅度减轻处罚；其他主动报告达成价格垄断协议的有关情况并提供重要证据的，可以按照不高于50%的幅度减轻处罚。 重要证据是指对政府价格主管部门认定价格垄断协议具有关键作用的证据。	**Article 14** Where an undertaking voluntarily reports to the Price Authority about the circumstances of the price monopoly agreement reached and provides material evidence, the Price Authority may discretionally reduce or exempt the penalty for that undertaking. The first undertaking which voluntarily reports about the circumstances of a price monopoly agreement and provides material evidence may be exempted from penalty; the second undertaking which voluntarily reports about the circumstances of a price monopoly agreement and provides material evidence may be granted at least a 50% reduction of penalty; other undertakings which voluntarily report about the circumstances of a price monopoly agreement and provide material evidence may be granted at most a 50% reduction of penalty. Material evidence refers to the evidence which will play a critical role for the Price Authority to find the existence of a price monopoly agreement.

第十五条 涉嫌价格垄断行为的经营者在被调查期间，可以提出中止调查的申请。 中止调查申请应当以书面形式提出，并载明下列事项： （一）　涉嫌垄断的事实； （二）　承诺采取消除行为后果的具体措施； （三）　履行承诺的时限； （四）　需要承诺的其他内容。	**Article 15** When undertakings are under investigation for suspected price monopoly conduct, they may apply for a suspension of the investigation. Application for suspension of the investigation shall be submitted in writing, with details of the following: (1)　facts concerning the suspected monopoly conduct; (2)　commitments to take concrete measures to eliminate the consequences of the suspected monopoly conduct; (3)　time limit of implementing the commitments; (4)　other issues that need to be committed.
第十六条 被调查的经营者承诺在政府价格主管部门认可的期限内采取具体措施消除行为后果的，政府价格主管部门可以决定中止调查，并制作中止调查决定书。 中止调查决定书应当载明被调查的经营者涉嫌违法的事实、承诺的具体内容、消除影响的措施和期限、不履行或者不完全履行承诺的法律后果等。	**Article 16** Where the investigated undertakings commit to take concrete measures to eliminate the consequences of their acts within the time limit approved by the Price Authority, the Price Authority may decide to suspend the investigation, and make a written decision to suspend the investigation. The decision to suspend the investigation shall set forth the facts concerning the suspected violations by the investigated undertakings, details about their commitment, measures, and time limit to eliminate the consequences, legal consequences if they fail to fulfill such commitments in whole or part, etc.
第十七条 决定中止调查的，政府价格主管部门应当对经营者履行承诺的情况进行监督。 经营者应当按照政府价格主管部门的要求，书面报告承诺履行情况。	**Article 17** Where suspension of the investigation is decided, the Price Authority shall supervise the implementation of the commitments by the undertakings. The undertakings shall report in writing to the Price Authority, as so required, the progress of implementing the commitments.

(Continued)

第十八条	**Article 18**
经营者履行承诺的，政府价格主管部门可以决定终止调查。	Where the undertakings have fulfilled their commitments, the Price Authority may decide to terminate the investigation.
有下列情形之一的，应当恢复调查： （一） 经营者在规定的时限内未履行承诺或者未完全履行承诺的； （二） 作出中止调查决定所依据的事实发生重大变化的； （三） 中止调查的决定是基于经营者提供的不完整或者不真实的信息作出的。	In the following circumstances, the investigation shall be resumed: (1) the undertakings fail to fulfill in whole or part the commitments within a specified time limit; (2) the facts upon which the decision to suspend depends the investigation have undergone substantial changes; (3) the decision to suspend the investigation was made on the basis of incomplete or untrue information provided by the undertakings.
第十九条	**Article 19**
行政机关和法律、法规授权的具有管理公共事务职能的组织滥用行政权力，实施排除、限制竞争行为的，政府价格主管部门可以向有关上级机关提出依法处理的建议： （一） 停止强制经营者从事价格垄断行为； （二） 废止含有排除、限制价格竞争内容的规定； （三） 对直接负责的主管人员和其他直接责任人员依法给予处分； （四） 纠正滥用行政权力行为的其他处理建议。	If administrative agencies and organizations designated by laws and regulations to manage public affairs abuse their administrative power to eliminate and/or restrict competition, the Price Authority may make a proposal to the relevant superior authority on the handling of the matter in accordance with the law: (1) to stop compelling undertakings to engage in price monopoly conduct; (2) to repeal a regulation that contains provisions eliminating and/or restricting price competition; (3) to discipline the persons in charge and the individuals who are directly responsible; (4) other proposals to rectify the abuse of administrative power.
法律、行政法规对行政机关和法律、法规授权的具有管理公共事务职能的组织滥用行政权力实施排除、限制竞争行为的处理另有规定的，依照其规定。	Where other laws or administrative regulations provide for the handling of abuses of administrative power by administrative agencies and organizations designated by laws and regulations to manage public affairs, those provisions shall govern.

第二十条 被调查人向政府价格主管部门提交书面说明、申请等资料的，应当由法定代表人、其他组织负责人或者个人签字并盖章。	**Article 20** Where the investigated person intends to submit an explanation or an application in writing to the Price Authority, such materials shall be signed by the legal representative or principal of the entity or the person and affixed with its seal.
第二十一条 经营者对政府价格主管部门作出的决定不服的，可以依法申请行政复议或者提起行政诉讼。	**Article 21** Where undertakings are dissatisfied with the decisions made by the Price Authority, they may apply for administrative review or file an administrative lawsuit in accordance with the law.
第二十二条 省、自治区、直辖市人民政府价格主管部门查处的案件，应当在作出处理决定后10个工作日内，将有关情况、案件调查终结报告及中止调查决定书、终止调查决定书、行政处罚决定书等报送国务院价格主管部门备案。 受委托的政府价格主管部门，应当在调查终结后5个工作日内，将有关情况、案件调查终结报告等报送委托机关。	**Article 22** Where the Price Authority of a province, an autonomous region, or a provincial level municipality investigates and handles a case, such Price Authority shall, within ten business days of making a decision on the case, file for record to the Price Authority of the State Council, the relevant information, final report on the investigation, decision to suspend the investigation, decision to terminate the investigation, and decision to impose administrative penalty. The Price Authority delegated to handle the case shall, within five business days of finalizing the investigation, submit the relevant information and the final report on investigation to the entrusting agency.
第二十三条 政府价格主管部门工作人员滥用职权、玩忽职守、徇私舞弊或者泄露执法过程中知悉的商业秘密，构成犯罪的，依法追究刑事责任；尚不构成犯罪的，依法给予处分。	**Article 23** Where the employees from the Price Authority abuse their power, neglect their duties, receive bribes and cheat, or disclose business secrets obtained during their enforcement activities, which constitutes a crime, criminal liability shall be pursued according to the law; if their conduct does not constitute a crime, administrative penalties shall be given in accordance with the law.

(Continued)

第二十四条 本规定对价格垄断行为调查程序和行政处罚程序未作规定的，依照《中华人民共和国行政处罚法》执行。	**Article 24** Issues relating to investigation procedures of price monopoly and procedures for administrative penalties not covered in these Rules herein shall be handled in accordance with the Law of the People's Republic of China on Administrative Penalties.
第二十五条 本规定由国家发展和改革委员会负责解释。	**Article 25** The provisions of these Rules shall be interpreted by the National Development and Reform Commission.
第二十六条 本规定自2011年2月1日起施行。	**Article 26** These Rules shall become effective as of February 1, 2011.

PART
C

JUDICIAL INTERPRETATIONS
司法解释

C-1

Rules by the Supreme People's Court on Certain Issues Relating to Application of Laws for Adjudicating Cases of Civil Disputes Caused by Monopoly Conduct

最高人民法院关于审理因垄断行为引发的民事纠纷案件应用法律若干问题的规定

(Promulgated by the Supreme People's Court on May 3, 2012, effective as of June 1, 2012)

（最高人民法院于2012年5月3日发布，自2012年6月1日起施行）

为正确审理因垄断行为引发的民事纠纷案件，制止垄断行为，保护和促进市场公平竞争，维护消费者利益和社会公共利益，根据《中华人民共和国反垄断法》、《中华人民共和国侵权责任法》、《中华人民共和国合同法》和《中华人民共和国民事诉讼法》等法律的相关规定，制定本规定。	In order to adjudicate correctly cases of civil monopoly disputes, to prevent monopoly conduct, to protect and promote fair market competition, and to safeguard the consumer interests and public interest, the Supreme People's Court has formulated these Rules in accordance with the Anti-Monopoly Law of the People's Republic of China, the Tort Liability Law of the People's Republic of China, the Contract Law of the People's Republic of China, and the Civil Procedure Law of the People's Republic of China, as well as other relevant laws and regulations.

(Continued)

第一条 本规定所称因垄断行为引发的民事纠纷案件（以下简称垄断民事纠纷案件），是指因垄断行为受到损失以及因合同内容、行业协会的章程等违反反垄断法而发生争议的自然人、法人或者其他组织，向人民法院提起的民事诉讼案件。	**Article 1** The cases of civil disputes caused by monopoly conduct ("civil monopoly disputes") in these Rules refer to those civil actions lodged with People's courts by natural persons, legal persons, or other organizations arising out of damages caused by monopoly conduct, and disputes over contractual terms and conditions, or articles of trade associations in violation of the Anti-Monopoly Law.
第二条 原告直接向人民法院提起民事诉讼，或者在反垄断执法机构认定构成垄断行为的处理决定发生法律效力后向人民法院提起民事诉讼，并符合法律规定的其他受理条件的，人民法院应当受理。	**Article 2** The People's court shall accept the case if the plaintiff directly files a civil lawsuit, or files the lawsuit after the decision convicting the monopoly conduct by the anti-monopoly enforcement authority comes into effect, and satisfies other requirement of acceptance in accordance with laws.
第三条 第一审垄断民事纠纷案件，由省、自治区、直辖市人民政府所在地的市、计划单列市中级人民法院以及最高人民法院指定的中级人民法院管辖。 经最高人民法院批准，基层人民法院可以管辖第一审垄断民事纠纷案件。	**Article 3** The first instance court for civil monopoly disputes shall be the intermediate People's courts of cities where the capital of a province, autonomous region, provincial level municipality, or specifically designated city in the state plan is located, or at other intermediate People's courts designated by the Supreme People's Court ("SPC"). When authorized by the SPC, the lower-level People's courts may hear in first instance civil monopoly disputes.
第四条 垄断民事纠纷案件的地域管辖，根据案件具体情况，依照民事诉讼法及相关司法解释有关侵权纠纷、合同纠纷等的管辖规定确定。	**Article 4** With respect to the territorial jurisdiction of civil monopoly disputes, it shall be determined on the specific circumstances of the case pursuant to the relevant provisions of the Civil Procedure Law and relevant judicial interpretations related to cases of tort or contract disputes.

第五条	**Article 5**
民事纠纷案件立案时的案由并非垄断纠纷，被告以原告实施了垄断行为为由提出抗辩或者反诉且有证据支持，或者案件需要依据反垄断法作出裁判，但受诉人民法院没有垄断民事纠纷案件管辖权的，应当将案件移送有管辖权的人民法院。	Where the cause of action for a case of civil dispute was not a monopoly dispute when the case was filed, but if there is evidence supporting the defendant's defense or counter-claim that the plaintiff engaged in monopoly conduct or that the case must be adjudicated under the Anti-Monopoly Law, the court accepting the case shall transfer it to the People's court having jurisdiction, if the court accepting the case has no jurisdiction over monopoly disputes cases.
第六条	**Article 6**
两个或者两个以上原告因同一垄断行为向有管辖权的同一法院分别提起诉讼的，人民法院可以合并审理。 两个或者两个以上原告因同一垄断行为向有管辖权的不同法院分别提起诉讼的，后立案的法院在得知有关法院先立案的情况后，应当在七日内裁定将案件移送先立案的法院；受移送的法院可以合并审理。被告应当在答辩阶段主动向受诉人民法院提供其因同一行为在其他法院涉诉的相关信息。	Where two, or more than two, plaintiffs have respectively filed lawsuits against the same defendant for the same monopoly conduct with the same court having jurisdiction, the People's court may combine such cases together for hearing. Where two, or more than two, plaintiffs have respectively filed lawsuits against the same defendant for the same monopoly conduct with different courts having jurisdiction, the court which accepts the case at a later time shall, upon learning of information about earlier acceptance of the case, rule within seven days that the case be transferred to the court having accepted the case earlier, which can decide whether to combine cases for hearing at its discretion. The defendant shall voluntarily provide relevant information to the court on related lawsuits arising out of the same conduct in another People's court during the defense stage.
第七条	**Article 7**
被诉垄断行为属于反垄断法第十三条第一款第（一）项至第（五）项规定的垄断协议的，被告应对该协议不具有排除、限制竞争的效果承担举证责任。	If the alleged monopoly conduct constitutes a monopoly agreement falling under items 1 to 5 of Article 13(1) of the Anti-Monopoly Law, the defendant shall bear the burden to prove that the alleged agreement does not have the effect of eliminating and/or restricting competition.

(Continued)

第八条 被诉垄断行为属于反垄断法第十七条第一款规定的滥用市场支配地位的，原告应当对被告在相关市场内具有支配地位和其滥用市场支配地位承担举证责任。 被告以其行为具有正当性为由进行抗辩的，应当承担举证责任。	**Article 8** If the alleged monopoly conduct constitutes an abuse of dominant market position falling under item 1 of Article 17 of the Anti-Monopoly Law, the plaintiff shall bear the burden to prove the defendant's dominant position in the relevant market and the abuse of such dominant market position. The defendant shall bear the burden of proving the existence of valid justification if it is raised as a defense.
第九条 被诉垄断行为属于公用企业或者其他依法具有独占地位的经营者滥用市场支配地位的，人民法院可以根据市场结构和竞争状况的具体情况，认定被告在相关市场内具有支配地位，但有相反证据足以推翻的除外。	**Article 9** If the alleged monopoly conduct is executed by public utility enterprises or other enterprises enjoying lawful monopoly position by way of abuses of dominant market position, the People's court may determine the defendant's dominant position in the relevant market based on market structure and competitive conditions unless such party can provide sufficient contrary evidence to prove otherwise.
第十条 原告可以以被告对外发布的信息作为证明其具有市场支配地位的证据。被告对外发布的信息能够证明其在相关市场内具有支配地位的，人民法院可以据此作出认定，但有相反证据足以推翻的除外。	**Article 10** The plaintiff can use information published by the defendant as evidence to prove the defendant's dominant market position. If such information supports a finding of a dominant position in the relevant market, the People's court may rule as such unless sufficient contrary evidence proves otherwise.
第十一条 证据涉及国家秘密、商业秘密、个人隐私或者其他依法应当保密的内容的，人民法院可以依职权或者当事人的申请采取不公开开庭、限制或者禁止复制、仅对代理律师展示、责令签署保密承诺书等保护措施。	**Article 11** Any evidence involving state secrets, business secrets, personal privacy, or other contents that shall be kept confidential in accordance with the law, the People's court may at its discretion or in response to a party's application decide to take protective measures such as a nonpublic trial, restricting or prohibiting photocopying, only exhibiting to authorized attorneys, or ordering a confidentiality covenant, etc.

第十二条 当事人可以向人民法院申请一至二名具有相应专门知识的人员出庭，就案件的专门性问题进行说明。	**Article 12** A party may apply to the People's court to have one or two professionals with relevant knowledge to explain specific questions of the case in court.
第十三条 当事人可以向人民法院申请委托专业机构或者专业人员就案件的专门性问题作出市场调查或者经济分析报告。经人民法院同意，双方当事人可以协商确定专业机构或者专业人员；协商不成的，由人民法院指定。 人民法院可以参照民事诉讼法及相关司法解释有关鉴定结论的规定，对前款规定的市场调查或者经济分析报告进行审查判断。	**Article 13** A party may apply to the People's court to entrust professional institutions or individuals to conduct market surveys or economic analysis on specific questions of a case. Upon approval by the People's court, both parties may negotiate to choose such professional institutions or individuals. If they fail to agree, the People's court may appoint such professional institutions or individuals as appropriate. The People's court may review and make its judgments of the above market survey results or economic analysis reports with reference to relevant provisions of appraisal conclusion in the Civil Procedure Law and relevant judicial interpretations.
第十四条 被告实施垄断行为，给原告造成损失的，根据原告的诉讼请求和查明的事实，人民法院可以依法判令被告承担停止侵害、赔偿损失等民事责任。 根据原告的请求，人民法院可以将原告因调查、制止垄断行为所支付的合理开支计入损失赔偿范围。	**Article 14** Where a defendant engages in monopoly conduct and causes loss to the plaintiff, the People's court may decide and order the defendant to bear civil liability such as ceasing infringement and compensating damages based on the plaintiff's claims and facts found in accordance with the law. Upon requests from the plaintiff, the People's court may incorporate the plaintiff's reasonable costs for investigation and prevention of the monopoly conduct into the amount of damages.
第十五条 被诉合同内容、行业协会的章程等违反反垄断法或者其他法律、行政法规的强制性规定的，人民法院应当依法认定其无效。	**Article 15** Where the alleged contractual terms and conditions, or articles of trade associations violate mandatory rules of the Anti-Monopoly Law or other laws and regulations, the People's court shall determine such provisions to be invalid.

(Continued)

第十六条	**Article 16**
因垄断行为产生的损害赔偿请求权诉讼时效期间，从原告知道或者应当知道权益受侵害之日起计算。	The statute of limitations for claiming damages against monopoly conduct is calculated from the date the plaintiff knew or should have known the infringement by the monopoly conduct.
原告向反垄断执法机构举报被诉垄断行为的，诉讼时效从其举报之日起中断。反垄断执法机构决定不立案、撤销案件或者决定终止调查的，诉讼时效期间从原告知道或者应当知道不立案、撤销案件或者终止调查之日起重新计算。反垄断执法机构调查后认定构成垄断行为的，诉讼时效期间从原告知道或者应当知道反垄断执法机构认定构成垄断行为的处理决定发生法律效力之日起重新计算。	Where the plaintiff reports potential monopoly conduct to the anti-monopoly enforcement authority, the statute of limitations shall be suspended from the date of said report. Where the anti-monopoly enforcement authority decides not to accept the case, to revoke the case, or decides to terminate the investigation, the statute of limitations shall restart from the date where the plaintiff knows or should have known the date of decision of non-acceptance, revocation, or termination of investigation. Where the anti-monopoly enforcement authority makes a finding of monopoly conduct after investigation, the statute of limitations shall be calculated from the date the plaintiff knew or should have known the effective date of the decision by the anti-monopoly enforcement authority.
原告起诉时被诉垄断行为已经持续超过二年，被告提出诉讼时效抗辩的，损害赔偿应当自原告向人民法院起诉之日起向前推算二年计算。	Where the alleged monopoly conduct has continued over two years when the plaintiff files the lawsuit and the defendant raises the defense of the expiry of the two-year statute of limitations, the amount of compensation for damages shall be calculated from the preceding two years before the date when the plaintiff first filed its lawsuit before the People's court.

PART
D

ADMINISTRATIVE DECISIONS
审查决定

MOFCOM

商务部审查决定

D-1

MOFCOM Announcement [2008] No. 95 Regarding the Conditional Approval of InBev's Acquisition of Anheuser-Busch

中华人民共和国商务部公告［2008］第95号
（商务部关于附条件批准英博集团公司收购AB公司
反垄断审查决定的公告）

(Published on November 18, 2008)

（2008年11月18日公布）

中华人民共和商务部收到英博集团公司(INBEV N.V./S.A.)收购AB公司(ANHEUSER-BUSCH COMPANIES INC.)的反垄断申报材料，经审查，决定如下：	The Ministry of Commerce of the People's Republic of China ("MOFCOM") has received an anti-monopoly notification regarding the acquisition of Anheuser-Busch Companies Inc. ("Anheuser-Busch") by InBev N.V./S.A. ("InBev"). After review, MOFCOM hereby decides as follows:
一、审查程序。 2008年9月10日，英博公司向商务部递交了申报材料。10月17日和10月23日，英博公司对申报材料进行了补充。10月27日，商务部对此项申报进行立案审查，并发出了立案通知。	**1 Review Process.** InBev submitted the anti-monopoly notification to MOFCOM on September 10, 2008, and supplemented with additional information and material respectively on October 17 and October 23, 2008. On October 27, 2008, MOFCOM accepted the notification for review and issued a notice for acceptance of the case.

(Continued)

二、审查决定。 立案后，商务部对申报材料进行了审查，并征求了政府有关部门的意见，听取了相关啤酒行业协会、国内主要啤酒生产企业、啤酒原料生产企业以及啤酒产品销售商的意见，根据反垄断法第28条的规定，决定对此项并购不予禁止。	**2 Review Decision.** Upon acceptance of the case, MOFCOM reviewed the notification documents and solicited comments from relevant governmental departments, and heard opinions from relevant beer trade associations, major domestic beer breweries, beer raw materials suppliers, and beer distributors. MOFCOM hereby decides not to prohibit the transaction in accordance with Article 28 of the Anti-Monopoly Law of the People's Republic of China.
三、附加的限制性条件。 鉴于此项并购规模巨大，合并后新企业市场份额较大，竞争实力明显增强，为了减少可能对中国啤酒未来市场竞争产生的不利影响，商务部对审查决定附加限制性条件，要求英博公司履行如下义务： 1、 不得增加AB公司在青岛啤酒股份有限公司现有27%的持股比例； 2、 如果英博公司的控股股东或控股股东的股东发生变化，必须及时通报商务部； 3、 不得增加英博公司在珠江啤酒股份有限公司现有28.56%的持股比例； 4、 不得寻求持有华润雪花啤酒（中国）有限公司和北京燕京啤酒有限公司的股份； 如果违反上述任何一项承诺，英博公司必须事先向商务部及时进行申报，商务部批准前，不得实施。	**3 Restrictive Conditions.** In view of the large scale of the contemplated acquisition, the relatively large market share of the new merged undertakings after the transaction, and the visibly enhanced competitive strength of the merged undertakings, MOFCOM imposes restrictive conditions to the transaction in order to mitigate any possible adverse effect over future competition in the Chinese beer market, and InBev is required to abide by and fulfill the following obligations. InBev shall: (1) not increase Anheuser-Busch's existing 27% share in Tsingtao Brewery Co., Ltd.; (2) report to MOFCOM any change in its controlling shareholders or the shareholders of the controlling shareholders; (3) not increase InBev's existing 28.56% share in the Zhujiang Brewery Co., Ltd.; (4) not seek to acquire stakes in China Resources Snow Brewery (China) Co., Ltd. or Beijing Yanjing Brewery Co., Ltd. InBev is required to report to MOFCOM in advance for approval of any action in violation of any of the above commitments, and no such actions shall be taken pending approval by MOFCOM.

本决定自公告之日起生效。 　　　　中华人民共和国商务部 　　　二〇〇八年十一月十八日	This decision shall become effective as of the date of its announcement. Ministry of Commerce November 18, 2008

D-2

MOFCOM Announcement [2009] No. 22 (MOFCOM Announcement Regarding the Prohibition of Coca-Cola's Acquisition of Huiyuan)

中华人民共和国商务部公告［2009年］第22号 （商务部关于禁止可口可乐公司收购中国汇源公司审查决定的公告）

(Published on March 18, 2009)

（2009年3月18日公布）

中华人民共和国商务部收到美国可口可乐公司(简称可口可乐)与中国汇源果汁集团有限公司(简称中国汇源公司)的经营者集中反垄断申报，根据《反垄断法》第三十条，现公告如下：	The Ministry of Commerce of the People's Republic of China ("MOFCOM") has received an anti-monopoly notification regarding a concentration of undertakings between the Coca-Cola Company ("Coca-Cola") and China Huiyuan Juice Group Limited ("Huiyuan"), and this announcement is made as follows in accordance with Article 30 of the Anti-Monopoly Law.
一、立案和审查过程。 2008年9月18日，可口可乐公司向商务部递交了申报材料。9月25日、10月9日、10月16日和11月19日，可口可乐公司根据商务部要求对申报材料进行了补充。11月20日，商务部认为可口可乐公司提交的申报材料达到了《反垄断法》第二十三条规定的标准，对此项申报进行立案审查，并通知了可口可乐公司。	**1. Acceptance and Review Process** Coca-Cola submitted its notification documents to MOFCOM on September 18, 2008, while additional and supplementary materials were submitted by Coca-Cola respectively on September 25, October 9, October 16, and November 19, 2008 in response to requests from MOFCOM. MOFCOM held subsequently on November 20, 2008, that the notification documents

由于此项集中规模较大、影响复杂，2008年12月20日，初步阶段审查工作结束后，商务部决定实施进一步审查，书面通知了可口可乐公司。在进一步审查过程中，商务部对集中造成的各种影响进行了评估，并于2009年3月20日前完成了审查工作。	submitted by Coca-Cola, as supplemented, met the requirements of Article 23 of the Anti-Monopoly Law, and the filing was accepted for review. Coca-Cola was informed accordingly. In view of the size of the transaction with complex effects and impact, MOFCOM decided on December 20, 2008, after the completion of its preliminary review, to proceed with a further review, and informed Coca-Cola of this decision in writing. During its further review, MOFCOM assessed the various effects of this concentration, and the review was completed before March 20, 2009.
二、审查内容。 根据《反垄断法》第二十七条，商务部从如下几个方面对此项经营者集中进行了全面审查： （一）　参与集中的经营者在相关市场的市场份额及其对市场的控制力； （二）　相关市场的市场集中度； （三）　经营者集中对市场进入、技术进步的影响； 四）　经营者集中对消费者和其他有关经营者的影响； （五）　经营者集中对国民经济发展的影响； （六）　汇源品牌对果汁饮料市场竞争产生的影响。	**2. Issues Reviewed** MOFCOM conducted a thorough review of the concentration in accordance with Article 27 of the Anti-Monopoly Law, which included: (1)　the market shares of the undertakings concerned by the concentration in the relevant market and their ability to control the market; (2)　the level of concentration in the relevant market; (3)　the effect of the concentration on the market entry and the progress of technologies; (4)　the effect of the concentration on consumers and other undertakings; (5)　the effect of the concentration on the development of the national economy; and (6)　the effect of the Huiyuan brand on the competition in the juice beverage market.
三、审查工作。 立案后，商务部对此项申报依法进行了审查，对申报材料进行了认真核实，对此项申报涉及的重要问题进行了深入分析，并通过书面征求意见、论证会、座谈会、听证会、实地调查、委托调查以及约谈当事人等方式，	**3. Review Process** Upon acceptance of the notification, MOFCOM duly reviewed and carefully verified the notification documents, and made an in-depth analysis of the important issues raised by the concentration. By way of written solicitation of opinions, validation meetings, workshops, hearings,

(*Continued*)

先后征求了相关政府部门、相关行业协会、果汁饮料企业、上游果汁浓缩汁供应商、下游果汁饮料销售商、集中交易双方、可口可乐公司中方合作伙伴以及相关法律、经济和农业专家等方面意见。

on-site visits, third party investigation, meeting with the parties, and through other means, MOFCOM also solicited comments and opinions from relevant governmental authorities, relevant trade associations, undertakings in the juice beverage industry, upstream suppliers of concentrate juice, downstream sellers of juice beverages, the parties to the concentration, the Chinese partners of Coca-Cola, as well as relevant legal experts, economic experts, and agricultural experts.

四、竞争问题。

审查工作结束后，商务部依法对此项集中进行了全面评估，确认集中将产生如下不利影响：

1、 集中完成后，可口可乐公司有能力将其在碳酸软饮料市场上的支配地位传导到果汁饮料市场，对现有果汁饮料企业产生排除、限制竞争效果，进而损害饮料消费者的合法权益。

2、 品牌是影响饮料市场有效竞争的关键因素，集中完成后，可口可乐公司通过控制"美汁源"和"汇源"两个知名果汁品牌，对果汁市场控制力将明显增强，加之其在碳酸饮料市场已有的支配地位以及相应的传导效应，集中将使潜在竞争对手进入果汁饮料市场的障碍明显提高。

3、 集中挤压了国内中小型果汁企业生存空间，抑制了国内企业在果汁饮料市场参与竞争和自主创新的能力，给中国果汁饮料市场有效竞争格局造成不良影响，不利于中国果汁行业的持续健康发展。

4. Competition Concerns

Upon completion of the review, MOFCOM made a thorough assessment of the concentration in accordance with the law, and determined that the concentration would have the following adverse effects:

(1) upon completion of the concentration, Coca-Cola would be able to leverage its dominance in the carbonated soft drinks market to the juice beverage market, which would eliminate and/or restrict competition by existing juice beverage companies, which, in turn, would damage the lawful interests of beverage consumers;

(2) brand is a key factor affecting effective competition in the beverage market. Two well-known juice brands "Minute Maid" and "Huiyuan" would become controlled by Coca-Cola upon completion of the concentration, and Coca-Cola's control over the juice beverage market would be therefore significantly strengthened, coupled with Coca-Cola's dominance in the carbonated drinks market and the associated leverage effect, the concentration would obviously raise the barriers for any potential competitor to enter the juice beverage market;

	(3) the concentration would squeeze out small and medium-sized juice producers in China, and limit local producers' ability to compete in the juice beverage market and to engage in proprietary innovation, which would have an adverse effect over effective competition in the Chinese juice beverage market, and would prove adverse to the sustained and sound development of the juice beverage market in China.
五、附加限制性条件的商谈。 为了减少审查中发现的不利影响，商务部与可口可乐公司就附加限制性条件进行了商谈。商谈中，商务部就审查中发现的问题，要求可口可乐公司提出可行解决方案。可口可乐公司对商务部提出的问题表述自己的看法，并先后提出了初步解决方案及其修改方案。经过评估，商务部认为可口可乐公司针对影响竞争问题提出的救济方案，仍不能有效减少此项集中产生的不利影响。	**5. Negotiation Regarding the Imposition of Restrictive Conditions** In an effort to mitigate the adverse effects revealed by the review, MOFCOM discussed with Coca-Cola the imposition of restrictive conditions. In the course of negotiations, MOFCOM requested Coca-Cola to propose a viable solution for the issues revealed in the review. Coca-Cola stated its position in respect of the issues raised by MOFCOM, and produced a preliminary proposal, followed by a revised proposal. Upon assessment, MOFCOM held that the remedies proposed by Coca-Cola to address the competition concerns could not yet effectively mitigate the adverse effects of the concentration.
六、审查决定。 鉴于上述原因，根据《反垄断法》第二十八条和第二十九条，商务部认为，此项经营者集中具有排除、限制竞争效果，将对中国果汁饮料市场有效竞争和果汁产业健康发展产生不利影响。鉴于参与集中的经营者没有提供充足的证据证明集中对竞争产生的有利影响明显大于不利影响或者符合社会公共利益，在规定的时间内，可口可乐公司也没有提出可行的减少不利影响的解决方案，因此，决定禁止此项经营者集中。	**6. Review Decision** In light of the above, MOFCOM held under Articles 28 and 29 of the Anti-Monopoly Law that the proposed concentration would have the effect of eliminating and/or restricting competition, and would adversely affect effective competition in the Chinese juice beverage market and the sound development of the juice industry. Given that the parties to the concentration did not provide adequate evidence to prove that the positive effects of the concentration obviously outweighed its

(Continued)

	adverse effects over competition, or to prove that the concentration served the public interest, nor did Coca-Cola submit within the specified time limit any viable solution to mitigate the adverse effects, it is hereby decided that the concentration shall be prohibited.
本决定自公告之日起生效。 中华人民共和国商务部 二〇〇九年三月十八日	This decision shall become effective as of the date of its announcement. Ministry of Commerce March 18, 2009

D-3

MOFCOM Announcement [2009] No. 28 Regarding the Conditional Approval of Mitsubishi Rayon's Acquisition of Lucite International

中华人民共和国商务部公告2009年第28号
（商务部关于附条件批准日本三菱丽阳公司收购璐彩特国际公司反垄断审查决定的公告）

(Published on April 24, 2009)

（2009年4月24日公布）

中华人民共和国商务部收到日本三菱丽阳公司（简称三菱丽阳公司）拟收购璐彩特国际公司（简称璐彩特公司）的经营者集中反垄断申报，根据《反垄断法》第三十条，现公告如下：

The Ministry of Commerce of the People's Republic of China ("MOFCOM") has received an anti-monopoly notification of a concentration of undertakings regarding the acquisition of Lucite International Company ("Lucite International") by Mitsubishi Rayon ("Mitsubishi Rayon"). This announcement is hereby made as follows in accordance with Article 30 of the Anti-Monopoly Law.

一、立案和审查过程。

2008年12月22日，日本三菱丽阳公司向商务部提交了申报材料。三菱丽阳公司根据商务部要求对申报材料进行了补充，2009年1月20日，商务部认为申报材料达到了《反垄断法》第二十三条规定的标准，对此项申报进行立案审查，并通知了三菱丽阳公司。鉴于双方在甲基丙烯酸甲酯（Methylmethacrylate，简称"MMA"）市场份额较高，

1. Acceptance and Review Process
Mitsubishi Rayon submitted its notification to MOFCOM on December 22, 2008, while additional and supplementary information was submitted by Mitsubishi Rayon at the request of MOFCOM. On January 20, 2009, MOFCOM held that the notification submitted met the requirements of Article 23 of the Anti-Monopoly Law, and the notification was accepted for review.

(Continued)

合并后导致的市场集中度变化幅度较大，且收购方因并购在MMA市场取得的市场支配力将产生纵向封锁效应，2009年2月20日，初步阶段审查工作结束后，商务部决定实施进一步审查，书面通知了三菱丽阳公司，进一步审查截止日为2009年5月20日。在进一步审查过程中，商务部对集中造成的各种影响进行了评估，并于2009年5月20日前完成了审查工作。	Mitsubishi Rayon was informed accordingly. Given that the market shares of the parties in Methylmethacrylate (hereinafter referred to as "MMA") are relatively high, and that the merger will cause great changes in the level of concentration in the relevant market, and that the market power gained by the acquiring party through such merger will result in vertical foreclosure effect. On February 20, 2009, after the conclusion of the preliminary review, MOFCOM decided to conduct a further review, which would expire on May 20, 2009. Mitsubishi Rayon was informed accordingly in writing. During the further review, MOFCOM assessed various effects of the concentration, and completed its review before May 20, 2009.
二、审查内容。 根据《反垄断法》第二十七条，商务部从如下几个方面对此项经营者集中进行了全面审查： （一）　参与集中的经营者在相关市场的市场份额及其对市场的控制力； （二）　相关市场的市场集中度； （三）　经营者集中对市场进入、技术进步的影响； （四）　经营者集中对消费者和其他有关经营者的影响； （五）　经营者集中对国民经济发展的影响； （六）　其他因素对市场竞争产生的影响。	**2. Issues Reviewed** MOFCOM conducted a thorough review of the concentration of undertakings in accordance with Article 27 of the Anti-Monopoly Law, which included: (1)　the market shares of the undertakings concerned by the concentration in the relevant market and their ability to control the market; (2)　the level of concentration in the relevant market; (3)　the effect of the concentration on the market entry and the progress of technologies; (4)　the effect of the concentration on consumers and other undertakings; (5)　the effect of the concentration on the development of the national economy; and (6)　other factors' effects on the competition in the market.

三、审查工作。	**3. Review Process**
立案后，商务部对此项申报依法进行了审查，对申报材料进行了认真核实，对此项申报涉及的重要问题进行了深入分析，并通过书面征求意见、论证会和座谈会以及约谈当事人等方式，先后征求了相关行业协会、MMA生产商、PMMA粒子生产商、PMMA板材生产商和集中交易双方等方面意见。	Upon acceptance of the notification, MOFCOM duly reviewed and carefully verified the notification documents, and made an in-depth analysis of the important issues raised by the proposed concentration. Through written solicitation of opinions, validation meetings, workshops, and meeting with the parties and other means, MOFCOM also solicited advice and opinions from the relevant trade association, MMA manufacturers, PMMA particle manufacturers, PMMA panel manufacturers, and parties to the concentration.
四、相关市场。	**4. Relevant Markets**
三菱丽阳公司和璐彩特公司的业务重叠主要是在MMA的生产和销售上。除MMA外，两家公司在某些特种甲基丙烯酸酯单体(SpMAs)、PMMA粒子和PMMA板材产品上也有少量重叠。因此，相关产品市场为MMA、SpMAs、PMMA粒子和PMMA板材。本项集中对除MMA外的其他三类产品市场影响很小。本项集中的相关地域市场为中国市场。	The major business overlap of Mitsubishi Rayon and Lucite International lies in the production and sales of MMA. In addition to MMA, slight overlaps also exist in some specialty methacrylate monomers (SpMAs), PMMA particle, and PMMA panel products. Therefore, the relevant markets shall be MMA, SpMAs, PMMA particles, and PMMA panel market. This concentration will cause little impact on the market of the latter three categories of products with the exception of MMA. The relevant geographic market concerned by this concentration shall be the Chinese market.
五、竞争问题。	**5. Competition Concerns**
经审查，商务部依法对此项集中进行了全面评估，确认集中将产生如下不利影响：	Upon completion of the review, MOFCOM made a thorough assessment of the transaction in accordance with the law, and confirmed that the transaction would have the following adverse effects:
从横向看，此次交易很可能会对中国MMA市场的有效竞争格局产生负面影响。双方合并后的市场份额达到64%，远远高于位于第二的吉林石化和位于第三的黑龙江龙新公司。凭借在MMA市场取得的支配地位，合并后三菱丽阳公司有能力在中国MMA市场排除和限制竞争对手。	Horizontally, this concentration will likely cause adverse effect upon the landscape of effective competition in the MMA market in China. After the merger, the parties will hold a 64%

(*Continued*)

从纵向看，由于三菱丽阳公司在MMA及其下游两个市场均有业务，交易完成后，凭借在上游MMA市场取得的支配地位，合并后三菱丽阳公司有能力对其下游竞争者产生封锁效应。	market share, far exceeding that of Jilin Petrochemical and Heilongjiang Longxin Company, respectively ranked second and third. With a dominant position in the MMA market after the merger, the combined Mitsubishi Rayon will have the capacity to eliminate and restrict competitors in the MMA market in China. Vertically, due to the fact that Mitsubishi Rayon is active in MMA and its two downstream markets, after the completion of the concentration, the combined Mitsubishi Rayon will have the capacity to foreclose competitors in the downstream market by way of its dominant position in the upstream MMA market.
六、附加限制性条件的商谈。 为了减少审查中发现的不利影响，商务部与集中双方就附加限制性条件进行了商谈。商谈中，商务部就审查中发现的问题，要求集中双方提出可行解决方案。集中双方对商务部提出的问题表述了自己的看法，并先后提出了初步解决方案及其修改方案。经过评估，商务部认为集中双方针对影响竞争问题提出的救济方案，可以减少此项集中产生的不利影响。	**6. Negotiation of Restrictive Conditions** In an effort to mitigate the adverse effects as revealed by the review, MOFCOM discussed with the parties the imposition of restrictive conditions. In the course of negotiations, MOFCOM asked the parties to propose a viable solution for the issues revealed in the review. The parties stated their positions in respect of the issues raised by MOFCOM, and produced a preliminary remedy proposal followed by a revised proposal. Upon assessment, MOFCOM held that the remedies proposed by the parties to address the competition concerns could mitigate the adverse effects of the concentration.
七、审查决定。 鉴于上述原因，根据《反垄断法》第二十八条和第二十九条，商务部认为，此项经营者集中具有排除、限制竞争效果，将对中国MMA市场及其下游市场有效竞争产生不利影响。鉴于在规定的时间内，集中双方提出了足以消除不利影响的解决方案，商务部决定接受集中双方所做承诺，附加限制性条件批准此项经营者集中，具体条件如下：	**7. Review Decision** In light of the above, MOFCOM held under Articles 28 and 29 of the Anti-Monopoly Law that this transaction would have the effect of eliminating and/or restricting competition, and would have an adverse effect on effective competition in the Chinese MMA market and the related downstream market.

（一） 产能剥离

璐彩特国际（中国）化工有限公司（简称璐彩特中国公司）将其年产能中的50%剥离出来，一次性出售给一家或多家非关联的第三方购买人（"第三方购买人"），剥离的期间为五年。第三方购买人将有权在五年内以生产成本和管理成本（即成本价格，不附加任何利润）购买璐彩特中国公司生产的MMA产品，该成本价由独立审计师作年度核实。

如果在剥离期限内产能剥离未能完成，集中双方同意商务部有权指派独立的受托人将璐彩特中国公司的100%股权出售给独立第三方（"全部剥离"）。

剥离应在拟议交易完成后的六个月内完成。如果璐彩特公司有合理理由提出延期申请，商务部有权将以上期限延长六个月（"剥离期限"）。

（二） 独立运营璐彩特中国公司直至完成产能剥离

在自拟议交易完成至完成产能剥离或完成全部剥离期间内（"独立运营期"），璐彩特中国公司与三菱丽阳公司在中国的MMA单体业务将独立运营，分别拥有各自的管理层和董事会成员。

在独立运营期内，集中双方将继续在相互竞争的基础上分别在中国销售MMA，两家公司不得相互交换有关中国市场的定价、客户及其他竞争性信息。

独立运营期内，集中双方违反承诺发生重大违反行为，应支付总金额介于人民币25万元和人民币50万元之间的罚款，具体金额由商务部根据相关重大违反行为的性质及其对中国市场竞争的影响决定。

（三） 未来五年不再收购也不再建新厂

Given that the parties to the concentration have proposed a solution within the specified time limit which would be sufficient to eliminate such adverse effect, MOFCOM decides to accept the commitments made by the parties to the concentration, and approves this concentration under the restrictive conditions outlined below:

(1) Divestiture of Production Capacity

Lucite International (China) Chemical Industry Co., Ltd. (hereinafter referred to as "Lucite China") shall divest 50% of its annual production capacity to one or more unaffiliated third party buyers ("Third Party Buyer(s)") under a one-off transaction. The duration for such divestiture shall be five years. Such Third Party Buyer(s) shall have the right to purchase at the production cost plus overheads (i.e. at cost, without any mark-up for profits) the MMA products manufactured by Lucite China over a period of five years, such at-cost price shall be subject to annual review and examination by an independent auditor.

The parties agree that if the specified production capacity is not divested before the specified divestiture deadline, MOFCOM shall have the right to appoint an independent trustee to sell and transfer the entire Lucite China equity interest to an independent third party ("Complete Divestiture").

The divestiture shall be completed within six months after closing of the contemplated transaction. If Lucite China has any reasonable cause to request on extension of the deadline, MOFCOM shall have the right to extend the above divestiture deadline by six months (the "Divestiture Deadline").

(2) Independent Operation until Completion of Capacity Divestiture

(Continued)

未经商务部事先批准，合并后三菱丽阳公司在拟议交易交割后五年内不得从事下列行为： 1、 在中国收购MMA单体、PMMA聚合物或铸塑板生产商。 2、 在中国新建生产MMA单体、PMMA聚合物或铸塑板的工厂。	During the period from closing of the contemplated transaction up to the completion of the capacity divestiture or the Complete Divestiture ("Period of Independent Operations"), the MMA monomer business of Lucite China and Mitsubishi Rayon in the Chinese market shall be run separately and independently by a separate team of management and board of directors. During the Period of Independent Operations, the parties shall each continue to sell MMA in China independently on a competitive basis, and no information about pricing, customers, or any other competitively sensitive information related to the Chinese market shall be exchanged between the parties. During the Period of Independent Operations, a total fine in the range of RMB 250,000 to RMB 500,000 will be imposed in case of any material breach of any commitment by the parties, and the specific amount of such fine shall be determined by MOFCOM in light of the nature of such material breach and its impact on competition in the Chinese market. (3) No More Acquisitions and No New Facilities in the Next Five Years Without prior approval by MOFCOM, the post-merger Mitsubishi Rayon shall not engage in any of the following activities over a period of five years after closing of the contemplated transaction: (i) acquisition of any MMA monomer, PMMA polymer, or cast sheet supplier in China; (ii) construction of any new facility in China to manufacture MMA monomer, PMMA polymer, or cast sheets.
本决定自公告之日起生效。 中华人民共和国商务部 二〇〇九年四月二十四日	This decision shall become effective as of the date of its announcement. Ministry of Commerce April 24, 2009

D-4

MOFCOM Announcement [2009] No. 76 Regarding the Conditional Approval of General Motors' Acquisition of Delphi

中华人民共和国商务部公告2009年第76号
（商务部关于附条件批准美国通用汽车公司收购美国德尔福汽车公司反垄断审查决定的公告）

(Published on September 28, 2009)

（2009 年9月28日公布）

中华人民共和国商务部收到美国通用汽车有限公司（简称通用汽车）拟收购美国德尔福公司（简称德尔福）的经营者集中反垄断申报，根据《反垄断法》第三十条，现公告如下：	The Ministry of Commerce of the People's Republic of China ("MOFCOM") has received an anti-monopoly notification of a concentration of undertakings regarding the acquisition of Delphi Corporation ("Delphi") by General Motors Company ("GM"). This announcement is hereby made as follows in accordance with Article 30 of the Anti-Monopoly Law ("AML").
一、立案和审查过程。 2009年8月18日，通用汽车向商务部提交了申报材料，并于8月28日、31日根据商务部要求对申报材料进行了补充。8月31日，商务部认为申报材料符合《反垄断法》第二十三条规定的标准，对此项申报进行初步审查，并通知通用汽车。在审查过程中，商务部对集中对市场竞争造成的各种影响进行了评估，并于2009年9月28日前完成审查工作。	**1. Acceptance and Review Process** GM submitted its notification to MOFCOM on August 18, 2009, and submitted supplemental information on August 28 and 31 at the request of MOFCOM. On August 31, MOFCOM held that the notification, as supplemented, met the requirements of Article 23 of the AML, and the notification was accepted for preliminary review. GM was informed accordingly.

(Continued)

	During the review, MOFCOM assessed various effects on market competition resulting from the concentration, and completed its review before September 28, 2009.
二、审查内容。 根据《反垄断法》第二十七条，商务部从如下几个方面对此项经营者集中进行了全面审查: （一）　参与集中的经营者在相关市场的市场份额及其对市场的控制力; （二）　相关市场的市场集中度; （三）　经营者集中对市场进入、技术进步的影响; （四）　经营者集中对消费者和其他有关经营者的影响; （五）　经营者集中对国民经济发展的影响; （六）　其他因素对市场竞争产生的影响。	**2. Issues Reviewed** MOFCOM conducted a thorough review of the concentration in accordance with Article 27 of the AML, which included: (1) the market shares of the undertakings concerned by the concentration in the relevant market and their ability to control the market; (2) the level of concentration in the relevant market; (3) the effect of the concentration on market entry and progress of technologies; (4) the effect of the concentration on consumers and other undertakings; (5) the effect of the concentration on the development of the national economy; and (6) other factors' effect on market competition.
三、审查工作。 立案后，商务部对此项申报依法进行了审查，对申报材料进行了认真核实，对此项申报涉及的重要问题进行了深入分析，并通过书面征求意见、召开座谈会以及约谈当事人等方式，先后征求了有关政府部门、相关行业协会、汽车生产商以及集中交易双方等方面意见。	**3. Review Process** Upon acceptance of the notification, MOFCOM duly reviewed and carefully verified the notification documents, and made an in-depth analysis of the important issues raised by the concentration. By way of written solicitation of opinions, workshops, and meetings with the parties, MOFCOM also solicited opinions from the relevant governmental departments, trade associations, auto manufacturers, and parties to the concentration.
四、相关市场。 集中交易双方的产品和业务没有横向重叠，但在上下游市场中存在纵向关系。因此，本案中根据交易双方各自的产品分别界定相关市场。	**4. Relevant Markets** The products and activities of the parties to the concentration do not overlap horizontally, but are vertically related in upstream and downstream markets.

就通用汽车的产品而言，相关产品市场界定为汽车乘用车市场和汽车商用车市场；两个相关产品市场的相关地域市场均为中国市场。就德尔福的产品而言，相关产品市场界定为10个独立的汽车零部件市场，它们分别是汽车电子电气传输系统市场、汽车连接系统市场、汽车电气中心市场、汽车热能系统市场、汽车娱乐和通信市场、汽车控制和安全市场、汽车安全系统市场、汽车汽油发动机管理系统市场、汽车柴油发动机管理系统市场、汽车燃料供给和蒸发产品市场；以上10个相关产品市场的相关地域市场均为中国市场。

Therefore, the relevant markets shall be defined according to the parties' respective products. As for GM's products, the relevant product markets are defined as the passenger vehicle market and the commercial vehicle market; the relevant geographic market shall be the Chinese market. As for Delphi's products, the relevant product markets are defined as ten separate auto parts markets, which are the electrical and electronic transmission system market, connection system market, electric center market, automobile thermal system market, entertainment and communication market, control and security market, safety system market, gas engine management systems market, diesel engine management system market, and fuel handling and evaporation market; the relevant geographic market for the above ten relevant product markets shall be the Chinese market.

五、竞争问题。

商务部依法对此项集中进行了全面评估，初步确认集中存在如下竞争关注：鉴于通用汽车在全球和中国汽车市场的领先地位，以及德尔福在全球和中国汽车零部件市场的领先地位和增长态势，考虑到中国相关市场的竞争状况，此项集中可能具有以下排除、限制竞争的效果：

（一）　德尔福是国内多家整车厂的独家供应商，鉴于集中实施后双方的控股关系和利益一致性，有必要消除集中对德尔福对国内其他汽车制造企业的供货稳定性、价格和质量可能带来的不利影响，从而避免因此排除、限制国内汽车市场的竞争；

（二）　鉴于集中实施后双方的控股关系和利益一致性以及通用汽车对德尔福董事会的介入，

5. Competition Concerns

After the overall assessment of this concentration by MOFCOM, it is preliminarily confirmed that the following competition concerns about the concentration may exist: in view of the leading position of GM in the worldwide and China-wide automobile markets, and Delphi's leading position and increasingly fast growth in the worldwide and China-wide auto parts market, and in light of the competitive conditions in the relevant markets in China, this concentration may have the effect of eliminating and/or restricting competition in the following aspects:

(1) whereas Delphi is the sole supplier to many domestic automobile OEMs, in light of the equity control and the congruence of interests between GM and Delphi post closing, it is necessary to

(Continued)

有必要确保通用汽车不获得德尔福掌握的国内其他汽车制造企业的研发技术、车型资料等竞争信息，从而避免因此排除、限制国内汽车市场的竞争；	eliminate potential adverse effects upon the stability, price, and quality of Delphi's supply to other domestic OEMs so as to avoid the elimination and restriction of competition in the domestic auto market;
（三）鉴于集中实施后双方的控股关系和利益一致性，国内其他汽车制造企业在转换零部件供应商时，有必要确保德尔福不会采取拖延和不配合策略，提高转换成本，从而避免因此排除、限制国内汽车市场的竞争；	(2) in light of the equity control and the congruence of interests between GM and Delphi post closing, as well as GM's involvement in the board of Delphi, it is necessary to ensure that GM will not access information in the possession of Delphi relating to the research & development of technology, and vehicle models of other domestic OEMs, so as to avoid the elimination and restriction of competition in the domestic auto market;
（四）基于集中实施后双方的控股关系和利益一致性，通用汽车可能未来增加自德尔福的汽车零部件采购，提高国内其他零部件企业进入通用汽车采购渠道的难度，使国内其他零部件企业和德尔福相比处于不利地位，从而排除、限制国内汽车零部件市场的竞争。	(3) in light of the equity control and the congruence of interests between GM and Delphi post closing, it is necessary to ensure that Delphi will not take delaying and uncooperative tactics when other domestic OEMs switch auto parts suppliers, whereby increasing the switching costs of those OEMs, so as to avoid the elimination and restriction of competition in the domestic auto market;
	(4) in light of the equity control and the congruence of interests between GM and Delphi post closing, GM may increase its purchasing from Delphi in future, while making it more difficult for other domestic auto parts suppliers to enter into GM's purchasing system, thereby putting domestic auto parts suppliers in a disadvantaged position compared to Delphi, which will eliminate and/or restrict competition in the domestic auto parts market.

六、附加限制性条件的商谈。 为了消除审查中确认的竞争关注，商务部与集中双方就附加限制性条件进行了商谈。商谈中，商务部就集中存在的竞争关注，要求集中双方提出可行的解决方案。集中双方对商务部提出的竞争关注陈述了自己的看法，并先后提出了初步解决方案及其修改方案。经过评估，商务部认为集中双方针对竞争关注提出的解决方案，可以消除此项集中可能产生的排除、限制竞争效果。	**6. Negotiation of Restrictive Conditions** In an effort to eliminate the competition concerns as identified by its review, MOFCOM discussed with the parties the imposition of restrictive conditions on the concentration. During the course of negotiations, MOFCOM asked the parties to propose a viable solution to the competition concerns resulting from the concentration. The parties stated their position in respect of the competition concerns raised by MOFCOM, and produced a preliminary proposal and followed by a revised proposal. Upon assessment, MOFCOM held that the remedy proposal raised by the parties to address the competition concerns could eliminate the likely effect of eliminating and/or restricting competition.
七、审查决定。 鉴于上述原因，根据《反垄断法》第二十八条和第二十九条，商务部认为，此项经营者集中可能具有排除、限制竞争的效果，对中国汽车整车市场及其上游汽车零部件市场的竞争产生不利影响。鉴于在规定时间内，集中双方提出了足以减少集中对竞争产生不利影响的解决方案，基本消除了商务部的竞争关注，商务部决定接受集中双方提出的解决方案，附加限制性条件批准此项经营者集中，具体条件如下： （一）　集中交易完成后，通用汽车、德尔福应当保证德尔福及其控股和实际控制的关联企业将继续对国内汽车厂商无歧视性地供货，并且承诺将一如既往地确保供货的及时性、可靠性及产品质量，确保在供货的价格和数量上依据市场规则和已达成的协议而定，不应附加会直接或间接排除、限制竞争的不合理条件；	**7. Review Decision** In light of the above, in accordance with Articles 28 and 29 of the AML, MOFCOM held that this concentration of undertakings may have the effect of eliminating and/or restricting competition, thus having adverse effect on the automobile vehicle market and the upstream auto parts market in China. Given that the parties to the concentration have proposed a solution within the specified time limit which would be sufficient to mitigate such adverse effect, which substantively eliminates MOFCOM's concerns, MOFCOM decided to accept the solution proposed by the parties to the concentration, and to approve this concentration under conditions as set forth below: (1)　post closing, GM and Delphi shall commit that Delphi and each of its respective affiliates under its actual control or in which it has a controlling share equity will continue to supply its

(Continued)

（二）　集中交易完成后，通用汽车不得非法寻求获得德尔福掌握的国内其他汽车厂商的竞争性保密信息，德尔福不得非法向通用汽车披露其掌握的国内其他汽车厂商的竞争性保密信息，双方不得以正式或非正式的方式非法相互交换和沟通第三方的竞争性保密信息；

（三）　集中交易完成后，通用汽车、德尔福应当保证德尔福及其控股和实际控制的关联企业应客户的合法要求，配合客户平稳转换供应商，不得故意拖延或设置、主张限制性条件，以提高其他整车厂商的转换成本，从而达到限制竞争的效果；

（四）　集中交易完成后，通用汽车应当对其所有汽车零部件的采购继续遵循多源供应和非歧视原则，在符合通用公司相关要求的条件下无歧视性地采购，不得专门制定对德尔福有利而对其他供应商不利的不合理条件。

自本决定生效之日起，通用汽车、德尔福应当定期向商务部报告其遵守上述限制性条件的情况，双方如有任何违反上述限制性条件的行为，商务部将依法予以处罚。

auto customers in China without discrimination, and is committed to continue timely and reliable supply and to maintain the quality of its products consistent with current practices, and is committed to ensure that prices and quantity of supply will be based on market conditions and agreed arrangements and shall not impose any other unreasonable conditions that directly or indirectly restrict or eliminate competition;

(2) post closing, GM commits not to illegally seek to obtain any competitively sensitive confidential information in the possession of Delphi relating to other domestic vehicle manufacturers, while Delphi commits not to illegally disclose any competitively sensitive confidential information in the possession of Delphi relating to other domestic vehicle manufacturers. The parties to the concentration are committed not to illegally exchange or communicate with each other any competitively sensitive confidential information of a third party whether by any formal or informal means;

(3) post closing, GM and Delphi shall commit that Delphi and each of its respective affiliates under its actual control or in which it has a controlling share equity will assist, if legitimately requested by a customer, its customers in smoothly switching suppliers without any intentional delays or imposition or insistence of any restrictive conditions aimed to raise the switching costs of other vehicle manufacturers with the effect of restricting competition;

	(4) post closing, GM commits to continue with its principle of multiple sourcing and non-discrimination with respect to the purchasing of all auto parts, and to conduct nondiscriminatory procurement provided the supplier meets the relevant requirements of GM, and not to specially formulate any unreasonable conditions favorable towards Delphi but unfavorable towards other suppliers. GM and Delphi shall report to MOFCOM regularly on their compliance with the above restrictive conditions as of the effective date of this decision, and in case of any breach by the parties of any of the above restrictive conditions, MOFCOM will impose penalties according to the law.
本决定自公告之日起生效。 中华人民共和国商务部 二〇〇九年九月二十八日	This decision shall become effective as of the date of its announcement. Ministry of Commerce September 28, 2009

MOFCOM Announcement [2009] No. 77 Regarding the Conditional Approval of Pfizer's Acquisition of Wyeth

中华人民共和国商务部公告［2009］第77号 （关于附条件批准辉瑞公司收购惠氏公司反垄断审查决定的公告）

(Published on September 29, 2009)

（2009年9月29日公布）

中华人民共和国商务部收到美国辉瑞公司（简称"辉瑞公司"）收购美国惠氏公司（简称"惠氏公司"）的经营者集中反垄断申报。经过审查，商务部决定附条件批准此项经营者集中。根据《中华人民共和国反垄断法》第三十条，现公告如下：	The Ministry of Commerce of the People's Republic of China ("MOFCOM") has received an anti-monopoly notification of a concentration of undertakings regarding the acquisition of Wyeth Inc. ("Wyeth") by Pfizer Inc. ("Pfizer"). After review, MOFCOM decides to approve this concentration under certain conditions. This announcement is hereby made as follows in accordance with Article 30 of the Anti-Monopoly Law ("AML").
一、立案和审查过程 2009年6月9日，商务部收到美国辉瑞公司收购惠氏公司经营者者集中申报申请，6月11日和14日收到补充材料，6月15日予以立案。根据《中华人民共和国反垄断法》和商务部有关经营者集中反垄断审查的相关规定，商务部对该案实施初步审查，初步审查工作截止日为7月15日。	**1. Acceptance and Review Process** MOFCOM received the anti-monopoly notification on June 9, 2009 in connection with Pfizer's contemplated acquisition of Wyeth, and received supplementary information respectively on June 11, and June 14, 2009. The filing was accepted by MOFCOM on June 15, 2009.

审查过程中，商务部发现此项集中在动物保健品领域存在限制或排除竞争问题，初步审查期满前，决定对该案实施进一步审查，该阶段审查工作截止日为2009年10月13日。	In accordance with the AML, and relevant MOFCOM regulations regarding the anti-monopoly review of concentrations of undertakings, MOFCOM made a preliminary review of the transaction, with the deadline for the preliminary review set for July 15, 2009. In the course of its review, MOFCOM found that the concentration raised concerns of restriction or elimination of competition in the field of animal health products, and decided before the deadline to enter into further review of the transaction, with the deadline for the further review set for October 13, 2009.
二、审查内容 根据《中华人民共和国反垄断法》第二十七条，商务部从以下几个方面对此项经营者集中进行了全面审查： （一）　参与集中的经营者在相关市场的市场份额及其对市场的控制力； （二）　相关市场的市场集中度； （三）　经营者集中对市场进入、技术进步的影响； （四）　经营者集中对消费者和其他有关经营者的影响； （五）　经营者集中对国民经济发展的影响。	**2. Issues Reviewed** MOFCOM conducted a thorough review of the transaction in accordance with Article 27 of the AML from the following perspectives: (1)　the market shares of the undertakings concerned by the concentration in the relevant market and their ability to control the market; (2)　the level of concentration in the relevant market; (3)　the effect of the concentration on the market entry and the progress of technologies; (4)　the effect of the concentration on consumers and other undertakings; and (5)　the effect of the concentration on the development of the national economy.
三、审查工作 立案后，商务部对申报材料进行了认真核实，对此项申报涉及的重要问题进行了深入分析，并通过召开论证会、座谈会、听证会和书面征求意见、实地调查以及约谈当事人等方式，先后征求了相关政府部门、行业协会、同业竞争者、上下游企业等方面	**3. Review Process** Upon acceptance of the notification, MOFCOM reviewed and carefully verified the notification documents, and made an in-depth analysis of the important issues raised by the filed concentration. By way of written solicitation of opinions, workshops, hearings, on-site visits, and meeting with the parties, and other means,

(Continued)

意见。针对审查中发现的个别产品存在的限制或排除竞争问题，商务部与申报方进行了充分磋商，并就消除不利竞争影响的解决方案达成共识。	MOFCOM also solicited opinions from the relevant governmental departments, trade associations, industry competitors, upstream and downstream players, and the parties to the transaction. In connection with the competition concerns of restriction or elimination of competition created by particular products as found in the review, MOFCOM had a full discussion with the notifying party and agreed upon solutions to eliminate the anti-competitive concerns.
四、竞争问题 （一）　相关市场。本交易所涉及的相关地域市场是中国境内市场（指中国大陆地区，不包括香港、澳门及台湾）。本交易所涉及的相关产品是人类药品和动物保健品，交易双方在中国境内市场存在如下重合产品：一是人类药品，具体包括 J1C（广谱青霉素）和 N6A（抗抑郁和情绪稳定剂）；二是动物保健产品，具体包括猪支原体肺炎疫苗、猪伪狂犬病疫苗以及犬用联苗。 （二）　竞争影响。调查表明，在上述两种人类药品领域以及猪伪狂犬病疫苗和犬用联苗两种动物保健品领域，合并后市场竞争结构没有发生实质性改变。但是，对于猪支原体肺炎疫苗而言，辉瑞和惠氏合并后市场竞争结构发生实质性改变，将产生限制或排除竞争的效果。 1、　市场份额明显增加。根据商务部掌握的数据，双方合并后在该市场的份额为49.4%（其中辉瑞为38%，惠氏为11.4%），远高于其他竞争对手，排名第二位的英特威市场份额只有18.35%，其他竞争者的市场份额均低于10%。合并后实体将有能力利用其规模效应扩大市场，进而控制产品价格。	**4. Competition Concerns** (1)　The relevant markets. The relevant geographic market involved in this transaction in the Chinese domestic market (for this purpose, it refers to the Mainland market, excluding Hong Kong, Macau, and Taiwan), and the relevant products include human drugs and animal health products. The merging parties have overlaps in the following product areas in the Chinese domestic market: (a) human drugs, specifically including J1C and N6A; and (b) animal health products, specifically including swine mycoplasma pneumonia vaccine, swine pseudo-rabies vaccine, and combination vaccine for dogs. (2)　Effect on competition. As shown by the investigation, there would be no substantial change in the structure of the post-merger market competition for the aforementioned two types of human drugs, and two of the animal health products, i.e. swine pseudo-rabies vaccine and combination vaccine for dogs. However, there would be substantial changes in the structure of the post-merger market

2、 市场集中度明显提高。根据商
务部掌握的数据，本项集中完
成后的赫氏指数为2182, 增量
为336。鉴于中国猪支原体肺
炎疫苗市场属于高度集中的市
场，此项集中将产生限制或排
除竞争效果。

3、 市场进入将更加困难。药品研
发的特点是成本高和周期长。
据统计，开发一种新产品大约
需要3年到10年的时间和250万
到1000万美元的投资。市场调
查显示，进入猪支原体肺炎疫
苗市场的技术壁垒更高。辉瑞
收购惠氏后，很可能利用其规
模优势进一步在中国扩张市
场，打压其他竞争者，限制其
他企业在该领域的发展。

competition with regard to swine mycoplasma pneumonia vaccine, which will have a restrictive or exclusionary anti-competitive effect.

(i) significant increase in market share. Based on the information available to MOFCOM, the post-merger market share of the merging parties in the swine mycoplasma pneumonia vaccine market will reach 49.4% (38% for Pfizer, and 11.4% for Wyeth), which is significantly higher than that of other competitors, with Intervet, the second largest competitor, having a market share of 18.35%, and other competitors having shares all below 10%. The post-merger entity will be able to expand its market share by virtue of its market scale, and would thereby control the product prices.

(ii) significant increase in the level of market concentration. Based on the information available to MOFCOM, the post-merger HHI (Herfindhal-Hirschman Index) would reach 2,182, with an increase of 336. In light of the highly concentrated market within China for the swine mycoplasma pneumonia vaccine, the concentration will have an effect of restricting or eliminating competition.

(iii) market entry made even more difficult. With the costly and long-drawn-out nature of drug research and development, it is estimated based on statistics, that a

(Continued)

new drug would require three to ten years to be developed and involves an investment ranging from US$2.5 million to US$10 million. As shown by market research, there is a higher technical barrier for entry into the swine mycoplasma pneumonia vaccine market. Upon merger, Pfizer may further expand its Chinese market share and marginalize other competitors by leveraging its scale, thereby restricting the development of other entities in this field.

五、审查决定	**5. Review Decision**

鉴于辉瑞公司收购惠氏公司后将对中国猪支原体肺炎市场产生限制竞争的效果，为了减少对该市场竞争产生的不利影响，商务部决定附条件批准此项集中，要求辉瑞公司履行如下义务：	In light of the restrictive effect of the contemplated Pfizer–Wyeth transaction on competition in the swine mycoplasma pneumonia vaccine market, MOFCOM decides to approve this concentration under certain conditions to mitigate its adverse effects over market competition. Under those conditions, Pfizer is required to perform the following obligations:
（一）　剥离在中国境内（指中国大陆地区，不包括香港、澳门及台湾）辉瑞旗下品牌为瑞倍适（Respisure）及瑞倍适-旺（Respisure One）的猪支原体肺炎疫苗业务。	(1)　Pfizer shall divest its Respisure and Respisure One swine mycoplasma pneumonia vaccines in China (Mainland China, excluding Hong Kong, Macau, and Taiwan);
（二）　被剥离业务包括确保其存活性和竞争性所需的有形资产和无形资产（包括知识产权）。	(2)　the divested businesses shall include both tangible and intangible assets (including intellectual property rights) required for their viability and competitiveness;
（三）　辉瑞公司必须在商务部批准此项集中后六个月内通过受托人为被剥离业务找到购买人并与之签订买卖协议。	(3)　Pfizer must within six months of MOFCOM's approval find a buyer for the divested businesses and enter into a sale and purchase agreement with the buyer through a trustee;
（四）　购买人应独立于集中双方，必须符合预先设定的资格标准，并需经商务部批准。	
（五）　如果辉瑞公司在商务部批准此项集中后六个月内未能找到购买人，商务部有权指定新的受托人以无底价方式处置被剥离业务。	

（六）	在六个月剥离期内，辉瑞公司应任命一名过渡期间经理，负责管理拟剥离业务。管理应以拟剥离业务利益最大化为原则，确保业务具有持续的可存活性、适销性和竞争力，并独立于双方保留的其他业务。	(4)	the buyer shall be independent of Pfizer and Wyeth, and must meet pre-determined standards as to its qualifications. The buyer must be approved by MOFCOM;
（七）	剥离后三年内，根据购买人的请求，辉瑞公司有义务向购买人提供合理的技术支持，协助其采购生产猪支原体肺炎疫苗所需的原材料，并对购买人的相关人员提供技术培训和咨询服务。	(5)	if Pfizer fails to find a buyer within the six-month period following the decision, MOFCOM will appoint a new trustee to dispose of the divested businesses without setting a minimum selling price;
		(6)	during this six-month period, Pfizer shall appoint a manager to manage the businesses in the interim so as to maximize the interests of the divested businesses, and to ensure the divested businesses maintain viability, merchantability, and competitiveness, and are separate from the other businesses retained by the merging parties;
		(7)	at the request of the purchaser, Pfizer shall within three years of the divestiture provide reasonable technical assistance to the purchaser, assist in the procurement of raw materials for production of swine mycoplasma pneumonia vaccines, and provide technical training and advice to the relevant personnel of the purchaser.
本决定自公告之日起生效. 中华人民共和国商务部 二〇〇九年九月二十九日		This decision shall become effective on the date of its announcement. Ministry of Commerce September 29, 2009	

D-6

MOFCOM Announcement [2009] No. 82 Regarding the Conditional Approval of Panasonic's Acquisition of Sanyo

中华人民共和国商务部［2009年］第82号公告 （关于附条件批准松下公司收购三洋公司反垄断审查决定的公告）

(Published on October 30, 2009)

（2009年10月30日公布）

中华人民共和国商务部收到松下株式会社（简称"松下公司"）与三洋电机株式会社（简称"三洋公司"）的经营者集中反垄断申报。经过审查，商务部决定附条件批准此项经营者集中。根据《中华人民共和国反垄断法》第三十条，现公告如下：

The Ministry of Commerce of the People's Republic of China ("MOFCOM") has received an anti-monopoly notification of a concentration of undertakings regarding the acquisition of Sanyo Electric Co., Ltd. ("Sanyo") by Panasonic Corporation ("Panasonic"). After review, MOFCOM decides to approve the concentration under certain conditions. This announcement is hereby made as follows in accordance with Article 30 of the Anti-Monopoly Law:

一、立案和审查程序

2009年1月21日，商务部收到松下公司收购三洋公司的经营者集中申报申请。经审查，商务部认为该申报材料不完整，要求申报方进一步补充完善。4月30日，申报方提交了补充材料。经审核，商务部认为经补充后的申报材料达到了法定标准，5月4日予以立案，开始初步审查。

1. Acceptance and Review Process

On January 21, 2009, MOFCOM received the notification for concentration of undertakings in connection with Panasonic's contemplated acquisition of Sanyo. After review of the notification, MOFCOM decided that the notification was incomplete and requested additional materials. On April 30, 2009, the

初步审查过程中，商务部认为此项收购导致合并后新企业在某些重合产品市场的份额明显增高，市场结构发生实质性改变，初步审查工作结束后，决定实施进一步审查，进一步审查截止日为9月3日。8月14日，商务部向申报方指出了审查发现的竞争问题，并要求其限期提出相应的解决方案。8月26日，申报方向商务部提出申请，请求延长进一步审查期限，以便准备解决上述竞争问题的具体方案。根据《中华人民共和国反垄断法》第二十六条，商务部决定将进一步审查期限延长60日，截止日为2009年11月3日。

notifying parties submitted supplemental filing materials. After review, MOFCOM believed the amended notification met the requisite standards under the relevant law, and on May 4 accepted the notification as a new case and started the preliminary review. During the preliminary review, MOFCOM found that the proposed merger would result in the merged entity having significant increase of market shares in some markets where the two companies had overlapped operations and would materially alter the structures in such markets. Therefore, after preliminary review, MOFCOM decided to undertake a further review and the deadline for such review was set as September 3. On August 14, MOFCOM informed the notifying parties with the competitive concerns in connection with the proposed concentration and required the notifying parties to submit plans to remedy these issues within a specified deadline. On August 26, the notifying parties requested for extension of the further review period in order to prepare for the detailed plan to address the competition concerns. Pursuant to Article 26 of the Anti-Monopoly Law, MOFCOM decided to extend the period of further review for another 60 days with a new deadline set as November 3, 2009.

二、审查内容

根据《中华人民共和国反垄断法》第二十七条，商务部从如下几个方面对此项经营者集中进行了全面审查：
(一)　参与集中的经营者在相关市场的市场份额及其对市场的控制力；
(二)　相关市场的市场集中度；
(三)　经营者集中对市场进入、技术进步的影响；

2. Issues Reviewed
MOFCOM conducted a thorough review of the concentration in accordance with Article 27 of the Anti-Monopoly Law, which included:
(1)　the market shares of the undertakings concerned by the concentration in the relevant market and their ability to control the market;
(2)　the level of concentration in the relevant market;

(Continued)

（四）　经营者集中对消费者和其他有关经营者的影响； （五）　经营者集中对国民经济发展的影响。	(3)　the effect of the concentration on the market entry and the progress of technologies; (4)　the effect of the concentration on consumers and other undertakings; and (5)　the effect of the concentration on the development of the national economy.
三、审查工作 立案后，商务部书面征求了相关政府部门、行业商会和协会的意见，对申报材料及相关补充材料的真实性、完整性进行了审核，要求申报方对特定问题进行了补充和澄清。审查中，商务部要求申报方就申报双方的重叠产品种类、销售数据、产品差异性、产品的定价方式与策略、分销模式、与下游用户的谈判、产能变化以及可能存在的纵向关系等问题提供相关文件与证据。为了解相关方面意见，商务部还向涉及不同产品的39家同行竞争者和下游用户发放了调查问卷，对个别企业进行了电话采访，并赴深圳等地进行了实地调查。针对审查中发现的限制或排除竞争问题，商务部与申报方进行了充分磋商，并就消除不利影响的解决方案达成共识。	**3. Review Process** After MOFCOM accepted the notification, it consulted with relevant governmental departments, trade associations, and organizations, examined and verified the authenticity and the completeness of the notification materials, as supplemented, and requested additional supplements and clarifications from the notifying parties on certain issues. During the review process, MOFCOM requested the notifying parties to submit relevant documents and evidence to address the following issues: overlapped product categories, sales data, product differences, ways and strategies for product pricing, type of distribution, negotiations with downstream users, changes in production capacity, and potential vertical relationships. In order to understand the opinions from relevant parties, MOFCOM has also conducted a survey of 39 competitors and downstream users of various products, conducted phone interviews with a few companies, and visited Shenzhen and other places for site visits. To address the potential restrictions on or elimination of competition in connection with the proposed concentration discovered during the review, MOFCOM has communicated and negotiated with the notifying parties to reach a mutually agreed resolution to prevent potential adverse consequences.

四、竞争问题

经审查，商务部确认此项集中将在以下三个产品市场产生限制或排除竞争影响：

（一）　硬币型锂二次电池

硬币型锂二次电池是用于手机、摄像机等电器的后备电源。经审查，该产品构成独立的产品市场，地域市场界定为世界市场。此项集中将在该产品市场产生限制或排除竞争影响，理由是：

第一，硬币型锂二次电池市场高度集中。申报双方分别是该市场的第一和第二大生产商，合并后松下公司占据61.6%的市场份额，导致下游用户的选择权受到很大限制。由于多数下游用户有从两家以上供应商采购产品的策略，合并导致的限制竞争效果将更为显著。

第二，合并后松下公司将具有单方面提价的能力。一方面，由于市场上竞争者非常有限，合并后松下公司的提价行为难以受到有效的竞争约束；另一方面，由于合并后松下提高价格行为对其他竞争者也可能是有利的，缺乏与松下进行有效竞争的动力。

第三，买方力量不足以消除上述限制竞争效果。虽然部分下游大型用户具有与合并后实体抗衡的买方力量，但此种买方力量并不能扩展至其他不具备同等议价能力的中小型用户。

（二）　民用镍氢电池

民用镍氢电池主要用于电动工具等电器的主电源。该产品构成独立的产品市场，相关地域市场为世界市场。此项集中将在该产品市场产生限制或排除竞争影响，理由是：

第一，民用镍氢电池市场是一个集中度较高的市场，且竞争者数量有限，合并后松下公司市场份额达46.3%，远高于其他竞争者，合并可能导致松下公司具有单方面提价的能力。

4. Competition Concerns

After review, MOFCOM determined that the proposed merger would eliminate and/or restrict competition in the following three markets.

(1)　Lithium coin-cell secondary batteries

Lithium coin-cell secondary batteries are a type of back-up source of power in electronics such as cellphones and camcorders. According to the review, this product constitutes an independent market and the geographic market was deemed to be worldwide. The proposed concentration would restrict or eliminate competition in this market because of the following:

First, the lithium coin-cell secondary battery market is highly concentrated. The two notifying parties to the proposed concentration were the number one and number two manufacturers in this market. After the merger, Panasonic would have 61.6% of the market share and would significantly restrict the choices of downstream users. As the majority of the downstream users have sourcing strategy to purchase products from more than two suppliers, the anti-competitive effect as a result of the merger would be more pronounced.

Secondly, after the proposed merger, Panasonic would have the ability to raise prices unilaterally. On the one hand, because there are limited competitors in this market, Panasonic's ability to raise prices would not be effectively constrained through competition. On the other, any post-merger price increased by Panasonic may likely be beneficial to other competitors, and they lack the motivation to effectively compete with Panasonic.

Thirdly, buyers' power cannot sufficiently offset the anti-competitive effect of the merger. Although some

(*Continued*)

第二，指定交易可能损害市场竞争。在调查中，商务部发现部分民用镍氢电池下游用户的需求方指定要求该下游用户使用三洋或松下品牌的电池产品。此种指定交易方式抑制了市场竞争，导致其他品牌的电池产品受到排挤，合并将进一步加剧此种限制竞争的效果。

第三，镍氢电池市场发展趋缓，较难吸引充分的市场进入抵消上述限制和排除竞争效果。

（三）　车用镍氢电池

车用镍氢电池是为混合动力汽车或纯电动汽车提供驱动动力的电池。此项集中将在该产品市场产生限制或排除竞争影响，理由是：

该市场高度集中，其中松下公司和丰田公司合资设立的企业————松下EV能源株式会社（简称"PEVE公司"）在该市场占77%的市场份额，具有绝对优势地位，加之市场上其他竞争者仅限于申报双方。合并将导致该市场竞争者数量进一步减少，松下公司很可能利用其在PEVE公司的影响力进一步削弱市场竞争。

large downstream users have the buyers' power to balance Panasonic's sellers' power after the merger, such buyers' power could not be extended to small and middle-sized users which do not have the equivalent bargaining power of the large users.

(2) Consumer nickel-metal-hydride batteries

Consumer nickel-metal-hydride (the "Ni-MH") batteries are chiefly used as the main battery for electrical appliances such as electric tools. This product constitutes an independent product market and its relevant geographic market is the worldwide market. The proposed concentration would restrict or eliminate competition in this market because of the following:

First, the concentration in the market of consumer Ni-MH is relatively high and there is a limited number of competitors. After the proposed merger, Panasonic's market share would reach 46.3%, much higher than any other competitor, which could give it the ability to unilaterally raise the prices of the product.

Secondly, brand designation may damage competition in this market. MOFCOM found in its investigation that companies buying from downstream users of consumer Ni-MH batteries require such downstream users to use Panasonic- or Sanyo-brand batteries. Such designation dampens competition in the market and marginalizes batteries of other brands. The proposed merger would further amplify the anti-competitive effect of such practice.

Thirdly, the Ni-MH battery market is experiencing slow growth and therefore cannot attract sufficient market entries to offset the effect of restricting or eliminating competition as described above.

(3) Automobile Ni-MH batteries

Automobile Ni-MH batteries are those providing driving power to hybrid or pure electric cars. The proposed concentration would restrict or eliminate competition in this market because of the following:

This market is highly concentrated. The joint venture of Panasonic and Toyota, Panasonic EV Energy Co., Ltd. ("PEVE"), has a 77% market share and enjoys the absolute leading position in this market. In addition, the only other competitors are the notifying parties, Panasonic and Sanyo. The proposed merger would further reduce competition in this market. Panasonic may use its power in PEVE to further reduce market competition.

五、附加限制性条件的商谈	**5. Negotiation of Restrictive Conditions**
为了解决上述竞争问题，根据《反垄断法》第二十九条的规定，2009年8月20日、8月26日、9月10日、9月24日、10月20日，商务部与申报方就救济方案进行了多次商谈。2009年10月22日，申报方提出了最终救济方案。经过评估，商务部确认该救济方案足以消除此项集中对中国市场造成的不利影响。	To address the competition issues as described above, MOFCOM and the notifying parties held several discussions respectively on August 20, August 26, September 10, September 24, October 20 regarding the plan of remedies according to Article 29 of the Anti-Monopoly Law. On October 22, 2009, the notifying parties submitted the final proposal of remedies. After assessment, MOFCOM determined that the proposal could preclude the adverse effect of the concentration in the Chinese market.
六、审查决定	**6. Review Decision**
鉴于松下公司与三洋公司的经营者集中将对硬币型锂二次电池、民用镍氢电池和车用镍氢电池等相关产品市场产生限制或排除竞争效果，为了减少集中对市场竞争产生的不利影响，商务部决定附条件批准此项集中，要求松下公司和三洋公司履行如下义务：	Because the proposed concentration of undertakings between Panasonic and Sanyo would result in a restriction or elimination of competition in the markets for lithium coin-cell secondary batteries, consumer Ni-MH batteries, and automobile Ni-MH batteries, MOFCOM decides to approve the concentration under conditions in order

(Continued)

（一）　关于硬币型锂二次电池

1、　剥离三洋公司目前全部的硬币型锂二次电池业务，即将三洋公司位于日本鸟取县岩见町的鸟取工厂的硬币形锂二次电池业务全部转让给独立第三方（购买人）。遴选购买人应按照有利于被剥离业务的发展和有利于市场竞争的原则进行，并需经商务部批准。三洋公司根据该购买人的需求，向购买人转让包括经营硬币形锂二次电池业务所需的生产设备、销售、研发部门及客户资源在内的相关资产；同时，三洋公司将许可购买人使用其所拥有的硬币型锂二次电池生产相关的专用知识产权。

2、　松下公司和三洋公司应在本次经营者集中完成日之后6个月内完成上述消除影响措施。如在该期限内未能实施完毕，可再延长6个月，但事前必须取得商务部批准。如果集中双方在该延长期内仍未能完成前述消除影响措施，则商务部有权指定独立受托人将前述拟剥离业务转让给独立第三方。

3、　从本次经营者集中完成之日至前述措施实施完毕止日的期间内，松下公司与三洋公司的相关事业主体独立运营，不得向对方披露有关价格、客户信息及其他竞争性信息，为履行法定义务而披露的信息不在此限。

（二）　关于民用镍氢电池

剥离三洋公司或松下公司其中一方的民用镍氢电池业务，具体剥离对象可由集中双方确定，具体剥离方案确定前须取得商务部批准。

1、　三洋将其在日本群马县高崎市的高崎工厂的民用镍氢电池业务转让给独立的第三方（购买人）；三洋将其在中国江苏省的苏州工厂生产的Sub-C•D型电池通过OEM形式供应给该购买人。

to mitigate the proposed concentration's adverse effect on market competition, and required Panasonic and Sanyo to fulfill the following obligations:

(1) regarding the lithium coin-cell secondary batteries

(i) Divest all of Sanyo's current lithium coin-cell secondary battery business, which is currently located at its Tottori factory in Iwami District, Tottori Prefecture, Japan and completely transfer or sell such business to an independent third party ("Buyer"). The selection of the Buyer shall be conducted in a way that would benefit the development of the divested business and market competition and shall be approved by MOFCOM. Sanyo will transfer or sell relevant assets required to conduct such business including production equipment, sales, R&D, and customer resources pursuant to the Buyer's needs. Meanwhile, Sanyo will permit the Buyer to use its specialized intellectual property related to lithium coin-cell secondary batteries production in its possession.

(ii) Sanyo and Panasonic shall complete the divestiture described above within six months after the merger is completed. If it is not completed within such time period, the deadline may be extended for another six months with MOFCOM's prior approval. If such divestiture is not completed within the extended period, MOFCOM will have the authority to appoint an independent trustee to transfer the business as described above to an independent third party.

三洋根据该购买人的需求，向
购买人转让包括经营民用镍氢
电池业务所需的生产设备、销
售、研发部门及客户资源在内
的资产，并许可该购买人使用
其拥有的民用镍氢电池生产相
关的知识产权；或者松下公司
将其在江苏省无锡工厂的民用
镍氢电池业务转让给购买人。
松下公司根据该购买人的需
求，向购买人转让包括经营民
用镍氢电池事业所需的生产设
备、销售、研发部门及客户资
源在内的资产，并许可该购买
人使用其拥有的民用镍氢电池
生产相关的知识产权。

遴选购买人应按照有利于被剥离业务
的发展和有利于市场竞争的原则进
行，并需经商务部批准。

2、 集中双方应在本次经营者集中
完成日之后6个月内实施前述
消除影响措施，如在该期限内
未能实施，在取得商务部认可
后，可再延长6个月。集中双
方如果在该延长期内仍未能实
施完毕前述消除影响措施，则
商务部有权指定独立的受托人
将前述拟剥离事业转让给独立
第三方。

3、 从本次经营者集中完成至前述
措施实施完毕的期间内，松下
公司与三洋公司的相关事业主
体独立运营，不得向对方披露
有关价格、客户的信息及其他
竞争性信息，为履行法定义务
而披露的信息不在此限。

(三) 关于车用镍氢电池

1、 关于松下公司剥离其车用镍氢
电池业务

第一，松下公司将其在日本国神奈
川县茅崎市的湘南工厂的HEV用镍氢
电池业务转让给独立第三方(购买
人)。遴选购买人应按照有利于被
剥离业务的发展和有利于市场竞争
的原则进行，并需经商务部批准。
松下公司根据该购买人的需求，

(iii) Between the date of the completion of the merger and the completion of the divestiture, Panasonic and Sanyo shall conduct related business independently and shall not disclose to each other any competitively sensitive information such as prices and customer information except for the disclosures pursuant to legal requirements or obligations.

(2) regarding consumer Ni-MH batteries

Divest the consumer Ni-MH battery business of either Sanyo or Panasonic, to be determined by the two parties of the merger. The detailed divestiture plan shall be approved by MOFCOM before it is finalized.

(i) Sanyo will transfer or sell its consumer Ni-MH battery business of its Takasaki factory located in Takasaki, Gunma Prefecture, Japan to an independent third party (the "Buyer"); Sanyo will transfer or sell its manufacturing facilities of Sub-C.D.-type batteries located in Suzhou, Jiangsu Province, China to such Buyer through the form of OEM. Sanyo will transfer or sell relevant assets required to conduct such business including production equipment, sales, R&D, and customer resources pursuant to the Buyer's needs. Meanwhile, Sanyo will permit the Buyer to use the intellectual property related to consumer Ni-MH battery production it owns; alternatively, Panasonic will transfer or sell its consumer Ni-MH battery business located in Wuxi, Jiangsu Province, China to the Buyer. Panasonic will transfer or sell relevant assets required to conduct such business including production equipment, sales, R&D, and customer resources

(Continued)

向购买人转让包括经营车用镍氢电池事业所需的生产设备、销售、研发部门及客户资源在内的资产，并许可该购买人使用其拥有的HEV用镍氢电池生产相关的知识产权。

第二，集中双方应在本次经营者集中完成日之后6个月内实施前述消除影响措施，如在该期限内未能实施完毕，在取得商务部认可后，可再延长6个月。集中双方如果在该延长期内仍未能实施完毕前述消除影响措施，则商务部有权指定独立的受托人将前述拟剥离事业转让给独立第三方。

第三，从本次经营者集中完成至前述措施实施完毕的期间内，松下公司与三洋公司的相关事业主体独立运营，不得向对方披露有关价格、客户的信息及其他竞争性信息，为履行法定义务而披露的信息不在此限。

2、 关于PEVE公司

第一，松下公司对PEVE的出资比例从目前的40%降到19.5%；

第二，松下公司放弃在PEVE股东大会的表决权；

第三，松下公司放弃对PEVE的董事委派权；

第四，放弃与PEVE的母公司丰田汽车的合资合同中关于车用镍氢电池业务的否决权；

第五，PEVE公司名称变更为不含"Panasonic"字样的公司名称。

前述措施应在本次经营者集中完成日之后6个月以内实施完毕，且在三年内对该措施内容不进行任何变更。终止该消除影响措施时，须获得商务部的认可。

pursuant to the Buyer's needs. Meanwhile, Panasonic will permit the Buyer to use the intellectual property related to consumer Ni-MH battery production it owns.

The selection of the Buyer shall be conducted in a way that would benefit the development of the divested business and market competition and shall be approved by MOFCOM.

(ii) Sanyo and Panasonic shall complete the divestiture described above within six months after the merger is completed. If it is not completed within such time period, the deadline may be extended for another six months with MOFCOM's prior approval. If such divestiture is not completed within the extended period, MOFCOM will have the authority to appoint an independent trustee to transfer the business as described above to an independent third party.

(iii) Between the date of the merger and completion of the divestiture, Panasonic and Sanyo shall conduct related business independently and shall not disclose to each other any competitively sensitive information such as prices and customer information except for the disclosures pursuant to legal requirements or obligations.

(3) regarding automobile Ni-MH batteries

(i) regarding Panasonic's divestiture of its automobile Ni-MH battery business

First, Panasonic will sell its HEV Ni-MH battery business of its Jounan factory located at Chigasaki, Kanagawa Prefecture, Japan to an independent third party (the "Buyer"). The selection of the Buyer shall be conducted in a way that would benefit the development of the divested business and market competition and shall be approved by MOFCOM. Panasonic will transfer or sell relevant assets required to conduct such business including production equipment, sales, R&D, and customer resources pursuant to the Buyer's needs. Meanwhile, Panasonic will permit the Buyer to use the intellectual property related to HEV Ni-MH battery production it owns.

Sanyo and Panasonic shall complete the divestiture described above within six months after the merger is completed. If it is not completed within such time period, the deadline may be extended for another six months with MOFCOM's prior approval. If such divestiture is not completed within the extended period, MOFCOM will have the authority to appoint an independent trustee to transfer the business as described above to an independent third party.

Between the date of the completion of the merger and the completion of the divestiture, Panasonic and Sanyo shall conduct related business independently and shall not disclose to each other any competitively sensitive information such as prices and customer information except for the disclosures pursuant to legal requirements or obligations.

(ii) regarding PEVE
first, Panasonic's capital contribution to PEVE shall be reduced from its current 40% to 19.5%;

secondly, Panasonic shall give up its voting rights at PEVE's shareholders' meetings;

(*Continued*)

	thirdly, Panasonic shall give up its rights to appoint a board member to PEVE's board of directors;
	fourthly, Panasonic will give up its veto rights relating to automobile Ni-MH battery business as part of the joint venture agreement with Toyota, another parent company of PEVE; and
	fifthly, PEVE shall change its company name to take out "Panasonic."
	These measures described above shall be implemented and completed within six months of the date of the merger and shall be effective for three years without any modification. Such measures may only be terminated with MOFCOM's consent.
本决定自公告之日起生效。 　　　　中华人民共和国商务部 　　　　二〇〇九年十月三十日	This decision shall become effective on the date of its announcement. Ministry of Commerce October 30, 2009

D-7

MOFCOM Announcement [2010] No. 53 Regarding the Conditional Approval of Novartis AG's Acquisition of Alcon Inc.

中华人民共和国商务部公告［2010年］第53号
（关于附条件批准诺华股份公司收购爱尔康公司反
垄断审查决定的公告）

(Published on August 13, 2010)

（2010年8月13日公布）

中华人民共和国商务部收到诺华股份公司(简称诺华)收购爱尔康公司(简称爱尔康)的经营者集中反垄断申报。经过审查，商务部决定附条件批准此项经营者集中。根据《中华人民共和国反垄断法》第三十条，现公告如下：	The Ministry of Commerce of the People's Republic of China ("MOFCOM") has received an anti-monopoly notification of a concentration of undertakings regarding the acquisition of Alcon Inc. ("Alcon") by Novartis AG ("Novartis"). After review, MOFCOM decides to approve this concentration under certain conditions. This announcement is made as follows in accordance with Article 30 of the Anti-Monopoly Law.
一、立案和审查程序 2010年4月20日，商务部收到诺华收购爱尔康的经营者集中申报申请，经审核，商务部认为申报材料达到了法定标准，予以立案，开始初步审查。初步审查过程中，商务部认为此项集中可能存在排除、限制竞争的问题，于5月17日决定实施进一步审查，进一步审查截止日期为8月14日。	**1 Acceptance and Review Process** MOFCOM received the notification on April 20, 2010 in connection with Novartis's contemplated acquisition of Alcon. After review of the notification, MOFCOM believed that the notification met the requisite standards under the relevant law, and accepted the notification as a new case and started preliminary review. During

(Continued)

	the preliminary review, MOFCOM found that the concentration raised concerns of restriction or elimination of competition, and decided to undertake a further review of the transaction on May 17, with the deadline for this further review set for August 14.
二、审查内容 根据《中华人民共和国反垄断法》第二十七条，商务部从如下几个方面对此项经营者集中进行了全面审查： （一）　参与集中的经营者在相关市场的市场份额及其对市场的控制力； （二）　相关市场的市场集中度； （三）　经营者集中对市场进入、技术进步的影响； （四）　经营者集中对消费者和其他有关经营者的影响； （五）　经营者集中对国民经济发展的影响。	**2 Issues Reviewed** MOFCOM conducted a thorough review of the transaction in accordance with Article 27 of the Anti-Monopoly Law from the following perspectives: (1)　the market shares of the undertakings concerned by the concentration in the relevant market and their ability to control the market; (2)　the level of concentration in the relevant market; (3)　the effect of the concentration on the market entry and the progress of technologies; (4)　the effect of the concentration on consumers and other undertakings; and (5)　the effect of the concentration on the development of the national economy.
三、审查工作 立案后，商务部书面征求了相关政府部门、行业协会的意见，对申报材料及相关补充材料的真实性、完整性进行了审核，要求申报方对特定问题进行了补充和澄清。审查中，商务部要求申报方就集中双方的重叠产品在中国和全球的市场份额情况、产品定价机制与销售模式、产品的性能和品质、行业监管政策以及市场参与者与申报方的关联关系等问题提供相关文件与证据。为了解相关方面意见，商务部还就关注问题向同行竞争者征求意见，对个别企业进行了电话调查。针对审查中发现的排除、限制竞争问题，商务部与申报方进行了充分磋商，并就消除不利影响的解决方案达成共识。	**3 Review Process** After MOFCOM accepted the notification, it consulted with relevant government agencies, trade associations, examined and verified the authenticity and the completeness of the notification materials, as supplemented, and requested additional information and clarifications from the notifying parties on certain issues. During the review process, MOFCOM requested the notifying parties to submit relevant documents and evidence to address the following issues: market shares of the overlapping products in China and worldwide, product pricing and sales model, product performance and quality, policy of industry supervision and management,

	and the relationships between market participants and the notifying parties. In order to understand the opinions from relevant parties, MOFCOM also obtained comments from competitors about relevant issues and conducted phone interviews with a few companies. To address the potential issues of restriction or elimination of competition in connection with the proposed concentration discovered during the review, MOFCOM has communicated and negotiated with the notifying parties to reach a mutually agreed resolution to prevent potential adverse consequences.
四、竞争问题 经审查，商务部认为此项集中可能在以下两个商品市场产生排除、限制竞争的不利影响： （一）　眼科抗炎/抗感染化合物 眼科抗炎/抗感染化合物适应症为抗炎和抗细菌，用于治疗眼睛发炎/眼部感染，特别适用于眼科手术后的眼睛发炎/眼部感染。经审查，该类产品构成独立的相关商品市场，诺华和爱尔康在中国销售的品牌分别为易妥芬和典必殊。申报材料表明，交易双方集中后在全球的市场份额超过55%，在中国的市场份额超过60%。目前，爱尔康在中国的市场份额超过60%，诺华在中国的市场份额不足1%。根据申报材料，诺华已经作出决策，将策略性地退出全球和中国市场。分析表明，诺华仍是中国市场竞争的参与者，如果诺华仅是为本次交易做出的策略性退出，在交易后有能力重新加大该产品在中国的投放，达到一定程度后，可能会在中国范围内会产生排除、限制竞争的效果。 （二）　关于隐形眼镜护理产品 申报材料表明，交易双方集中后在全球的市场份额接近60%，远高于其他竞争对手。在中国境内双方的市场份	**4 Competition Concerns** After review, MOFCOM decides that the concentration may have adverse effect of restricting or eliminating competition in the following two markets: A. Ophthalmologic Anti-Inflammatory/ 　　Anti-Infective Combinations Ophthalmologic anti-inflammatory/ anti-infective combinations are indicated for anti-inflammatory and anti-bacterial treatment and are useful for the treatment of eye-inflammation/ eye infections, especially for eye-inflammation/eye infections after an ophthalmologic operation. According to the review, the products constitute an independent relevant product market and the respective brands sold in China by Novartis and Alcon are Infectoflam and TobraDex. The notification materials indicate that post-concentration, the global market shares of the parties to the transaction will exceed 55% and their market shares in China will exceed 60%. At present, the market share of Alcon in China exceeds 60% while Novartis holds less than 1% market share in China.

(Continued)

额接近20%，集中后的企业将成为中国市场中第二大企业。 海昌隐形眼镜有限公司（简称海昌）为中国市场中第一大生产和销售企业，市场份额超过30%。

审查查明，2008年，诺华的全资子公司上海视康贸易有限公司（简称上海视康）与海昌签署了《销售和分销协议》，海昌成为上海视康在中国境内唯一的经销商。通过该协议双方建立了战略性合作伙伴关联关系。

该协议有可能导致集中后的企业和海昌在销售此类产品时，在产品价格、数量、销售区域等方面进行协调，从而可能具有排除、限制竞争的效果。

According to the notification materials, Novartis has made the decision to strategically withdraw from the global and Chinese market. As shown by analysis, Novartis is still competing in China. If Novartis decided to withdraw from the market strategically only for this transaction, it still has the capability to market the products again after the transaction on an even larger scale. If the marketing reaches a certain extent, it may restrict or eliminate competition in China.

B. Contact Lens Care Products

The notification materials indicate that, post-concentration, the parties' global market share nearly reaches 60% and is much higher than other competitors. The market share of the two parties in China is nearly 20% and, post-concentration, the combined entity will be the second largest one in China. Haichang Contact Lenses Co., Ltd. ("Haichang"), which has a market share of more than 30%, is the largest competitor in the fields of production and sale in China.

As shown by the investigation, Shanghai Shikang Trading Co., Ltd. ("Shanghai Shikang"), a wholly owned subsidiary of Novartis, signed a Sales and Distribution Agreement with Haichang in 2008, which made Haichang the sole distributor of Shanghai Shikang in the territory of China. Shanghai Shikang and Haichang have set up a strategic affiliated partnership.

This agreement may lead to the result that when, post-concentration, the combined entity and Haichang market said products, they can coordinate in the aspects of price, quantity, market zone, etc., and may eliminate and/or restrict competition.

五、附加限制性条件的商谈	**5 Negotiation of Restrictive Conditions**
为了解决上述竞争问题，根据《反垄断法》第二十九条的规定，2010年8月6日、8月9日，商务部与申报方就限制性条件进行了多次商谈。2010年8月9日，申报方提出了减少集中对竞争产生不利影响的最终救济措施。经过评估，商务部认为该最终救济措施可以减少此项集中对中国市场可能造成的不利影响。	To address the competition issues described above, MOFCOM and the notifying parties held several discussions respectively on August 6 and August 9, 2010 regarding the restrictive conditions according to Article 29 of the Anti-Monopoly Law. On August 9, 2010, the notifying parties submitted the final plan of remedies to mitigate the adverse effect of the concentration. After assessment, MOFCOM determined that the final plan was sufficient to mitigate the adverse effect of the concentration over the Chinese market.
六、审查决定	**6 Review Decision**
鉴于诺华与爱尔康的经营者集中可能对眼科抗炎/抗感染化合物和隐形眼镜护理商品市场产生排除、限制竞争效果，为了减少集中对市场竞争产生的不利影响，商务部决定附条件批准此项集中，要求诺华和爱尔康履行如下义务：	Because the proposed concentration of undertakings between Novartis and Alcon would result in restriction or elimination of competition in ophthalmological anti-inflammatory/anti-infective compounds and contact lenses care products, MOFCOM decided to approve the concentration under certain conditions in order to mitigate the proposed concentration's adverse effect on market competition, and required Novartis and Alcon to fulfill the following obligations:
（一）　关于眼科抗炎/抗感染化合物。	1 Ophtalmological Anti-Inflammatory/Anti-Infective compounds
截止2010年底，诺华全面停止向中国销售易妥芬产品；同时，在商务部审查决定生效之日起5年内，诺华不得重新将易妥芬产品或以新名称出现的同样产品投放中国市场，不得将其在本交易割前所拥有的，诺华在中国之外的其他国家销售的眼科抗炎/抗感染化合物产品投放中国市场。在此5年期内，自审查决定生效之日起的每一周年，诺华应向商务部汇报履行承诺的情况。	By the end of 2010, Novartis shall cease the sale of Infectoflam in China; at the same time, within five years of the effective date of MOFCOM's review decision, Novartis shall not re-launch Infectoflam or the same products under a new name into China. Novartis shall not launch the ophthalmic anti-inflammatory/anti-infective compounds that it owned and sold in other countries before closing of this transaction, into China. In this five-year period, Novartis shall report to MOFCOM about the performance of these commitments
（二）　关于隐形眼镜护理产品。	
在商务部审查决定生效之日起12个月内，诺华终止上海视康与海昌隐形眼镜公司之间的《销售和分销协议》。诺华应在终止《销售和分销协议》一周之内向商务部汇报履行承诺的情况。	

(Continued)

	every anniversary after the date when the review decision becomes effective.
	2 Contact Lenses Care Products
	Within 12 months of the effective date of MOFCOM's review decision, Novartis shall terminate the Sales and Distribution Agreement between Shanghai Shikang and Haichang. Novartis shall report to MOFCOM about the performance of these commitments within one week of its termination of the Sales and Distribution Agreement.
自本决定生效之日起，商务部有权对上述限制性条件的实施进行监督检查；诺华应当根据商务部《关于实施经营者集中资产或业务剥离的暂行规定》，委托监督受托人对其履行义务的情况进行监督。	From the date this decision comes into effect, MOFCOM has the right to supervise and inspect the implementation of the above restrictive conditions. Novartis shall, according to the Interim Provisions on Asset or Business Divestiture during the Implementation of Concentrations of Undertakings, entrust a supervision trustee to supervise its performance of the obligations.
本决定自公告之日起生效。 中华人民共和国商务部 二〇一〇年八月十三日	This decision shall become effective as of the date of its announcement. Ministry of Commerce August 13, 2010

D-8

MOFCOM Announcement [2011] No. 33 Regarding the Conditional Approval of the Acquisition of Public Joint-Stock Company Silvinit by Public Joint-Stock Company Uralkali

中华人民共和国商务部[2011]第33号公告(关于附条件批准乌拉尔开放型股份公司吸收合并谢尔维尼特开放型股份公司反垄断审查决定的公告）

(Published on June 2, 2011)

（2011年6月2日公布）

中华人民共和国商务部(以下简称商务部)收到乌拉尔开放型股份公司(以下简称乌钾或申报方)吸收合并谢尔维尼特开放型股份公司(以下简称谢钾)的经营者集中反垄断申报，根据《中华人民共和国反垄断法》（以下简称《反垄断法》)和相关规定对该项经营者集中进行了审查，决定对该项经营者集中附加限制性条件。现公告如下：

The Ministry of Commerce of the People's Republic of China ("MOFCOM") has received an anti-monopoly notification of a concentration of undertakings regarding the acquisition of public joint-stock company Silvinit ("Silvinit") by public joint-stock company Uralkali ("Uralkali" or the "notifying party"). MOFCOM reviewed the concentration in accordance with the Anti-Monopoly Law of the People's Republic of China ("AML") and relevant rules, and decided to approve the concentration under certain conditions. The decision is hereby announced as follows:

一、立案和审查过程

2011年3月14日，商务部收到了申报方提交的符合《反垄断法》第二十三条规定的文件、资料，对该项经营者集中申报予以立案，进行初步审查。

1 Acceptance and Review Process
On March 14, 2011, MOFCOM received relevant notification documents and materials from the notifying party which were in compliance with the requirements of Article 23 of the AML. Upon

(Continued)

4月12日，商务部作出了对该项经营者集中实施进一步审查的决定。6月2日，商务部作出了对该项经营者集中附加限制性条件的决定。

在审查过程中，商务部对申报方提交的文件、资料及补交的文件、资料的真实性、完整性和准确性进行了审核，要求申报方对参与集中双方重叠产品的种类和品质、生产和资源分布、定价机制和销售模式、各方在中国和全球的市场份额以及行业发展现状和前景等信息进行了澄清、说明和补充。

商务部书面征求了有关政府部门、行业协会等各方面的意见，并通过书面和座谈会方式，向相关生产商、贸易商以及行业专家了解了相关产品、钾资源分布、相关市场界定、市场结构以及生产、运营和贸易模式等方面的信息。

acceptance of the filing and preliminary review, MOFCOM decided on April 12 to have a further review of the proposed concentration. On June 2, MOFCOM issued its decision granting conditional anti-monopoly approval of the proposed concentration.

In the course of review, MOFCOM checked the documents, materials, and supplemental information submitted by the notifying party for authenticity, completeness, and accuracy, and requested the notifying party to provide clarification, explanation, and supplemental information regarding, *inter alia*, the type and nature of overlapping products between the merging parties, the distribution of production and resources, their pricing mechanisms and sales models, the parties' respective market shares in China and worldwide, and the current status and future prospects of the industry's development.

MOFCOM solicited in writing comments from relevant governmental departments and trade associations, collected information in writing and through workshops with relevant producers, trading companies, and industry experts regarding the relevant products, distribution of the potassium resources, definition of the relevant market, market structure, as well as the production, operations, and trading model.

二、竞争分析

商务部根据《反垄断法》第二十七条规定的因素，对该项经营者集中进行了审查，深入分析了该项经营者集中对市场竞争的影响，认为其可能具有排除、限制竞争的不利影响。

2 Competition Analysis
MOFCOM reviewed the proposed concentration in accordance with the factors listed in Article 27 of the AML, and after an in-depth analysis of the effect of the proposed concentration on market competition, MOFCOM believes that the proposed concentration may have the adverse effect of eliminating and/or restricting competition.

商务部认定氯化钾为相关商品市场。氯化钾主要作为钾肥使用。钾肥包括氯化钾、硫酸钾、硝酸钾、磷酸二氢钾、硫酸钾镁肥等。氯化钾通常是其他形式钾肥和复合肥的原料。从商品特性、用途等因素分析，氯化钾与其他钾肥产品之间不具有较为紧密的替代关系。商务部考察了全球氯化钾市场和中国氯化钾市场的情况。基于中国氯化钾进口现状，还考虑了中国氯化钾进口市场，包括氯化钾海运贸易市场和边境贸易市场。

商务部审查了相关市场的市场份额、市场集中度以及乌钾吸收合并谢钾后的公司对市场的控制力。氯化钾生产依赖钾资源的自然分布。在全球范围内，钾资源主要集中在少数国家，其中全球前三大钾资源拥有国合计约占世界总储量的80%以上。全球氯化钾的生产和销售主要集中于少数几家企业。本项经营者集中完成后将产生全球第二大的氯化钾出口供应商，市场份额将超过全球市场的1/3，其与全球第一大供应商合计约占全球氯化钾供应量的70%。中国对国际氯化钾市场依赖度较高，目前有一半左右的氯化钾需求依赖海运贸易和边境贸易进口，其中进口量的一半以上来源于谢钾、乌钾及其关联贸易公司。

该项经营者集中实施后，谢钾作为一个有竞争实力的供应商被乌钾吸收合并，相关市场的集中度将进一步提高。一方面，合并后的公司将拥有更多的钾资源和更强大的生产、供应及出口能力，对国际氯化钾市场将拥有更强的市场控制力，可能对包括中国市场在内的全球氯化钾海运贸易市场竞争产生不利影响。 同时，该项经营者集中也增加了全球范围内氯化钾供应商协调生产和销售的可能性，可能具有排除、限制竞争的效果。另一方面，边境贸易是中国进口氯化钾的重要途径。 中国1/3左右的进口氯化钾来自与乌钾和谢钾的边境贸易。 该项经营者集中实施后，

MOFCOM holds that the relevant product market in this case is potassium chloride, which is mainly used as a potassium fertilizer. Potassium fertilizers include, among others, potassium chloride, potassium sulfate, potassium nitrate, potassium dihydrogen phosphate, and magnesium-potassium sulfate fertilizer. Potassium chloride is usually used as raw materials for other forms of potassium fertilizers and compound fertilizers. According to an analysis of the product's properties, applications, and other factors, there is no close substitutability between potassium chloride and other potassium fertilizer products. MOFCOM researched the global and domestic market for potassium chloride. Due to the current circumstances of Chinese potassium chloride importation, MOFCOM also considered the Chinese import market for potassium chloride, including the ocean transport market and the border trade market for potassium chloride.

MOFCOM reviewed the market share and level of market concentration in the relevant market as well as the post-merger market power of the combined company after absorption of Silvinit by Uralkali. The production of potassium chloride relies on the natural distribution of potassium resources. Globally, potassium resources are primarily concentrated in a few countries, and the world top three potassium reserve countries approximately account for over 80% of the total reserve in the world. The production and sale of potassium chloride in the world are primarily concentrated in the hands of a few companies. The proposed concentration will create the world's second largest export provider of potassium chloride, and its market share will account for

(*Continued*)

中国以边境贸易方式进口氯化钾将由乌钾和谢钾两家公司供应变为合并后的公司独家供应，这可能对中国氯化钾边境贸易市场具有排除、限制竞争效果。

商务部审查了氯化钾市场进入的难易程度。进入氯化钾市场主要受制于：是否拥有商业上可开采钾矿资源以及开发新矿或扩展现有设施所需资金量。审查发现，钾矿资源主要集中在现存氯化钾生产商手中，开发新矿或扩展现有设施所需资金量大、时间长，同时伴随较大的产业、技术、地质和环境等风险。其他竞争者市场进入难度较大。

此外，基于中国对氯化钾进口的依赖以及氯化钾市场结构现状，该项经营者集中将对中国农业等相关产业产生一定影响。

over one-third of the global market, and, together with the largest provider, it will account for around 70% of the world supply of potassium chloride. China depends heavily on the international potassium chloride market, and currently about half of the demand for potassium chloride in China relies on import by ocean trade and border trade; over half of such imports are sourced from Silvinit, Uralkali and their affiliated trading companies.

Upon implementation of the proposed concentration, Silvinit, as a separate competitive force, will be absorbed by Uralkali, and the concentration in the relevant market will be further aggravated. On one hand, the combined company will hold more potassium resources; possess stronger production, supply, and export capacity; and gain a stronger market power over the international market for potassium chloride, which may have an adverse effect on the competition in the global ocean trade market for potassium chloride (including the Chinese market). At the same time, the proposed concentration also increases the likelihood of global suppliers of potassium chloride coordinating their production and sales, which may have the effect of eliminating and/or restricting competition. On the other hand, border trade is an important means for importation of potassium chloride in China, and about one-third of imported potassium chloride is sourced from border trades with Uralkali and Silvinit. Upon implementation of the proposed concentration, China's importation of potassium chloride by border trade will change from supply by Uralkali and Silvinit as separate entities to sole supply by the combined company, which may have the effect of eliminating or restricting competition in the border trade market for potassium chloride in China.

MOFCOM reviewed the barriers to enter the potassium chloride market, and such barriers mainly included the availability and possession of commercially exploitable potassium resources, and funding required to develop new mines or expand current facilities. After review, it found that potassium resources are mainly concentrated in the hands of existing producers of potassium chloride, and that developing new mines or expanding existing facilities requires large amounts of time and money and is accompanied by considerable industrial, technical, geological, and environmental risks. The barriers to entry are high.

In addition, on account of China's dependence on importation of potassium chloride and the current market structure for potassium chloride, the proposed concentration will have certain effects on relevant industries in China, including agriculture.

三、附加限制性条件的商谈

为解决上述竞争问题，根据《反垄断法》第二十九条的规定，商务部于5月11日向申报方提出了竞争关注，申报方提出了就竞争关注提交相应解决方案的意向。5月13日、5月17日、5月18日和5月20日，商务部就申报方提交的解决方案与其进行了数轮商谈。5月20日，申报方提出了减少该项经营者集中对竞争产生不利影响的解决方案。经过评估，商务部认为上述解决方案可以减少该项经营者集中对竞争产生的不利影响，接受了申报方提出的上述解决方案。

3 Negotiation of Restrictive Conditions

In order to resolve the above competitive issues, MOFCOM expressed its competition concerns to the notifying party on May 11 under Article 29 of the AML, in response to which the notifying party indicated its intention to propose remedies to address the competition concerns. Various negotiations were held with the notifying party on May 13, May 17, May 18, and May 20 in connection with the proposal. On May 20, the notifying party submitted a proposal which was aimed at mitigating the adverse effect of the proposed concentration on the market competition. After evaluation, MOFCOM held that the submitted

(Continued)

	proposal could mitigate the adverse effect of the proposed concentration on market competition, and therefore accepted the proposal submitted by the notifying party.
四、审查决定 商务部认为，乌钾吸收合并谢钾的经营者集中可能对中国氯化钾市场产生排除、限制竞争的效果。为了减少该项经营者集中对市场竞争产生的不利影响，商务部决定对该项集中附加限制性条件，经营者自本公告之日起可以实施集中，但须履行如下义务： （一） 合并后的公司应继续保持目前的氯化钾销售做法和程序，交易后继续以直接贸易方式对中国市场销售氯化钾，并继续通过铁路运输和海上运输方式为中国市场稳定可靠、尽心尽力地供应氯化钾产品。 （二） 合并后的公司应一如既往地为中国市场提供种类齐全和数量充足的氯化钾产品，包括氧化钾含量为60%和62%的氯化钾产品（包括白色的白钾和粉色的红钾）。此外，合并后的公司应一如既往地供应中国用户，在种类和数量上满足其在农业、工业和特殊工业用途在内的各种用途。 （三） 合并后的公司应维持惯常的协商程序，价格谈判应充分考虑与中国客户交易的历史情况与现状，以及中国市场的特殊性。惯常的协商包括现货销售（按每笔交易或按月度）或合同销售（半年或年度）而进行的价格协商。 （四） 自审查决定生效之日起的每半年或应商务部要求，合并后的公司应向商务部汇报履行承诺的情况。 商务部有权对限制性条件的实施进行监督检查。合并后的公司应当根据商务部对本案适用的相关规定，	**4 Review Decision** MOFCOM holds that the proposed concentration of Uralkali and Silvinit may have the effect of eliminating and/or restricting competition in the Chinese market for potassium chloride. In order to mitigate the adverse effect of the proposed concentration on market competition, MOFCOM decides to approve the proposed concentration subject to certain restrictive conditions. As from the date of this announcement, the undertakings may proceed with the concentration subject to compliance with the following obligations: (1) the combined company shall continue to maintain existing sales practices and procedures with respect to potassium chloride, and will continue to sell potassium chloride to Chinese markets via direct trading, and stably, reliably, and with the utmost effort supply potassium chloride products to the Chinese market by rail and sea. (2) the combined company shall continue as before to supply a complete array of potassium chloride products in sufficient quantities to the Chinese market, including potassium chloride products with 60% and 62% K_2O (including white Potassium White, and pink Potassium Red). In addition, the combined company shall continue as before to supply its Chinese customers, to meet their various demands, both in terms of category and quantity, for all applications including agricultural, industrial, and special industrial purposes.

委托监督受托人对其履行义务的情况进行监督。合并后的公司如有任何违反上述限制性条件的行为，商务部有权依法予以处罚。	(3) the combined company shall continue to maintain the customary negotiation process, and the pricing negotiation shall fully consider the history and current circumstances of its dealings with Chinese customers and the uniqueness of the Chinese market. The customary negotiations include pricing negotiations for spot sale (by transaction or month) and contract sale (semi-annual or annual). (4) as from the effective date of this decision, the combined company shall report its adherence to its commitments on a semi-annual basis or at the request of MOFCOM. MOFCOM shall have the right to inspect, monitor, and oversee the implementation of the restrictive conditions. The combined company shall appoint a supervision trustee to supervise its performance of the obligations in accordance with the relevant requirements that MOFCOM has applied in connection with the concentration. In the event of any violation by the combined company of any of the above-mentioned restrictive conditions, MOFCOM shall have the right to punish such violation in accordance with law.
本决定自公告之日起生效。 　　　　中华人民共和国商务部 　　　　二〇一一年六月二日	This decision shall become effective as of the date of its announcement. Ministry of Commerce June 2, 2011

MOFCOM Announcement [2011] No. 73 Regarding the Conditional Approval for the Acquisition of Savio Macchine Tessili S.P.A. by Penelope Company Limited

商务部公告2011年第73号关于附条件批准佩内洛普有限责任公司收购萨维奥纺织机械股份有限公司反垄断审查决定的公告

(Published on October 31, 2011)

（2011年10月31日公布）

中华人民共和国商务部（以下简称商务部）收到佩内洛普有限责任公司（以下简称佩内洛普）收购萨维奥纺织机械股份有限公司（以下简称萨维奥）的经营者集中反垄断申报。经审查，商务部决定附加限制性条件批准此项经营者集中。根据《中华人民共和国反垄断法》（以下简称《反垄断法》）第三十条，现公告如下：

The Ministry of Commerce of the People's Republic of China ("MOFCOM") has received an anti-monopoly notification of a concentration of undertakings regarding the acquisition of Savio Macchine Tessili S.P.A. ("Savio") by Penelope Company Limited ("Penelope"). After review, MOFCOM decides to approve this concentration of undertakings subject to restrictive conditions. The following announcement is hereby made under Article 30 of the Anti-Monopoly Law of the People's Republic of China ("AML"):

一、立案和审查程序

2011年7月14日，商务部收到佩内洛普收购萨维奥经营者集中申报。经审核，商务部认为该申报材料不完备，要求申报方予以补充。9月5日，商务部确认经补充的申报材料符合《反垄断法》第二十三条的要求，对该项经营者集中申报开始立案审查。

1 Acceptance and Review Process

A notification of concentration of undertakings was received by MOFCOM on July 14, 2011 concerning Penelope's contemplated acquisition of Savio. After review, MOFCOM concluded that the notification was incomplete and required the

经初步审查，商务部认为此项集中将对自动络筒机电子清纱器市场具有或可能具有排除、限制竞争效果。9月15日，商务部向申报方提出了对此项集中的竞争关注。9月23日，申报方向商务部提交了解决方案。9月30日，商务部决定实施进一步审查，截止日期为12月29日。在进一步审查过程中，商务部对申报方提出的解决方案进行了评估，认为该方案能够解决此项集中产生的竞争问题。10月31日，商务部作出了对该项经营者集中附加限制性条件的决定。

审查过程中商务部征求了有关政府部门、行业协会、同业竞争者和下游企业的意见。

二、竞争分析

商务部根据《反垄断法》第二十七条规定的因素，对此项经营者集中进行了审查，深入分析了此项经营者集中对市场竞争的影响，认为其可能具有排除、限制竞争的不利影响。

收购方佩内洛普是专为此次交易成立的工具公司。佩内洛普的全资控股股东Alpha Private Equity Fund V（以下简称Alpha V）是一家私募股权基金，投资领域涉及有色金属回收利用，家用纺织品销售、纺织机械生产和销售等。

notifying party to submit supplemental information. On September 5, 2011, MOFCOM confirmed that the filing, as supplemented, met the requirements of Article 23 of the AML, and started the review of this concentration.

After a preliminary review, MOFCOM concluded that this concentration has or may have the effect of eliminating and/or restricting competition in the market for electronic yarn clearers for automatic winders. On September 15, MOFCOM raised its anti-competitive concerns to the notifying party. On September 23, the notifying party submitted its proposed solutions to MOFCOM. On September 30, MOFCOM decided to have a further review until December 29, 2011. During the further review, MOFCOM assessed the solutions proposed by the notifying party and accepted that the proposed solution could solve the competition issues arising from the concentration. On October 31, 2011, MOFCOM issued its decision to grant approval for this concentration of undertakings subject to restrictive conditions.

In the review process, MOFCOM solicited opinions from relevant governmental departments, trade associations, competitors in the same industry, and downstream enterprises.

2 Competition Analysis
MOFCOM reviewed the concentration in accordance with the factors specified in Article 27 of the AML, and made an in-depth analysis of the effect of the concentration on market competition, on the basis of which MOFCOM concluded that this transaction may likely have an adverse effect by restricting or eliminating competition in the market.

The acquiring party, Penelope, is a special purpose vehicle set up specifically for this transaction.

(Continued)

Alpha V持有乌斯特技术有限公司（以下简称乌斯特）27.9%的股份，是乌斯特的第一大股东。 被收购方萨维奥是一家纺织机械生产商，主要生产自动络筒机、自动络筒机电子清纱器、转杯纺纱机和倍捻机等产品。络菲兄弟有限公司（以下简称络菲）是萨维奥的全资子公司。

经调查，商务部发现乌斯特和络菲是全球仅有的两家自动络筒机电子清纱器制造商。自动络筒机电子清纱器是装配于自动络筒机的监控装置，功能是探测出纱线质量瑕疵后进行自动修补。该装置能够在极短的时间内高速处理纱线质量瑕疵，其他装置无法实现此项功能。自动络筒机电子清纱器市场构成单独市场。

商务部对此项集中涉及的自动络筒机电子清纱器市场竞争状况、供求关系、采购模式和市场进入等问题进行了调查，利用第三方信息对申报方提供的数据进行了核实，并就有关问题咨询了行业专家的意见。商务部重点对Alpha V是否可能参与或影响乌斯特的经营活动进行了审查，内容包括乌斯特的股权结构、股东大会表决机制、股东大会历史出席记录、董事会的组成和表决机制等。商务部认为，不能排除Alpha V参与或影响乌斯特经营活动的可能性。

自动络筒机电子清纱器市场高度集中。作为仅有的两家自动络筒机电子清纱器制造商，乌斯特和络菲2010年在全球市场的份额分别为52.3%和47.7%，在中国市场的份额与此类似。此项集中完成后，乌斯特和络菲有可能通过Alpha V协调其经营活动，排除、限制自动络筒机电子清纱器市场的竞争。同时，Alpha V也有可能通过对乌斯特和络菲的控制和影响从事上述排除、限制竞争行为。

商务部对自动络筒机电子清纱器的市场进入进行了调查。调查发现，有关专利、专有技术和商业秘密对研发和生产自动络筒机电子清纱器具有关键作用，

Penelope is wholly owned by Alpha Private Equity Fund V ("Alpha V"), a private equity fund investing in, among other industry sectors, the recycling of non-ferrous metals, sales of household textiles, and production and sales of textile machinery. Alpha V is also the largest shareholder, with a 27.9% equity stake, in Uster Technologies Co., Ltd. ("Uster"). The target of the acquisition, Savio, is a producer of textiles machinery which includes, among other things, automatic winders, electronic yarn clearers for automatic winders, rotor spinning machines, and two-for-one twisters. Loepfe Brothers Ltd. ("Loepfe") is a wholly owned subsidiary of Savio.

During the investigation, MOFCOM found that Uster and Loepfe are the only two manufacturers of electronic yarn clearers for automatic winders in the world. An electronic yarn clearer is a monitoring and control device installed on an automatic winder to detect and automatically repair any defect in the yarns. It has the unique function to expeditiously treat yarn defects within an extremely short time, and other devices are unable to conduct the same function. The market for electronic yarn clearers for automatic winders constitutes a separate market.

MOFCOM made relevant investigations regarding, among other aspects, the competitive conditions, demand and supply, type of procurement and market entry in the market of electronic yarn clearers for automatic winders, verified the data provided by the notifying party with information from third parties, and consulted with industry experts regarding relevant issues. In its review, MOFCOM focused on the possibility for Alpha V to participate in or influence the operations of Uster. MOFCOM's review

自动络筒机电子清纱器技术已受专利等知识产权的保护，新企业进入这一市场难度很大。同时，规模经济对包括自动络筒机电子清纱器在内的纺织机械行业十分重要，新的市场进入者很难在短期内形成规模经济。调查未发现最近三年有新的企业成功进入这一市场。证据表明，2009年曾有企业合作研发自动络筒机电子清纱器，但其产品未获客户认可，2010年未取得市场份额。商务部认为自动络筒机电子清纱器市场进入难度很大。

综上，商务部认为此项集中将对自动络筒机电子清纱器市场具有或可能具有排除、限制竞争的效果。

covered the shareholding structure of Uster, the voting mechanism at Uster shareholders' meetings, the historical attendance of Uster shareholders' meetings, as well as the composition and voting mechanisms of Uster's board of directors. MOFCOM concluded that the possibility for Alpha V to participate in or influence the operations of Uster could not be ruled out.

The market for electronic yarn clearers for automatic winders is highly concentrated. As the only two producers of electronic yarn clearers for automatic winders in the world, Uster and Loepfe respectively have global market shares of 52.3% and 47.7%, with a similar market share split in China, for 2010. After the concentration, Uster and Loepfe are likely to coordinate their business activities through Alpha V, in order to restrict or eliminate competition in the market for electronic yarn clearers for automatic winders. At the same time, Alpha V is also likely to engage in activities restricting or eliminating competition by way of its control and influence over Uster and Loepfe.

MOFCOM investigated market entry for electronic yarn clearers for automatic winders. The investigation found that the relevant patents, know-how, and business secrets play a key role in the research, development, and production of electronic yarn clearers for automatic winders, and the relevant technologies are protected by patents and other intellectual property rights, which is a significant barrier for new entrants. In addition, economies of scale are quite important in the industry of textile machinery including electronic yarn clearers, and it is very difficult for new entrants to establish economies of scale in a short time. The investigation did not find any successful

(Continued)

	case of new entry into this market during the past three years. Evidence shows that there were companies collaborating to research and develop electronic yarn clearers for automatic winders in 2009, but their product did not receive customer recognition, and did not win any market share in 2010. MOFCOM concluded that there are considerable difficulties for new entry into the market of automatic yarn clearers for automatic winders. In summary, MOFCOM concluded that this concentration will or is likely to have the effect of restricting or eliminating competition in the market for electronic yarn clearers for automatic winders.
三、附加限制性条件的商谈 商务部与申报方就如何消除上述竞争问题进行了多轮商谈。9月23日，Alpha V的最终控制实体Apef Management Company 5 Limited（以下简称Apef 5）提交了最终解决方案。经过评估，商务部认为该解决方案可以消除此项经营者集中对竞争的不利影响。	**3 Negotiations of Restrictive Conditions** MOFCOM and the notifying party held multiple rounds of negotiations regarding how to address the above competition concerns. On September 23, Apef Management Company 5 Limited ("Apef 5"), the ultimate controlling entity of Alpha V, submitted the final remedy proposal. After evaluation, MOFCOM concluded that the proposal could preclude the adverse effects of this concentration on competition.
四、审查决定 鉴于佩内洛普收购萨维奥后对自动络筒机电子清纱器市场具有或可能具有排除、限制竞争效果，商务部决定附加限制性条件批准此项集中，要求Alpha V的最终控制实体Apef 5履行如下义务： （一）　商务部作出审查决定起6个月内将其持有乌斯特的股份转让给独立第三方。 （二）　向商务部报告受让方的身份、交易量以及交易日期，确保转让乌斯特的股份不会产生新的排除、限制竞争问题。	**4 Review Decision** Considering that the acquisition of Savio by Penelope has or may have the effect of eliminating and/or restricting competition in the market for electronic yarn clearers for automatic winders, MOFCOM decides to approve this concentration subject to restrictive conditions, and requested Alpha V's ultimate controlling entity Apef 5 to perform the following obligations: (1)　to transfer its shares in Uster to an independent third party within six months of the date of this decision by MOFCOM;

（三） 转让乌斯特的股份完成前不得参与或影响乌斯特经营管理活动。 （四） 根据商务部《关于实施经营者集中资产或业务剥离的暂行规定》（商务部公告2010年第41号），委托独立的监督受托人对转让股份进行监督。 自本决定生效之日起，商务部有权对上述限制性条件的实施进行监督检查。	(2) to report to MOFCOM the identity of the buyer, and the amount and date of the transaction, to ensure that such transfer of Uster shares will not give rise to new competitive concerns regarding the restriction or elimination of competition; (3) not to participate in or influence the operations and management of Uster prior to completion of the transfer; and (4) to appoint an independent supervision trustee to supervise the equity transfer in accordance with the Interim Provisions on Asset or Business Divestiture during the Implementation of Concentrations of Undertakings (MOFCOM Announcement [2010] No. 41). As from the effective date of this decision, MOFCOM has the right to monitor and inspect the implementation of the above restrictive conditions.
本决定自公告之日起生效。 中华人民共和国商务部 二〇一一年十月三十一日	This decision shall become effective as of the date of its announcement. Ministry of Commerce October 31, 2011

D-10

MOFCOM Announcement [2011] No. 74 Regarding the Anti-Monopoly Review Decision for Conditional Approval of the Contemplated Joint Venture between GE (China) Co., Ltd. and China Shenhua Coal to Liquid and Chemical Co., Ltd.

商务部公告2011年第74号 关于附条件批准通用电气（中国）有限公司与中国神华煤制油化工有限公司设立合营企业反垄断审查决定的公告

(Published on November 10, 2011)

（2011年11月10日公布）

中华人民共和国商务部（以下简称商务部）收到通用电气（中国）有限公司（以下简称通用中国）与中国神华煤制油化工有限公司（以下简称神华煤制油）设立合营企业的经营者集中反垄断申报。经审查，商务部决定附加限制性条件批准此项经营者集中。根据《中华人民共和国反垄断法》（以下简称《反垄断法》）第三十条，现公告如下：	The Ministry of Commerce of the People's Republic of China ("MOFCOM") has received an anti-monopoly notification of a concentration of undertakings regarding the establishment of a joint venture between GE (China) Co., Ltd. ("GE China") and China Shenhua Coal to Liquid and Chemical Co., Ltd. ("CSCLC"). After review, MOFCOM decides to approve this concentration under certain conditions. The decision is hereby announced in accordance with Article 30 of the Anti-Monopoly Law of the People's Republic of China ("AML").

一、立案和审查程序	**1 Acceptance and Review Process**
2011年4月13日，商务部收到通用中国与神华煤制油设立合营企业经营者集中申报。经审核，商务部认为该申报文件、资料不完备，要求申报方予以补充。5月16日，商务部确认经补充的申报文件、资料符合《反垄断法》第二十三条的要求，对该项经营者集中申报予以立案并开始初步审查。	On April 13, 2011, MOFCOM received an anti-monopoly notification for the contemplated joint venture between GE China and CSCLC. After review, MOFCOM decided that the notification documents and materials were incomplete, and requested additional information. On May 16, 2011, MOFCOM confirmed that the notification documents, as supplemented, complied with the requirement of Article 23 of the AML, accepted the notification into the docket, and started the preliminary review.
经审查，商务部认为此项集中对水煤浆气化技术许可市场可能具有排除、限制竞争效果。6月15日，商务部决定对此项集中实施进一步审查。9月13日，商务部决定延长进一步审查期限。	After review, MOFCOM determined that this concentration is likely to have the effect of restricting or eliminating competition in the licensing market for coal-water slurry gasification technology. On June 15, 2011, MOFCOM decided to conduct further review of the concentration. On September 13, MOFCOM decided to extend the period of further review.
审查过程中，商务部征求了政府有关部门、行业协会、同业竞争者的意见，利用第三方信息对申报方提供的数据进行了核实，就有关问题咨询了行业专家的意见。	In the process of review, MOFCOM solicited comments from relevant governmental departments, trade associations, and other competitors in the market, and verified the information that the notifying party submitted against third party information, and solicited opinions from industry experts regarding relevant issues.
二、竞争分析	**2 Competition Analysis**
商务部根据《反垄断法》第二十七条规定的因素，对此项经营者集中进行了审查，深入分析了此项经营者集中对市场竞争的影响，认为其可能具有排除、限制竞争的不利影响。	On the basis of the factors specified in Article 27 of the AML, MOFCOM reviewed the concentration of undertakings, and conducted an in-depth analysis of the effect of this concentration on market competition, and concluded that it is likely to have adverse effects that may restrict or eliminate competition.

(Continued)

参与设立合营企业一方通用中国是通用电气公司在中国设立的外商投资公司。通用基础设施技术公司是通用电气公司的子公司，在本次交易中负责向拟设立合营企业许可通用水煤浆气化技术。参与设立合营企业的另一方神华煤制油主要从事煤炭液化、煤化工项目及配套项目的开发经营。神华煤制油的母公司神华集团有限责任公司（以下简称神华集团）是综合性能源企业，以煤炭、电力、热力的生产和供应，以及铁路、港口运输服务为主营业务。

拟设立合营企业的业务主要是向工业和电力项目提供水煤浆气化技术许可和工程服务。水煤浆气化技术是将固体形态的煤炭转变成水煤浆，经过再加工生产出一氧化碳和氢气等混合气体的一种煤气化技术。水煤浆气化技术与其他煤气化技术在技术工艺、原料煤要求和进料方式等方面存在显著区别，水煤浆气化技术许可市场构成相关商品市场。拟设立合营企业营业范围限于中国，且国内水煤浆气化技术需求方选择技术提供方的范围限于中国国内，此项集中的相关地域市场为中国市场。

中国水煤浆气化技术许可市场集中度较高，仅有通用基础设施技术公司水煤浆气化技术、兖矿华东理工多喷嘴对置式水煤浆气化技术与西北化工研究院多元料浆气化技术三家主要竞争者，其中通用基础设施技术公司水煤浆气化技术市场份额最高。

水煤浆气化技术对原料煤的灰分含量、灰熔点度和内水含量有特定要求，技术需求方新建水煤浆气化项目必须具备可靠的原料煤的供应。我国神府地区（含内蒙古自治区鄂尔多斯和陕西省榆林地区）的煤质能够适应水煤浆气化技术的要求。神华集团在神府地区的煤矿所产煤炭占该地区煤炭总产量的份额最高，且质量管理严格、煤质稳定。神华集团神府地区煤矿所产煤炭被多个水煤浆气化技术项目用作原料煤。

One party to the joint venture, GE China, is a foreign invested company incorporated by GE in China. GE Infrastructure Technology Company is a subsidiary of GE and, in the context of this joint venture, it is responsible for licensing the coal-water slurry gasification technology to the contemplated joint venture. The other party to the joint venture, CSCLC, primarily engages in the development and operation of coal liquefaction, coal chemical projects, and associated projects. The parent company of CSCLC, Shenhua Group Co., Ltd. ("Shenhua Group"), is a comprehensive energy enterprise focusing on the production and supply of coal, electricity, and heat, as well as railway and port transportation services.

The contemplated joint venture will primarily provide technology licensing and engineering services of coal-water slurry gasification to industrial and electrical power projects. The coal-water slurry gasification technology is a coal gasification technology to transform coal from its solid form into coal-water slurry, which will be further processed to produce a mixture of gases, including carbon monoxide and hydrogen, etc. Since coal-water slurry gasification technology is significantly different from other coal gasification technologies in terms of technological processes, requirements for raw coals, feeding method, etc., the licensing market for coal-water slurry gasification technology constitutes the relevant product market. Since the operational scope of the contemplated joint venture is limited to China, and the scope in which domestic users of coal-water slurry gasification technology choose technology suppliers is limited to inside China, the relevant geographic market for this concentration is the Chinese market.

2010年，神华集团是水煤浆气化技术原料煤的最大供应商。此外，神华集团神府地区煤炭外运主要依靠自营铁路和煤炭码头，运输成本较低。

商务部对水煤浆气化技术许可市场进入进行了调查。调查发现，水煤浆气化技术是多项复杂技术的集合体，涉及的工艺技术和工程技术需经过长期实践才能成熟，未经过充分试验的新技术存在很高的商业风险。进入水煤浆气化技术许可市场，必须寻找愿意承担部分首套示范装置成本的技术使用方，新的技术许可方进入这一市场难度很大。水煤浆气化技术科技含量高，涉及大量专利保护。技术研发和实现工业化应用周期很长。商务部认为水煤浆气化技术许可市场进入难度很大。

综上，神华集团是水煤浆气化技术原料煤的最大供应商，通用基础设施技术公司在水煤浆气化技术市场份额最高。通用中国与神华煤制油设立合营企业从事水煤浆气化技术许可，可能利用神华集团原料煤优势，通过控制原料煤的供应，限制水煤浆气化技术许可市场的竞争。

The market for the licensing of coal slurry gasification technologies in China is highly concentrated, with only three major competitors, including GE Infrastructure Technology Company with its coal-water slurry gasification technology, Yankuang East China Science and Technology with its technology of coal-water slurry gasification with opposed multi-burners, and Northwest Chemical Research Institute with its multi-element slurry gasification technology. The coal-water slurry gasification technology of GE Infrastructure Technology Company has the highest market share.

Coal-water slurry gasification technology has specific requirements regarding the ash content, ash fusion point, and water content of the raw coal, and a newly built coal-water slurry gasification project by a technology user must have a reliable supply of raw coal. The quality of coal in the Shenfu area in China (including Erdos in Inner Mongolia Autonomous Region and Yulin region in Shaanxi Province) is able to meet the requirements for coal-water slurry gasification technology. The coal production of Shenhua Group in the Shenfu area accounts for the largest share in this area, and Shenhua applies strict quality management and the quality of the coal produced is reliable and stable. The coal produced by Shenhua Group from the Shenfu area was used by many coal-water slurry gasification projects as raw coal. In 2010, Shenhua Group was the largest supplier of raw coal for coal-water slurry gasification technology. In addition, the coal produced by Shenhua Group from the Shenfu area was mainly transported by self-operated railway and coal wharf operated, and the freight costs are relatively low.

(Continued)

| | MOFCOM investigated the entry in the licensing market for coal-water slurry gasification technology. The investigation revealed that the coal-water slurry gasification technology is a combination of many complex technologies, and the process and engineering technologies involved could only become mature after a long period of practice, and there are significant commercial risks for new technologies that have not been sufficiently tested. To enter the licensing market for coal-water slurry gasification technology, it is necessary to seek a technology user who is willing to share part of the costs for the first set of demonstrative equipment, and thus it is very difficult for the new licensor of the technology to enter this market. The coal-water slurry gasification technology is technology intensive, and protected by a large number of patents. There is a long period for the R&D and industrialized application of the technology. MOFCOM concluded that there are significant difficulties for new entry into the licensing market for licensing of coal-water slurry gasification technology. |
| | In summary, Shenhua Group is the largest supplier of the raw coal for coal-water slurry gasification technology, and GE Infrastructure Technology Company has the largest share in the market for coal slurry gasification technology. The joint venture between GE China and CSCLC to provide licensing of coal-water slurry gasification technology may restrict competition in the licensing market of coal-water slurry gasification technology, by taking Shenhua Group's advantage in raw coal and by controlling the supply of raw coal. |

三、附加限制性条件的商谈 商务部向申报方提出了此项集中可能存在的限制竞争问题，并要求申报方作出解释说明，提出解决问题的措施。经多次商谈，10月28日，神华集团和神华煤制油提交了最终解决方案。经评估，商务部认为，神华集团和神华煤制油提交的最终解决方案可以解决竞争关注。	**3 Negotiation of Restrictive Conditions** MOFCOM raised the anti-competitive concerns about the concentration to the notifying party, and requested the notifying party to provide explanations and propose solutions. After many rounds of discussion, a final remedy proposal was submitted by Shenhua Group and CSCLC on October 28, 2011. After evaluation, MOFCOM concluded that the final proposal submitted by Shenhua Group and CSCLC could resolve the anti-competitive concerns.
四、审查决定 鉴于通用中国与神华煤制油设立合营企业对中国水煤浆气化技术许可市场可能具有限制竞争影响，商务部决定附加限制性条件批准此项集中，要求神华集团和神华煤制油履行如下义务： 通用中国与神华煤制油设立合营企业，从事水煤浆气化技术许可，不得利用限制供应水煤浆气化技术原料煤，或者以供应原料煤为条件，迫使技术需求方使用该合营企业的技术，或者提高使用其他技术的成本。 商务部有权对上述限制性条件的实施进行监督检查。	**4 Review Decision** Considering that the joint venture between GE China and CSCLC may restrict competition in the licensing market of coal-water slurry gasification technology in China, MOFCOM decided to approve this concentration subject to restrictive conditions, and requested Shenhua Group and CSCLC to perform the following obligations: GE China and CSCLC, which would establish the joint venture to license coal-water slurry gasification technology, must not compel technology users into using the joint venture's technology, or raise the costs of using other alternative technologies, by restricting the supply of raw coal for the coal-water slurry gasification technology, or by conditioning the license on the supply of raw coal. MOFCOM has the power to supervise and inspect the implementation of the above restrictive conditions.
本公告自发布之日起生效。 商务部 二〇一一年十一月十日	This decision shall become effective as of the date of its announcement. Ministry of Commerce November 10, 2011

MOFCOM Announcement [2011] No. 90 Regarding the Conditional Approval of the Acquisition of the Hard Disk Drive Business of Samsung Electronics Co., Ltd. by Seagate Technology plc

商务部公告2011年第90号 关于附条件批准希捷科技公司收购三星电子有限公司硬盘驱动器业务反垄断审查决定的公告

(Published on December 12, 2011)

（2011年12月12日公布）

中华人民共和国商务部（以下简称商务部）收到希捷科技公司（以下简称希捷或申报方）收购三星电子有限公司（以下简称三星，与希捷合称交易双方）硬盘驱动器（以下简称硬盘）业务的经营者集中反垄断申报。经审查，商务部决定附加限制性条件批准此项经营者集中。根据《中华人民共和国反垄断法》（以下简称《反垄断法》）第三十条，现公告如下：	The Ministry of Commerce of the People's Republic of China ("MOFCOM") has received an anti-monopoly notification of a concentration of undertakings regarding the acquisition by Seagate Technology plc ("Seagate" or the "notifying party") of the hard disk drive ("HDD") business of Samsung Electronics Co., Ltd. ("Samsung", together with Seagate, "Parties"). After review, MOFCOM decides to approve this concentration under certain conditions. The decision is hereby announced in accordance with Article 30 of the Anti-Monopoly Law of the People's Republic of China ("AML"):
一、立案和审查程序 2011年5月19日，商务部收到希捷收购三星硬盘业务经营者集中申报。经审核，商务部认为该申报文件、	**1 Acceptance and Review Process** On May 19, 2011, MOFCOM received the notification of a concentration of undertakings regarding the acquisition of Samsung's HDD business by Seagate.

材料不完备，要求申报方予以补交。6月13日，商务部确认经补交的申报文件、资料符合《反垄断法》第二十三条的要求，对该项经营者集中申报予以立案并开始初步审查。

经初步审查，商务部认为此项集中对硬盘市场可能具有排除、限制竞争效果。7月13日，商务部决定对此项集中实施进一步审查。10月11日，商务部决定延长进一步审查期限，截止日期为12月12日。

审查过程中，商务部对申报方提交的文件、资料的真实性、完整性和准确性进行了审核，书面征求了相关政府部门、行业协会和下游企业等方面的意见，向生产商、客户、相关专家了解了相关产品、相关市场界定、市场结构、交易模式、市场发展前景等方面的信息，委托专家对此项集中中的竞争影响进行了分析评估。

After review, MOFCOM held that the notification documents and materials submitted were incomplete, and thus required the notifying party to submit further necessary documents and materials. On June 13, MOFCOM acknowledged that the documents and materials submitted as supplemented met the requirements set out in Article 23 of the AML, and decided to accept the filing of a concentration of undertakings, with preliminary review being carried on accordingly.

Upon preliminary review, MOFCOM held that the concentration might have an effect of eliminating and restricting competition on the HDD market. On July 13, MOFCOM decided to carry out a further review of the concentration. On October 11, MOFCOM decided to extend the period of further review, with a deadline of December 12.

During the review, MOFCOM reviewed the authenticity, completeness, and accuracy of the documents and materials submitted by Seagate, sought opinions and comments in writing from relevant government departments, trade association, downstream enterprises, etc., collected information from manufacturers, customers, and relevant experts in respect of the relevant products, the definition of and relevant markets, market structures, trading mode, market development prospect, etc., and engaged experts to carry out the analysis and assessment on the effect of the concentration on competition.

二、竞争分析

根据《反垄断法》及其相关规定，商务部对此项集中涉及的硬盘行业市场状况、采购模式、产能利用、产品创新、买方议价能力、市场进入和对消费者影响等内容进行了审查，分析了在上述相关

2 Competition Analysis

In accordance with the AML and other relevant provisions, MOFCOM reviewed the status of the HDD market, procurement mode, production capacity usage, product innovation, buyer's bargaining power, market entry, effect on consumers, etc.

(Continued)

商品市场中此前发生的交易、特定期间市场价格变化等情况，综合评估了此项经营者集中对市场竞争等方面的影响。

（一） 集中交易和相关市场。
根据希捷和三星签署的《资产购买协议》，希捷将收购三星硬盘业务相关资产。希捷是一家从事硬盘等数字存储产品生产和销售的企业。目标资产是三星专门用于硬盘研发、生产和销售的所有厂房、设备和其他资产。

硬盘是以磁存储技术为基础的存储设备，通常作为计算机和其他消费电子产品中最重要的辅助存储介质使用。硬盘与固态硬盘、闪存等其他辅助存储设备在容量、价格、用途等方面差异明显，硬盘市场构成单独的相关商品市场。按终端应用不同，硬盘市场可以分为企业级应用、台式电脑应用、便携式电脑应用和消费电子产品应用等细分的相关商品市场。硬盘的采购和供应在全球市场范围内展开，本项集中的相关地域市场为全球市场。

（二） 市场状况。
经调查，商务部发现硬盘市场呈现以下特征：

第一，市场集中度较高。近二十年来，硬盘市场集中度不断提高。目前，在硬盘市场上仅存希捷、西部数据、日立存储、东芝和三星5家生产商。2010年，上述5家生产商在全球市场的份额分别约为33%、29%、18%、10%和10%，在中国市场的份额与此类似。

第二，硬盘产品同质化明显。各硬盘厂商的硬盘产品之间差异不大，下游用户能在较短时间内转换供应商，且成本很低。

第三，硬盘市场透明度较高。硬盘厂商和主要买家数量均较少，产品同质化明显，竞争者对相互之间的技术、成本、生产和销售状况等情况均比较了解。

as related to the concentration, analysis of prior trading on the markets of above relevant products, market price changes during certain periods, etc., and an overall appraisal of the effect of the concentration of undertakings on market competition, etc.

(1) The Concentration and the Relevant Markets

According to the Asset Purchase Agreement between Seagate and Samsung, Seagate will purchase the assets related to Samsung's HDD business. Seagate is an enterprise engaged in the production and sale of digital storage products such as HDD, etc. The target assets consist of all the factory buildings, equipment, and other assets of Samsung specifically dedicated to the development, production, and sale of HDD.

HDD is the storage device based on magnetic memory technology, usually used as the most important accessory storage medium of computers and other consumer electronic products. HDD is quite different from solid-state disks, flash memories, and other accessory storage equipment in terms of capacity, price, usage, etc., and the HDD market constitutes a separate relevant product market. For different end-use purposes, the HDD market may be divided further into sub-relevant product markets of HDDs for enterprise applications, desk computer applications, portable laptop computer applications, consumer electronic product applications, etc. The sale and supply of HDD are being carried out in the worldwide market, and the concentration hereunder has the global market as its relevant geographic market.

(2) Market Status

After investigation, MOFCOM finds that the HDD market has the following characteristics:

硬盘厂商能凭借相关事实和经验确定竞争对手的产品价格或价格区间。同时，硬盘厂商经常共用相同的分销商，通过分销渠道了解其他品牌硬盘产品信息较容易。

第四，大型电脑生产商是硬盘产品的主要下游客户。硬盘产品销售主要包括对大型电脑生产商的销售和经过分销商向下游用户的销售，其中大型电脑生产商是硬盘的主要客户，其与硬盘生产商之间的交易价格决定了硬盘的市场价格。

（三）　采购模式。
为获得并保持竞争性价格，大型电脑生产商在硬盘采购中通常采用不公开竞标方式，按季度同多个硬盘生产商进行双边谈判。为保证供应的连续性和安全性，大型电脑生产商最终将总需求按照价格等因素在2至4家硬盘生产商之间按一定比例分配。在单次竞标中，最具竞争力的要约一般会获得较大订单份额，次之会获得较小订单份额，再次的可能拿不到订单。这种采购模式促使硬盘生产商为了获得订单和获得更大的订单份额而竞争。因此，维持大型电脑生产商目前的采购模式对保持硬盘市场的竞争非常重要。

（四）　产能利用。
调查发现，硬盘行业产能利用率较高。特别是2008年第四季度以来，随着市场需求的增加，所有硬盘生产商的产能利用率均持续上升。2010年第四季度全部5家硬盘生产商的平均产能利用率约90%，剩余产能有限。

（五）　产品创新。
调查发现，创新对硬盘行业影响重大。率先推出创新产品可以获得较高的市场份额和利润，在其他竞争者推出同类产品后，该产品利润率即显著降低。硬盘生产商需要通过不断创新降低成本，创新是硬盘生产商的重要竞争手段。调查还发现，硬盘市场的竞争是维持产品创新的重要前提，排除或限制竞争行为将显著降低硬盘生产商的创新意愿和创新速度。

First, the level of market concentration is relatively high. Over the last 20 years, the level of concentration in the HDD market has increased. At present, there are only five manufacturers on the HDD market: Seagate, Western Digital, Hitachi Storage, Toshiba, and Samsung. In 2010, the above five manufacturers had respectively 33%, 29%, 18%, 10%, and 10% of the global market, with a similar market percentage in the Chinese market.

Secondly, HDD products are homogeneous in nature. The HDD manufacturers are not that much different from each other in terms of their HDD products, and downstream customers may change suppliers easily in a relatively short time, with low cost.

Thirdly, the HDD market has a relatively high degree of transparency. Both HDD manufacturers and the main buyers are relatively limited in number, products are obviously homogeneous, and competitors know each other relatively well in terms of technology, cost, production, and sales status, etc. HDD manufacturers may figure out, by relevant facts and experiences, the product price or price scope of their competitors. Also, HDD manufacturers often use the same distributors, which enable them to know easily, through the distribution channels, information on HDD products of other brands.

Fourthly, large-scale computer manufacturers are the main downstream clients of HDD products. The HDD products are mainly sold to large-scale computer manufacturers, and also to downstream customers through distributors, and of the two, the large-scale computer manufacturers are the main customers, and the market price is actually determined by the trading price between them and the HDD manufacturers.

(Continued)

（六）　买方议价能力和对消费者影响。

调查发现，硬盘厂商主导下游分销商的销售价格，分销商对硬盘厂商不具有抵消性的购买力量。对于大型电脑生产商，硬盘厂商的涨价如不是针对特定企业，一般不会遭到大型电脑生产商的反对。大型电脑生产商有能力通过提高电脑产品的价格，将硬盘价格的上涨转嫁给最终消费者，因此缺乏行使抵消性购买力量的意愿。最终消费者高度分散，对硬盘和电脑价格的上涨没有议价能力。

受2011年7月以来泰国洪灾影响，西部数据硬盘产能受损并率先提高硬盘价格。此后，包括交易双方在内的其他硬盘厂商也提高了产品价格，部分硬盘产品涨价幅度超过100%。调查发现，在其他条件未见明显变化的情况下，个人电脑的销售价格相应上涨，电脑生产商向最终消费者直接转嫁了硬盘的价格上涨负担。

（七）　市场进入。

调查发现，知识产权及其他专有知识对硬盘行业至关重要，特别是非知识产权的核心技术、工艺流程和技术队伍构成进入该市场的实质性障碍。规模经济在相关市场中同样重要，新进入者如无法达到一定的生产和销售量则无法生存，而要达到相应规模则需要高额的生产、研发和市场开拓投资，潜在风险巨大。近十年来，没有新的竞争者进入相关市场。据此，商务部认为硬盘市场进入难度很大。

（八）　此项集中对相关商品市场和消费者的影响。

在硬盘市场，交易双方均是重要的生产商，此项集中将减少一个重要的竞争者。考虑到前述大型电脑生产商的采购模式，此项集中增加了剩余硬盘制造商同时获得订单的可能性，削弱了前述采购模式对硬盘生产商的竞争压力。同时，由于硬盘市场透明度较高，硬盘厂商有能力预判其他竞争者的行为，此项集中也进一步增加了市场竞争者通过协调从事排除、限制竞争行为的可能性。

(3) Procurement Mode

In order to obtain and maintain a competitive price, large-scale computer manufacturers often adopt the mode of non-open bidding in procurement of HDD, having bilateral negotiations for each quarter with several manufacturers. In order to guarantee the continuity and safety of supply, large-scale computer manufacturers will ultimately divide their total demand among two to four manufacturers, at a certain ratio, according to factors such as price, etc. In a single bidding, the most competitive offer will usually win a relatively big share of the order, the less competitive one may win a relatively small share of the order, while leaving the rest of the bidders with no orders. Their procurement mode compels HDD manufacturers to compete with each other in order to get orders and get a larger share of orders. Therefore, it is very important to maintain the present procurement mode of large-scale computer manufacturers, in order to keep competition on the HDD market.

(4) Capacity Usage

The investigation found that the HDD industry has a relatively high capacity usage rate. In particular, since the fourth quarter of 2008, all HDD manufacturers have had their production capacity usage rate increasing continuously. In the fourth quarter of 2010, all five HDD manufacturers had their production capacity average usage rate about 90%, with only limited spare capacity left.

(5) Product Innovation

The investigation finds that innovation has an important influence on the HDD industry. Manufacturers who launch new and innovative products may first get a higher market share, and when other competitors launch products of the same category, the profit rate of that product category will drop substantially. HDD manufacturers have to reduce

目前，中国是全球最大的个人电脑消费国之一，此项集中将对中国消费者利益造成不利影响。

（九）　审查结论。

综上，商务部认为此项集中将对硬盘市场产生排除、限制竞争的效果。

their costs through constant innovation, and innovation is indeed an important means for HDD manufacturers to compete. The investigation also found that competition on the HDD market is an important precondition for the maintenance of product innovation, and any act of elimination of or restriction on competition will substantially reduce the manufacturers' innovation motivation and innovation speed.

(6) Buyer's Bargaining Power and Impact on Consumers

The investigation found that HDD manufacturers guide the selling price for downstream distributors, while distributors do not have the purchasing power to offset such guidance from manufacturers. For large-scale computer manufacturers, if the price increase by HDD manufacturers is not set against specific enterprises, they usually do not oppose such price increase. As large-scale computer manufacturers have the ability to transfer the cost of such HDD price increases to end-use consumers by raising the selling price of their own computer products, they lack the willingness to exercise their offsetting purchasing strength. The end-use consumers are highly dispersed, having no price bargaining powers against the price rises of HDD and computers.

Affected by the floods in Thailand, since July 2011 Western Digital has suffered a loss in its HDD production capacity and raised the selling price of its HDD. Thereafter, other HDD manufacturers, including the parties, raised the selling price of their products, too. The price of some HDD products has even increased by more than 100%. The investigation found that, under a situation of no obvious changes in other conditions, personal computers also have their selling price increased accordingly, as computer manufacturers transfer the

(*Continued*)

burden of such HDD price increases directly to the end-users.

(7) Market Entry

Upon investigation, it was found that intellectual property rights and other know-how are of primary importance to the HDD industry. In particular, such non-IP elements as core technologies, manufacturing processes, and technical teams constitute material market entry barriers. Economies of scale also play an important role in the relevant market and newcomers will not be able to survive if they cannot reach a certain degree of productivity and sales, but to achieve the relevant scale requires massive production, research and investment in market expansion, which poses a huge potential risk. In the past decade, there has been no new competitor into the relevant market; therefore, MOFCOM believes it is quite difficult to enter the HDD market.

(8) Effect of the Concentration on the Relevant Product Market and Consumers

In the HDD market, both parties are important manufacturers, therefore this concentration will eliminate an important competitor. Given the procurement mode of large computer manufacturers, this concentration will enhance the possibility of the remaining HDD manufacturers to obtain purchase orders and reduce the competitive pressure of such procurement mode on HDD manufacturers. Meanwhile, as the HDD market is relatively more transparent, HDD manufacturers are able to predict the action of other competitors, and this concentration will further enhance the possibility of market competitors to eliminate and/or restrict competition through coordination. At present, China is one of the major PC consumer countries

	in the world and this concentration will have adverse effects on Chinese consumers.
	(9) Conclusion of Review
	In summary, MOFCOM believes that this concentration will have the effect of eliminating and/or restricting competition on the HDD market.
三、附加限制性条件的商谈 在审查期间，商务部向交易双方指出了本项集中将产生的排除、限制竞争效果，并就如何消除上述竞争问题进行了多轮商谈。交易双方先后提出了多轮解决方案。经评估，商务部认为，交易双方提交的最终解决方案能够减少此项经营者集中对竞争产生的不利影响。	**3 Negotiation on Restrictive Conditions** During the review, MOFCOM pointed out to both parties that the concentration will have the effect of eliminating and and/or restricting competition and held several rounds of negotiations on how to preclude such competition issues. The two parties put forward a few proposals. Upon assessment, MOFCOM thinks that the final remedy proposal submitted by the two parties could mitigate the adverse effect of this concentration of undertakings on competition.
四、审查决定 审查认为，希捷收购三星硬盘业务对硬盘市场具有排除、限制竞争影响，商务部决定附加限制性条件批准此项集中，申报方应履行如下义务： （一） 在相关市场上维持三星硬盘作为一个独立竞争者而存在，包括但不限于以下内容： 第一，交易完成后，希捷将组建独立的子公司，负责对原三星公司生产线生产的硬盘产品（以下简称三星产品）独立定价，并以三星品牌独立销售。希捷和三星的销售团队均应向监督受托人报备，接受本决定项下的监督。 第二，在前述独立销售团队组建并实际开展相关业务之前的过渡期内，应当由三星的原销售团队继续销售三星产品。过渡期内的销售不得损害三星产品的竞争力。过渡期内三星继续销售的安排和月度销售情况应当向监督受托人报告，接受本决定项下的监督。	**4 Review Decision** The investigation determined that Seagate's acquisition of Samsung's HDD business will have the effect of eliminating and/or restricting competition on the HDD market; therefore, MOFCOM decides to approve this concentration under certain conditions, and the notifying party shall fulfill the following obligations: (1) Samsung remains as an independent competitor in the relevant market, including but not limited to: First, upon completion of the transaction, Seagate will set up an independent subsidiary responsible for the independent pricing of HDD products from Samsung's previous production line ("Samsung Products") as well as independent sales under the Samsung brand. The sales teams of both Seagate and Samsung shall report to the supervision trustee and be subject to supervision under this decision.

(Continued)

第三，交易完成后，希捷应当保持三星产品定价销售团队的完全独立性，在三星产品定价销售团队与希捷其他产品定价销售团队之间建立防火墙，防止双方交换竞争性信息。竞争性信息是指任何可能导致竞争者之间协调彼此经营行为的信息，特别是任何有关产品价格、产量、客户、竞标等方面的信息。三星产品的销售团队只能指定一名负责人向希捷指定的一名负责人汇报。前述两负责人的人选及变更应事先向监督受托人报备，两负责人不得在两团队之间沟通竞争性信息。两负责人之间的任何信息沟通情况均应事先或同时报告监督受托人，接受本决定项下的监督。

第四，希捷应当确保维持三星生产线的独立运行，三星产品生产线应当使用三星的设备、流程和生产系统。希捷可以对三星产品生产线进行技术支持和改造，以提高三星产品的生产效率和竞争力。此种技术支持和改造不得对三星产品的产量或产能施加任何限制性影响，并应向监督受托人进行事先和事后报告，接受本决定项下的监督。

第五，希捷应当确保三星产品独立建立并严格执行合理的产品定价机制。前述定价机制的确立和任何修改，任何偏离该机制的定价行为均应向监督受托人报告，并说明理由，接受本决定项下的监督。

第六，希捷应当针对三星产品设立独立的研发中心。希捷可以给予该研发中心以技术支持，包括允许其采用希捷的标准流程，以提高三星产品的生产效率和竞争力。前述技术支持和任何信息及人员交流均应事先或即时向监督受托人报备，接受本决定项下的监督。

（二）希捷应履行本审查决定作出后6个月内继续维持和扩大三星产品产能的承诺，之后应当根据市场需求状况合理确定三星产品的产能和产量。希捷和三星产品的产能及产量情况应当按月向监督受托人报告。

Secondly, during the transitional period before these sales teams are established and conduct relevant business, Samsung's existing sales team shall continue to sell Samsung Products. The sales during the transitional period shall not jeopardize the competitiveness of Samsung Products. During the transitional period, Samsung shall report to the supervision trustee of the arrangement of continuous sales and monthly sales and will be subject to supervision under this decision.

Thirdly, upon completion of the transaction, Seagate shall maintain the full independence of the Samsung sales team's product pricing and set up a firewall between the sales teams of Samsung and Seagate to prevent the two teams from exchanging competitively sensitive information. Competitively sensitive information means any information that may lead to coordination of their respective business operations between competitors, especially information on product price, clients, and competitive bidding. The sales team of Samsung shall designate only one person responsible for reporting to the person in charge designated by Seagate. The nominees of these two persons and any change thereto shall be reported to the supervision trustee for recording in advance and the two persons in charge shall not communicate between the two teams regarding information on competition. Furthermore, any communication between the two persons shall be reported to the supervision trustee beforehand or simultaneously and be subject to supervision under this decision.

Fourthly, Seagate shall ensure independent operation of Samsung's production line and the production line of Samsung shall use Samsung's equipment, process, and production

（三）　集中完成后，希捷不得实质性改变当前的商业模式，强制或变相强制客户从希捷或任何受希捷控制的公司排他性地采购其硬盘产品。

（四）　集中完成后，希捷不得迫使东电化(中国)投资有限公司(以下简称东电化)排他性地向希捷或任何其他受希捷控制的公司供应硬盘磁头，或限制东电化向其他硬盘生产商供应磁头的数量。

（五）　希捷承诺，本决定作出后三年内每年投资至少8亿美元，且将以希捷近年一贯的速度，继续在创新领域投入研发资金的承诺，以确保给客户带来更多创新性产品和解决方案。

（六）　根据商务部《关于实施经营者集中资产或业务剥离的暂行规定》(商务部公告2010年第41号)，希捷委托独立的监督受托人对希捷履行上述义务的情况进行监督。

本决定实施12个月后，希捷可以向商务部提出解除上述第（一）、（二）项义务的申请。该申请应说明本决定项下附加限制性条件的实施情况和解除上述第(一)、(二)项义务的理由并提供相关证据。商务部将依申请并根据市场竞争状况作出是否解除的决定。

为履行上述义务，希捷应当在监督受托人确定一周内提交详细的操作方案并报商务部批准后实施。

商务部有权通过监督受托人或自行监督检查希捷履行上述义务的情况。希捷未适当履行上述义务，商务部有权根据《反垄断法》相关规定作出处理。

system. Seagate may carry out technical support and innovation to Samsung's production line in order to improve productivity and competitiveness of the Samsung Products. Such technical support and innovation shall not exert any restrictive effect on the column and capability of the Samsung Products and shall be reported to the supervision trustee beforehand and afterwards and be subject to supervision under this decision.

Fifthly, Seagate shall ensure that it will independently set up and strictly implement a reasonable pricing mechanism for Samsung Products. The establishment of such pricing mechanism and any change thereto, including any deviation from such pricing mechanism, shall be reported to the supervision trustee, stating the reasons, and shall be subject to supervision under this decision.

Sixthly, Seagate shall set up an independent R&D center in respect of Samsung Products. Seagate may provide technical support to such R&D center, including allowing the use of Seagate's standard process in an effort to improve the productivity and competitiveness of Samsung Products. The aforementioned technical support and information exchange shall be reported to the supervision trustee beforehand or simultaneously and shall be subject to supervision under this decision.

(2)　Seagate shall honor its commitments to maintain and expand the production capacity of Samsung Products within six months after the decision of the review. The production capacity and productivity of both the Seagate products and the Samsung Products shall be reported to the supervision trustee on a monthly basis.

(Continued)

	(3) Upon completion of the concentration, Seagate shall not materially change the current commercial mode by compelling clients or compelling clients in a disguised form to exclusively purchase HDD products from Seagate or from companies controlled by Seagate.
	(4) Upon completion of the concentration, Seagate shall not compel TDK China Co., Ltd. to exclusively supply HDD heads to Samsung or companies controlled by Seagate, or limit the number of HDD heads supplied by TDK China Co., Ltd. to other HDD manufacturers.
	(5) Seagate undertakes that, within three years of this decision, Seagate shall invest at least US$800,000,000 each year and shall continue to honor its commitment to funding research and development in innovation at its usual speed of recent years, in order to bring about more innovative products and solutions to clients.
	(6) In accordance with the Interim Provisions on Asset or Business Divestiture during the Implementation of Concentrations of Undertakings (MOFCOM Announcement [2010] No. 41), Seagate shall entrust an independent supervision trustee to supervise the performance of Seagate's obligations.
	Twelve months after the implementation of this decision, Seagate may request MOFCOM to terminate the obligations under preceding items (1) and (2). Such request shall describe the implementation of the restrictive conditions under this decision and cite reasons for release of the obligations under preceding items (1) and (2), together with the relevant evidence.

	MOFCOM shall, depending on the competitive conditions of the market, decide whether to release such obligation or not.
	For purposes of fulfilling the aforesaid obligations, Seagate shall, within one week of deciding the supervision trustee, come up with a detailed operation proposal and submit the same to MOFCOM for approval and implementation thereafter.
	MOFCOM has the power to supervise and examine Seagate's performance of its obligations through the supervision trustee or on its own. Should Seagate fail to properly perform its obligations, MOFCOM has the right to handle such issues in accordance with the relevant provisions of the AML.
本公告自发布之日起生效。 商务部 二〇一一年十二月十二日	This decision shall become effective as of the date of its announcement. Ministry of Commerce December 12, 2011

D-12

MOFCOM Announcement [2012] No. 6 Regarding the Conditional Approval of the Establishment of a Joint Venture by Henkel Hong Kong and Tiande Chemical

商务部公告2012年第6号 关于附加限制性条件批准汉高香港与天德化工组建合营企业经营者集中反垄断审查决定的公告

(Published on February 9, 2012)

（2012年2月9日公布）

中华人民共和国商务部收到汉高香港控股有限公司（以下简称汉高香港）与天德化工控股有限公司（以下简称天德化工）组建合营企业的经营者集中反垄断申报。经审查，商务部决定附加限制性条件批准此项经营者集中。根据《中华人民共和国反垄断法》（以下简称《反垄断法》）第三十条，现公告如下：	The Ministry of Commerce of the People's Republic of China ("MOFCOM") has received an anti-monopoly notification of a concentration of undertaking regarding the establishment of a joint venture by Henkel Hong Kong Holding Limited (hereinafter referred to as "Henkel Hong Kong") and Tiande Chemical Holding Limited (hereinafter referred to as "Tiande Chemical"). After review, MOFCOM decides to approve this concentration of undertakings under certain conditions. In accordance with Article 30 of the Anti-Monopoly Law of the People's Republic of China ("AML"), it is hereby announced as follows:
一、立案和审查程序 2011年8月8日，商务部收到汉高香港与天德化工组建合营企业的经营者集中申报。	**1 Acceptance and Review Process** On August 8, 2011, MOFCOM received the notification of a concentration of undertakings concerning the establishment of a joint venture

经审核，商务部认为该申报材料不完备，要求申报方予以补充。9月26日，商务部确认经补充的申报材料符合《反垄断法》第二十三条的要求，对该项经营者集中申报开始立案审查。

经初步审查，商务部认为此项集中可能对氰基丙烯酸酯单体市场具有排除、限制竞争的效果。10月25日，商务部决定实施进一步审查，2012年1月19日，商务部决定延长进一步审查期限，截止日期为3月19日。在进一步审查过程中，商务部向申报方提出了对此项集中的竞争关注，申报方向商务部提交了解决方案。商务部对申报方提交的解决方案进行了评估，认为该方案可以减少此项集中对竞争产生的不利影响。

在审查过程中，商务部征求了有关政府部门、行业协会、同业竞争者和下游企业的意见，了解了相关市场界定、市场结构、行业特征及未来发展趋势等方面的信息。

between Henkel Hong Kong and Tiande Chemical. Through review and verification, MOFCOM believed that the notification materials were incomplete and requested the notifying party to supplement. On September 26, MOFCOM confirmed that the supplemented notification materials satisfied the requirements of Article 23 of the AML, and accepted such case for review.

After its preliminary review, MOFCOM believed that such concentration may have the effect of eliminating and/or restricting competition in the market of cyanoacrylate monomers. On October 25, MOFCOM decided to conduct a further review and on January 19, 2012, MOFCOM decided to extend the period of further review to March 19. During its further review, MOFCOM raised competition concerns in relation to the concentration to the notifying parties and the notifying parties submitted remedy proposals. After review, MOFCOM believed that such proposals could mitigate the concentration's adverse effects on competition.

During the review, MOFCOM solicited comments from relevant governmental departments, opinions of trade associations, business competitors, and downstream enterprises, and learned information concerning market definition, market structure, industrial features, and future development trends.

二、竞争分析

商务部根据《反垄断法》第二十七条规定的因素，对此项经营者集中进行了审查，深入分析了此项经营者集中对市场竞争的影响，认为其可能具有排除、限制竞争的不利影响。

本交易所涉产品主要为氰乙酸乙酯、氰基丙烯酸酯单体和氰基丙烯酸酯粘合剂。 上述三种产品在工业生产中处于产业链的上、中、下游。

2 Competition Analysis

Based on the elements set forth in Article 27 of the AML, MOFCOM reviewed this concentration of undertakings, thoroughly analyzed the effects of such concentration on market competition, and held that it may have the adverse effect of eliminating and/or restricting competition.

The main products involved in this transaction are ethyl cyanoacetate,

(Continued)

根据用途特性、生产和使用上的替代性以及进出口状况等因素，商务部认定氰乙酸乙酯、氰基丙烯酸酯单体和氰基丙烯酸酯粘合剂分别构成独立的相关商品市场。相关地域市场均为全球市场。鉴于本项交易所涉产品的市场分布特征，商务部同时考察了本项交易对中国市场竞争状况的影响。

商务部审查了相关市场的市场份额、市场集中度、市场控制力、市场进入，重点评估了氰乙酸乙酯和氰基丙烯酸酯单体市场的竞争关联关系和交易可能产生的排除、限制竞争效果。

在氰乙酸乙酯市场中，全球有两大供应商，天德化工是其中之一。两大供应商均在中国境内生产氰乙酸乙酯产品，面向全球销售，各占全球和中国市场份额约45-50%，市场集中度指数HHI大于4050，市场集中度很高。商务部考察了氰乙酸乙酯市场的进入条件。氰乙酸乙酯由氰化物和氯乙酸合成生成。氰化物和氯乙酸均属危险化学品，生产氰乙酸乙酯环境污染较大，其生产、运输、储存、销售受到严格监管。由于国家管制及环保要求，其他国家生产氰乙酸乙酯的工厂已基本关闭，目前全球仅有包括天德化工在内的两家规模较大的中国企业生产，氰乙酸乙酯市场进入非常困难。天德化工在氰乙酸乙酯市场具有较强的市场控制力。

在氰基丙烯酸酯单体市场中，全球约70%以上的氰基丙烯酸酯单体在中国境内生产。目前，氰基丙烯酸酯单体市场的竞争相对充分。拟设立的合营企业以氰乙酸乙酯为原材料生产氰基丙烯酸酯单体。交易前，天德化工不生产氰基丙烯酸酯单体，汉高香港的母公司汉高股份有限及两合公司（以下简称汉高股份）生产氰基丙烯酸酯单体，其产品主要自用于生产下游产品氰基丙烯酸酯粘合剂。汉高股份在氰基丙烯酸酯单体市场和粘合剂市场具备品牌、技术、资金和人才优势。

cyanoacrylate monomers, and cyanoacrylate adhesive. These three products stay in the upper, middle, and lower reaches of the industrial chain. Considering the elements such as use features, the substitutability in manufacture and use and the import and export status, MOFCOM confirmed that ethyl cyanoacetate, cyanoacrylate monomers, and cyanoacrylate adhesive respectively constitute independent product markets. The relevant geographic market for all of the three products is worldwide. In view of the market distribution features of the products involved in this transaction, MOFCOM simultaneously investigated the effect of this transaction on competitive situations in China.

MOFCOM reviewed the market share, level of market concentration, market control and market entry in the relevant markets, and mainly assessed the relationship between the markets of ethyl cyanoacetate and cyanoacrylate monomers in respect of competition as well as the effect of eliminating and/or restricting competition this transaction may cause.

In the market of ethyl cyanoacetate, there are two main suppliers in the world, and Tiande Chemical is one of them. Both suppliers manufacture ethyl cyanoacetate products within China, sell the products globally, and each has a 45–50% share respectively in global and Chinese markets. The market concentration index, HHI, is higher than 4050 and therefore the level of market concentration is high. MOFCOM also investigated the market entry criteria for ethyl cyanoacetate. Ethyl cyanoacetate is synthesized by cyanide and chloroacetic acid, both of which are dangerous chemicals. The manufacture of ethyl cyanoacetate will

本交易拟设合营企业德高控股有限公司（以下简称德高控股），并通过德高控股新设子公司潍坊德高创新材料有限责任公司（以下简称潍坊德高）生产氰乙酸乙酯的下游产品氰基丙烯酸酯单体。本项交易前，汉高股份向天德化工采购氰乙酸乙酯的数量约占天德化工氰乙酸乙酯产量的5%；此次新设合营企业所需氰乙酸乙酯的绝大部分将从天德化工购买，两者加总约占天德化工氰乙酸乙酯产能的四分之一。拟议合营企业成立后，鉴于天德化工与合营企业的关联关系以及天德化工在原材料氰乙酸乙酯市场上的控制力，天德化工在销售氰乙酸乙酯产品时，可能会对合营企业和其他氰基丙烯酸酯单体生产企业采取区别性的供给策略，从而将天德化工在氰乙酸乙酯市场上的优势延伸到合营企业，削弱其他氰基丙烯酸酯单体生产企业的市场竞争力，对氰基丙烯酸酯单体市场产生排除、限制竞争的影响。

cause severe environmental pollution, and its manufacture, transport, storage, and sales are strictly regulated. Due to state control and environmental protection requirements, nearly all the factories manufacturing ethyl cyanoacetate in other countries are closed. At present, there are only two large-scale Chinese enterprises, including Tiande Chemical, that are producing such products, therefore market entry is quite difficult. Tiande Chemical has a strong control over the ethyl cyanoacetate market.

In the market of cyanoacrylate monomers, over 70% of cyanoacrylate monomers in the world market are manufactured within China. At present, there is relatively sufficient competition in the cyanoacrylate monomers market. The joint venture to be established will manufacture cyanoacrylate monomers with ethyl cyanoacetate as the raw material. Before the transaction, Tiande Chemical did not manufacture cyanoacrylate monomers, while Henkel AG & CoKGaA (hereinafter referred to as "Henkel AG"), the parent company of Henkel Hong Kong, manufactures cyanoacrylate monomers, which are mainly used to produce cyanoacrylate adhesive, a downstream product. Henkel AG enjoys the advantages of brand, technology, capital, and talents in both the cyanoacrylate monomers market and cyanoacrylate adhesive market.

In this transaction, the joint venture named Degao Holding Limited Company (hereinafter referred to as "Degao Holding") is proposed to be established and Weifang Degao Innovative Materials Co., Ltd. (hereinafter referred to as "Weifang Degao"), the newly established subsidiary of Degao Holding, will manufacture cyanoacrylate monomers,

(Continued)

the lower reach products of ethyl cyanoacetate. Before this transaction, the quantity of ethyl cyanoacetate purchased by Henkel AG from Tiande Chemical is around 5% of the output of Tiande Chemical. Most of the ethyl cyanoacetate needed by the joint venture to be established shall also be purchased from Tiande Chemical. The quantity of the above two purchases shall amount to 25% of the ethyl cyanoacetate production capacity of Tiande Chemical. After the joint venture is established, considering the association relationship between Tiande Chemical and the joint venture as well as Tiande Chemical's control over the market of the raw material, ethyl cyanoacetate, when selling ethyl cyanoacetate, Tiande Chemical is likely to adopt different supply strategies for the joint venture and other cyanoacrylate monomers manufacturers, and so to extend the advantages of Tiande Chemical in the market of ethyl cyanoacetate to the joint venture and undermine the market competitiveness of other cyanoacrylate monomers manufacturers. Consequently, it shall have the effect of eliminating and/or restricting competition on the market of cyanoacrylate monomers.

三、附加限制性条件的商谈

商务部与申报方就如何解决上述竞争问题进行了多轮商谈。2012年1月13日，交易双方提交了最终解决方案。经过评估，商务部认为，该解决方案可以减少此项经营者集中对竞争的不利影响。

3 Negotiation of Restrictive Conditions
MOFCOM and the notifying parties conducted several rounds of negotiations to discuss how to solve the above competition issue. On January 13, 2012, the two parties to the transaction submitted the final remedy proposal. After evaluation, MOFCOM believes that such proposal could mitigate the adverse effects of such concentration on competition.

四、审查决定

鉴于汉高香港与天德化工组建合营企业，可能会对氰基丙烯酸酯单体市场产生排除、限制竞争的效果，商务部决定附加限制性条件批准此项集中，要求交易双方履行如下义务：

(一) 天德化工应基于公允、合理和不歧视的原则，向下游所有客户供应氰乙酸乙酯。包括：不得以不合理的高价销售产品，不得给予潍坊德高更优惠的供货条件，不得与汉高股份和潍坊德高沟通竞争性信息等。

(二) 自审查决定生效之日起每年或应商务部要求，交易双方及时向商务部汇报其履行上述承诺的情况。

(三) 交易双方应根据商务部相关规定，委托独立的监督受托人，对交易双方履行上述义务的情况进行监督。

为履行上述义务，交易双方应当在监督受托人确定后，尽快提交履行上述义务的详细操作方案并报商务部批准后实施。

本决定自公告之日起生效。

中华人民共和国商务部

二〇一二年二月九日

4 Review Decision

Considering that the establishment of a joint venture between Henkel Hong Kong and Tiande Chemical is likely to eliminate and/or restrict competition in the market of cyanoacrylate monomers, MOFCOM decides to approve this concentration under certain conditions and requires the two parties to fulfill the following obligations:

(1) Tiande Chemical shall provide ethyl cyanoacetate to all lower reach clients under the principles of fairness, reasonableness, and non-discrimination, including not selling products at an unreasonably high price, not providing Weifang Degao with more preferential supply conditions, and not exchanging competitively sensitive information with Henkel AG and Weifang Degao.

(2) As from the effective date of this decision, the two parties shall report their fulfillment of the above commitments to MOFCOM on a yearly basis or upon the request of MOFCOM.

(3) The parties shall, according to the relevant regulations, entrust an independent supervision trustee to supervise the performance of the above obligations by the parties.

In order to fulfill the above obligations, the two parties shall, after the supervision trustee is decided, submit a detailed proposal for performing the above obligations in a prompt manner to MOFCOM and implement it after being approved by MOFCOM.

This decision shall become effective as of the date of its announcement.

Ministry of Commerce

February 9, 2012

MOFCOM Announcement [2012] No. 9 Regarding the Conditional Approval of the Acquisition of Hitachi Global Storage Technologies by Western Digital Corp.

商务部公告2012年第9号 关于附加限制性条件批准西部数据收购日立存储经营者集中反垄断审查决定的公告

(Published on March 2, 2012)

（2012年3月2日公布）

中华人民共和国商务部收到西部数据收购日立存储的经营者集中反垄断申报。经审查，商务部决定附加限制性条件批准此项经营者集中。根据《中华人民共和国反垄断法》（以下简称《反垄断法》）第三十条，现公告如下：	The Ministry of Commerce of the People's Republic of China ("MOFCOM") has received an anti-monopoly notification of a concentration of undertaking regarding the acquisition of Hitachi Global Storage Technologies (hereinafter referred to as "Hitachi Storage") by Western Digital Corp. (hereinafter referred to as "Western Digital"). After review, MOFCOM decides to approve this concentration of undertakings under certain conditions. In accordance with Article 30 of the Anti-Monopoly Law of the People's Republic of China ("AML"), it is hereby announced as follows:
一、立案和审查程序 2011年4月2日，商务部收到西部数据收购日立存储的经营者集中申报。经审核，商务部认为该申报文件、材料不完备，要求申报方予以补充。	**1 Acceptance and Review Process** On April 2, 2011, MOFCOM received the notification of a concentration of undertakings concerning the acquisition of Hitachi Storage by Western Digital.

5月10日，商务部确认经补充的申报文件、资料符合《反垄断法》第二十三条的要求，对该项经营者集中申报予以立案审查。

经初步审查，商务部认为此项集中对硬盘驱动器（以下简称硬盘）市场可能具有排除、限制竞争效果。6月8日，商务部决定对此项集中实施进一步审查。9月7日，经申报方同意，商务部决定延长进一步审查期限，截止时间为11月6日。11月1日，西部数据以案件事实产生重大变更为由申请撤回申报，商务部审查后予以同意，审查程序终止。11月7日，商务部对西部数据重新申报的经营者集中予以立案审查。12月7日，商务部决定对此项集中实施进一步审查，截止日期为2012年3月6日。

审查过程中，商务部对申报方提交的文件、资料的真实性、完整性和准确性进行了审核，书面征求了相关政府部门、行业协会和下游企业等方面的意见，实地调研了生产企业，向客户、行业专家了解了相关产品、相关市场界定、市场结构、交易模式、市场发展前景等方面的信息，委托专家对此项集中的竞争影响进行了分析评估。

After review and verification, MOFCOM believed that the notification documents and materials were incomplete and requested the notifying party to supplement. On May 10, MOFCOM confirmed that the supplemented notification documents and materials satisfied the requirements of Article 23 of the AML, and accepted the case for review.

After its preliminary review, MOFCOM believed that this concentration may have the effect of eliminating and/or restricting competition in the market of HDD drives (hereinafter referred to as "HDD"). On June 8, MOFCOM decided to conduct a further review. On September 7, with the consent of the notifying party, MOFCOM decided to extend the period of further review to November 6. On November 1, Western Digital applied to withdraw the notification for the reason that the facts had materially changed, and MOFCOM agreed to such withdrawal after review, and the review procedure was terminated. On November 7, MOFCOM accepted the notification of a concentration of undertakings re-notified by Western Digital. On December 7, MOFCOM decided to conduct a further review on their concentration and the deadline was set for March 6, 2012.

During the review, MOFCOM reviewed and verified the authenticity, completeness, and accuracy of the documents and materials submitted by the notifying party, solicited comments in writing from relevant governmental departments, the opinions of trade associations and downstream enterprises, conducted on-site investigations of the manufacturers, learned the information concerning the relevant products, the relevant market definition, market structure, transaction modes, and

(Continued)

market development prospects from clients and industrial experts, and entrusted experts to analyze and assess the impact of such concentration on competition.

二、竞争分析	**2 Competition Analysis**
根据《反垄断法》及其相关规定，商务部对此项集中涉及的硬盘行业市场状况、采购模式、产能利用、产品创新、买方议价能力、市场进入和集中对消费者影响等内容进行了审查，考虑了在上述相关商品市场中此前发生的交易、特定期间市场价格变化等情况，综合评估了此项经营者集中对市场竞争等方面的影响。	According to the AML and the relevant regulations, MOFCOM reviewed the market situation of the HDD industry involved in such concentration, the purchase modes, utilization of production capacity, product innovation, buyers' bargaining ability, market entry, and the impact of the concentration on consumers, took into consideration the previous transactions that occurred in the relevant product market and the changes of the market prices during certain periods, and comprehensively assessed the impact of such concentration of understandings on market competition.
（一） 集中交易和相关市场。	**1. The concentration and the relevant market**
根据西部数据、西部数据爱尔兰公司（西部数据全资子公司）、日立公司和Viviti Technologies Ltd.（日立公司全资子公司，以下简称Viviti公司）签署的《股权购买协议》，西部数据将收购Viviti公司全部股权。西部数据是从事硬盘等数字存储产品的生产和销售企业。Viviti公司作为控股公司直接持有Hitachi Global Storage Technologies Netherlands B.V.公司，并通过该公司间接持有Hitachi Global Storage Technologies Singapore Pte. Ltd.等公司从事硬盘业务。	According to the Equity Purchase Agreement signed by Western Digital, Western Digital Ireland Company (the wholly owned subsidiary of Western Digital), Hitachi Company, and Viviti Technologies Ltd. (the wholly owned subsidiary of Hitachi) (hereinafter referred to as "Viviti"), Western Digital shall acquire all equity of Viviti. Western Digital is an enterprise engaged in manufacturing and selling digital storage products such as HDDs. As a holding company, Viviti directly owns Hitachi Global Storage Technologies Netherlands B.V., and, through such company, indirectly owns Hitachi Global Storage Technologies Singapore Pte. Ltd. to conduct its HDD business.
硬盘是以磁存储技术为基础的存储设备，通常作为计算机和其他消费电子产品中最重要的辅助存储介质使用。硬盘与固态硬盘、闪存等其他辅助存储设备在容量、价格、用途等方面差异明显，硬盘市场构成单独的相关商品市场。按终端应用不同，硬盘市场可以分为企业级应用、台式电脑应用、便携式电脑应用和消费电子产品应用等细分的相关商品市场。硬盘的采购和供应在全球市场范围内展开，本项集中的相关地域市场为全球市场。	An HDD is a kind of storage device based on magnetic storage technology, and is usually used as the most important secondary

（二） 市场状况。

经调查，商务部发现硬盘市场呈现以下特征：

第一，市场集中度较高。近二十年来，硬盘市场集中度不断提高。目前，在硬盘市场上仅存希捷、西部数据、日立存储、东芝和三星5家生产商（2011年12月，商务部批准希捷收购三星硬盘业务，但要求三星硬盘作为独立的竞争者继续存在）。2010年，上述5家生产商在全球市场的份额分别约为33%、29%、18%、10%和10%，在中国市场的份额与此类似。

第二，硬盘产品同质化明显。各硬盘厂商的硬盘产品之间差异不大，下游用户能在较短时间内转换供应商，且成本很低。

第三，硬盘市场透明度较高。硬盘厂商和主要买家数量均较少，产品同质化明显，竞争者对相互之间的技术、成本、生产和销售状况等情况均比较了解。硬盘厂商能凭借相关事实和经验确定竞争对手的产品价格或价格区间。同时，硬盘厂商经常共用相同的分销商，通过分销渠道了解其他品牌硬盘产品信息较容易。

第四，大型电脑生产商是硬盘产品的主要下游客户。硬盘产品销售主要包括对大型电脑生产商的销售和经过分销商向下游用户的销售，其中大型电脑生产商是硬盘的主要客户，其与硬盘生产商之间的交易价格决定了硬盘的市场价格。

（三） 采购模式。

为获得并保持竞争性价格，大型电脑生产商在硬盘采购中通常采用不公开竞标方式，按季度同多个硬盘生产商进行双边谈判。为保证供应的连续性和安全性，大型电脑生产商最终将总需求按照价格等因素在2至4家硬盘生产商之间按一定比例分配。在单次竞标中，最具竞争力的要约一般会获得较大订单份额，次之会获得较小订单份额，再次的可能拿不到订单。

storage media for computers and other consumer electronics. HDD is quite distinctive from solid-state disk, flash memory, and other secondary storage devices in relation to volume, price, and use, and therefore the HDD market constitutes a separate product market. According to the different end uses, the HDD market could be classified into relevant product markets for enterprise use, desktop use, notebook computer use, and consumer electronics use. The purchase and supply of HDDs are conducted globally. The relevant geographic market of this concentration is the global market.

2. Market Situation

Through investigation, MOFCOM found that the HDD market had the following features:

i. The level of market concentration is high. Over the last 20 years, the market concentration of HDD has kept increasing. At present, only five manufacturers are active on the market, that is, Seagate, Western Digital, Hitachi Storage, Toshiba, and Samsung (in December 2011, MOFCOM approved the acquisition of the hard disk business of Samsung by Seagate, but required Seagate to still keep Samsung HDD as an independent competitor). In 2010, the shares of the above five manufacturers in the global market were respectively 33%, 29%, 18%, 10%, and 10%, and shares in the Chinese market are similar.

ii. The homogenization of HDD products is obvious. There are few differences between the HDD products of the manufacturers, and so the downstream users can change suppliers within a short time at a low cost.

iii. The transparency of the HDD market is relatively high. There are

(Continued)

这种采购模式促使硬盘生产商为了获得订单和获得更大的订单份额而竞争。因此，维持大型电脑生产商目前的采购模式对保持硬盘市场的竞争非常重要。

（四）　产能利用。

调查发现，硬盘行业产能利用率较高。2008年第四季度以来，随着市场需求的增加，所有硬盘生产商的产能利用率均持续上升。2010年第四季度全部5家硬盘生产商的平均产能利用率约90%，剩余产能有限。2011年的泰国洪灾导致部分产能暂时无法利用，市场供应进一步紧张。

（五）　产品创新。

调查发现，创新对硬盘行业影响重大。率先推出创新产品可以获得较高的市场份额和利润，在其他竞争者推出同类产品后，该产品利润率即显著降低。硬盘生产商需要通过不断创新降低成本，创新是硬盘生产商的重要竞争手段。调查还发现，硬盘市场的竞争是维持产品创新的重要前提，排除或限制竞争行为将显著降低硬盘生产商的创新意愿和创新速度。

（六）　买方议价能力和对消费者影响。

调查发现，硬盘厂商主导下游分销商的销售价格，分销商对硬盘厂商不具有抵消性的购买力量。对于大型电脑生产商，硬盘厂商的涨价如不是针对特定企业，一般不会遭到大型电脑生产商的反对。大型电脑生产商有能力通过提高电脑产品的价格，将硬盘价格的上涨转嫁给最终消费者，因此，缺乏行使抵消性购买力量的意愿。最终消费者高度分散，对硬盘和电脑价格的上涨没有议价能力。

受2011年泰国洪灾影响，西部数据硬盘产能受损并率先提高硬盘价格。此后，包括交易双方在内的其他硬盘厂商也提高了产品价格，部分硬盘产品涨价幅度超过100%。

a few HDD manufacturers and a small number of main purchasers, the products are identical, and each competitor has a clear knowledge of the technologies, costs, manufacturing, and sales status of other competitors. The HDD manufacturers can rely on relevant facts and experiences to estimate the product prices or price ranges of competitors. Meanwhile, the HDD manufacturers often share the same distributors, so it is easy to learn information about the HDD products of other brands through distribution channels.

iv. Those large computer manufacturers are the main downstream clients of HDD products. The HDD products are mainly sold to large computer manufacturers and to downstream users through distributors. The former are the main clients of HDDs and the prices for the transactions between such enterprises and the HDD manufacturers would determine the market price of HDDs.

3. Purchase Modes

In order to obtain and keep a competitive price, a large computer manufacturer usually adopts private bidding to purchase HDDs and conducts bilateral negotiations with several HDD manufacturers on a quarterly basis. To ensure the continuous and safe supply of HDDs, large computer manufacturers will finally proportionally allocate their total demand among two to four HDD manufacturers based on price and other factors. During any single bidding, the most competitive offer will obtain a larger order share, while the less competitive offer may

调查发现，在其他条件未见明显变化的情况下，个人电脑的销售价格相应上涨，电脑生产商将硬盘价格上涨转嫁给了最终消费者。

（七） 市场进入。

调查发现，知识产权及其他专有知识对硬盘行业至关重要，特别是非知识产权的核心技术、工艺流程和技术队伍构成进入该市场的实质性障碍。规模经济在相关市场中同样重要，新进入者如无法达到一定的生产和销售量则无法生存，而要达到相应规模则需要高额的生产、研发和市场开拓投资，潜在风险巨大。近十年来，没有新的竞争者进入相关市场。据此，商务部认为硬盘市场进入难度很大。

（八） 此项集中对相关商品市场和消费者的影响。

在硬盘市场，交易双方都是重要的生产商。鉴于前述大型电脑生产商的采购模式，此项集中将减少一个重要的竞争者，加大了剩余硬盘生产商均获得订单的机会，削弱了采购过程中硬盘生产商之间的竞争压力。西部数据和日立存储均是相关市场内的重要创新者，此项集中将增强交易双方通过推迟新产品投入市场时间、延长原有产品生命周期等方式放缓创新速度的可能性。同时，由于硬盘市场透明度较高，硬盘厂商有能力预判其他竞争者的行为，此项集中也将进一步增加市场竞争者通过协调从事排除、限制竞争行为的可能性。目前，中国是全球最大的个人电脑消费国之一，此项集中将对中国消费者利益造成不利影响。

（九） 审查结论。

综上，商务部认为此项集中将对硬盘市场产生排除、限制竞争的效果。

get a smaller share or even no order at all. Such a purchase mode makes HDD manufacturers compete to obtain more orders and a larger share of orders. Therefore, keeping the present purchase mode of the large computer manufacturers is critical to the maintenance of competition in the HDD market.

4. Utilization of Production Capacity

It has been found that the utilization rate of production capacity is high in the HDD industry. Since the fourth quarter of 2008, with the increase in market demand, the utilization rates of the production capacity of all HDD manufacturers have kept increasing. In the fourth quarter of 2010, the average utilization rate of the production capacity of all five HDD manufacturers was around 90%, and the remaining capacity was limited. The flood in Thailand in 2011 led to temporary failure in the use of parts of the production capacity and so caused a further shortage of market supply.

5. Product Innovation

Through investigation, it has been found that the influence of innovation in the HDD industry is significant. Any manufacturer who first introduces an innovative product will obtain a larger market share and more profits. After other competitors also introduce similar products, the profit margin of such product will decrease significantly. The HDD manufacturers need to keep innovating to lower costs. Innovation is an important competition means for HDD manufacturers. It is also found that the competition in HDD market is an important premise for product innovation. The effect of eliminating and/or restricting competition will obviously undermine the innovation incentives of the HDD manufacturers and also slow down innovation.

(Continued)

6. Buyers' Bargaining Power and the Impact on Consumers

Through investigation, it has been found that HDD manufacturers have significant influence in determining the selling prices of HDDs to the downstream distributors, and distributors have no countervailing buyer power against HDD manufacturers. For large computer manufacturers, if the price increase made by any HDD manufacturer is not against certain enterprises, they will not object to such increase. The large computer manufacturers have the power to pass on such increase in the prices of HDDs to end consumers by raising the prices of computer products. Therefore, they do not have the incentive to exercise countervailing buyer power. The end consumers are highly scattered, and have no bargaining power against the increase of prices of HDDs and computer products.

Due to the Thailand floods in 2011, the production capacity of Western Digital's HDD was affected and Western Digital first raised the prices of HDDs. Following it, other HDD manufacturers including the parties to this transaction also raised the prices of their products, and some even raised the price by over 100%. It has been found through investigation that the sales prices of personal computers were raised accordingly with other conditions unchanged and the computer manufacturers passed on the increase in HDD prices to the end consumers.

7. Market Entry

It has been found through investigation that intellectual property and other know-how are critical to the HDD industry. In particular, such non-IP elements as core technologies, manufacturing processes, and technology teams constitute material market entry barriers. Economies of scale are also important in the relevant market. New entrants cannot survive if they cannot reach a certain quantity in both production and sales. But in order to achieve such scale, they need to make huge investments in production, R&D, and market expansion, and so will potentially face great risks. In the last ten years, no new competitors entered the relevant market. Therefore, MOFCOM believes that it is difficult to enter the HDD market.

8. The Effect of the Concentration on the Relevant Market and Consumers

In the HDD market, both parties to this transaction are important manufacturers. In consideration of the purchase process of the large computer manufacturers, the concentration will cause one important competitor to leave such market, increase the chances of the remaining HDD manufacturers to get orders, and so mitigate the competition between the HDD manufacturers during the purchase process. Both Western Digital and Hitachi Storage are important innovators in the relevant markets. This concentration will increase the possibility for the two parties to slow down innovation by postponing the launch of any new products and prolonging the life cycle of original products. Also, due to the high transparency in the HDD market, HDD manufacturers can predict the behavior of other competitors, and this concentration can further increase the possibility for market competitors to coordinate to eliminate and/or restrict competition. Nowadays, China is one of the largest PC consumer countries in the world. This concentration will have an adverse effect on the interests of Chinese consumers.

(Continued)

	9. Review Conclusion Based on the above, MOFCOM believes that this concentration will have the effect of eliminating and/or restricting competition in the HDD market.
三、附加限制性条件的商谈 在审查期间，商务部向申报人指出了本项集中将产生的排除、限制竞争效果，并就如何消除上述竞争问题进行了多轮商谈。申报人先后提出了多个解决方案，并向商务部提交了欧盟附加限制性条件批准此项集中的书面文件。经评估，商务部认为，申报人提交的最终解决方案，包括按照欧盟要求向独立第三方出售Viviti公司全部3.5英寸硬盘资产内容的解决方案，能够减少此项经营者集中对竞争产生的不利影响。	**3 Negotiation of Restrictive Conditions** During the review, MOFCOM pointed out to the notifying party that the concentration would eliminate and/or restrict competition and conducted several rounds of negotiations to discuss how to solve such competition issues. The notifying party made several remedy proposal, and submitted the written document issued by the EU to approve the concentration under certain conditions. Through evaluation, MOFCOM believes that the final remedy proposal submitted by the notifying party, including the solution containing the divestiture of all 3.5-inch HDD assets to an independent third party according to the requirements of the EU, could mitigate the adverse effect of such concentration on competition.
四、审查决定 审查认为，西部数据收购Viviti公司对硬盘市场具有排除、限制竞争影响，商务部决定附加限制性条件批准此项集中，西部数据（包括西部数据及其关联公司，下同）、日立公司和Viviti公司（包括Viviti公司及其关联公司，下同）应履行如下义务： （一）　　　集中完成后，在相关市场上维持Viviti公司作为一个独立的竞争者存在，包括但不限于以下内容： 第一，维持Viviti公司交易前的状态，确保Viviti公司维持独立的法人地位并独立开展业务，包括但不限于研发、生产、采购、营销、售后、行政、财务、投资、人事任命等方面。为确保上述独立性，西部数据和Viviti公司应事先制定保障措施，报告监督受托人并经商务部批准后实施，接受本决定项下的监督。	**4 Review Decision** After review, it is believed that the acquisition of Viviti by Western Digital shall have the effect of eliminating and/or restricting competition in the market of HDD. MOFCOM decides to approve this concentration under certain conditions and requires Western Digital (including Western Digital and its affiliates, hereinafter the same), Hitachi, and Viviti (including Viviti and its affiliates, hereinafter the same) to fulfill the following obligations: (1)　After the concentration, Viviti shall be kept as an independent competitor in the relevant market, including but not limited to the following:

第二，集中完成后，Viviti公司应当继续使用既有的生产线和相关生产团队生产硬盘产品，并由原销售团队以HGST生产商的名义（交易完成后，Viviti公司直接持有的Hitachi Global Storage Technologies Netherlands B.V.公司及项下的关联公司中的Hitachi Global Storage Technologies或日立环球存储科技将改为HGST），以交易前使用的TRAVELSTAR和ULTRASTAR品牌，以独立和合理的定价机制继续独立销售硬盘产品。西部数据和Viviti公司互不沟通或干预对方的生产、定价和销售等事宜。为确保实现上述目标，西部数据和Viviti公司应当事先制定保障措施，特别是双方应当建立防火墙，确保双方不会交换竞争性信息。竞争性信息是指任何可能导致竞争者之间协调彼此经营行为的信息，特别是任何有关产品成本、价格、产量、客户、竞标等方面的信息。上述措施报告监督受托人并经商务部批准后实施，接受本决定项下的监督。

第三，集中完成后，西部数据对Viviti公司行使股东权利履行股东义务不得损害两公司的独立性，不得排除或限制两公司之间的竞争。西部数据任何行使股东权利履行股东义务的事项均应事先报告监督受托人，其中涉嫌损害两公司独立性、排除或限制两公司间竞争的，应当事先报商务部批准。双方应当事先制定保障措施，特别是应当建立防火墙，报告监督受托人并经商务部批准后实施，接受本决定项下的监督。

第四，西部数据和Viviti公司应各自维持相互独立的研发机构。双方可在硬盘产品研发方面进行合作，以提高双方的生产效率和竞争力，但不得以此沟通竞争性信息、损害两公司的独立性、排除或限制两公司之间的竞争。西部数据和Viviti公司应当就研发合作事项事先提交具体方案，报告监督受托人并经商务部批准后实施。实施过程中的任何信息及人员交流等事项均应事先向监督受托人报备，接受本决定项下的监督。

i. To keep Viviti in the same status as before the transaction, and ensure that Viviti acts as an independent legal person and independently carries out businesses, including but not limited to the following aspects: R&D, manufacture, purchase, marketing, post-sale, administration, finance, investment, and staffing. To ensure the above independence, Western Digital and Viviti shall stipulate the safeguard measures in advance, report such measures to the supervision trustee and implement them after being approved by MOFCOM, and accept the supervision under this decision.

ii. After the concentration, Viviti shall keep using the existing production line and the relevant production team to produce HDD products, and such products shall be sold independently by the original sales team in the name of the manufacturer, HGST (after the transaction, the name of Hitachi Global Storage Technologies Netherlands B.V. directly held by Viviti, and the affiliate, Hitachi Global Storage Technologies, shall be changed into HGST), with the original brands TRAVELSTAR and ULTRASTAR, and under an independent and reasonable pricing mechanism. Western Digital or Viviti shall not communicate or intervene with the issues concerning production, pricing, and sales of the other party. To guarantee the realization of the above goals, Western Digital and Viviti shall stipulate certain safeguard measures in advance. In particular, the parties shall establish a firewall to ensure that the parties shall not exchange competitively sensitive information. Competitively sensitive

(Continued)

（二）	西部数据和Viviti公司应当根据市场需求状况合理确定产能产量。西部数据和Viviti公司产品的产能和产量情况应当按月向监督受托人报告，接受本决定项下的监督。	
（三）	集中完成后，西部数据和Viviti公司不得实质性改变此前的商业模式，强制或变相强制客户从两公司排他性地采购其硬盘产品。	
（四）	西部数据和Viviti公司将以近年一贯的速度，继续在创新领域投入研发资金，以确保给客户带来更多创新性产品和解决方案。	
（五）	在满足（一）条件的基础上，西部数据承诺，在本审查决定公布之日起6个月内，向第三方剥离Viviti公司主要3.5英寸硬盘资产。剥离上述资产的交易，按照《反垄断法》、《关于实施经营者集中资产或业务剥离的暂行规定》等相关规定办理。	
（六）	根据商务部《关于实施经营者集中资产或业务剥离的暂行规定》，西部数据应委托独立的监督受托人对西部数据履行上述义务的情况进行监督。	

本决定实施24个月后，西部数据可以向商务部提出解除上述第（一）、（二）项义务的申请。该申请应说明本决定项下附加限制性条件的实施情况和解除上述义务的理由并提供相关证据。商务部将依申请并根据市场竞争状况作出是否解除的决定。

为履行上述义务，西部数据应当在监督受托人确定一周内提交详细的操作方案并报商务部批准后实施。

商务部有权通过监督受托人或自行监督检查西部数据履行上述义务的情况。西部数据未适当履行上述义务，商务部有权根据《反垄断法》相关规定作出处理。

information refers to any information which is likely to cause the competitors to coordinate their operating activities, especially any information concerning product cost, price, output, clients, and bidding. These measures shall be reported to the supervision trustee and implemented after being approved by MOFCOM, and they shall be under the supervision determined by this decision.

iii. After the transaction, Western Digital shall exercise its shareholder rights and perform shareholder obligations vis-à-vis Viviti, but shall not prejudice the independence of the two companies, nor eliminate and/or restrict competition between the two companies. The matters concerning the exercise of the shareholder rights or the performance of the shareholder obligations by Western Digital shall be reported to the supervision trustee in advance. The matters suspected of prejudicing the independence of the two companies or eliminating and/or restricting competition between the two companies shall be reported in advance to MOFCOM for approval. The parties shall stipulate the safeguard measures in advance. Especially, a firewall is necessary. These measures shall be reported to the supervision trustee and implemented after being approved by MOFCOM, and shall be supervised as prescribed under this decision.

iv. Western Digital and Viviti shall keep their independent organization in R&D. The parties may cooperate in the research and development of HDD products to improve productivity efficiency and competitiveness, but shall not rely on such cooperation to exchange

	competitively sensitive information, prejudice the independence of the two companies, or eliminate and/or restrict competition between the two companies. Western Digital and Viviti shall submit in advance a specific proposal on R&D cooperation, report it to the supervision trustee, and implement it after its being approved by MOFCOM. Any matter concerning information or personnel exchange during the implementation of such proposal shall be submitted to the supervision trustee for record in advance and shall be supervised as prescribed under this decision.
	(2) Western Digital and Viviti shall reasonably determine production capacity and output based on market demand. The capacity and output of Western Digital and Viviti shall be reported to the supervision trustee on a monthly basis and shall be supervised as prescribed under this decision.
	(3) After the concentration, Western Digital and Viviti shall not materially change the original business modes, nor compel clients or compel clients in a disguised form, to exclusively purchase HDD products from them.
	(4) Western Digital and Viviti shall continue to make R&D investments in innovation at a speed consistent with recent years to bring more innovative products and solutions to clients.
	(5) Upon satisfaction of the conditions in paragraph (1), Western Digital commits that it shall, within six months after the announcement of this decision, divest the main 3.5-inch HDD assets of Viviti to a third party. Such asset divestiture shall be conducted according to the provisions of the AML, and the Interim

(*Continued*)

Provisions on Asset or Business Divestiture during the Implementation of Concentrations of Undertakings.

(6) According to MOFCOM's Interim Provisions on Asset or Business Divestiture during the Implementation of Concentrations of Undertakings, Western Digital shall entrust an independent supervision trustee to supervise the fulfillment of the above obligations by Western Digital.

After 24 months after the effective date of this decision, Western Digital may apply to MOFCOM to cancel the obligations in paragraphs (1) and (2) above. Such application shall specify the status on the fulfillment of the restrictive conditions under this decision and the reasons for cancelling the above obligations, and provide the relevant supporting documents. MOFCOM shall determine whether to cancel such obligations according to the application as well as the market competitive conditions.

In order to fulfill the above obligations, Western Digital shall submit a detailed proposal for fulfilling the above obligations within one week after the supervision trustee is determined, and implement such proposal after being approved by MOFCOM.

MOFCOM shall have the right to inspect the fulfillment of the above obligations by Western Digital through the supervision trustee or through supervision by itself. If Western Digital fails to properly fulfill the above obligations, MOFCOM shall have the right to handle it according to the provisions of the AML.

本公告自发布之日起生效。 中华人民共和国商务部 二〇一二年三月二日	This decision shall become effective as of the date of its announcement. Ministry of Commerce March 2, 2012

D-14

MOFCOM Announcement [2012] No. 25 Regarding the Conditional Approval of Google's Acquisition of Motorola Mobility

商务部公告2012年第25号 关于附加限制性条件批准谷歌收购摩托罗拉移动经营者集中反垄断审查决定的公告

(Published on May 19, 2012)

（2012年5月19日公布）

中华人民共和国商务部（以下简称商务部）收到谷歌公司（以下简称谷歌）收购摩托罗拉移动公司（以下简称摩托罗拉移动）的经营者集中反垄断申报。经审查，商务部决定附加限制性条件批准此项经营者集中。根据《中华人民共和国反垄断法》（以下简称《反垄断法》）第三十条，现公告如下：	The Ministry of Commerce of the People's Republic of China ("MOFCOM") has received an anti-monopoly notification of a concentration of undertakings regarding the acquisition of Motorola Mobility Holdings, Inc. ("Motorola Mobility") by Google Inc. ("Google"). After review, MOFCOM decides to approve this concentration of undertakings under certain conditions. This announcement is hereby made as follows according to Article 30 of the Anti-Monopoly Law ("AML").
一、立案和审查程序 2011年9月30日，商务部收到谷歌收购摩托罗拉移动的经营者集中申报。经审核，商务部认为该申报文件、材料不完备，要求申报方予以补充。11月21日，商务部确认经补充的申报文件、资料符合《反垄断法》第二十三条的要求，对该项经营者集中申报予以立案并开始初步审查。	**1. Acceptance and Review Process** On September 30, 2011, MOFCOM received the notification of a concentration in respect of Google's proposed acquisition of Motorola Mobility. After review of the notification, MOFCOM found that the notification was incomplete and requested the notifying party to submit

(Continued)

经初步审查，商务部认为此项集中对中国移动智能终端操作系统市场可能具有排除、限制竞争效果。本案进入进一步审查延长阶段。12月21日，商务部决定对此项集中实施进一步审查。2012年3月20日，经申报方同意，商务部决定延长进一步审查期限。

审查过程中，商务部征求了相关政府部门、行业协会和下游企业的意见，并就技术问题咨询了有关专家，对申报方提交的文件、资料的真实性、完整性和准确性进行了审核。

supplementary materials. On November 21, MOFCOM believed that the notification as supplemented met the requirements set by Article 23 of the AML, and accepted the notification and started its preliminary review.

During its preliminary review, MOFCOM found that the concentration may have the effect of eliminating and/or restricting competition in the Chinese market for the operating systems for smart mobile devices. On December 21, MOFCOM decided to start its further review of the notification. On March 20, 2012, upon consent of the notifying party, MOFCOM extended the period of its further review.

During the review process, MOFCOM solicited opinions from the relevant governmental departments, trade associations, and downstream companies and consulted experts on technical issues in relation to the transaction. It also reviewed the authenticity, completeness, and accuracy of the materials and documents submitted by the notifying party.

二、竞争分析

根据《反垄断法》及其相关规定，商务部对此项集中涉及的相关市场状况、安卓系统的免费开源问题、谷歌公平对待终端制造商问题、摩托罗拉移动专利许可问题、市场进入等进行了审查，综合评估了此项集中对相关市场竞争等方面的影响。

（一）集中交易。

2011年8月15日，谷歌与摩托罗拉移动签订收购协议。根据该协议，谷歌将收购摩托罗拉移动的全部股份，收购完成后摩托罗拉移动将成为谷歌的全资子公司。谷歌主要经营互联网搜索引擎和在线广告服务，并提供在线服务和软件产品。谷歌开发了移动智能设备操作系统安卓，并以开源、免费的方式提供给移动智能设备制造商使用。摩托罗拉移动是移动设备制造商，产品主要包括手机和平板电脑。

2. Competition Analysis
According to the AML and related provisions, MOFCOM reviewed the issues in relation to the status of the relevant markets involved in this concentration, free and open-source access to the Android system, Google's fair treatment of mobile device manufacturers, licensing of Motorola Mobility patents, market entry, etc., and comprehensively assessed the effect of this concentration on competition in the relevant markets.

(1) The Transaction of Concentration
On August 15, 2011, Google and Motorola Mobility entered into an acquisition agreement under which Google would acquire all the equity of Motorola Mobility so that Motorola Mobility would become a wholly owned subsidiary of Google post-transaction.

（二）　相关市场。

移动智能终端和移动智能终端操作系统构成本案的相关商品市场。

移动智能终端是指具备开放的操作系统平台，个人电脑级的处理能力，高速接入能力和丰富的人机交互界面的智能终端，目前主要是指智能手机，还包括平板电脑、智能电视等。移动智能终端已经成为互联网业务的关键入口和主要创新平台，其操作系统平台的开放性、人机交互体验的独特性和携带的便捷性显著区别于个人电脑、功能手机等其他产品，构成一个独立的市场。

移动智能终端操作系统是管理移动智能终端硬件与软件资源的程序，其与电脑操作系统等其他产品差异明显，构成单独的相关商品市场。

移动智能终端及其操作系统市场具有全球市场的特征。商务部在审查中考虑了全球市场的竞争状况，但重点考察了中国市场状况。

（三）　相关市场状况。

移动智能终端市场和其操作系统市场呈现出不同的竞争状况。移动智能终端市场集中度相对分散、竞争激烈，市场不断推陈出新，更新换代频繁，各制造商均面临较大的竞争压力。调查表明，摩托罗拉移动相对于其他竞争者并不具备明显优势。

与上述市场显著不同，移动智能终端操作系统市场是一个高度集中的市场。最新数据表明，2011年第四季度，仅谷歌开发的安卓系统就占据73.99%中国市场份额，此外，诺基亚的塞班系统占12.53%，苹果的iOS占10.67%，三者合计占据97.19%的中国市场份额。考虑到安卓系统超高的市场份额、移动智能终端制造商对安卓系统的高度依赖性、谷歌公司雄厚的财力和技术开发能力以及很高的市场进入门槛，商务部认定安卓系统在移动智能终端操作系统市场占据市场支配地位。

Google mainly engages in the internet search engine business and online advertisement services. It also provides online services and software products. Google has developed the Android system, an operating system for smart mobile devices, and made such system available to manufacturers of smart mobile devices free of charge and in open source. Motorola Mobility is a manufacturer of mobile devices, which mainly include cellphones and tablet PCs.

(2) Relevant Markets

The relevant markets are those for smart mobile devices and for the operating systems for such devices.

Smart mobile devices refer to the smart terminal devices with open platforms for operating systems, PC-level processing capacity, high-speed access ability, and man-machine interfaces ("MMI"). Currently, they mainly include smart phones, tablet PCs, and smart TVs. Smart mobile devices have become a critical access to and a main innovation platform for the internet business. They are distinguished from other products such as PCs and feature phones because the platforms for the smart mobile device operating systems are open, the MMI experience is unique, and the devices are easily portable. Smart mobile devices constitute an independent product market.

Smart mobile device operating systems are programs that manage the hardware and software of smart mobile devices. They are significantly different from other products such as computer operating systems and constitute an independent product market.

The markets for smart mobile devices and their operating systems are both global in nature. MOFCOM considered the competition status in the global market, but focused on the review of the Chinese market.

(Continued)

由于诺基亚已经宣布逐步放弃塞班系统，苹果手机售价普遍远高于安装安卓系统的智能手机，而微软公司开发的WINDOWS PHONE操作系统尚处于起步阶段，因此安卓系统的市场支配地位预计在未来相当一段时间内将继续维持和巩固。

（四）　安卓系统的免费、开源问题。

目前，安卓系统已经形成完整的生态产业链，移动智能终端制造商、软件开发商、最终用户均对安卓系统形成依赖性。终端制造商必须依据安卓系统对产品进行设计开发，软件开发商依据安卓系统进行研发，而开发出的应用软件仅适用于安卓系统而无法适用于其他操作系统。最终用户由于使用习惯等原因也会对安卓系统形成相当程度的依赖。调查发现，对于移动智能终端制造商而言，更换操作系统成本巨大：必须更改相关硬件和软件以适应新的操作系统，同时，操作系统的更改还可能导致用户体验的差别，存在较大的商业风险。

安卓系统的免费、开源特征是其在较短时间内取得市场支配地位的重要原因，在相当一段时间内维持安卓系统的免费、开源对于保护相关方的合理预期和正当利益至关重要。谷歌在此项集中完成后改变安卓系统目前免费、开源的商业模式将对相关各方产生重大不利影响。

（五）　谷歌公平对待终端制造商问题。

此项集中完成后，摩托罗拉移动成为谷歌的全资子公司。鉴于谷歌在移动智能终端操作系统上具有的市场支配地位，谷歌有动机也有能力给予摩托罗拉移动优于其他移动智能终端制造商的待遇，如先于其他制造商向摩托罗拉移动提供最新开发的安卓系统。调查中，商务部发现，谷歌在推出新版的安卓系统前，会首先非指向性地选择一个移动智能终端制造商合作，以测试新版安卓系统与终端硬件设备的适应性。

(3) Status of the Relevant Markets

The markets for smart mobile devices and their operating systems feature different competition status. The market for smart mobile devices is relatively segmented and fiercely competitive with a fast high updating frequency, where all manufacturers face considerable competition pressure. The investigation shows that Motorola Mobility possesses no apparent advantage compared with its competitors.

Obviously different from the above market, the market for smart mobile device operating systems is highly concentrated. The latest data indicate that the Android system developed by Google had a market share of 73.99% in China in the fourth quarter of 2011, while the Symbian system developed by Nokia had 12.53%, and iOS developed by Apple had 10.67%. These three collectively accounted for 97.19% of the Chinese market. Considering Android's significant market share, the high dependence on Android by device manufacturers, Google's strong financial resources and R&D capability and significantly high market entry barriers, MOFCOM concluded that Google has a dominant market position in the market for smart mobile device operating systems. Since Nokia has stated its intention to gradually give up the Symbian system, iPhone prices are normally far above those of smartphones with the Android system, and the Windows Phone operating system is just under early development by Microsoft, the Android system is expected to remain dominant for a very long time in the future.

(4) Free and Open-source access to the Android system

At present, the Android system has formed a complete industry chain. Smart mobile device manufacturers,

被选中的终端制造商将有机会先于其他制造商获得新版安卓系统，从而在移动智能终端的市场竞争中处于有利地位。此项集中完成后，谷歌将有可能仅选择摩托罗拉移动作为测试对象。谷歌对移动智能终端制造商的差别待遇将扭曲该市场的竞争，使摩托罗拉移动之外的其他终端制造商处于不利的竞争地位。

（六）　摩托罗拉移动专利许可问题。

摩托罗拉移动拥有众多手机领域的专利，相当一部分专利属于核心专利。谷歌收购摩托罗拉移动的主要目的就是拥有这些手机专利。此项集中完成后，谷歌将同时拥有强大的软硬件开发和集成能力，借助其在移动智能终端市场的支配地位，谷歌有动机也有能力在专利许可中向相对方附加不合理的许可条件，这将对相关市场的竞争造成损害，并最终损害消费者的利益。

（七）　市场进入。

如前所述，移动智能终端操作系统市场是一个高度集中的市场，安卓系统、塞班系统和苹果iOS占据了97%以上的市场份额，其他经营者所占份额极为有限，属边缘竞争者。

移动智能终端操作系统的开发需要雄厚的技术和资金实力，高度集中的市场对新进入者形成了极高的进入壁垒。一个移动智能终端操作系统是否能够取得成功，关键取决于与该操作系统相匹配的软件开发环境是否友好、是否能够吸引软件开发者。优秀的应用开发环境可以大大降低开发门槛，提高开发效率，提升用户体验，进而吸引众多软件开发者，最终具有良好用户体验的应用软件吸引消费者和潜在购买者。以移动智能终端操作系统为基础开发的应用软件数量的多寡、用户体验的优劣已经成为不同操作系统之间竞争的关键要素之一。

software developers, and end users have become dependent on the Android system. Device manufacturers have to design and develop their products in line with the Android system. Software developers also develop their products in line with the Android system, and the application software so developed is only compatiable with the Android system rather than other systems. End users, due to their formed use habits, are highly dependent on the Android system as well. The investigation shows that the costs for smart mobile device manufacturers to switch operating systems is significant; they need to replace the related hardware and software to suit the new system. Meanwhile, there are considerable commercial risks in changing the operating system as it may lead to different user experience.

The Android system has quickly obtained its dominance in the market largely because it is accessible, free of charge, and in open source. It is critically important to keep it free and in open source for quite a long period so as to protect the reasonable expectations and legitimate interests of the related parties. Any change by Google to such free and open-source commercial mode post-transaction may lead to significant adverse effect on the related parties.

(5) Google's Fair Treatment of Device Manufacturers

After this concentration, Motorola Mobility would become Google's wholly owned subsidiary. Given Google's dominance in the market for smart mobile device operating systems, Google has the incentive and is capable of giving more favorable treatment to Motorola Mobility than to other smart mobile device manufacturers. For example, it may provide the latest developed Android system to Motorola

(Continued)

目前，典型的移动智能终端操作系统软件开发环境包括安卓开发环境、苹果开发环境和微软开发环境。数量庞大的安卓应用和苹果应用已经成功吸引了绝大多数软件开发者以及消费者，转换开发环境不仅需要软件开发者适应新的技术要求，还将面临失去众多消费者的巨大商业风险；而且，对于消费者而言，改变操作系统意味着熟悉新的操作界面、更换智能终端等额外成本。可见，安卓系统和苹果系统已经形成完整的、具有强大市场吸引力和良好口碑的系统，无论市场的边缘竞争者还是新进入者，都面临极高的进入门槛。在可预期的未来，市场进入难以减轻或消除上述排除、限制竞争效果。

Mobility earlier than to others. During the investigation, MOFCOM found that, before its announcement of a new version of the Android system, Google would randomly select a smart mobile device manufacturer to test the compatibility of the new version to smart devices. The selected device manufacturer had priority in obtaining the new version of Android compared to other manufacturers, and was thus competitively advantaged in the smart mobile device market. After completion of this concentration, Google may choose Motorola Mobility as the only manufacturer for the applicability test. This discriminatory treatment by Google would distort competition in the market for smart mobile devices and put device manufacturers other than Motorola Mobility at a competitive disadvantage.

(6) Motorola Mobility's Patent Licensing

Motorola Mobility owns a large number of patents for cellphones, many of which are essential patents. The main purpose of Google for the transaction resides in the acquisition of Motorola Mobility's patents. Post-transaction, Google would have strong capabilities in both software development and integration. Based on its dominance in the market for smart mobile device operating systems, Google would have the incentive and ability to impose unreasonable terms and conditions in the licensing of Motorola Mobility's patents, adversely affecting competition in relevant markets, and ultimately harming consumers.

(7) Market Entry

As mentioned above, the market for smart mobile device operating systems is highly concentrated, where Android, Symbian, and iOS systems collectively

	possess a market share of over 97% and other undertakings are marginal competitors with very limited market shares.
	The development of smart mobile device operating systems requires strong technology and financial capabilities, and the market is highly concentrated with extremely high entry barriers. The success of a smart mobile device operating system significantly depends on whether the development environment for software applicable to the operating system is supportive, and whether it can attract software developers. An excellent application and development environment can significantly lower the entry barriers, increase development efficiencies, enhance user experience, and further attract more software developers. Ultimately, application software providing excellent user experience can attract consumers and potential customers. The number of application software developed based on smart mobile device operating systems and the quality of user experience has become a critical factor in the competition among different operating systems.
	So far, the typical development environment for software applicable to smart mobile device operating systems includes Android, Apple iOS, and Microsoft. The large number of Android and iOS applications have successfully attracted most software developers and consumers. Change in the development environment not only requires software developers to get used to new technological requirements, but also to face huge commercial risks of losing many consumers. Moreover, from the perspective of customers, switching to a new operating system means extra

(Continued)

	costs for adapting to the new operating interface, changing the smart mobile device, etc. Therefore, Android and Apple iOS have built up integrated and market-appealing systems with a good reputation. Both marginal competitors in the market and new entrants have to face extremely high entry barriers. In the foreseeable future, market entries can hardly mitigate or eliminate the above effect of restricting or eliminating competition.
三、附加限制性条件的商谈 在审查期间，商务部向谷歌指出了此项集中将产生的排除、限制竞争效果，并就如何解决上述竞争问题进行了多轮商谈。2012年5月15日，谷歌向商务部提交了解决竞争问题的最终承诺。经评估，商务部认为，该承诺能够减少此项集中对竞争产生的不利影响。	**3. Negotiation of Restrictive Conditions** During the review, MOFCOM pointed out the effect of eliminating and/or restricting competition this concentration may have, and held several rounds of negotiations with Google to address the competition issues identified above. On May 15, 2012, Google submitted its final commitments to MOFCOM. After assessment, MOFCOM believes that the commitments can mitigate the adverse competitive effect of this concentration.
四、审查决定 经审查，商务部认为谷歌收购摩托罗拉移动具有排除、限制竞争影响。根据谷歌向商务部作出的承诺，商务部决定附加限制性条件批准此项集中。谷歌应当履行如下义务： (一) 谷歌将在免费和开放的基础上许可安卓平台，与目前的商业做法一致。安卓平台是指用于移动设备的当前及未来版本的开源软件堆栈，包括以目前发布于 http://code.google.com/android/ 的形式存在的且在义务期内(除非这些义务被修改或解除)于该网站或后继网站上可获得的操作系统、中间件及关键开源应用程序在内。本项义务不影响谷歌对与安卓平台相关的软件(包括但不限于在安卓平台上运行的应用程序)保持闭源或使之闭源的权力。	**4. Review Decision** After review, MOFCOM held that Google's proposed acquisition of Motorola Mobility would have an effect of eliminating and/or restricting competition. In view of the commitments Google made to MOFCOM, MOFCOM decides to approve this concentration under the condition that Google fulfills the following obligations: (1) Google will license the Android platform free of charge and in open source, which is consistent with its current commercial practice. The Android platform refers to current and future versions of open-source software stacks used for mobile devices, including operating systems, middlewares, and key open-source

本项义务不影响谷歌就其提供的与安卓平台相关的产品和服务(包括但不限于在安卓平台上运行的应用程序)寻求付款或其他对价的能力。

(二) 谷歌应当在安卓平台方面以非歧视的方式对待所有原始设备制造商。本项义务仅适用于已经同意不对安卓平台进行分化或衍生的原始设备制造商。本项义务不适用于谷歌提供、许可或分销与安卓平台相关的产品和服务(包括但不限于在安卓平台上运行的应用程序)的方式。

(三) 本次交易后,谷歌应当继续遵守摩托罗拉移动在摩托罗拉移动专利方面现有的公平、合理和非歧视(FRAND)义务。

(四) 根据商务部《关于实施经营者集中资产或业务剥离的暂行规定》(商务部公告2010年第41号),谷歌委托独立的监督受托人对谷歌履行上述义务的情况进行监督。

对于第(一)项和第(二)项义务,自商务部决定之日起5年内有效。如果市场状况或市场竞争发生变化,则谷歌可以向商务部申请变更或解除此2项义务。如果谷歌不再控制摩托罗拉移动,则此2项义务失效。

自商务部决定发布之日起5年内,谷歌应当每6个月就其遵守上述义务的情况向商务部和监督受托人报告。5年期满后,商务部可以继续评估中国移动智能终端操作系统市场的状况,并根据评估状况依法作出决定。

商务部有权通过监督受托人或者自行监督检查谷歌履行上述义务的情况。谷歌未适当履行上述义务时,商务部有权根据《反垄断法》相关规定作出处理。

applications currently published on <http://code.google.com/android/> and available on this website or its successors during the obligation period (unless such obligations are modified or removed). This obligation shall not affect Google's right to keep or ability to keep closed-source the software related to the Android platform (including but not limited to applications operated on the Android platform). This obligation shall not affect Google's ability to request payment or other consideration for the provision of the products and services related to the Android platform (including but not limited to applications operated on the Android platform).

(2) Google will treat all original equipment manufacturers (OEMs) in a non-discriminatory manner with respect to the provision of the Android platform. This obligation only applies to OEMs that have accepted not to differentiate or derive from the Android platform. This obligation does not apply to the form of Google's provision, licensing, or distribution of products and services related to the Android platform (including but not limited to applications operated on the Android platform).

(3) Google will continue to comply with the obligations Motorola Mobility currently undertakes with respect to its patents, to license them on fair, reasonable, and non-discriminatory (FRAND) terms.

(4) According to the Interim Provisions on Asset or Business Divestiture during Implementation of Concentrations of Undertakings (MOFCOM Announcement [2010] No. 4), Google will appoint an independent supervision trustee to supervise its performance of the above obligations.

(Continued)

	Obligations (1) and (2) are imposed for five years from the date of this decision. If any change happens to the market circumstances or market competition, Google may request MOFCOM to change or terminate these two obligations. When Google no longer controls Motorola Mobility, these two obligations will be no longer in force. Within five years from the date of this decision, Google will report to MOFCOM and the supervision trustee on its performance of the above obligations every six months. After five years, MOFCOM may continue to evaluate the conditions of the Chinese market for smart mobile device operating systems, and may make further decisions based on the result of its evaluation and in accordance with the law. MOFCOM may, through the supervision trustee or on its own, supervise and inspect Google's performance of the above obligations. If Google fails to duly perform the above obligations, MOFCOM may deal with such failures according to the relevant provisions of the AML.
本公告自发布之日起生效。 　　　　中华人民共和国商务部 　　　　二〇一二年五月十九日	This decision shall become effective as of the date its announcement. Ministry of Commerce May 19, 2012

MOFCOM Announcement [2012] No. 35 Regarding the Conditional Approval of the Acquisition of Goodrich by United Technologies

商务部公告2012年第35号 关于附加限制性条件批准联合技术收购古德里奇经营者集中反垄断审查决定的公告

(Published on June 15, 2012)

（2012年6月15日公布）

中华人民共和国商务部收到联合技术公司（以下简称联合技术）收购古德里奇公司（以下简称古德里奇）的经营者集中反垄断申报。经审查，商务部决定附加限制性条件批准此项经营者集中。根据《中华人民共和国反垄断法》（以下简称《反垄断法》）第三十条，现公告如下：	The Ministry of Commerce of the People's Republic of China ("MOFCOM") has received an anti-monopoly notification of a concentration of undertakings for the acquisition of Goodrich Corporation ("Goodrich") by United Technologies Corporation ("UTC"). After review, MOFCOM decides to approve this concentration under conditions. This announcement is hereby made as follows according to Article 30 of the Anti-Monopoly Law ("AML").
一、立案和审查程序 2011年12月12日，商务部收到联合技术收购古德里奇的经营者集中申报。经审核，商务部认为该申报材料不完备，要求申报方予以补充。2012年2月6日，商务部确认经补充的申报材料符合《反垄断法》第二十三条的要求，对该项经营者集中申报开始立案审查。	**1. Acceptance and Review Process** On December 12, 2011, MOFCOM received the notification of a concentration in connection with UTC's proposed acquisition of Goodrich. After review of the notification, MOFCOM found that the notification was incomplete and requested the notifying party to submit supplemental materials.

(Continued)

经初步审查，商务部认为此项集中可能对飞机交流发电系统市场具有排除、限制竞争的效果。3月2日，商务部决定实施进一步审查，5月31日，商务部决定延长进一步审查期限，截止日期为7月30日。 审查过程中，商务部对申报方提交的文件、资料的真实性、完整性和准确性进行了审核，书面征求了有关政府部门、同业竞争者和下游客户的意见，了解相关产品信息、市场参与者情况、市场结构状况、行业特征及未来发展趋势等，并就相关情况进行了实地调研。	On February 6, 2012, MOFCOM believed that the notification as supplemented met the requirements set by Article 23 of the AML, and accepted the notification and started its review. Upon preliminary review, MOFCOM found that the concentration may have an effect of eliminating and/or restricting competition in the market for aircraft AC power generation systems. On March 2, MOFCOM decided to start a further review of the notification. On May 31, 2012, MOFCOM decided to extend the period of further review with a new deadline of July 30. During the review process, MOFCOM reviewed the authenticity, completeness, and accuracy of the documents and materials submitted by the notifying party, solicited comments in writing from relevant governmental departments, competitors, and downstream customers, collected information about the relevant products, market participants, market structure, industry features, future development trend, etc., and conducted on-site investigations in respect of the relevant matters.
二、竞争分析 商务部根据《反垄断法》第二十七条规定的因素，对此项经营者集中进行了全面审查，深入分析了此项经营者集中对相关市场竞争可能产生的影响，认为其对飞机交流发电系统市场具有排除、限制竞争的影响。 （一）　相关市场。 商务部重点审查了本交易所涉横向重叠的产品，主要包括飞机电源系统、飞机照明系统、飞行控制作动系统和飞机发动机控制系统。　这四大系统均为飞机及飞机发动机的重要组成部件。	**2. Competition Analysis** According to Article 27 of the AML, MOFCOM conducted a comprehensive review of the concentration, thoroughly analyzed the potential impact of the concentration on competition in the relevant markets, and found that the concentration may have an effect of eliminating and/or restricting competition in the market for aircraft AC power generation systems. **(1) Relevant Markets** MOFCOM focused its review on the horizontal overlapping products involved in the transaction, mainly including aircraft electrical power systems, aircraft lighting systems, actuation systems for flight control, and aircraft engine control systems.

根据产品的特征和用途等需求特性、生产和使用上的供给特性以及下游客户在实践中的招标情况等，商务部认定交流发电系统、飞机舱内照明系统、辅助飞行控制作动系统、旋翼飞机飞行控制作动系统、水平安定面配平作动器、导弹作动系统、发动机电子控制系统、燃油计量装置、主燃油泵分别构成独立的相关商品市场。这些相关商品的供应商均在全球范围内从事业务活动，向全球范围内的客户进行销售。同时，相关商品所面对的下游客户都是采用全球采购策略，客户在全球范围内选择供应商。另外，相关商品的价格是基于全球定价，不同地域间不存在明显价差。因此，商务部认定上述商品的相关地域市场均为全球市场。

（二）　竞争评估。

商务部综合考察了相关市场的市场份额、市场集中度、市场控制力、市场进入、研发和创新等因素，重点评估了本交易在全球交流发电系统市场上可能产生的排除、限制竞争效果。

在飞机交流发电系统市场中，全球共有包括联合技术和古德里奇在内的6家供应商。交易前联合技术和古德里奇的市场份额分别为72%和12%，位居市场前两名。交易后双方合计市场份额为84%，市场份额远远高于其他竞争者。交易后市场集中度HHI指数为7158，交易后HHI指数增加值为1728。

调查发现，2007年至2011年飞机制造商对交流发电系统的多次招投标中，联合技术获得了绝大多数的市场机会，古德里奇是市场中为数不多的飞机交流发电系统的中标供应商，市场上其他竞争者的存在不能对交易双方构成有效的竞争约束。联合技术拥有飞机交流发电系统的领先技术，本交易将进一步强化联合技术的市场控制力，减少下游客户在全球范围内选择相关商品的供应商数量，将在全球交流发电系统市场上产生排除、限制竞争的效果。

All of these four types of systems are important components of aircrafts and aircraft engines. MOFCOM assessed the demand features based on the product characteristics and intended use, the supply features based on the production and application, as well as the practice of bidding invitations by downstream customers. MOFCOM found that each of the following products constitutes an independent product market: AC power generation systems, aircraft cabin lighting systems, auxiliary flight control actuation systems, rotary-wing aircraft flight control actuation systems, horizontal stabilizer trim actuators, missile actuation systems, electronic engine control systems, fuel metering devices, and main fuel pumps. The suppliers of the above relevant products sell their products to customers across the world. Meanwhile, all the downstream customers of the relevant products adopt a global procurement strategy and select suppliers worldwide. In addition, relevant products are priced on a global basis without significant regional differences. Therefore, MOFCOM found that the relevant geographic market for each of the above relevant products is worldwide.

(2) Competition Assessment

MOFCOM comprehensively assessed such factors as market share, level of market concentration, market power, market entry, R&D and innovation in the relevant markets, and focused its assessment on the effect of eliminating and/or restricting competition that the transaction may have on the global market for AC power generation systems.

In the market for aircraft AC power generation systems, there are, in total, six suppliers in the world, including UTC and Goodrich. Before the transaction, the market shares of UTC and Goodrich were 72% and 12%, respectively, ranking as the top two in the market.

(*Continued*)

（三） 市场进入。

飞机交流发电系统的供应商通常需要根据不同飞机平台的要求"量身打造"适合的产品。供应商要具备雄厚的资金和技术实力，才能满足飞机产品前期研发成本高，研发周期长，技术难度大，投资回收期长的要求。同时，交流发电系统产品具有相对较长的生命周期，一旦某一飞机平台确定使用某一交流发电产品，在未来的一段时间将不做改变，这种情况甚至可能长达数十年。新飞机平台的出现以及技术革新可能为新的市场进入者提供机会。对市场进入者的高要求、市场机会的有限性和不可控性，导致交流发电系统市场进入门槛较高。

Post-transaction, the combined market share of the parties would be 84%, far exceeding the market shares of their competitors. Post-transaction, the HHI in the relevant market would be 7158, increased by 1728.

The investigation showed that, from 2007 to 2011, UTC secured most of the market opportunities in many biddings by aircraft manufacturers for AC power generation systems, Goodrich was one of the few other suppliers of aircraft AC power generation systems that won such bids, and their competitors in the market were unable to impose effective competitive constraint on them. UTC has advanced technologies for aircraft AC power generation systems. This transaction would further strengthen the market power of UTC, reduce the number of suppliers of the relevant product available to downstream customers, and eliminate and/or restrict competition on the global market for AC power generation systems.

(3) Market Entry

Suppliers of aircraft AC power generation systems usually need to customize suitable products based on requirements of different aircraft platforms. In order to cope with the high R&D costs in the early stage, long R&D cycles, technical difficulty, and long investment recovery period associated with aircraft products, suppliers need to have strong financial and technical resources. Meanwhile, AC power generation system products have relatively long life cycles; once a particular AC power generation product is used on an aircraft platform, it will remain there for a long time, sometimes decades. While new aircraft platforms and technical renovation may provide opportunities to new market entrants, the entry barriers into the market

	for AC power generation systems are relatively significant as there are high requirements on the entrants and the market opportunities are limited and out of the entrants' control.
三、附加限制性条件的商谈 商务部与申报方就如何解决上述竞争问题进行了多轮商谈。2012年6月6日，交易双方提交了最终解决方案。经过评估，商务部认为，该解决方案可以减少此项经营者集中在飞机交流发电系统市场对竞争产生的不利影响。	**3. Negotiation of Restrictive Conditions** To address the competition concerns as described above, MOFCOM and the notifying party held several discussions. On June 6, 2012, the parties to the transaction submitted the final proposal. After assessment, MOFCOM determined that the proposal is sufficient to mitigate the adverse effects of the concentration on competition in the market for aircraft AC power generation systems.
四、审查决定 鉴于联合技术收购古德里奇，将对飞机交流发电系统市场产生排除、限制竞争的效果，商务部决定附加限制性条件批准此项集中，要求交易双方履行如下义务： （一）剥离古德里奇的电源系统业务，包括古德里奇位于英国Pitstone和美国特温斯堡的交流发电系统业务、低压直流发电系统业务和配电系统业务，以及古德里奇在其与泰雷兹航电系统公司的合资公司爱罗雷克中60%的权益。联合技术和古德里奇应根据买方的需求，向买方转让确保上述被剥离业务存活性和竞争性所需的有形资产和无形资产（包括但不限于生产设备、销售部门、研发部门、客户服务及相关知识产权）。 （二）联合技术应在商务部批准此项集中后6个月内根据商务部《关于实施经营者集中资产或业务剥离的暂行规定》为被剥离业务找到购买人并与之签订买卖协议。经申请，上述期限可延长至9个月。	**4. Review Decision** Because the proposed acquisition of Goodrich by UTC would have an effect of eliminating and/or restricting competition in the market for aircraft AC power generation systems, MOFCOM decides to approve this concentration under certain conditions and requires UTC and Goodrich to fulfill the following obligations: (1) Goodrich's electric power systems business shall be divested, including the AC generation systems business, low-voltage DC generation systems business, and electric distribution systems business located in Pitstone, U.K. and Twinsburg, U.S., as well as Goodrich's 60% interest in the Aerolec Joint Venture between Goodrich and Thales Avionics Electrical Systems SA (collectively, "Divestment Business"). At the request of the buyer(s), UTC and Goodrich shall transfer the tangible and intangible assets (including but not limited to production equipment, sales

(Continued)

如在该期限内未能找到购买人并签订协议，则商务部有权指定剥离受托人在3个月内以无底价方式为被剥离业务找到购买人并签订买卖协议。

(三) 在剥离完成之前，联合技术和古德里奇应当按照商务部《关于实施经营者集中资产或业务剥离的暂行规定》第十二条的要求履行相应义务。

(四) 剥离完成后1年内，根据购买人的请求，联合技术和古德里奇有义务向购买人提供合理的技术支持，协助其进行电源系统的制造、装配、测试、维修和大修等业务，并对购买人的相关人员提供技术培训和咨询服务。

(五) 参与集中的经营者应当按照商务部《关于实施经营者集中资产或业务剥离的暂行规定》的要求委托监督受托人，对其履行义务的情况进行监督。

商务部将依据相关法律法规对上述限制性条件的实施进行监督检查。当事方如有任何违反上述限制性条件的行为，商务部将依法予以处罚。

divisions, R&D divisions, customer services, and relevant IPs) that are necessary to ensure the viability and competitiveness of the Divested Business.

(2) UTC shall identify buyer(s) and sign a purchase agreement for the sale of the Divestment Business within six (6) months after the approval of the proposed concentration by MOFCOM in accordance with the Interim Provisions on Asset or Business Divestiture during the Implementation of Concentrations of Undertakings. Upon application, such period can be extended to nine (9) months. If UTC fails to identify a buyer and execute the relevant agreement within the prescribed period, MOFCOM shall have the right to designate a divestiture trustee to find buyer(s) and enter into purchase agreements for divestiture of the Divestment Business without a minimum price within three (3) months.

(3) Before the completion of the transfer of the Divested Business, UTC and Goodrich shall fulfill their obligations as required by Article 12 of the Interim Provisions on Asset or Business Divestiture during the Implementation of Concentrations of Undertakings.

(4) UTC and Goodrich shall, within one (1) year after the divestiture and upon the request from the buyer(s), provide the buyer(s) with reasonable technical support; assist the buyer(s) in the manufacturing, assembly, test, maintenance and overhaul, and other activities with respect to electric systems; and provide the relevant personnel of the buyer(s) with technical trainings and consultation services.

	(5) The undertakings concerned by the concentration shall, in accordance with relevant provisions set out in the Interim Provisions on Asset or Business Divestiture during the Implementation of Concentrations of Undertakings, engage a supervision trustee to supervise the fulfillment of their obligations.
	MOFCOM will supervise and inspect the fulfillment of the above restrictive conditions in accordance with the relevant laws and regulations. In case of any breach by the parties of any of the above restrictive conditions, MOFCOM will impose penalties according to law.
本决定自公告之日起生效。 中华人民共和国商务部 二〇一二年六月十五日	This decision shall become effective as of the date of its announcement. Ministry of Commerce June 15, 2012

MOFCOM Announcement [2012] No. 49 Regarding the Conditional Approval of Walmart's Acquisition of 33.6% of Newheight Holdings

商务部公告2012年第49号 关于附加限制性条件批准沃尔玛公司收购纽海控股33.6%股权经营者集中反垄断审查决定的公告

(Published on August 13, 2012)

（2012年8月13日公布）

中华人民共和国商务部（以下简称商务部）收到沃尔玛公司收购纽海控股有限公司（以下简称纽海控股）33.6%股权的经营者集中反垄断申报。经审查，商务部决定附加限制性条件批准此项经营者集中。根据《中华人民共和国反垄断法》（以下简称《反垄断法》）第三十条，现公告如下：

The Ministry of Commerce of the People's Republic of China ("MOFCOM") has received an anti-monopoly notification of a concentration of undertakings regarding Walmart's acquisition of 33.6% of Newheight Holdings Ltd. ("Newheight Holdings"). After review, MOFCOM hereby decides to approve this concentration of undertakings under certain conditions. In accordance with Article 30 of the Anti-Monopoly Law of the People's Republic of China ("AML"), it is announced as follows.

一、立案和审查程序

2011年12月16日，商务部收到沃尔玛公司收购纽海控股33.6%股权的经营者集中申报。经审核，商务部认为该申报文件、材料不完备，要求申报方予以补充。2012年2月16日，商务部确认经补充的申报文件、资料符合《反垄断法》第二十三条的要求，对该项经营者集中申报予以立案并开始初步审查。

1. Acceptance and Review Process

On December 16, 2011, MOFCOM received the notification of Walmart's acquisition of 33.6% of Newheight Holdings. Upon examination of the notification, MOFCOM found the submitted documents and materials incomplete and required the notifying party to provide supplemental materials. On February 16, 2012, MOFCOM

经初步审查，商务部认为此项集中对中国B2C网上零售市场可能具有排除、限制竞争效果。本案进入进一步审查延长阶段。2012年3月16日，商务部决定对此项集中实施进一步审查。2012年6月13日，经申报方同意，商务部决定延长进一步审查期限。

审查过程中，商务部征求了相关政府部门、行业协会和相关企业的意见，了解了相关市场界定、行业特征及未来发展趋势等方面信息，并对申报方提交的文件、资料的真实性、完整性和准确性进行了审核。

confirmed that the notification, as supplemented, met the requirements of Article 23 of the AML, accepted the notification, and started a preliminary review.

During the preliminary review, MOFCOM believed that this concentration may have an effect of eliminating and/or restricting competition in the B2C online retail market in China. On March 16, 2012, MOFCOM decided to undertake a further review of this concentration. On June 13, 2012, with the consent of the notifying party, MOFCOM decided to extend the period of further review.

During the review process, MOFCOM consulted with the relevant governmental departments, trade associations and enterprises, and collected information in relation to market definition, industry features and the development trends. It also examined and verified whether the submitted documents and materials are authentic, complete, and accurate.

二、竞争分析

根据《反垄断法》第二十七条，商务部对此项经营者集中进行了综合评估，深入分析该项经营者集中对市场竞争的影响，认为其可能具有排除限制竞争的效果。

2011年11月24日，沃尔玛公司及其全资子公司GEC 2 PTE. LTD.（以下简称GEC 2）与纽海控股、纽海控股的售股股东中国平安保险海外（控股）有限公司、美国自然人于刚先生、澳大利亚自然人刘峻岭先生，纽海控股的全资子公司新岗岭有限公司（以下简称新岗岭香港）及新岗岭香港的全资子公司纽海信息技术（上海）有限公司（以下简称纽海上海），以及上海益实多电子商务有限公司（益实多）及其售股股东深圳市平安创新有限公司签订了《购股协议》（以下简称协议）。

2. Competition Analysis
In accordance with Article 27 of the AML, MOFCOM made a comprehensive assessment of this concentration and an in-depth analysis of the possible impact of this concentration on the market, and found that this concentration may have an effect of eliminating and/or restricting competition.

On November 24, 2011, Walmart, along with its wholly owned subsidiary GEC 2 PTE. LTD. ("GEC 2"), entered into a share purchase agreement (the "Agreement") with Newheight Holdings and Newheight Holdings' selling shareholders China Ping An Insurance Overseas (Holdings) Limited, U.S. individual Mr. Gang YU, Austrian individual Mr. Junling LIU, Newheight

(Continued)

根据协议，沃尔玛公司将通过其全资子公司GEC 2对纽海控股的持股比例从17.7%增加至51.3%。纽海控股将通过全资子公司新岗岭香港和纽海上海持有益实多的网上购物平台"1号店"（以下简称益实多1号店）的网上直销业务。交易完成后，沃尔玛公司将成为纽海控股的控股股东，并通过纽海控股取得对益实多1号店网上直销业务的控制权。

沃尔玛公司是全球和中国连锁超级市场的主要竞争者，其在采购、仓储、产品线、门店网络、服务和物流以及品牌等方面存在竞争优势，业务主要为实体超市。益实多1号店是目前中国最大的网上超市，拥有上千个供应商，数百个品牌合作商。销售商品涉及食品饮料、美容护理、厨卫清洁、电器等十大类，共计十万多种商品。益实多1号店业务范围包括网上直销业务和增值电信业务。根据双方经营范围、经营模式及特点、需求和供给替代等方面因素，商务部认为B2C网上零售市场为相关商品市场。同时，考虑到消费习惯、运输、关税等因素，相关地域市场为中国市场。

调查显示，网上零售涉及支付、仓储、配送、营销、网络平台等多个环节，其中物流和服务是制约网络零售商发展的关键因素。沃尔玛公司在中国实体零售市场具备成熟的仓储配送系统、广泛的供货渠道和较高的品牌知名度。交易完成后，沃尔玛公司有能力将其在实体市场的竞争优势传导至益实多1号店的网上零售业务。集中产生的综合效应将实质性增强并购后实体在网上零售行业的竞争实力。为此，商务部对本案可能涉及的中国增值电信业务市场进行了延伸调查。调查结果表明，并购后实体如通过益实多1号店进入增值电信业务市场，将有能力依托现有实体零售市场与网上零售业务的综合竞争优势迅速扩展业务，在增值电信业务市场取得优势地位，实质性增强其对网络平台用户的议价权，从而在中国增值电信业务市场可能具有排除或限制竞争效果。

Corporation Limited ("Newheight Hong Kong", a wholly owned subsidiary of Newheight Holdings), and Newheight Information & Technology (Shanghai) Co., Ltd. ("Newheight Shanghai", a wholly owned subsidiary of Newheight Hong Kong), as well as Shanghai Yishiduo E-commerce Co., Ltd. ("Yishiduo") and Yishiduo's selling shareholder Shenzhen Ping An Innovation Capital Investment Co., Ltd.

According to the Agreement, Walmart will, through its wholly owned subsidiary GEC 2, increase its shareholding in Newheight Holdings from 17.7% to 51.3%. Newheight Holdings will, through its wholly owned subsidiaries Newheight Hong Kong and Newheight Shanghai, own the online direct sales business of Yishiduo's online shopping platform "Yihaodian" ("Yihaodian"). Once the transaction is completed, Walmart will become the controlling shareholder of Newheight Holdings and obtain control over the direct sales business of Yihaodian through Newheight Holdings.

Walmart is a major competitor in the global and Chinese market for supermarket chains, with its competitive advantages in regard to procurement, warehousing, product lines, shop network, services, logistics, and brands. Its major business is the operation of real supermarkets. Yihaodian is currently the largest online supermarket in China, which has over one thousand suppliers and cooperates with several hundred brands. It offers more than 100,000 products in ten major categories ranging from food and beverages, beauty and care, kitchen and bathroom ware to electrical appliances. The business scope of Yihaodian includes online direct sales and value-added telecommunication services. In view of the parties' business scope, operation model and

| | features as well as demand and supply substitution, MOFCOM believes that B2C online retail is the relevant product market. Meanwhile, considering consumption habit, transportation, and tariff, the relevant geographic market is China. |
| | As the investigation shows, online retail business involves many segments such as payment, warehousing, delivery, marketing, and online platform, of which logistics and services are the key factors hindering the development of online retailers. In the Chinese physical retail store market, Walmart has mature warehousing and delivery systems, broad supply channels and high brand awareness. Post-transaction, Walmart will be able to leverage its competitive advantages in the physical store market to Yihaodian's online retail business. The comprehensive effect generated from the concentration will materially strengthen the competitiveness of the merged entity in the online retail market. Therefore, MOFCOM extended its investigation to a market possibly related to this case, the market of value-added telecommunication services in China. As the investigation results show, if the merged entity enters into the market of value-added telecommunication services through Yihaodian, benefiting from its present competitiveness in the physical store retail market and the online retail business, it will be able to rapidly expand its business, obtain a superior position in the market of value-added telecommunication services, and materially enhance its bargaining power against online platform users, which may have an effect of eliminating and/or restricting competition in the market of value-added telecommunication services. |

(*Continued*)

三、附加限制性条件的商谈 在审查期间，商务部向申报方提出了此项集中可能产生的竞争问题。2012年7月3日，沃尔玛公司向商务部提交了解决竞争问题的最终承诺。经评估，商务部认为，该承诺能够减少此项集中对市场竞争可能产生的不利影响。	**3. Negotiations of Restrictive Conditions** During the review process, MOFCOM communicated with the notifying party about the possible competition concerns arising from the concentration. On July 3, 2012, Walmart submitted to MOFCOM its final commitments to resolve the competition concerns. Upon assessment, MOFCOM believes that these commitments can mitigate the possible adverse effect of the concentration on market competition.
四、审查决定 经审查，商务部认为沃尔玛公司通过收购纽海控股33.6%股权，取得对益实多1号店网上直销业务的控制权可能具有排除、限制竞争效果。根据沃尔玛公司向商务部作出的承诺，商务部决定附加限制性条件批准此项集中。沃尔玛公司应当履行如下义务： （一）　纽海上海此次收购，仅限于利用自身网络平台直接从事商品销售的部分。 （二）　在未获得增值电信业务许可的情况下，纽海上海在此次收购后不得利用自身网络平台为其他交易方提供网络服务。 （三）　本次交易完成后，沃尔玛公司不得通过VIE架构从事目前由上海益实多电子商务有限公司（益实多）运营的增值电信业务。 商务部有权通过监督受托人或者自行监督检查沃尔玛公司履行上述义务的情况。沃尔玛公司未适当履行上述义务时，商务部有权根据《反垄断法》相关规定作出处理。	**4. Review Decision** After review, MOFCOM held that Walmart's acquisition control over the online direct sale business of Yihaodian through acquiring 33.6% of Newheight Holdings may have the effect of eliminating and/or restricting competition. In view of the commitments made by Walmart to MOFCOM, MOFCOM decides to approve this concentration under certain conditions, whereby Walmart shall perform the following obligations: (1)　The acquisition in respect of Newheight Shanghai shall be limited to the product sales business that is directly operated through the use of its self-owned online platform. (2)　Post-transaction, without obtaining permit for the business of value-added telecommunication services, Newheight Shanghai may not use its self-owned online platform to provide online services to other transaction parties. (3)　Post-transaction, Walmart may not through the use of VIE structures engage in the business of value-added telecommunication services that are currently operated by Shanghai Yishiduo E-commerce Co., Ltd. (Yishiduo).

	MOFCOM may, through the supervision trustee or on its own, supervise and inspect Walmart's performance of the above obligations. If Walmart fails to duly perform the above obligations, MOFCOM may deal with such failure according to the relevant provisions of the AML.
本公告自发布之日起生效。 　　　　　　中华人民共和国商务部 　　　　　　二〇一二年八月十三日	This announcement shall become effective as of the date of its issuance. Ministry of Commerce August 13, 2012

MOFCOM Announcement [2012] No. 87 Regarding the Conditional Approval of the Joint Venture between ARM Holdings, Giesecke & Devrient, and Gemalto

商务部公告2012年第87号 关于附加限制性条件批准安谋公司、捷德公司和金雅拓公司组建合营企业经营者集中反垄断审查决定的公告

(Published on December 6, 2012)

（2012年12月6日公布）

中华人民共和国商务部收到安谋公司、捷德公司和金雅拓公司组建合营企业的经营者集中反垄断申报。经审查，商务部决定附加限制性条件批准此项经营者集中。根据《中华人民共和国反垄断法》（以下简称《反垄断法》）第三十条，现公告如下：	The Ministry of Commerce of the People's Republic of China ("MOFCOM") has received an anti-monopoly notification of a concentration of undertakings regarding the establishment of a joint venture between ARM Holdings Plc. ("ARMH"), Giesecke & Devrient GmbH ("G&D), and Gemalto N.V. ("Gemalto"). After review, MOFCOM decides to approve this concentration of undertakings under conditions. The decision is hereby announced as follows in accordance with Article 30 of the Anti-Monopoly Law of the People's Republic of China ("AML"):
一、立案和审查程序 2012年5月4日，商务部收到安谋公司、捷德公司和金雅拓公司组建合营企业的经营者集中申报。	**1. Acceptance and Review Process** On May 4, 2012, MOFCOM received an anti-monopoly notification for the establishment of a joint venture between ARMH, G&D, and Gemalto.

经审核，商务部认为该申报材料不完备，要求申报方予以补充。6月28日，商务部确认经补充的申报材料符合《反垄断法》第二十三条的要求，对该项经营者集中立案审查。

经初步审查，商务部认为此项集中可能对可信执行环境（Trusted Execution Environment，以下简称TEE）市场具有排除、限制竞争的效果。7月27日，商务部决定实施进一步审查，10月25日，商务部决定延长进一步审查期限，截止日期为12月24日。在进一步审查过程中，商务部向申报方提出了对此项集中的竞争关注，申报方向商务部提交了解决方案。商务部对申报方提交的解决方案进行了评估，认为该方案可以减少此项集中对竞争产生的不利影响。

审查过程中，商务部对申报方提交的文件资料的真实性、完整性和准确性进行了审核，征求了有关政府部门、行业协会、同业竞争者和下游企业的意见。

After review, MOFCOM decided that the notification documents and materials were incomplete, and requested additional information. On June 28, 2012, MOFCOM confirmed that the notification documents, as supplemented, met the requirements set forth in Article 23 of the AML, accepted the notification, and started its preliminary review.

After a preliminary review, MOFCOM determined that this concentration may have the effect of eliminating and/or restricting competition in the market of Trusted Execution Environment ("TEE"). On July 27, MOFCOM decided to conduct further review of the concentration. On October 25, MOFCOM decided to extend the period of further review to December 24. During the further review, MOFCOM raised competition concerns in relation to the concentration to the notifying parties and the notifying parties submitted proposals to address these concerns. After review of the final proposal, MOFCOM believed that the proposal could mitigate the adverse competitive effects of this concentration.

During the review, MOFCOM reviewed and verified the authenticity, completeness, and accuracy of the documents and materials submitted by the notifying parties, and solicited comments from relevant governmental departments, trade associations, business competitors, and downstream enterprises.

二、竞争分析

商务部根据《反垄断法》第二十七条规定的因素，对此项经营者集中进行了审查，深入分析了此项集中对市场竞争的影响，认为其对TEE市场可能具有排除、限制竞争的不利影响。

2. Competition Analysis

In accordance with Article 27 of the AML, MOFCOM conducted a comprehensive review of the concentration, thoroughly analyzed the potential competitive effects of the concentration, and found that the concentration may have an effect of eliminating and/or restricting competition in the TEE market.

(Continued)

本次交易由安谋公司、捷德公司和金雅拓公司共同出资成立合营企业，从事TEE的整合研发和推广。TEE是一种安全解决方案，可以在设备的应用处理器中建立一个在操作系统周围运行的独立的执行环境，对可信应用程序的资源和数据进行保护。

安谋公司主要从事家用电子产品应用处理器知识产权授权业务。家用电子产品应用处理器安装在家用电子产品芯片内，支持应用程序在操作系统中运行。安谋公司的业务与合营企业即将开展的业务存在纵向关系。安谋公司在家用电子产品应用处理器知识产权授权业务上具有业界公认的市场地位，拥有较强的市场控制力。合营企业在下游开展的对TEE进行研发和整合业务依赖于安谋公司的TrustZone技术，而TrustZone技术属于安谋公司应用处理器知识产权授权内容。合营企业组建后，安谋公司可能利用其在家用电子产品应用处理器知识产权授权市场拥有的控制力歧视合营企业以外的其他TEE技术研发者，或通过对自有知识产权的特殊设计降低第三方的TEE性能，使其他竞争者不能公平参与竞争，从而对TEE市场产生排除、限制竞争的效果。

同时，在应用处理器市场，企业必须具有相当的研发实力和经验，拥有相应的知识产权，市场进入非常困难。

The joint venture to be established by ARMH, G&D, and Gemalto is to engage in the integration of R&D and promotion of TEE. TEE is a security solution which can establish an independent execution environment operating around the operating system in a device's application processor, in order to protect the resources and data of the trusted applications.

ARMH is primarily engaged in the licensing of intellectual property related to application processors for consumer electronics. An application processor for consumer electronics is installed in the chip of the consumer electronics, which supports the applications' operation in the operating system. ARMH's business and the business to be conducted by the joint venture are in a vertical business relationship. ARMH has an industry-wide recognized market position in the licensing of intellectual property related to application processors for consumer electronics and it has a relatively strong market power. The R&D and integration business of the joint venture to be conducted downstream will rely on the TrustZone technology of ARMH which is among ARMH's intellectual property licensing related to application processors. After the establishment of the joint venture, ARMH could take advantage of its market power in the market of the licensing of intellectual property related to application processors for consumer electronics, to discriminate against researchers and developers of TEE technology other than the joint venture or degrade the performance of TEE for a third party through special designs of its own intellectual property, so as to preclude other competitors from fair competition, eliminating and/or restricting competition in the TEE market.

	Meanwhile, it is very difficult to enter the market of application processors as companies must have comparable R&D capacity and experience and own relevant intellectual property.
三、附加限制性条件的商谈 商务部与申报方就解决上述竞争问题进行了多次商谈。11月8日，交易方提交了解决方案。经过评估，商务部认为，该解决方案可以减少此项经营者集中对竞争的不利影响。	**3. Negotiation of Restrictive Conditions** MOFCOM and the notifying parties held multiple rounds of negotiation regarding how to address the above competition concerns. On November 8, the transaction parties submitted the final remedy proposal. After evaluation, MOFCOM concluded that the proposal could mitigate the adverse competitive effects of this concentration.
四、审查决定 鉴于本次交易可能会对TEE市场产生排除、限制竞争的效果，商务部决定附加限制性条件批准此项集中，要求交易各方履行如下义务： 1、　本次交易完成后，安谋公司将本着无歧视性原则，及时发布基于安谋公司应用处理器TrustZone技术之上研发TEE所必需的安全监控代码及其他信息，包括相关许可、授权的标准及条件。 2、　安谋公司不得通过对自有知识产权的特殊设计降低第三方TEE的性能。 安谋公司的上述义务自商务部决定之日起8年内有效。安谋公司应当每年就其遵守上述义务情况向商务部报告。如果外部环境或合营企业发生重大变化，安谋公司可以向商务部申请变更或解除上述义务。 商务部可以自行或者通过监督受托人监督检查安谋公司履行上述义务情况。当事方如有违反上述限制性条件的行为，商务部将依据《反垄断法》相关规定予以处罚。	**4. Review Decision** In view that this transaction may have an effect of eliminating and/or restricting competition in the TEE market, MOFCOM decides to approve it under conditions and requires the parties to fulfill the following obligations: (1) Post transaction, ARMH must, in a non-discriminatory manner, timely release the security monitoring codes and other information (including relevant permits, and licensing standards and conditions) that are necessary for TEE R&D based on ARMH's TrustZone technology related to application processors. (2) ARMH must not degrade the performance of TEE for a third party through special designs of its own intellectual property. The above obligations are imposed for eight years from the date of this decision. ARMH shall report to MOFCOM on its performance of the above obligations every year. If any significant change happens to the external environment or to the joint venture, ARMH may request MOFCOM to change or terminate the above obligations.

(Continued)

	MOFCOM may, through the supervision trustee or on its own, supervise and inspect ARMH's performance of the above restrictive conditions. If ARMH fails to duly perform the above restrictive conditions, MOFCOM may deal with such failures according to the relevant provisions of the AML.
本决定自公告之日起生效。 中华人民共和国商务部 二〇一二年十二月六日	This decision shall become effective as of the date of its announcement. Ministry of Commerce December 6, 2012

MOFCOM Announcement [2013] No. 20 Regarding the Conditional Approval of the Acquisition of Xstrata plc by Glencore International plc

商务部公告2013年第20号关于附加限制性条件批准嘉能可国际公司收购斯特拉塔公司经营者集中反垄断审查决定的公告

(Published on April 16, 2013)

（2013年4月16日公布）

中华人民共和国商务部(以下简称商务部)收到嘉能可国际公司(Glencore International plc，以下简称嘉能可)收购斯特拉塔公司(Xstrata plc，以下简称斯特拉塔)的经营者集中反垄断申报。经审查，商务部决定附加限制性条件批准此项经营者集中。根据《中华人民共和国反垄断法》(以下简称《反垄断法》)第三十条，现公告如下：	The Ministry of Commerce of the People's Republic of China ("MOFCOM") has received an anti-monopoly notification of a concentration of undertakings regarding the acquisition of Xstrata plc ("Xstrata") by Glencore International plc ("Glencore"). After review, MOFCOM decides to approve this concentration of undertakings under restrictive conditions. This announcement is made as follows in accordance with Article 30 of the Anti-Monopoly Law of the People's Republic of China ("AML").
一、立案和审查程序 2012年4月1日，商务部收到嘉能可收购斯特拉塔经营者集中反垄断申报。经审核，商务部认为该申报文件、资料不完备，要求申报方予以补充。5月17日，商务部确认经补充的申报文件、资料符合《反垄断法》第二十三条的要求，对此项经营者集中申报予以立案并开始初步审查。	**1. Acceptance and Review Process** On April 1, 2012, MOFCOM received a notification of a concentration of undertakings concerning the acquisition of Xstrata by Glencore. Through review and verification, MOFCOM believed that the notification materials were incomplete and requested the notifying party to supplement.

(Continued)

6月15日，商务部决定对此项经营者集中实施进一步审查。经进一步审查，商务部认为此项经营者集中对铜精矿、锌精矿和铅精矿市场可能具有排除、限制竞争的效果。9月14日，经申报方同意，商务部决定延长进一步审查期限，截止时间为11月13日。在上述审查期间，申报方就商务部提出的竞争问题提交了两轮解决方案，经审查均不能有效解决该案竞争问题。11月6日，申报方申请撤回案件并于11月23日重新申报。11月29日，商务部予以立案。12月28日，商务部决定对此项经营者集中实施进一步审查。2013年3月29日，经申报方同意，商务部决定延长进一步审查期限。

审查过程中，商务部对申报方提交的文件、资料的真实性、完整性和准确性进行了审核，向政府有关部门、相关行业协会、下游客户、同业竞争者以及行业专家征求了意见，多次召开座谈会，核实了相关数据信息。

On May 17, MOFCOM confirmed that the supplemented notification materials satisfied the requirements of Article 23 of the AML, accepted this case, and started a preliminary review. On June 15, MOFCOM decided to conduct a further review of the concentration. After the further review, MOFCOM believed that this concentration may have the effect of eliminating and/or restricting competition in the markets of copper concentrate, zinc concentrate, and lead concentrate. On September 14, with the consent of the notifying party, MOFCOM decided to extend the period of further review to November 13. During the further review, the notifying party submitted two rounds of remedy proposals to address the competition concerns raised by MOFCOM. After review, MOFCOM believed that they were insufficient to effectively address those competition concerns. On November 6, the notifying party withdrew the case and resubmitted a notification on November 23. On November 29, the resubmitted notification was accepted by MOFCOM. On December 28, MOFCOM decided to conduct a further review of this concentration of undertakings. On March 29, 2013, with the consent of the notifying party, MOFCOM decided to extend the period of further review.

During the review, MOFCOM reviewed and verified the authenticity, completeness, and accuracy of the documents and materials submitted by the notifying party, solicited comments from relevant governmental departments, trade associations, downstream customers, competitors, and industrial experts, held several discussion meetings, and verified the relevant data and information.

二、竞争分析 商务部按照《反垄断法》及配套规定，对此项经营者集中进行了审查，深入分析了此项经营者集中对市场竞争的影响，认为其在铜精矿、锌精矿和铅精矿市场可能具有排除、限制竞争的效果。	**2. Competition Analysis** In accordance with the AML and its implementing rules, MOFCOM reviewed this concentration of undertakings, conducted an in-depth analysis of the effect of this concentration on market competition, and held that it may have an adverse effect of eliminating and/or restricting competition in the markets of copper concentrate, zinc concentrate, and lead concentrate.
（一）　交易概况。 收购方嘉能可在泽西注册成立，总部位于瑞士，在伦敦证交所和香港联交所上市。嘉能可主要有金属及矿石、能源、农产品三个业务部门。其中，金属及矿石业务部包括锌、铜、铅，氧化铝、铝，铁合金、镍矿砂、钴、铁矿石三个商品部门。嘉能可是全球最大的有色金属及矿产品供货商，拥有成熟的全球营运经验和营销网络，在全球铜精矿、锌精矿和铅精矿第三方贸易市场具有较强控制力。嘉能可的采矿、冶炼、精炼及加工、物流及存储的全产业链优势使其能够在全球范围内供应商品。嘉能可在中国不拥有或运营生产性资产，目前在中国设有7家从事贸易和仓储的实体。 被收购方斯特拉塔在英国伦敦注册成立，总部位于瑞士，在伦敦证交所和瑞士证交所上市。斯特拉塔是全球第五大多元化矿业集团及金属公司，是全球重要的实体资产运营商，主要生产合金、煤炭、铜、镍和锌等大宗商品。斯特拉塔是全球第四大铜生产商，矿山储量丰富，冶炼能力较强。斯特拉塔在中国境内销售焦煤、动力煤、铁合金、精铜、铜精矿等商品。斯特拉塔在中国设有一家生产不锈钢产品的合营企业及两家从事贸易的实体。	(1) Overview of the Transaction The acquirer, Glencore, was incorporated in Jersey, headquartered in Switzerland, and is listed on the London Stock Exchange and the Hong Kong Stock Exchange. Glencore has three main business segments, namely metals and minerals, energy products, and agricultural products. Among them, the metals and minerals segment includes three commodity divisions, namely zinc, copper and lead, alumina and aluminum, and ferroalloy, nickel ore sand, cobalt and iron ore. Glencore is the largest supplier of non-ferrous metals and minerals in the world with sophisticated global operating experience and marketing networks, and has a strong control power in the global third party trade markets of copper concentrate, zinc concentrate, and lead concentrate. Glencore's preponderance in the whole industrial chain of mining, smelting, refining, as well as processing, logistics, and storage enables it to supply products all over the world. Glencore does not own or operate any production assets in China, and at present it has set up seven entities in China engaged in trade and warehousing.

(Continued)

嘉能可目前持有斯特拉塔33.65%的股权。通过本交易，收购其未持有的斯特拉塔全部已发行在外的股份。交易完成后，嘉能可将持有斯特拉塔100%的股份。	The acquired party, Xstrata, was incorporated in London, U.K., headquartered in Switzerland, and is listed on the London Stock Exchange and the SWX Swiss Exchange. Xstrata is the fifth largest diversified mining group and metal company in the world and is an important operator of tangible assets in the world, which mainly produces bulk commodities such as alloy, coal, copper, nickel, and zinc. Xstrata is the fourth largest copper producer in the world with rich mine reserves and a strong smelting capacity. In China Xstrata sells commodities such as coking coal, steam coal, ferroalloy, refined copper, and copper concentrate. Xstrata has set up a joint venture in China producing stainless steel products and two entities engaging in trading. Glencore currently has 33.65% shares in Xstrata and will acquire all outstanding shares of Xstrata through this transaction. After the transaction, Glencore will own 100% shares in Xstrata.
(二) 相关市场。 嘉能可和斯特拉塔在多个市场存在横向重叠或纵向关系，具体包括铬矿、锌精矿、锌金属、铅精矿、铅金属、铜精矿、再生铜、精铜、镍矿砂、钴中间产品、精钴、海运动力煤、海运焦煤等商品的生产、供应、贸易和第三方贸易市场。 本次交易涉及的相关商品均在全球范围内进行交易，目前全球范围内有很多国际性竞争者参与相关商品的生产或供应。嘉能可和斯特拉塔均为国际上重要的相关商品生产商和供应商，本次交易对全球市场具有重要影响。中国市场是嘉能可矿产品的最大市场，也是斯特拉塔矿产品的主要市场，此项经营者集中对中国市场将产生较大影响。	(2) The Relevant Markets Glencore and Xstrata overlap with each other horizontally or vertically in several markets, including the production, supply, trading, and third party trading markets of commodities such as chrome ore, zinc concentrate, zinc metal, lead concentrate, lead metal, copper concentrate, secondary copper, refined copper, nickel ore sand, cobalt intermediate products, refined cobalt, seaborne thermal coal, and seaborne coking coal. The relevant products involved in this transaction are all traded worldwide, and at present, there are many international competitors participating in the production or supply of the relevant products in the world.

此项经营者集中涉及的相关商品中，中国是铜精矿、铅精矿和锌精矿的主要进口国，铜精矿、锌精矿、铅精矿进口量占总供应量比例较高，2011年分别达到68.5%、28.7%和27.3%，集中双方在全球和中国铜精矿、铅精矿和锌精矿生产、供应市场份额也较高。其他商品进口量占总供应量比例较低，且集中双方在相关市场的份额较低。本案重点审查了此项经营者集中对铜精矿、铅精矿和锌精矿市场的影响。铜精矿、铅精矿和锌精矿分别是指由含铜、锌、铅矿石经破碎、球磨、浮选等工艺生产的达到一定标准的含铜、锌、铅量较高的矿石。

商务部对此项经营者集中从铜精矿、铅精矿和锌精矿的生产、供应、贸易和第三方贸易等角度进行了分析。其中，生产是指相关产品的加工制造。供应是指供应商对终端客户的实物销售。贸易包括贸易商对终端客户的实物销售，以及对其他转售方的销售。第三方贸易是指第三方贸易商从生产商采购商品并在公开市场的转售，通过第三方贸易商销售的商品不包括各国国内生产并消费且不出口的商品，以及生产商直接向终端用户销售的商品。此项经营者集中前，嘉能可从斯特拉塔采购部分铜精矿、铅精矿和锌精矿，本案中斯特拉塔的市场份额不包括销售给嘉能可，并由嘉能可销售给终端客户的销售量所占市场份额。

Glencore and Xstrata are both important producers and suppliers of the relevant products in the world, and this transaction has a significant impact on the global market. China is the largest market for Glencore's mineral products, and is also a major market for Xstrata's mineral products. This concentration of undertakings will have a great impact on the Chinese market.

In terms of the relevant products involved in this concentration, China is a major importing country of copper concentrate, lead concentrate, and zinc concentrate. The import volumes of these products account for a high percentage of the total supplies, which were 68.5%, 28.7%, and 27.3%, respectively, in 2011. In addition, both parties to the concentration have large shares in the global and Chinese production and supply markets of copper concentrate, lead concentrate, and zinc concentrate. With respect to other products, the imports account for a small percentage of the total supplies, and the parties to the concentration have smaller shares in those relevant markets. The review focused on the effect of the concentration on the markets of copper concentrate, lead concentrate, and zinc concentrate. Copper concentrate, lead concentrate, and zinc concentrate respectively refer to ores meeting certain standards and having a high content of copper, lead, and zinc that are produced from copper, lead, and zinc ores through processes such as crushing, pellet grinding, and flotation.

MOFCOM analyzed the concentration in respect of production, supply, trading, and third party trade of copper concentrate, lead concentrate, and zinc concentrate. Production means the processing and manufacturing of the relevant products.

(Continued)

	Supply means physical commodity sales from suppliers to end customers. Trading means physical commodity sales from traders to end customers, and sales to other resellers. Third party trade means resale of products to the public market by a third party trader who sources products from producers. The products sold through third party traders do not include the products that are produced and consumed domestically and are not exported, nor the products that are sold to end customers directly by producers. Prior to the concentration, Glencore sourced from Xstrata part of its copper concentrate, lead concentrate, and zinc concentrate. In this case, Xstrata's market share does not include the shares of the products it sold to Glencore that are then sold to end customers through Glencore.
(三) 铜精矿市场竞争分析。 1、此项经营者集中将增加嘉能可控制的含铜资源量。 嘉能可2011年拥有的含铜资源量超过0.17亿吨，权益矿铜产量为18.9万吨。斯特拉塔2011年拥有的含铜资源量超过1亿吨，权益矿铜产量为95.2万吨。新建项目及扩产项目完成后，2015年将新增权益矿铜产量约45万吨。斯特拉塔还有三座将于2018年至2019年投产的铜矿山资产，预计投产后产能每年新增权益矿铜产量120万吨。此项经营者集中完成后，嘉能可目前的权益矿铜产量约为110万吨，2015年将可能超过150万吨，2018年至2019年将有更大幅度的增长。 从集中双方占有的含铜资源量以及权益矿铜产量来看，嘉能可收购斯特拉塔完成后拥有的含铜资源量将超过1.17亿吨，权益矿铜产量将大幅增加。	(3) Competition Analysis of the Copper Concentrate Market (i) This concentration will increase the copper resources under Glencore's control In 2011, Glencore had more than 17 million tons of copper resources and an equity copper output of 189,000 tons. In 2011, Xstrata had more than 100 million tons of copper resources and an equity copper output of 952,000 tons. After the completion of new projects and expansion projects, the equity copper output will increase by around 450,000 tons in 2015. Xstrata has three copper mines assets, which will start production between 2018 and 2019 and are expected to increase Xstrata's equity copper output by 1,200,000 tons every year. After the concentration, Glencore's current equity copper output will be approximately 1,100,000 tons, and it may exceed 1,500,000 tons in 2015 and will increase more quickly in 2018 and 2019.

	Judging from the copper resources and equity copper output owned by the parties to the concentration, after the acquisition of Xstrata, Glencore will own more than 117 million tons of copper resources and its equity copper output will largely increase.
2、此项经营者集中将增强嘉能可对铜精矿市场的控制力。 嘉能可和斯特拉塔均为全球重要的铜精矿生产和供应商。2011年嘉能可和斯特拉塔在全球铜精矿生产市场的份额分别为1.5%和6.1%,合并份额为7.6%,居第三位;在全球铜精矿供应市场的份额分别为5.3%和4%,合并份额为9.3%,居第一位;在中国铜精矿供应市场的份额分别为9%和3.1%,合并份额为12.1%,居第一位。嘉能可是全球最大的以第三方形式采购有色金属及矿产品的实物供应商,拥有全球营运网络和营运经验。与主要竞争者相比,嘉能可的主要优势集中在商品营销、物流、风险管理等领域。嘉能可的全球营运网络使其拥有稳健的全球采购、分销能力以及客户资源。2010年嘉能可在全球铜精矿第三方贸易市场份额达30%,居第一位。2011年在全球铜精矿贸易市场的份额约为9.5%,居第四位。此项经营者集中将全面增强嘉能可在铜精矿生产、供应和贸易市场的控制力。 中国是全球铜精矿的主要需求国,目前铜精矿需求占全球总需求的50%左右。2011年中国铜精矿进口量占国内总供应量的68.5%,且存在进一步上升的趋势。2011年嘉能可和斯特拉塔向中国出口的铜精矿分别占中国进口总量的13.3%和4.5%,合计达17.8%。中国市场是集中双方的主要市场,2011年嘉能可和斯特拉塔分别有53.7%和17%的铜精矿销往中国市场。嘉能可在中国市场拥有健全的营销网络和丰富的客户资源,随着嘉能可控制的权益矿铜产量的增加,其铜精矿产能和供应能力可能大幅提高。	(ii) This concentration will increase Glencore's ability to control the copper concentrate market Glencore and Xstrata are both important producers and suppliers of copper concentrate in the world. In 2011, Glencore and Xstrata's shares in the global production market of copper concentrate were 1.5% and 6.1%, respectively, and their combined market share was 7.6%, ranking third in the world; their shares in the global supply market of copper concentrate were 5.3% and 4%, respectively, and their combined market share was 9.3%, ranking first in the world. Their shares in the Chinese supply market of copper concentrate were 9% and 3.1%, respectively, and their combined market share was 12.1%, ranking first in China. Glencore is the world's largest physical commodity supplier of non-ferrous metals and minerals sourced from third parties, with global operation networks and operating experience. Compared with major competitors, Glencore's major advantages lie in areas such as product marketing, logistics, and risk management. Glencore's global operation networks enable it to own steady global sourcing and distribution capability and customer resources. In 2010, Glencore's share in the global third party trade market of copper concentrate reached 30%, ranking first in the world. In 2011, Glencore's share in the global trade market of copper concentrate was about 9.5%, ranking fourth in the world.

(Continued)

This concentration will comprehensively increase Glencore's ability to control the production, supply, and trade markets of copper concentrate.

China is the major consumer country of copper concentrate in the world, and its demand for copper concentrate accounts for about 50% in the total global demand. In 2011, the import volume of copper concentrate into China accounted for 68.5% of the total supply volume in the country and this percentage will likely increase in the future. In 2011, Glencore's and Xstrata's exports of copper concentrate to China accounted for 13.3% and 4.5%, respectively, 17.8% in aggregate, of the total import volume of China. China is a major market for the parties to the concentration. In 2011, Glencore and Xstrata sold 53.7% and 17%, respectively, of their copper concentrate to China. Glencore has a sound marketing network and rich customer sources in China, and with the increasing equity copper output controlled by Glencore, its production and supply capacity of copper concentrate may improve greatly.

3、此项经营者集中将强化嘉能可对铜产业链的整合。 嘉能可从事铜精矿的生产、供应和贸易，其主营业务为铜精矿第三方贸易；斯特拉塔主营业务为铜精矿生产和供应。嘉能可收购斯特拉塔后将强化其在铜精矿上下游市场的纵向整合。此项集中将降低其他贸易商获得斯特拉塔铜精矿供应的可能性，并加强嘉能可在铜精矿贸易市场的地位。 再生铜与铜精矿具有一定程度的替代性，精铜是铜精矿的下游产品。嘉能可和斯特拉塔还是全球再生铜和精铜市场的主要竞争者。2011年，嘉能可和斯特拉塔在全球再生铜生产市场的合并份额居第一位；嘉能可在全球和	(iii) This concentration will intensify Glencore's integration of the copper industry chain Glencore is active in the production, supply, and trading of copper concentrate, and its main business is third party trade of copper concentrate; Xstrata's main business is the production and supply of copper concentrate. The acquisition of Xstrata by Glencore will intensify Glencore's vertical integration in the upstream and downstream markets of copper concentrate. This concentration will reduce the possibility for other traders to source copper concentrate from Xstrata, and will strengthen Glencore's position in the trade market of copper concentrate.

中国再生铜供应市场的份额均居第三位。斯特拉塔2011年没有从事再生铜供应。2011年，嘉能可和斯特拉塔在全球精铜生产市场的合并份额居第三位；在全球精铜供应市场的合并份额居第二位；在中国精铜供应市场的合计份额居第二位。 嘉能可是全球重要的有色金属期货交易商，对金融市场，特别是期货市场具有很强的影响力。嘉能可拥有多个伦敦期货交易所注册仓库，在铜金属现货市场参与度很高。目前国际通行的铜精矿定价由伦敦金属交易所铜金属报价和加工费决定，从铜产业链的角度看，铜精矿受铜金属价格影响较大。嘉能可收购斯特拉塔完成后，将增强影响铜金属和铜精矿价格的能力。	Secondary copper and copper concentrate are substitutable with each other to a certain degree, and refined copper is a downstream product from copper concentrate. Glencore and Xstrata are also main competitors in the global markets of secondary copper and refined copper. In 2011, Glencore and Xstrata's combined share ranked first in the global market of secondary copper; Glencore's share ranked third in both the global and Chinese markets of secondary copper. Xstrata was not present in the supply of secondary copper in 2011. In 2011, Glencore and Xstrata's combined share ranked third in the global production market of refined copper, the second in the global supply market of refined copper, and the second in the Chinese supply market of refined copper. Glencore is an important dealer of non-ferrous metals futures in the world, and it has a strong influence on the financial market especially in the futures market. Glencore has several warehouses registered on the London Metal Exchange, and it participates actively in the spot market of copper metals. As a current standard international practice, the pricing of copper concentrate is determined by copper metal quotation at the London Metal Exchange and its processing cost, and from the point of the copper industry chain, the price of copper concentrate is considerably affected by the price of copper metals. After the acquisition of Xstrata, Glencore's influence on the pricing of copper metals and copper concentrate will be enhanced.
4、此项经营者集中可能改变原有竞争格局下的合同条件。 斯特拉塔是铜精矿生产商，通过矿山合同向客户供应铜精矿。矿山合同是指铜精矿生产商与客户签订的合同期限为1年以上的长期合同。矿山合同	(iv) This concentration may change the contractual terms existing in the original competition landscape Xstrata is a producer of copper concentrate, and supplies copper concentrate to customers through

(Continued)

大部分条款固定，仅有加工费等与价格相关的极少量的条款由买卖双方按约定周期续订。

嘉能可作为铜精矿贸易商，主要通过贸易商长期合同和现货合同向客户供应铜精矿。贸易商长期合同是为了满足没有矿山合同或矿山合同很少的客户的特定需求签订的。贸易商长期合同的加工费受现货市场左右，年度数量、品质、装期和回收率等原本固定的条款，都会因买卖双方对加工费条件预期不同而大幅波动。现货合同是指以当时的现货价格临时订立的短期合同，合同期限一般为3个月以下。

对客户而言，矿山合同在交易价格、矿石质量、加工费水平等方面通常优于贸易商合同和现货合同。此次集中完成后，嘉能可有能力利用对铜精矿市场的控制力以及在铜产业链方面的优势，将斯特拉塔原来的矿山合同转为贸易商合同或现货合同，对铜精矿客户将产生不利影响。

mine contracts. A mine contract is a long-term contract entered into between a copper concentrate producer and customers, which has a term of at least one year. Most provisions of a mine contract are fixed, and only very limited provisions relating to pricing such as processing charges are to be periodically renewed by the buyer and the seller.

As a trader of copper concentrate, Glencore supplies copper concentrate to customers mainly through trader long-term contracts and spot contracts. A trader long-term contract is entered into to meet specific demand of customers that have no or very few mine contracts. The processing charges under a trader long-term contract are affected by the spot market, and the provisions originally agreed upon in connection with annual volume, quality, shipping date, and recovery rate change significantly depending on different expectations of the buyer and the seller on the processing charges. A spot contract is a short-term contract entered into for the time being at the current spot price, and its term is normally less than three months.

As for customers, a mine contract is normally more favorable than trader contracts and spot contracts in terms such as the trading price, ore quality, and processing costs. After this concentration, Glencore will be able to use its control power over the market of copper concentrate and its advantages in the copper industry chain to replace Xstrata's original mine contracts with trader contracts or spot contracts, which will adversely affect copper concentrate customers.

5、此项经营者集中对铜精矿市场进入的影响。

铜金属储量有限且分布集中，现有大型铜矿山掌握在少数行业领先的铜业公司手中，

(v) The effect of this concentration on the entry into the copper concentrate market

The reserve of copper metal is limited and its allocation is concentrated, and the existing large copper mines

铜精矿市场是资本密集型行业，无论是获得铜资源探矿权，还是建设铜的采矿、选矿及加工都需要投入巨额资金，资金壁垒是进入铜精矿市场的重大障碍。铜精矿行业为资源型行业，各国日趋严格的环保政策和产业政策提高了铜精矿市场的进入难度。向中国市场出口铜精矿的主要生产商包括必和必拓公司、美国自由港迈克墨伦铜金矿公司、英美资源集团，该市场近5年没有重要的新市场进入者。

进入全球铜精矿贸易市场需要具备获取铜精矿资源的渠道以及全球营销网络，进入难度较大。向中国市场出口铜精矿的主要贸易商包括嘉能可、荷兰托克有限公司、马克瑞士公司等，近5年没有重要的新市场进入者。

此项经营者集中完成后，嘉能可控制的含铜资源量将大幅增加，将提高潜在市场竞争者进入相关市场的难度。在5年内，新的市场进入难以减轻或消除此项经营者集中引起的排除、限制竞争的效果。

are under the control of a few leading copper companies. The largest barrier to entry into the copper concentrate market is the unavailability of certain scale copper resources. The copper concentrate market is of a capital intensive industry, and enormous amounts of funds are required to acquire copper resource exploration rights or for copper mining, beneficiation, and processing. Financing is the largest barrier to entry into the copper concentrate market. The copper concentrate industry is a resource-oriented industry. Increasingly strict environmental protection policies and industry policies worldwide have increased the difficulty of entry into the copper concentrate market. Major producers exporting copper concentrate into China include BHP Billiton Ltd., Freeport-McMoRan Copper & Gold Inc., and Anglo American plc. There has been no significant new market entrant in the past five years.

It is rather difficult to enter into the global trading market of copper concentrate, which requires sourcing channels of copper concentrate resources and a global marketing network. Major traders exporting copper concentrate into China include Glencore, Trafigura AG, The Mark Rich Group, etc. There has been no significant new market entrant in the past five years.

After this concentration, copper resources controlled by Glencore will increase significantly, which will make it even more difficult for potential market competitors to enter into the relevant markets. Within five years, new market entrants are unlikely to mitigate or eliminate the effect of eliminating and/or restricting competition caused by this concentration.

(Continued)

6、此项经营者集中对铜精矿消费者的影响。

目前，中国铜精矿高度依赖进口，中国主要铜冶炼厂的集中度低，议价能力较弱。中国中小铜冶炼企业数量占铜冶炼企业总数的90%，生产规模小，议价能力更弱。此次集中完成后，嘉能可将增强谈判能力，进一步削弱冶炼和加工企业的谈判议价地位。中国铜冶炼企业买方力量较弱，难以抵消此项经营者集中引起的排除、限制竞争的效果。

综上，此项经营者集中完成后，嘉能可控制的含铜资源量将大幅度提高，斯特拉塔丰富的矿山储量和冶炼能力将进一步强化嘉能可的铜产业链优势，增强嘉能可对铜精矿生产、供应和贸易等环节的控制力，可能改变现有竞争格局下的供应条件，提高市场进入难度，最终损害下游消费者利益。

(vi) The effect of this concentration on consumers of copper concentrate

At present, the sourcing of copper concentrate in China depends heavily on imports, while major copper smelters in China have a low degree of concentration and have a weak bargaining power. In China, small and middle-sized copper smelting enterprises account for 90% of the total number of copper smelting enterprises, and their production scale is small and bargaining power is even weaker. After this concentration, Glencore will enhance its negotiation power, and this will further weaken the negotiation and bargaining power of smelting and processing enterprises. Chinese copper smelting enterprises have a weak buyer power, and therefore cannot counteract the effect of eliminating and/or restricting competition caused by this concentration.

In conclusion, after this concentration, copper resources controlled by Glencore will increase significantly, and Xstrata's rich mine reserves and smelting capacity will further strengthen Glencore's preponderance in the copper industry chain, thus increasing Glencore's ability to control the production, supply, and trading of copper concentrate. It may change the supply terms existing in the current competition landscape, increase the difficulty of entry into the market, and, finally, impair the interests of downstream consumers.

(四)锌精矿市场竞争分析。

1、此项经营者集中将提高嘉能可对锌精矿市场的控制力。

斯特拉塔是全球最大的锌精矿生产商，2011年在全球锌精矿生产市场占有7.6%的份额。嘉能可是全球第五大锌精矿生产商，2011年在全球锌精矿生产市场占有3.6%的份额。

(4) Competition Analysis of the Zinc Concentrate Market

(i) This concentration will enhance Glencore's ability to control the zinc concentrate market

Xstrata is the largest zinc concentrate producer in the world, and had a 7.6% market share in the global production market of zinc concentrate in 2011.

集中双方合并市场份额为11.2%，与相关市场第二位竞争者(市场份额为6.1%)相比具有明显优势。

嘉能可是全球最大的锌精矿供应商，2011年在全球锌精矿供应市场占有13.1%的份额，居第一位。斯特拉塔2011年在全球锌精矿供应市场占有4.7%的份额。集中双方合并份额为17.9%，与相关市场第二位竞争者(市场份额为6.4%)相比具有明显优势。嘉能可是中国锌精矿供应市场的最大供应商，2011年占有9%的份额，与相关市场第二位竞争者(市场份额为5.3%)相比具有明显优势，斯特拉塔2011年在中国市场没有供应锌精矿。

嘉能可在锌精矿市场同样拥有全球性的采购、分销能力以及客户资源。与主要竞争者相比在商品营销、物流、风险管理领域具有优势。2010年嘉能可在全球锌精矿第三方贸易市场占有50%的份额，居第一位；2011年在全球锌精矿贸易市场占有23.9%的份额，居第一位。

中国锌精矿进口量占总供应量比例较高，2011年28.7%的锌精矿需要进口。中国市场是嘉能可的锌精矿的主要市场，2011年嘉能可向中国出口的锌精矿占其全球总销售量的42.5%，在中国锌精矿进口市场上占有33.3%的份额。

此项经营者集中将显著增强嘉能可在锌精矿生产、供应市场的地位，进一步强化嘉能可对锌精矿贸易市场的控制力。

Glencore is the fifth largest zinc concentrate producer in the world, and had a 3.6% market share in the global production market of zinc concentrate in 2011. The combined market share of the parties was 11.2%, indicating a clear advantage compared to the competitor in the second place with a market share of 6.1%.

Glencore is the largest zinc concentrate producer in the world, and had a 13.1% market share in the global supply market of zinc concentrate in 2011, ranking first. Xstrata had a 4.7% market share in the global supply market of zinc concentrate in 2011. The combined market share of the parties was 17.9%, indicating a clear advantage compared to the competitor in the second place with a market share of 6.4%. Glencore is the largest supplier in the Chinese supply market of zinc concentrate with a 9% market share in 2011, indicating clear advantage compared to the competitor in the second place with a market share of 5.3%. Xstrata did not supply zinc concentrate in the Chinese market in 2011.

Glencore also possesses global sourcing, distribution capability, and customer resources in the zinc concentrate market, and has a significant advantage in respect of products marketing, logistics, and risk management compared to major competitors. In 2010, Glencore ranked first with a 50% market share in the global third party trading market of zinc concentrate; in 2011, Glencore ranked first with a 23.9% market share in the global zinc concentrate trading market.

There is a relatively high percentage of imported zinc concentrate among the total supply in China. 28.7% of zinc concentrate was imported in 2011. The Chinese market is Glencore's major market for zinc concentrate, to

(*Continued*)

	which Glencore exported 42.5% of its total global sales in 2011, accounting for 33.3% of the Chinese import market.
	This concentration will significantly strengthen Glencore's position in the production and supply markets of zinc concentrate, and further increase Glencore's ability to control the zinc concentrate trading market.
2、 此项经营者集中将强化嘉能可对锌产业链的整合。	(ii) This concentration will intensify Glencore's integration of the zinc industry chain
此项经营者集中完成后，嘉能可将实现在锌精矿生产、供应和贸易市场的纵向整合。锌金属是锌精矿的下游产品。嘉能可和斯特拉塔还是全球锌金属重要的生产、供应和贸易商。2011年嘉能可和斯特拉塔在全球锌金属生产市场的合并份额居第二位，在全球锌金属供应市场的合并份额居第一位。	After this concentration, Glencore will realize the vertical integration in the production, supply, and trading markets of zinc concentrate. Zinc metal is a downstream product from zinc concentrate. Glencore and Xstrata are also important producers, suppliers, and traders of zinc metal in the world. In 2011, Glencore and Xstrata's combined market share ranked second in the global production market of zinc metal, and ranked first in the global supply market of zinc metal.
此项经营者集中完成后，嘉能可在锌精矿生产、供应、贸易，锌金属生产、供应、现货交易和期货交易等环节的影响力均大为增强，由于锌精矿受锌金属价格影响较大，嘉能可在收购斯特拉塔完成后，将增强影响锌金属和锌精矿价格的能力。	After this concentration, Glencore will largely increase its ability to influence the production, supply, and trading of zinc concentrate and the production, supply, spot trading, and futures trading of zinc metal. Since zinc concentrate is considerably affected by the price of zinc metal, Glencore will enhance its ability to influence the pricing of zinc metal and zinc concentrate after its acquisition of Xstrata.
综上，斯特拉塔虽然目前在中国市场没有供应锌精矿，但此项经营者集中完成后，斯特拉塔的锌精矿生产能力将增强嘉能可在锌精矿供应和贸易市场的控制力，强化嘉能可对锌产业链的整合，对中国下游锌冶炼企业将产生不利影响。	In conclusion, although Xstrata currently does not supply zinc concentrate in the Chinese market, after the completion of this concentration, Xstrata's production capacity of zinc concentrate will enhance Glencore's control power over the supply and trading markets of zinc concentrate and intensify Glencore's integration of the zinc industry chain after the consummation of this concentration, causing adverse effects on

锌精矿市场进入受资源分布、资金壁垒和环保、产业政策的限制，进入难度较大。目前在中国从事锌精矿贸易的主要竞争者包括嘉能可、荷兰托克有限公司等少数贸易商，近5年没有重要的新市场进入者。中国锌冶炼企业自有原料企业少，生产规模小，买方力量弱，主要通过现货合同进口锌精矿，在交易过程中处于不利地位，加工费明显低于全球基准价格。市场进入和买方力量难以抵消此项经营者集中对竞争的不利影响。

the downstream Chinese zinc smelting enterprises.

It is rather difficult to enter into the zinc concentrate market due to the restraints in respect of resources allocation, finance barriers, and environmental and industrial policies. At present, major competitors engaged in zinc concentrate trading in China include only a few traders such as Glencore and Trafigura AG, and there has been no significant new entrant in the past five years. Few of the Chinese zinc smelting enterprises have self-supply of raw materials. They only have a small scale in production and weak buyer bargaining power, and mainly import zinc concentrate through spot contracts. They are disadvantaged in trading and their processing charges are significantly lower than the global benchmark prices. Market entries and buyer power can hardly set off the adverse effects on competition resulted from this concentration.

(五) 铅精矿市场竞争分析。

1、 此项经营者集中将提高嘉能可对铅精矿市场的控制力。

斯特拉塔是全球第二大铅精矿生产商，2011年在全球铅精矿生产市场占有5.2%的份额。嘉能可2011年在全球铅精矿生产市场占有1.6%的份额。集中双方合并市场份额为6.8%，居全球第一位。

嘉能可是全球最大的铅精矿供应商，2011年在全球铅精矿供应市场占有7.4%的份额。斯特拉塔2011年在全球铅精矿供应市场占有0.2%的份额。集中双方合并份额为7.6%，居全球第一位。2011年，嘉能可在中国铅精矿供应市场占有9%的份额，居第二位，斯特拉塔在中国市场没有供应铅精矿。

嘉能可拥有全球铅精矿采购、分销能力以及客户资源，2010年在全球第三方铅精矿贸易市场占有45%的份额，居第一位；2011年在全球铅精矿贸易市场占有21.9%的份额，居第二位。

(5) Competition Analysis of the Lead Concentrate Market

(i) This concentration will enhance Glencore's ability to control the lead concentrate market

Xstrata is the second largest producer of lead concentrate in the world, and had a 5.2% market share in the global production market of lead concentrate in 2011. Glencore had a 1.6% market share in the global production market of lead concentrate in 2011. The combined market share of the parties was 6.8% and ranked first globally.

Glencore is the largest lead concentrate supplier in the world, and had a 7.4% market share in the global supply market of lead concentrate in 2011. Xstrata had a 0.2% market share in the global supply market of lead concentrate in 2011. The combined market share of the parties was 7.6% and ranked first globally. In 2011, Glencore ranked second in the Chinese supply market

(Continued)

中国铅精矿进口量占总供应量比例较高，2011年27.3%的铅精矿需要进口。中国市场是嘉能可的铅精矿的主要市场，2011年嘉能可向中国市场出口的铅精矿占其全球总销售量的64.3%，在中国铅精矿进口市场占有21.7%的份额。 此项经营者集中将显著增强嘉能可在铅精矿生产、供应市场的地位，进一步强化嘉能可对铅精矿贸易市场的控制力。	of lead concentrate with a 9% market share, while Xstrata did not supply lead concentrate to the Chinese market. Glencore possesses global sourcing, distribution capability, and customer resources for lead concentrate. In 2010, Glencore ranked first with a 45% market share in the global third party trading market of lead concentrate; in 2011, Glencore ranked second with a 21.9% market share in the global trading market of lead concentrate. There is a relatively high percentage of imported lead concentrate among the total supply in the Chinese market. 27.3% of lead concentrate was imported in 2011. The Chinese market was Glencore's major market for lead concentrate, to which Glencore exported 64.3% of its global sales, accounting for 21.7% of the Chinese import market of lead concentrate. This concentration will significantly strengthen Glencore's position in the manufacture and supply markets of lead concentrate, and further enhance Glencore's ability to control the trading market of lead concentrate.
2、 此项经营者集中将强化嘉能可对铅产业链的整合。 此项经营者集中完成后，嘉能可将实现在铅精矿生产、供应和贸易市场的垂直整合。铅金属是铅精矿的下游产品。嘉能可和斯特拉塔还是全球铅金属重要的生产、供应和贸易商。2011年嘉能可和斯特拉塔在全球铅金属生产市场的合并份额居第一位；在全球铅金属供应市场的合并份额居第二位。此项经营者集中完成后，嘉能可在铅精矿生产、供应、贸易，以及铅金属生产、供应等市场均有重要影响力。 综上，斯特拉塔虽然目前在中国市场没有供应铅精矿，但此项经营者集中完成后，斯特拉塔的铅精矿生产能	(ii) This concentration will intensify Glencore's integration of the lead industry chain After this concentration, Glencore will realize the vertical integration of the manufacture, supply, and trading markets of lead concentrate. Lead metal is a downstream product from lead concentrate. Glencore and Xstrata are also important lead metal producers, suppliers, and traders in the world. In 2011, Glencore and Xstrata's combined market share ranked first in the global production market of lead metal, and ranked second in the global supply market of lead metal. After this concentration, Glencore will have a material influence on the production,

力将增强嘉能可在铅精矿供应和贸易市场的控制力，强化嘉能可对铅产业链的整合，增强嘉能可对铅精矿的价格影响力，对中国铅冶炼企业具有不利影响。	supply, and trading markets of lead concentrate, as well as the production and supply markets of lead metal. In conclusion, although Xstrata currently does not supply lead concentrate in the Chinese market, after this concentration, Xstrata's production capacity of lead concentrate will enhance Glencore's ability to control the supply and trading markets of lead concentrate, intensify Glencore's integration of the lead industry chain, and strengthen Glencore's influence in the pricing of lead concentrate, causing adverse effects on the Chinese lead smelting enterprises.
铅精矿市场进入受资源分布、资金要求、营销网络和环保、产业政策的限制，进入难度较大。目前在中国从事铅精矿贸易的主要竞争者包括嘉能可、托克、马克瑞士等少数贸易商，近5年没有重要的新市场进入者。中国铅冶炼企业生产规模偏小，买方力量较弱。大部分冶炼企业通过现货合同进口铅精矿，在交易过程中处于不利地位，加工费明显低于全球基准价格。市场进入和买方力量难以抵消此项经营者集中对竞争的不利影响。	It is rather difficult to enter the lead concentrate market due to the restraints in respect of resources allocation, finance requirement, marketing network, and environmental and industrial policies. At present, there are only a few major competitors engaged in lead concentrate trading in China, including Glencore, Trafigura, and Marc Rich, and there have been no significant new entrants in the last five years. The Chinese lead smelting enterprises have a rather small scale in production and weak buyer bargaining power, and mainly import lead concentrate through spot contracts. They are disadvantaged in trading and their processing charges are significantly lower than the global benchmark prices. Market entries and buyer power can hardly set off the adverse effects on competition resulted from this concentration.
(六) 审查结论。 此项经营者集中将消除中国铜精矿、锌精矿和铅精矿市场的重要竞争者或潜在竞争者斯特拉塔，显著增加嘉能可掌握的相应矿产资源量，进一步强化嘉能可在相关产业的纵向整合程度，提高其对铜精矿、铅精矿和锌	(6) Review Conclusion This concentration will eliminate Xstrata as an important or potential competitor in the Chinese copper concentrate, zinc concentrate, and lead concentrate markets, which will significantly increase Glencore's mineral resources, further intensify its vertical

(Continued)

精矿等大宗商品市场的控制力。此项经营者集中对铜精矿、铅精矿和锌精矿市场可能具有排除、限制竞争的效果。	integration in the relevant industries, and enhance its ability to control the commodity markets of copper concentrate, zinc concentrate, and lead concentrate. This concentration is likely to have the effect of eliminating and/or restricting competition in the copper concentrate, zinc concentrate, and lead concentrate markets.
三、附加限制性条件的商谈 审查期间，商务部向申报方指出了此项经营者集中可能具有的排除、限制竞争的效果，并就如何减少集中对竞争产生的不利影响进行了多轮商谈。嘉能可先后提出多个解决方案。经评估，商务部认为，嘉能可于2013年4月12日向商务部提交的《嘉能可国际公司收购斯特拉塔公司全部已发行股份的交易救济承诺方案》（以下简称最终救济方案）能够减少此项经营者集中对竞争产生的不利影响。	**3. Negotiations of Restrictive Conditions** During its review, MOFCOM pointed out to the notifying party the effects of eliminating and/or restricting competition that will result from this concentration, and held several rounds of negotiations on how to mitigate these adverse effects on competition. Glencore has put forward several proposals. After review, MOFCOM believed that the "Remedy Proposal on Glencore's Acquisition of All the Outstanding Shares of Xstrata" (the "Final Remedy Proposal") submitted on April 12, 2013 by Glencore is capable of mitigating the adverse effects on competition that will result from this concentration.
四、审查决定 审查认为，嘉能可收购斯特拉塔对中国铜精矿、锌精矿和铅精矿市场可能具有排除、限制竞争的效果，商务部决定基于嘉能可最终救济方案的承诺附加限制性条件批准此项经营者集中，嘉能可和斯特拉塔应履行如下义务：	**4. Review Decision** After review, MOFCOM finds that the concentration may have the effect of eliminating and/or restricting competition on the Chinese markets of copper concentrate, zinc concentrate, and lead concentrate. Therefore, it approves this concentration under the restrictive conditions as included in the Final Remedy Proposal. Glencore and Xstrata shall fulfill the following obligations:
（一）铜精矿市场。 1、 剥离铜精矿资产。 嘉能可应当剥离本交易后其在拉斯邦巴斯(Las Bambas)，即斯特拉塔目前正在开发的位于秘鲁的铜矿项目中持有的全部权益（以下简称拉斯邦巴斯项目）。	(1) Copper Concentrate Market (i) Divestment of a copper concentrate asset Glencore shall sell all of its post-transaction ownership interest in Las Bambas, a copper project ("Las Bambas") currently being developed by Xstrata.

自本公告公布之日起3个月内，嘉能可应当启动出售拉斯邦巴斯项目的程序并公布其出售要约公告。随后，应定期向商务部报告其寻找潜在买方的情况。嘉能可应尽其合理的最佳努力于2014年8月31日前向商务部提交关于潜在买方的详细情况。2014年9月30日之前，除非经商务部同意延期，嘉能可应当与经商务部同意的买方签订具有约束力的出售协议。2015年6月30日之前，嘉能可应当完成上述出售协议项下拉斯邦巴斯项目的转让交割。	Glencore will start the sale process and make a public announcement of its offer to sell its ownership interest in Las Bambas within three months of the date of this announcement, and will thereafter keep MOFCOM regularly updated regarding its search for potential purchasers. Glencore will use its reasonable best efforts to provide MOFCOM with details of potential purchaser(s) for Las Bambas by August 31, 2014. Glencore will enter into a binding sale and purchase agreement with the purchaser approved by MOFCOM by September 30, 2014, unless an extension is granted by MOFCOM. Glencore will complete the transfer of Las Bambas under such agreement by June 30, 2015.
如嘉能可未能于2014年9月30日之前按上述要求与经商务部同意的买方签订具有约束力的出售协议，或者签署协议但未于2015年6月30日之前完成协议项下拉斯邦巴斯项目的转让交割，除非经商务部同意，嘉能可应当委任剥离受托人，分别自2014年10月1日或者2015年7月1日起3个月内，无底价拍卖商务部指定的其在下述任一项目中的全部权益:坦帕坎(Tampakan)、芙蕾达河(Frieda River)、埃尔帕琼(El Pachón)或阿伦布雷拉(Alumbrera)。	If Glencore fails to enter into a binding sale and purchase agreement by September 30, 2014, or it has entered into such an agreement but fails to complete the transfer of Las Bambas by June 30, 2015 then, unless otherwise agreed by MOFCOM, Glencore must appoint a divestiture trustee to sell by way of auction its ownership interest in one of Tampakan, Frieda River, El Pachón, or Alumbrera, as designated by MOFCOM, at no minimum price within three months from October 1, 2014 or July 1, 2015, as the case may be.
2、 维持集中前铜精矿的交易条件。	(ii) Maintenance of the trading terms existing before the concentration
2013年至2020年12月31日，嘉能可应每年向中国客户提供不低于最低数量的铜精矿长期合同报盘。2013年最低数量为90万干公吨铜精矿。其中，不低于20万干公吨报盘的价格应按照主要矿山企业和主要冶炼厂在年度供货谈判中协商达成的年度基准价提供，其余70万干公吨报盘的价格应参照上述价格提供。在上述期限内，自2014年1月1日起，如嘉能可年度铜精矿生产预算发生增减，则其向中国客户提供上述最低数量报盘应按比例进行调整。	For a period from 2013 to December 31, 2020, Glencore will continue to offer to supply Chinese customers with a minimum volume of copper concentrate annually under long-term contracts. Such minimum volume for 2013 will be 900,000 dry metric tons of copper concentrate. The price for a minimum of 200,000 dry metric tons of copper concentrate will be offered in accordance with the applicable annual benchmark price agreed between major

(Continued)

	miners and major smelters during annual supply negotiations and the price for the remaining 700,000 dry metric tons of copper concentrate will be offered with reference to the applicable annual benchmark price. In the above period, starting from January 1, 2014, if there is an increase or reduction in Glencore's forecast copper concentrate production, the minimum volume of copper concentrate to be offered for supply to Chinese customers will be adjusted pro rata.
(二) 锌精矿和铅精矿市场。 2013年至2020年12月31日，嘉能可应当继续向中国客户提供锌精矿和铅精矿长期合同和现货合同报盘，其报盘条件(包括与价格相关的条件)应公平、合理，并在考虑产品质量、数量、交货期、付款条件、买方信誉以及其他相关因素的情况下与当时通行的国际市场条款一致。	(2) Zinc Concentrate and Lead Concentrate Markets For a period from 2013 to December 31, 2020, Glencore will continue to offer to supply Chinese customers with zinc concentrate and lead concentrate through long-term contracts and spot contracts, the offered terms of which, including those in relation to price, will be fair and reasonable and in accordance with prevailing international market terms after taking into account product quality, volume, delivery period, payment conditions, buyer creditworthiness, and any other relevant circumstances.
(三) 限制性条件的监督执行。 限制性条件的监督执行除按本公告办理外，最终救济方案对嘉能可也具有法律约束力。 嘉能可应当根据商务部《关于实施经营者集中资产或业务剥离的暂行规定》委托独立的监督受托人，对嘉能可履行公告义务及承诺的情况进行监督。 嘉能可应自本公告发布之日起每季度结束后的15天内，向商务部和监督受托人书面报告拉斯邦巴斯项目剥离义务履行情况。嘉能可应当自本公告发布之日起每日历年度结束后45天内，向商务部和监督受托人书面报告长期供应义务履行的情况。	(3) Supervision and Enforcement on the Restrictive Conditions The supervision and enforcement of the restrictive conditions shall be conducted in accordance with this announcement and the Final Remedy Proposal is legally binding on Glencore as well. Glencore shall appoint an independent supervision trustee in accordance with MOFCOM's Interim Provisions on Asset or Business Divestiture during the Implementation of Concentrations of Undertakings, to supervise Glencore's performance of the above obligations and commitments Within 15 days after the end of each quarter following this announcement,

	Glencore will provide written reports to MOFCOM and the supervision trustee demonstrating that it is complying with the divestment commitment regarding Las Bambas. Within 45 days after the end of each calendar year following this announcement, Glencore will provide written reports to MOFCOM and the supervision trustee demonstrating that it is complying with the long-term supply commitments.
本公告自发布之日起生效。 中华人民共和国商务部 2013年4月16日	This decision shall become effective on the date of its announcement. Ministry of Commerce April 16, 2013
附件：嘉能可国际公司收购斯特拉塔公司全部已发行股本的交易救济承诺方案	Attachment: Remedy Proposal on Glencore's Acquisition of All the Outstanding Shares of Xstrata

嘉能可国际公司收购斯特拉塔公司全部已发行股本的交易救济承诺方案

Remedy Proposal on Glencore's Acquisition of All the Outstanding Shares of Xstrata

2013年4月12日

April 12, 2013

目录　内容	**Contents**
第一章：救济承诺全文	**Chapter One　Full Text of the Commitments**
第一部分　定义	Section 1　Definitions
第二部分　救济承诺	Section 2　Commitments
第三部分　经批准的买方	Section 3　Approved Purchaser
第四部分　受托人	Section 4　Trustees
第五部分　救济承诺的复审/终止	Section 5　The Review Clause
第二章：救济承诺工作方案拟议大纲	**Chapter Two　Proposed Outline of the Work Plan for the Commitments**
第一章：救济承诺全文 本救济承诺是就中华人民共和国商务部("商务部")根据《反垄断法》审查嘉能可国际公司("嘉能可")收购斯特拉塔公司("斯特拉塔")(统称"嘉能可")的交易("本交易")而做出的。 作为商务部批准本交易的一项条件，嘉能可特此做出以下救济承诺("救济承诺")。	**Chapter One Commitments** These commitments are made in connection with the review by the Ministry of Commerce of the People's Republic of China ("**MOFCOM**") of the acquisition (the "**Transaction**") of Xstrata plc ("**Xstrata**") by Glencore International plc ("**Glencore**") (Xstrata and Glencore together referred to as "**Glencore**") in accordance with the Anti-Monopoly Law. As a condition to MOFCOM's approval of the Transaction, Glencore hereby commits as follows (the "**Commitments**"):
第一部分 定义 关联企业:由嘉能可控制的企业。 备选剥离资产:坦帕坎(Tampakan)，芙蕾达河(Frieda River)、埃尔帕琼(El Pachón)或阿伦布雷拉(Alumbrera)。	**Section 1 Definitions** **Affiliated Undertakings**: undertakings controlled by Glencore. **Alternative Divestment Asset**: Tampakan, Frieda River, El Pachón, or Alumbrera.

阿伦布雷拉:斯特拉塔在Minera Alumbrera公司所持的50%控制权益,该公司通过与Yacimientos Mineros de Agua de Dionisio签订协议有权开采Bajo de la Alumbrera铜金矿。

适用的年度基准价:主要矿山企业和主要冶炼厂在年度供货谈判中协商达成的加工费和精炼费,作为铜精矿供货的年度基准价格并载于铜行业公开刊物。

经批准的买方:根据第16段所列标准经商务部批准的作为剥离资产收购方的实体。

中国客户:交货地址位于中华人民共和国(就本救济承诺而言,不包括台湾、香港和澳门)的铜精矿、锌精矿或铅精矿(视情况而定)的客户。

铜精矿资产剥离承诺:第1段至第5段规定的承诺。

铜精矿供应承诺:第9段和第11段规定的承诺。

成本:应包括可辨认的、可直接归属于资产方面的支出以及嘉能可和斯特拉塔就拉斯班巴斯在本交易前或本交易后所发生及将要发生的费用。

- 就一项资产而言,成本系为购置或建造资产时所付出的对价的公允价值,包括使资产到达场所和达到预定可使用状态前所发生的可归属于该项资产的支出和拆除、弃置时所发生的直接费用。资产是指企业过去交易或事项形成的、由企业拥有或者控制的、预期会给企业带来经济利益的资源。
- 费用是指由于资产流出、资产损耗或者形成负债而引起的经济利益减少,会导致所有者权益减少,而与向所有者分配利润无关。负债是指企业过去的交易或V益流出企业的现实义务。

Alumbrera: 50% controlling interest held by Xstrata in Minera Alumbrera, a company that has mining rights in the Bajo de la Alumbrera copper-gold mines under an agreement with Yacimientos Mineros de Agua de Dionisio.

Applicable Annual Benchmark Price: the processing charges and refining charges agreed in annual supply negotiations between the Major Miners and the Major Smelters are the annual benchmark prices for copper concentrate supply, which are published in copper industry publications.

Approved Purchaser: an entity that has been approved by MOFCOM in accordance with the requirements set out in paragraph 16 to acquire the Divestment Asset.

Chinese Customers: the customers of copper concentrate, zinc concentrate, or lead concentrate (as the case may be) with a delivery address within the territory of the People's Republic of China (excluding Taiwan, Hong Kong, and Macao for the purpose of this Remedy Proposal).

Copper Concentrate Asset Divestiture Commitments: the Commitments set out in paragraphs 1 to 5.

Copper Concentrate Supply Commitments: the Commitments set out in paragraphs 9 to 11.

Cost: includes any identifiable expenses that are directly attributable to the assets, as well as expenses that have been or will be incurred by Glencore and Xstrata in connection with Las Bambas before or after the Transaction.

- With respect to an asset, the Cost is the fair value of the consideration paid when purchasing or building that asset, including expenses attributable to such asset incurred before such asset was moved to the site and became fit for the expected use,

(Continued)

- 资产、费用和负债的定义是根据国际会计准则理事会于2010年9月公布的《财务报表的概念框架2010》作出的。
- 就拉斯班巴斯而言，成本应包括但不限于以下内容：
  - 购买采矿权而产生的成本（包括所有期权付款）；
  - 与资源勘探有关而产生的成本（包括钻孔工程和所有可行性研究）；
  - 与所有环境及社会影响评估有关而产生的成本；
  - 购买项目所需的所有土地和其他地面使用权而产生的成本；
  - 为取得必要许可而支付的与该项目有关的许可费；
  - 就项目向所有顾问（包括律师、咨询顾问和工程人员）支付的成本；
  - 向被任命开展土建工程、预开采及建设厂房和相关基础设施（包括供水用坝、管道、公路、尾矿坝）的承包商支付的成本；
  - 为项目购买、运输和建造所有不动产、厂房及设备而产生的成本；
  - 与升级物流基础设施（包括港口、铁路和公路）有关而支付的成本；
  - 与嘉能可和斯特拉塔为项目雇用的雇员有关的成本，包括工资、奖金、养老金和其他款项；
  - 与嘉能可和斯特拉塔的其他雇员向项目提供服务有关的成本；
  - 与受项目影响的社区安置有关的成本；
  - 与项目融资有关的资本化费用；及
  - 与汇兑差额有关的成本。

决定：商务部公布的经营者集中附加限制性条件批准的决定。

剥离资产：拉斯邦巴斯(Las Bambas)或商务部指定的资产（视情况而定）。

剥离交易：嘉能可对剥离资产所有权权益进行的剥离。

剥离受托人：一个或一个以上（独立于嘉能可）的自然人或法人，经商务部批准并经嘉能可委托，获得嘉能可排他性授权，在第7段所规定的情形下出售商务部指定资产。

as well as direct expenses caused by dismantlement and disposal of that asset. An asset is a resource resulted from the entity's past transactions or events, that is owned or controlled by the entity and from which economic benefits are expected to flow to the entity.

- Expenses are decreases in economic benefits in the form of outflows or depletions of assets or incurrences of liabilities that result in decreases in equity, other than those relating to distributions to equity participants. A liability is a present obligation of the entity arising from the entity's prior transactions or events, the settlement of which is expected to result in an outflow from the entity of economic benefits.
- The asset, expenses, and liability are defined in accordance with the Conceptual Framework for Financial Reporting 2010 published by the International Accounting Standards Board in September 2010.
- With respect to Las Bambas, the Cost includes but is not limited to:
  - the costs incurred for the purchase of mining rights (including all payments for options);
  - the costs incurred in connection with resources exploration (including drilling projects and all feasibility studies);
  - the costs incurred in connection with all environmental and social evaluations;
  - the costs incurred for all the acquisitions of lands and other land use rights that are necessary for the project;
  - the royalties paid to obtain necessary licenses for the project;
  - the costs paid to all advisors (including lawyers, consultants, and engineering staff) for the project;

埃尔帕琼:斯特拉塔在位于阿根廷圣胡安省的埃尔帕琼开发项目中所持的100%的权益。

芙蕾达河:斯特拉塔在其与高原太平洋矿业公司(Highlands Pacific Limited)的合营公司中所持的81.82%的权益,斯特拉塔通过该合营企业管理位于巴布亚新几内亚西北部的桑道恩省和东塞皮克省边界附近的Horse-Ivaal-Trukai及相邻的铜金矿项目。

嘉能可:指嘉能可国际公司及其关联企业,嘉能可国际公司的注册地址为Queensway House, Hilgrove Street, St. Helier, JE1 1ES, Jersey,其总部位于瑞士,Baarermattstrasse 3, 6341 Baar。

嘉能可铜精矿生产预算:是指供应承诺期内每年嘉能可就其控制的资产所作年度预算中列出的其控制的资产下一年度铜精矿生产预算的总量。

拉斯邦巴斯:当前由斯特拉塔拉斯邦巴斯有限公司(Xstrata Las Bambas S.A.)正在开发的位于秘鲁的Cotabambas省和Grau省的项目(及相关设施)。

拉斯邦巴斯剥离期:根据各自适用的情况,指自本交易决定公布之日起至2014年9月30日止,或至2015年6月30日止的期间。

铅精矿供应承诺:第14段和第15段规定的承诺。

长期合同:指在该合同项下采购的精矿的交货期超过三个月的合同。

主要矿山企业:例如,必和必拓公司(BHP Billiton)、美国自由港麦克墨伦铜金矿公司(Freeport)、安托法加斯塔集团(Antofoagasta)、智利国家铜公司(Codelco)和巴布亚新几内亚OK Tedi公司(OK Tedi),或其它任何将来参与铜精矿年度基准价格谈判的矿山企业。

- the costs paid to contractors appointed to carry out civil works, pre-mining, and plant construction as well as related infrastructure (including dams for water supply, pipes, roads, and tailing dams);
- the costs incurred for the purchase, transportation, and construction of real estate, plants, and equipment for the project;
- the costs paid in connection with the upgrade of logistics infrastructure (including ports, railways, and roads);
- the costs related to employees hired by Glencore and Xstrata particularly for the project, including salaries, bonuses, pensions, and other payments;
- the costs related to the services provided by other employees of Glencore and Xstrata for the project;
- the costs related to resettlement of communities affected by the project;
- the capitalized expenses related to the project financing; and
- the costs related to exchange gains or losses.

Decision: the decision published by MOFCOM to conditionally approve the concentration of undertakings.

Divestment Asset: Las Bambas or an asset designated by MOFCOM (as the case may be).

Divestiture Transaction: the divestiture of Glencore's Ownership Interest in the Divestment Asset.

Divestiture Trustee: one or more natural or legal person(s), independent from Glencore, who is approved by MOFCOM and exclusively appointed by Glencore to sell the MOFCOM Designated Asset under the scenario set out in paragraph 7.

El Pachón: the 100% interest held by Xstrata in the El Pachón development project located in San Juan, Argentina.

(Continued)

主要冶炼厂:例如，奥鲁比斯
(Aurubis)、泛太平洋铜业公司(Pan
Pacific Copper)、LS日光铜业公司(LS
Nikko)、江西铜业集团公司和铜陵有
色集团，或其它任何将来参与铜精矿
年度基准价格谈判的冶炼企业。

委托协议:就每一受托人而言，委任
该受托人的条款。

最低价:在即将签订关于购买拉斯邦
巴斯的有约束力的买卖协议时分别计
算的，关于嘉能可在拉斯邦巴斯中所
持所有权权益的不低于下列价格中较
高者的价格:(1)由估值专家确定的嘉
能可在拉斯邦巴斯中所持所有权权益
的公平市场价格，以及(2)嘉能可和
斯特拉塔在本交易前及本交易后就嘉
能可在拉斯邦巴斯中所持所有权权益
所发生及将要发生的所有成本之和(
经嘉能可审计师审计并由监督受托人
确认)。

最低数量:大致相等于嘉能可和斯特
拉塔在2011年和2012年通过长期合
同供应给中国客户的铜精矿合计平
均数量的数量，即900,000千公吨铜
精矿。

商务部指定资产:商务部依据第8段所
指定的，嘉能可将被要求剥离其所持
所有权权益的备选剥离资产。

商务部受托人剥离期:根据各自适用
的情况，自2014年10月1日或者自
2015年7月1日起三个月的期间。

所有权权益:嘉能可对剥离资产持有
的有效所有权权益。

现货合同:指在该合同项下采购的精
矿的交货期为三个月或少于三个月
的合同。

Frieda River: the 81.82% interest held by Xstrata in the joint venture with Highlands Pacific Limited, through which Xstrata manages Horse-Ivaal-Trukai and the adjacent copper-gold mining project located near the boundary between Sandaun and East Sepik in Papua New Guinea.

Glencore: Glencore International plc and its Affiliated Undertakings. Glencore's registered address is Queensway House, Hilgrove Street, St. Helier, JE1 1ES, Jersey and is headquartered at Baarermattstrasse 3, 6341 Baar, Switzerland.

Glencore's Copper Concentrate Production Budget: the total budget of copper concentrate production for the next year as listed in the annual budget made by Glencore each year in the Supply Commitment Period in connection with all assets under its control.

Las Bambas: the project (and related facilities) currently being developed by Xstrata Las Bambas S.A. in Cotabambas and Grau, Peru.

Las Bambas Divestiture Period: a period starting from the announcement date of the Decision on the Transaction and ending on September 30, 2014 or June 30, 2015, as the case may be.

Lead Concentrate Supply Commitments: the commitments set out in paragraphs 14 and 15.

Long-term Contract: a contract under which the delivery period of the purchased concentrate is more than three months.

Major Miners: for example, BHP Billiton, Freeport, Antofoagasta, Codelco, and OK Tedi, or any other miner that participates in future negotiations of the annual benchmark price for copper concentrate.

监督受托人:一个或一个以上(独立于嘉能可)的自然人或法人,经商务部批准并经嘉能可委托,其承担监督嘉能可遵守决定规定的条件和义务的职责。	**Major Smelters**: for example, Aurubis, Pan Pacific Copper, LS Nikko, Jiangxi Copper Corporation, and Tongling Nonferrous Metals Group Co., Ltd., or any other smelter that participates in future negotiations of the annual benchmark price for copper concentrate.
供应承诺期:自2013年1月1日起8年的期间。	**Mandate**: the entrustment terms in respect of each Trustee.
供应承诺:指铜精矿供应承诺、锌精矿供应承诺和铅精矿供应承诺。	**Minimum Price**: the price of Glencore's Ownership Interest in Las Bambas, which is calculated when a binding sale and purchase agreement for Las Bambas is to be entered into, and which shall not be lower than the higher of: (1) the fair market price of Glencore's Ownership Interest in Las Bambas as determined by the Valuation Experts, and (2) the total of all the Costs that have been or will be incurred by Glencore and Xstrata in connection with Glencore's Ownership Interest in Las Bambas prior to or following the Transaction, as audited by Glencore's auditor and confirmed by the Supervision Trustee.
坦帕坎:斯特拉塔在菲律宾合资公司Sagittarius矿业公司中所持有的62.5%的权益。	
本交易:嘉能可收购斯特拉塔所有已发行但现在并非由嘉能可持有的股份。	
受托人:监督受托人和/或剥离受托人。	
估值专家:为计算最低价,由嘉能可选择并经监督受托人确认的两家独立的投资银行,以确定拉斯邦巴斯的公平市场价格。	**Minimum Volume**: a volume that is generally equal to the average volume of copper concentrate supplied to Chinese Customers under Long-term Contracts by both Glencore and Xstrata in 2011 and 2012, namely 900,000 dry metric tons of copper concentrate.
斯特拉塔公司:斯特拉塔公司,注册地址为瑞士Bahnhofstrasse 2, 6301 Zug。	**MOFCOM Designated Asset**: the Alternative Divestment Asset designated by MOFCOM in accordance with paragraph 8, with respect to which Glencore will be requested to divest its Ownership Interest.
锌精矿供应承诺:第12段和第13段规定的承诺。	**MOFCOM Trustee Divestiture Period**: a three-month period starting from October 1, 2014 or July 1, 2015, as the case may be.

(Continued)

	Ownership Interest: Glencore's valid ownership interest in the Divestment Asset.
	Spot Contract: a contract under which the delivery period for the purchased concentrate is three months or less.
	Supervision Trustee: one or more natural or legal person(s), independent from Glencore, who is approved by MOFCOM and appointed by Glencore to take the responsibility of supervising Glencore's compliance with the conditions and obligations attached to the Decision.
	Supply Commitment Period: a period of eight years starting from January 1, 2013.
	Supply Commitments: the copper concentrate supply commitments, zinc concentrate supply commitments, and lead concentrate supply commitments.
	Tampakan: the 62.5% interest held by Xstrata in the joint venture Sagittarius Mining Inc. in the Philippines.
	Transaction: the acquisition by Glencore of all the outstanding shares of Xstrata that are not currently owned by Glencore.
	Trustee(s): the Supervision Trustee and/or the Divestiture Trustee.
	Valuation Experts: two independent investment banks chosen by Glencore and confirmed by the Supervision Trustee to determine the fair market price of Las Bambas, so as to calculate the Minimum Price.
	Xstrata: Xstrata plc with its registered address at Bahnhofstrasse 2, 6301 Zug, Switzerland.
	Zinc Concentrate Supply Commitments: the commitments set out in paragraphs 12 and 13.

第二部分救济承诺 作为商务部批准本交易的一项条件，嘉能可谨此提出下文所列的一揽子救济措施承诺，以解决商务部在审查本交易过程中提出的关注。这些关注涉及向中国客户供应铜精矿、锌精矿和铅精矿。	**Section 2 Commitments** Glencore hereby respectfully proposes as follows a package of Commitments as a condition to MOFCOM's approval of the Transaction, so as to address the concerns raised by MOFCOM during the review of the Transaction. Those concerns relate to the supply of copper concentrate, zinc concentrate, and lead concentrate to Chinese Customers.
I. 铜精矿资产剥离承诺 嘉能可剥离拉斯邦巴斯 1.　嘉能可将在拉斯邦巴斯剥离期内以不低于最低价的价格（除非经嘉能可同意）向经批准的买方出售其在拉斯邦巴斯中的所有权权益。 2.　嘉能可应在本交易决定公布之日起3个月内启动其在拉斯邦巴斯中所有权权益的出售程序，并在此期间内就出售其在拉斯邦巴斯中的所有权权益的意向发布公告。 3.　嘉能可应尽其合理的最佳努力于2014年8月31日前向商务部提交关于其在拉斯邦巴斯中所有权权益潜在买方的详细情况。 4.　嘉能可应于2014年9月30日前就以不低于最低价的价格（除非经嘉能可同意）转让所有权权益与经批准的买方签订具有约束力的买卖协议，并包含其它在国际并购市场上该等性质的交易所常用的惯常条款和条件。 5.　具有约束力的买卖协议签订后，嘉能可应于2015年6月30日前向经批准的买方完成其在拉斯邦巴斯中的所有权权益转让。 嘉能可剥离拉斯邦巴斯的报告承诺 6.　嘉能可应在拉斯邦巴斯资产剥离期内，于本交易决定公布之日起每季度结束后的15天内向商务部和监督受托人提交一份书面报告说明其对铜精矿资产剥离承诺的履行情况；特别是，自本交易决	**I. Copper Concentrate Asset Divestiture Commitments** **Glencore's Divestiture of Las Bambas** 1.　Glencore will, within the Las Bambas Divestiture Period, sell its Ownership Interest in Las Bambas to an Approved Purchaser at a price not lower than the Minimum Price (unless otherwise agreed by Glencore). 2.　Glencore will start the process to sell its Ownership Interest in Las Bambas within three months after the announcement date of this Decision, and will, within the same period, make a public announcement of its offer to sell its Ownership Interest in Las Bambas. 3.　Glencore will use its reasonable best efforts to provide MOFCOM with details of the potential purchaser(s) of its Ownership Interest in Las Bambas by August 31, 2014. 4.　By September 30, 2014, Glencore will sign a binding sale and purchase agreement with the Approved Purchaser for the transfer of its Ownership Interest at a price not lower than the Minimum Price (unless otherwise agreed by Glencore), which will include other customary terms and conditions generally adopted for a transaction of such nature in the international merger market.

(*Continued*)

定公布之日起，嘉能可应定期向商务部报告其寻找拉斯邦巴斯所有权权益的潜在买方的情况。	5. After the execution of the binding sale and purchase agreement, Glencore will complete the transfer of its Ownership Interest in Las Bambas to the Approved Purchaser by June 30, 2015. **Commitments to Report Glencore's Divestiture of Las Bambas** 6. During the Las Bambas Divestiture Period, within 15 days after the end of each quarter following this Decision, Glencore will provide written reports to MOFCOM and the Supervision Trustee demonstrating that it is complying with the Copper Concentrate Asset Divestiture Commitments; particularly, following this Decision, Glencore will keep MOFCOM regularly updated regarding its search for potential purchasers of its Ownership Interest in Las Bambas.
II. 剥离受托人剥离备选剥离资产 7. 如嘉能可未能(1)按第4段规定于2014年9月30日前就其在拉斯邦巴斯的所有权权益签订具有约束力的买卖协议；或(2)按第5段规定于2015年6月30日前完成其在拉斯邦巴斯的所有权权益转让交割，除非经商务部同意，则嘉能可应在上述任一情形发生后两个工作日内根据第18至第27段规定的程序向商务部提交委任剥离受托人的提议。剥离受托人应根据第31段的规定在商务部受托人剥离期内无底价出售嘉能可在商务部指定资产中的所有权权益。 8. 商务部应在不迟于前述第7段所列情形发生后1周内确定商务部指定资产。	**II. Diverting Alternative Divestment Asset by the Divestiture Trustee** 7. If Glencore fails to (1) enter into a binding sale and purchase agreement in respect of its Ownership Interest in Las Bambas by September 30, 2014 in accordance with paragraph 4 or (2) complete the transfer of its Ownership Interest in Las Bambas by June 30, 2015 in accordance with paragraph 5, unless otherwise approved by MOFCOM, Glencore will submit its proposal to MOFCOM for appointing a Divestiture Trustee in accordance with the procedures set out in paragraphs 18 to 27 within two business days after either of the above circumstances occurs. The Divestiture Trustee shall sell Glencore's Ownership Interest in

	the MOFCOM Designated Asset by way of auction at no minimum price within the MOFCOM Trustee Divestiture Period in accordance with paragraph 31. 8. MOFCOM will determine the MOFCOM Designated Asset no later than one week after the occurrence of the circumstances set out in paragraph 7 above.
III. 铜精矿供应承诺 9. 在供应承诺期间内，嘉能可应继续向中国客户提供不低于最低数量的铜精矿长期合同报盘。 10. 在根据第9段提供的铜精矿的长期合同报盘中，不低于200,000干公吨的铜精矿报盘的价格每年按照适用的年度基准价向中国客户提供，700,000干公吨的铜精矿报盘的价格参照适用的年度基准价向中国客户提供。 11. 在供应承诺期内，2013年嘉能可应向中国客户提供不低于900,000干公吨的铜精矿长期合同报盘；自2014年1月1日起，如在供应承诺期内任何一年嘉能可的铜精矿生产预算与2011和2012年嘉能可及斯特拉塔合计铜精矿产量的平均值（即3,400,000干公吨）相比发生变化，则该年度根据第9段和第10段的规定向中国客户提供的铜精矿长期合同报盘的最低数量应按相同的百分比进行调整。	**III. Copper Concentrate Supply Commitments** 9. In the Supply Commitment Period, Glencore will continue to offer to supply Chinese Customers with the Minimum Volume of copper concentrate under Long-term Contracts. 10. In the offer to supply copper concentrate under Long-term Contracts made in accordance with paragraph 9, the price for a minimum of 200,000 dry metric tons of copper concentrate will be offered to Chinese Customers every year in accordance with the Applicable Annual Benchmark Price and the price for 700,000 dry metric tons of copper concentrate will be offered to Chinese Customers with reference to the Applicable Annual Benchmark Price. 11. During the Supply Commitment Period, Glencore will offer to supply Chinese Customers with no less than 900,000 dry metric tons of copper concentrate under Long-term Contracts in 2013; starting from January 1, 2014, if there is any change to Glencore's Copper Concentrate Production Budget in any year during the Supply Commitment Period compared to the average of the aggregate copper concentrate output of Glencore

(Continued)

	and Xstrata in 2011 and 2012 (i.e. 3,400,000 dry metric tons), the Minimum Volume of copper concentrate to be offered for supply to Chinese Customers in accordance with paragraphs 9 and 10 in that year will be adjusted pro rata.
IV. 锌精矿供应承诺 12. 在供应承诺期内，嘉能可应继续向中国客户提供锌精矿长期合同和现货合同报盘。 13. 在供应承诺期内，嘉能可锌精矿的报盘条件（包括与价格相关的条件）应公平、合理，并且应当在考虑到产品质量、数量、交货期、付款条件、买方信誉以及其他任何相关因素的情况下，与当时的国际市场条款一致。	**IV. Zinc Concentrate Supply Commitments** 12. During the Supply Commitment Period, Glencore will continue to offer to supply Chinese Customers with zinc concentrate through Long-term Contracts and Spot Contracts. 13. During the Supply Commitment Period, Glencore's terms of the offer to supply zinc copper concentrate, including those in relation to price, will be fair and reasonable and in accordance with prevailing international market terms after taking into account product quality, volume, delivery period, payment conditions, buyer creditworthiness, and any other relevant circumstances.
V. 铅精矿供应承诺 14. 在供应承诺期内，嘉能可将继续向中国客户提供铅精矿长期合同和现货合同报盘。 15. 在供应承诺期内，嘉能可铅精矿的报盘条件（包括与价格相关的条件）应公平、合理，并且应当在考虑到产品质量、数量、交货期、付款条件、买方信誉以及其他任何相关因素的情况下，与当时的国际市场条款一致。	**V. Lead Concentrate Supply Commitments** 14. During the Supply Commitment Period, Glencore will continue to offer to supply Chinese Customers with lead concentrate through Long-term Contracts and Spot Contracts. 15. During the Supply Commitment Period, Glencore's terms of the offer to supply lead copper concentrate, including those in relation to price, will be fair and reasonable and in accordance with prevailing international market terms after taking into account product quality, volume, delivery period, payment conditions, buyer creditworthiness, and any other relevant circumstances.

第三部分 经批准的买方

16. 为了获得商务部的批准，剥离资产的买方必须符合以下条件:
    (a) 买方必须独立于嘉能可，且不持有嘉能可的实质性权益;
    (b) 买方必须具有必要的资源、能力和意愿以维持和开发剥离资产;
    (c) 向该买方出售剥离资产不会导致排除或限制竞争;
    (d) 若必要且相关，如果剥离交易需要获得其他监管部门的批准，买方必须符合获得其他监管部门批准的条件。

(有关买方的上述标准以下称为"买方要求")。

17. 嘉能可与经批准的买方之间达成的最终具有约束力的买卖协议应以商务部的批准为前提条件。当嘉能可与买方达成协议后，嘉能可应向商务部和监督受托人提交一份有全套相关文件支持且经论证的提案，包括最终协议的副本。嘉能可应能够向商务部证明买方符合买方要求，剥离资产将按照符合救济承诺的方式进行出售。在作出该等批准前，商务部有权核实买方达到买方条件，并且剥离资产将以符合救济承诺的方式进行出售。

Section 3 Approved Purchaser

16. In order to be approved by MOFCOM, the purchaser of the Divestment Asset must satisfy the following conditions:
    (a) the purchaser must be independent of Glencore and hold no substantive interest in Glencore;
    (b) the purchaser must have the necessary resources, capability, and incentive to maintain and develop the Divestment Asset;
    (c) the sale of the Divestment Asset to the purchaser will not result in the elimination or restriction of competition;
    (d) to the extent that it is necessary and relevant, if the Divestiture Transaction is subject to approvals from other regulatory authorities, the purchaser must satisfy the conditions to such approvals.

(The above criteria for the purchaser are referred to as the "**Purchaser Requirements**").

17. The final binding sale and purchase agreement between Glencore and the Approved Purchaser shall be conditional on MOFCOM's approval. As soon as Glencore comes to an agreement with the purchaser, Glencore will submit to MOFCOM and the Supervision Trustee a verified proposal supported by a complete set of documents, including a copy of the final agreement. Glencore shall demonstrate to MOFCOM that the purchaser meets the Purchaser Requirements and that the Divestment Asset is being sold in a manner consistent with the Commitments. Before MOFCOM approves, it has the authority to verify that the purchaser fulfills the

(*Continued*)

	Purchaser Requirements and that the Divestment Asset is being sold in a manner consistent with the Commitments.
第四部分　受托人 **I. 委任程序** 18. 根据第22段至27段所列明的程序，嘉能可应委任一名或一名以上的监督受托人和一名剥离受托人（如适用），以履行其各自在救济承诺项下的职责。 19. 受托人应独立于嘉能可，具备必要的资质履行其委托协议，例如投资银行、顾问或者审计师，且当时不存在以后也不会有实质性的利益冲突。受托人由嘉能可支付薪酬，该付款不应妨碍受托人独立和有效的履行其委托协议。 20. 嘉能可应委任估值专家。第19段中所列的要求应参照适用于估值专家。 21. 为避免疑问，监督受托人不应是估值专家之一。 嘉能可委任受托人的提议 22. 在本交易决定公布起15个工作日内，嘉能可应向商务部提交一份提议，其中包括列有三名或三名以上的嘉能可拟委任为监督受托人的清单。 23. 在按照第7段要求嘉能可提议剥离受托人之日前，嘉能可应向商务部提交一份提议，列出三名嘉能可拟委任为剥离受托人的清单，以供商务部批准。 24. 每一提议应包含足够的信息供商务部核实各拟议受托人是否满足第19段规定的要求，并且应包括: 　(a) 有关该等受托人的拟议委托协议的完整条款，委托协议应包含能使受托人履行救济承诺下的职责的所有必要条款； 　(b) 工作方案大纲，该工作方案大纲架应说明受托人打算如何履行其任务。	**Section 4 Trustees** **I. Appointment Procedure** 18. Glencore will, in accordance with the procedures set out in paragraphs 22 to 27, appoint one or more Supervision Trustees and one Divestiture Trustee (where applicable) to carry out their respective functions specified in the Commitments. 19. The Trustees shall be independent from Glencore, possess the necessary qualifications to carry out their Mandate, such as an investment bank or consultant or auditor, and shall neither have nor become exposed to a material conflict of interest. The Trustees shall be remunerated by Glencore in a way that does not impede the independent and effective fulfillment of their Mandate. 20. Glencore will appoint the Valuation Experts and the requirements set out in paragraph 19 shall apply to Valuation Experts with reference. 21. To avoid doubt, the Supervision Trustee shall not be one of the Valuation Experts. **Glencore's Proposal on the Appointment of Trustees** 22. Within 15 business days after the announcement of the Decision, Glencore shall submit a proposal to MOFCOM, including a list of three or more persons whom Glencore proposes to appoint as the Supervision Trustees. 23. No later than the date Glencore shall propose the Divestiture Trustee in accordance with paragraph 7, Glencore shall submit

商务部对受托人的批准

25. 嘉能可应根据经商务部批准的委托协议，在商务部批准之日起1周内通过书面协议委任受托人。

嘉能可提出的新提案

26. 如果所有可能被委任的拟议受托人均被否决，嘉能可应根据第22至24段规定的要求和程序，在被通知否决之日起的一周内提交至少三人作为拟议受托人人选。

商务部提名的受托人

27. 如果所有后续提出的可能被委任的拟议受托人最终均被商务部否决，商务部应提名一名受托人，嘉能可应根据商务部批准的委托协议委任或使其被委任为受托人。

a proposal to MOFCOM with a list of three persons whom Glencore proposes to appoint as the Divestiture Trustee for MOFCOM's approval.

24. Each proposal shall contain sufficient information for MOFCOM to verify that the proposed Trustee fulfills the requirements set out in paragraph 19 and shall include:

   (a) the full terms of the proposed Mandate in respect of such Trustee, which shall include all provisions necessary to enable the Trustee to fulfill its duties under the Commitments;

   (b) the outline of a work plan, which shall describe how the Trustee intends to carry out its assigned tasks.

MOFCOM's Approval of the Trustees

25. Glencore will, in accordance with the Mandate approved by MOFCOM, appoint the Trustee(s) in writing within one week of the approval date.

Glencore's New Proposal

26. If none of the proposed Trustees is approved, Glencore shall submit a list of at least three proposed Trustees within one week of being informed of the rejection, in accordance with the requirements and procedures set out in paragraphs 22 to 24.

Trustees Nominated by MOFCOM

27. If all further proposed Trustees are rejected by MOFCOM, MOFCOM shall nominate a Trustee, whom Glencore shall appoint, or cause to be appointed, in accordance with the Mandate approved by MOFCOM.

(Continued)

II. 受托人职责	**II. Functions of the Trustees**
28. 为保障救济承诺得到遵守，每一受托人应承担其特定的职责。为确保商务部决定所附的条件和义务得到遵守，商务部可自行，或应嘉能可的请求，向受托人作出命令或指示。	28. Each Trustee shall assume its specified duties in order to ensure compliance with the Commitments. MOFCOM may, on its own initiative or at the request of Glencore, give any orders or instructions to the Trustee in order to ensure compliance with the conditions and obligations attached to the Decision.
监督受托人关于供应承诺的一般责任和义务	**General duties and obligations of the Supervision Trustee relating to the Supply Commitments**
29. 监督受托人应：	29. The Supervision Trustee shall:
(a) 监督并确保在供应承诺期内对供应承诺的遵守；	(a) supervise and ensure compliance with the Supply Commitments in the Supply Commitment Period;
(b) 在其向商务部提交的第一份报告中提出详细的工作方案，详述其将如何监督供应承诺的义务和条件的履行情况；	(b) propose in its first report to MOFCOM a detailed work plan describing how it intends to supervise compliance with the obligations and conditions relating to the Supply Commitments;
(c) 承担监督受托人在决定所附条件和义务项下的其他职能；	(c) assume the other functions assigned to the Supervision Trustee under the conditions and obligations attached to the Decision;
(d) 向嘉能可建议监督受托人认为为确保嘉能可遵守供应承诺的条件和义务所必要的合理采取的措施；	(d) propose to Glencore such measures as the Supervision Trustee considers reasonably necessary to ensure Glencore's compliance with the conditions and obligations relating to the Supply Commitments;
(e) 在供应承诺期届满前的每个日历年度内，在自收到嘉能可的报告后15日内向商务部提交一份书面报告，同时，如商务部批准，向嘉能可提供该书面报告的非保密版本。该报告应包含嘉能可实质遵守供应承诺项下的各项义务的情况；和	(e) in each calendar year before the Supply Commitment Period expires, provide to MOFCOM, sending Glencore a non-confidential copy at the same time if approved by MOFCOM, a written report within 15 days after receipt of the report from Glencore, which shall include the information on Glencore's
(f) 如监督受托人基于合理理由认为嘉能可未遵守这些供应承诺的某一重要条款，其应立即书面报告商务部，同时，如商务部批准，向嘉能可提供该书面报告的非保密版本。	
监督受托人关于铜精矿资产剥离承诺的一般责任和义务	
30. 监督受托人应：	
(a) 监督并确保铜精矿资产剥离承诺的遵守；	

(b) 承担监督受托人在决定所附铜精矿资产剥离承诺的条件和义务项下的其他职责；

(c) 向嘉能可建议监督受托人认为为确保嘉能可遵守铜精矿资产剥离承诺的条件和义务所必要的合理采取的措施；

(d) 审查并评估剥离程序的进度，并按照剥离程序的不同阶段，确认潜在买方收到关于铜精矿资产剥离承诺的充分信息；

(e) 每季度就嘉能可对铜精矿资产剥离承诺的实质遵守情况向商务部提交一份综合报告，同时，如商务部批准，向嘉能可提供该报告的非保密版本。该等报告应当在收到嘉能可根据第6段所提供的报告之日起7日内提交。

(f) 如剥离受托人基于合理理由认为嘉能可未遵守铜精矿资产剥离承诺的某一重要条款，则应立即书面报告商务部，同时，如商务部批准，向嘉能可提供该书面报告的非保密版本；以及

(g) 审查和评估由嘉能可的审计师出具的，为确定最低价而进行的关于嘉能可和斯特拉塔在本交易前及本交易后就拉斯邦巴斯产生及将要发生的所有成本之和的审计结果的确认，并在需要时向嘉能可的审计师进一步进行核实，以使其能够为商务部核查这些成本。

剥离受托人在商务部受托人剥离期内的责任与义务

31. 在适用剥离受托人的情况下，嘉能可应授权剥离受托人全权负责剥离事务。剥离受托人应以无底价拍卖的方式以最利于快速出售的条款和条件出售商务部指定资产。买方必须满足16条规定的买方要求，经商务部批准同意后，嘉能可应与其签署协议，

compliance with the various obligations under the Supply Commitments; and

(f) promptly report in writing to MOFCOM, sending Glencore a non-confidential copy at the same time if approved by MOFCOM, if it concludes on reasonable grounds that Glencore is failing to comply with a material undertaking of the Supply Commitments.

General duties and obligations of the Supervision Trustee relating to the Copper Concentrate Asset Divestiture Commitments

30. The Supervision Trustee shall:
    (a) supervise and ensure compliance with the Copper Concentrate Asset Divestiture Commitments;
    (b) assume the other functions assigned to the Supervision Trustee under the conditions and obligations relating to the Copper Concentrate Asset Divestiture Commitments as attached to the Decision;
    (c) propose to Glencore such measures as the Supervision Trustee considers reasonably necessary to ensure Glencore's compliance with the conditions and obligations relating to the Copper Concentrate Asset Divestiture Commitments;
    (d) review and evaluate the progress of the divestiture process and, pursuant to different stages of the divestiture process, confirm that the potential purchasers have received sufficient information relating to the Copper Concentrate Asset Divestiture Commitments;

(Continued)

协议条款由剥离受托人与买方商定。剥离受托人在出售商务部指定资产时应保护嘉能可的合法财务权益，且不违反剥离受托人以无底价方式无条件剥离的义务。

32. 在商务部受托人剥离期内（或商务部另行要求的期限内），剥离受托人应每个月向商务部提交一份综合报告，以汇报剥离程序的进展情况。该等报告应于每个月结束后的15日内提交，并且，如商务部批准，向嘉能可提供该等报告的非保密版本。

(e) provide MOFCOM, sending Glencore a non-confidential copy at the same time if approved by MOFCOM, with a comprehensive quarterly report on Glencore's compliance with the Copper Concentrate Asset Divestiture Commitments; such reports shall be submitted within seven days upon receipt of the report provided by Glencore in accordance with paragraph 6.

(f) promptly report in writing to MOFCOM, sending Glencore a non-confidential copy at the same time if approved by MOFCOM, if it concludes on reasonable grounds that Glencore is failing to comply with a material undertaking of the Copper Concentrate Asset Divestiture Commitments; and

(g) review and evaluate the confirmation issued by Glencore's auditor on the result of the auditing (conducted to determine the Minimum Price) of the total of all the Costs that have been or will be incurred by Glencore and Xstrata in connection with Las Bambas prior to and following the Transaction, and further verify with Glencore's auditor when necessary, so as to enable itself to examine such Costs for MOFCOM.

Duties and obligations of the Divestiture Trustee in the MOFCOM Trustee Divestiture Period

31. Where a Divestiture Trustee is applicable, Glencore shall grant the Divestiture Trustee an exclusive mandate to carry out the divestiture. The Divestiture Trustee shall sell the MOFCOM

	Designated Asset by auction at no minimum price with the terms and conditions that are most favorable for a quick sale. The purchaser must satisfy the Purchaser Requirements set out in paragraph 16. Upon MOFCOM's approval, Glencore shall execute an agreement with the purchaser, the term of which shall be mutually agreed by the Divestiture Trustee and the purchaser. The Divestiture Trustee shall protect Glencore's legitimate financial interests when selling the MOFCOM Designated Asset and shall not breach its obligation to unconditionally divest such asset at no minimum price.
	32. In the MOFCOM Trustee Divestiture Period (or otherwise at MOFCOM's request), the Divestiture Trustee shall provide MOFCOM with a comprehensive monthly report on the progress of the divestiture process. Such reports shall be submitted within 15 days after the end of every month with a non-confidential copy to Glencore if approved by MOFCOM.
III. 嘉能可的责任和义务 33. 嘉能可应向受托人提供并促使其顾问向受托人提供为使受托人能履行其任务而由受托人合理要求的所有配合、协助和信息。受托人应享有全面和完整的权限接触嘉能可与救济承诺相关的、为履行其在救济承诺项下的职责所必要的该等账目、记录和文件。嘉能可应按要求向受托人提供任何文件的复印件。嘉能可应在其办公地点为受托人提供一间或多间办公室，且为了向受托人提供受托人履行其任务所需的所有信息，嘉能可应出席相关会议。	**III. Duties and Obligations of Glencore** 33. Glencore shall provide and shall cause its advisors to provide with all such cooperation, assistance, and information as the Trustee may reasonably require to perform its tasks. The Trustee shall have full and complete access to Glencore's books, records, and documents that are related to the Commitments and are necessary for fulfilling its duties under the Commitments. Glencore shall provide the Trustee upon request with copies of any document. Glencore shall make

(Continued)

34. 嘉能可应按照受托人的合理请求向其提供所有管理或行政支持，以履行其在救济承诺项下的职责。这应包括目前在公司总部层面提供的所有与救济承诺相关的行政支持职能。经受托人合理请求，嘉能可应向受托人提供或者促使其顾问向受托人提供其向剥离资产潜在买方提供的相关信息。嘉能可应告知受托人有关可能买方的情况，提交一份潜在买方清单，及时告知受托人剥离进程中的任何进展。

35. 嘉能可应在救济承诺下合理要求的范围内，授予或促使其关联企业授予剥离受托人经正当签署的全面委托权限，使其能够有效执行出售、交割，以及剥离受托人认为实现商务部指定资产的交割所必要或合适的所有行为和声明，包括任命顾问协助出售程序。经剥离受托人请求，嘉能可应促使为了进行有效出售和交割所需要的文件得以适当签署。

36. 嘉能可应赔偿每一受托人及其雇员和代理人（每一方称为"被赔偿方"），使每一被赔偿方不受损害。嘉能可特此同意每一被赔偿方不应就履行救济承诺项下的受托人职责产生的任何责任向嘉能可承担任何责任，除非该等责任出于受托人、受托人的雇员、代理人或顾问的故意失职、轻率、重大过失或恶意。

37. 在嘉能可承担费用的情况下，如果受托人认为任命顾问是其履行其委托协议项下的职责和义务所必需或合适的，经嘉能可批准（此等批准不能无理由地拒绝或拖延），每一受托人可以任命顾问（尤其是关于公司财务或法律方面的建议），但受托人发生的任何费用或其他花销应是合理的。如果嘉能可拒绝批准受托人提议的顾问人选，商务部可以在与嘉能可商谈后，批准任命该等顾问。只有受托人有权向顾问发出指示。

available to the Trustee one or more offices on its working premises and shall be available for meetings in order to provide the Trustee with all information necessary for the performance of its tasks.

34. Glencore shall provide the Trustee with all managerial and administrative support that it may reasonably request to fulfil its duties under the Commitments. This shall include all administrative support functions relating to the Commitments which are currently carried out at headquarters level. Glencore shall provide and shall cause its advisors to provide the Trustee, on request, with the information submitted to potential purchasers. Glencore shall inform the Trustee on possible purchasers, submit a list of potential purchasers, and keep the Trustee informed of all developments in the divestiture process.

35. Glencore shall, to the extent reasonably required under the Commitments, grant or procure the Affiliated Undertakings to grant comprehensive powers of attorney, duly executed, to the Divestiture Trustee to effect the sale, the closing, and all actions and declarations which the Divestiture Trustee considers necessary or appropriate to achieve the closing of the MOFCOM Designated Asset, including the appointment of advisors to assist with the sale process. Upon request of the Divestiture Trustee, Glencore shall cause the documents required for effecting the sale and closing to be duly executed.

36. Glencore shall indemnify each Trustee and its employees and agents (each an **Indemnified Party**") and hold each Indemnified

38. 在剥离交易完成之前，且在遵守第40段至第41段规定的情况下，嘉能可应：
   (a) 确保潜在买方能够以公平合理的方式充分接触剥离资产的相关信息，以使潜在买方能够评估剥离资产的价值、范围以及潜力；
   (b) 基于买方要求提供必要的支持，以保证剥离资产的顺利过渡和平稳运营；以及
   (c) 向买方转让剥离资产并及时迅速地办理相关法律手续。

39. 当剥离资产是运营矿山时，在完成剥离交易前，且在遵守第40段至第41段规定的情况下，嘉能可应：
   (a) 如经要求，保持剥离资产独立于其他业务，以最有利于剥离业务的方式管理剥离资产；
   (b) 不从事可能对剥离资产造成不利影响的任何行为，如雇用其员工、或者获取其商业秘密或其他保密信息；以及
   (c) 如因管理剥离资产和履行上述义务的需要，可任命临时人员，并确保管理人员在相关受托人的监督下履行其职责，该等人员的任命或更换应经相关受托人的批准。

40. 就拉斯邦巴斯而言，第39段规定的要求仅在其成为运营矿山后适用，并直至嘉能可根据第1段至第5段规定将其剥离，或拉斯邦巴斯剥离期届满时为止。

41. 第38段以及第39段（如适用）的要求，仅在商务部根据第8段规定指定了商务部指定资产后，才适用于具体的备选剥离资产。

Party harmless against, and hereby agrees that an Indemnified Party shall have no liability to Glencore for any liabilities arising out of the performance of the Trustee's duties under the Commitments, except to the extent that such liabilities result from the willful default, recklessness, gross negligence, or bad faith of the Trustee, its employees, agents, or advisors.

37. At the expense of Glencore, the Trustee may appoint advisors (in particular for corporate finance or legal advice), subject to Glencore's approval (this approval not to be unreasonably withheld or delayed) if the Trustee considers the appointment of such advisors necessary or appropriate for the performance of its duties and obligations under the Mandate, provided that any fees and other expenses incurred by the Trustee are reasonable. Should Glencore refuse to approve the advisors proposed by the Trustee, MOFCOM may approve the appointment of such advisors instead, after consultations with Glencore. Only the Trustee shall be entitled to issue instructions to the advisors.

38. Prior to the completion of the Divestiture Transaction and subject to the provisions of paragraphs 40 and 41, Glencore shall:
   (a) ensure that the potential purchasers have full access to the relevant information of the Divestment Asset in a fair and reasonable manner, so to enable the potential purchasers to evaluate the value, scope, and potentials of the Divestment Asset;

(Continued)

(b) upon request by the purchaser, provide necessary support to ensure smooth transition and stable operation of the Divestment Asset; and

(c) transfer the Divestment Asset to the purchaser and undertake relevant legal formalities in a timely and prompt manner.

39. If the Divestment Asset is a mine in operation, prior to the completion of the Divestiture Transaction and subject to the provisions of paragraphs 40 and 41, Glencore shall:

(a) upon request, keep the Divestment Asset independent from other businesses and manage the Divestment Asset in the best interest of the divestment business;

(b) not carry out any act that might have an adverse impact on the Divestment Asset, such as hiring its employees, or obtaining its business secrets or other confidential information; and

(c) if necessary for managing the Divestment Asset and fulfilling the above obligations, appoint temporary staff and ensure that the management staff fulfill their duties and obligations under the supervision of the relevant Trustee. The appointment and replacement of such staff shall be subject to approval by the relevant Trustee.

40. In respect of Las Bambas, the requirements set out in paragraph 39 shall be applicable only after it has become a mine in operation and until it has been divested by Glencore in accordance with paragraphs 1 to 5 or until the Las Bambas Divestiture Period expires.

	41. The requirements in paragraphs 38 and 39 (if applicable) shall be applicable to the specific Alternative Divestment Asset only after MOFCOM has designated the MOFCOM Designated Asset in accordance with paragraph 8.

IV. 受托人的更换、解除和再委任
 	
42. 如果受托人停止履行其在救济承诺项下的职责，或者由于任何其他合理理由，包括受托人出现利益冲突的情形：
  (a) 在听取受托人的意见后，商务部可以要求嘉能可更换受托人；或者
  (b) 在获得商务部的事前批准的情况下，嘉能可可以更换受托人。
 	
43. 如果受托人按照第42段的规定被更换，可以要求该受托人继续履行其职责直至新的受托人就职，该受托人应向新任受托人全面转交所有相关信息。新任受托人应根据第18至27段规定的程序进行委任。
 	
44. 除按照第42段进行的更换外，只有在受托人被委托监督的所有救济承诺都得以执行之后，且经商务部解除受托人的职责之后，受托人才应停止其受托人职责。然而，如果随后发现相关救济可能并未完全和适当履行，商务部可以随时要求再次委任监督受托人。
	IV. Replacement, Discharge and Reappointment of the Trustee
	42. If the Trustee ceases to perform its functions under the Commitments or for any other good cause, including the exposure of the Trustee to a conflict of interest:
	  (a) MOFCOM may, after hearing the Trustee, require Glencore to replace the Trustee; or
	  (b) Glencore, with the prior approval of MOFCOM, may replace the Trustee.
	43. If the Trustee is removed according to paragraph 42, the Trustee may be required to continue its functions until a new Trustee is in place and the Trustee shall fully hand over all the relevant information to the new Trustee. The new Trustee shall be appointed in accordance with the procedure referred to in paragraphs 18 to 27.
	44. Besides the removal according to paragraph 42, the Trustee shall cease to act as Trustee only after MOFCOM has discharged it from its duties after all the Commitments with which the Trustee has been entrusted have been implemented. However, MOFCOM may at any time require the reappointment of the Supervision Trustee if it subsequently appears that the relevant remedies might not have been fully and properly implemented.

(Continued)

第五部分 救济承诺的复审/终止	**Section 5 The Review Clause**
45. 经嘉能可请求并出示合理理由，商务部可以在适当情况下对救济承诺中预定的时限予以变更。嘉能可必须说明变更的原因。	45. MOFCOM may, where appropriate, in response to a request from Glencore showing good cause, change the time periods foreseen in the Commitments. Glencore must explain the reasons for such change.
46. 经嘉能可请求并出示合理理由，商务部可以在适当的情况下变更或免除嘉能可在救济承诺项下的义务。嘉能可必须提供变更或解除义务的理由。	46. MOFCOM may, where appropriate, in response to a request from Glencore showing good cause, modify or waive the obligations under the Commitments. Glencore must explain the reasons for such modification or waiver.
第二章:救济承诺工作方案拟议大纲	**Chapter Two Proposed Outline of the Work Plan for the Commitments**
1 委任监督受托人	**1. Appointment of the Supervision Trustee**
嘉能可将委任一个或一名以上的独立的监督受托人。委任监督受托人的程序和条款已在救济承诺中列明。监督受托人将负责监督嘉能可遵守供应承诺以及铜精矿资产剥离承诺的情况。	Glencore shall appoint one or more independent Supervision Trustees. The procedure and terms for the appointment of the Supervision Trustees are set out in the Commitments. The Supervision Trustee shall be responsible for supervising Glencore's compliance with the Supply Commitments and the Copper Concentrate Asset Divestiture Commitments.
2 铜精矿资产剥离承诺	**2. Copper Concentrate Asset Divestiture Commitments**
监督受托人需在接受委任之日起30个工作日内向商务部提交一份详细的工作方案，说明其将如何监督嘉能可遵守铜精矿资产剥离承诺的要求。	The Supervision Trustee shall, within 30 business days after it accepts the appointment, submit to MOFCOM a detailed work plan, describing how it intends to carry out the supervision of Glencore's compliance with the requirements under the Copper Concentrate Asset Divestiture Commitments.
工作方案的准确范围和条款将由监督受托人(经与商务部及嘉能可磋商后)决定。	
3 供应承诺 **(a) 详细的工作方案**	The exact scope and specific terms of the work plan shall be determined by the Supervision Trustee (after consultation with MOFCOM and Glencore).
监督受托人将需要在接受委任之日起30个工作日内向商务部提交一份详细的工作方案，阐述其将如何监督嘉能可遵守供应承诺的要求。	
尽管工作方案的准确范围和条款将由监督受托人(经与商务部和嘉能可的磋商)决定，嘉能可在下文中列出了其认为应作为该工作方案一部分的要点	

（这些要点也表明了工作方案是有效且可执行的）。这些要点如下：

(b) 铜精矿供应承诺

嘉能可承诺每年向监督受托人提供嘉能可就其控制的相关资产所作的下一年度铜精矿生产预算，以便能够让监督受托人确定并量化嘉能可铜精矿生产预算的百分比变化。这能够使监督受托人确定是否需要更改嘉能可自2014年1月1日起根据铜精矿供应承诺须向中国客户提供的铜精矿长期合同报盘的最低数量。

嘉能可承诺，在供应承诺期内每年结束后的45天内，向监督受托人提供一份报告，该报告将：

- 详细说明嘉能可在上一年中向中国客户提供的铜精矿长期合同报盘的总量，以及按长期合同向中国客户实际供应的铜精矿总量。
- 包括证据表明嘉能可在上一年中按长期合同向中国客户提供的铜精矿报盘以及实际供应的铜精矿的价格条款。

(c) 锌精矿与铅精矿供应承诺

嘉能可承诺，在供应承诺期内每年结束后的45天内，向监督受托人提供一份报告，该报告将：

- 详细说明嘉能可在上一年中通过长期合同和现货合同向中国客户提供的铅精矿和锌精矿报盘的总量，以及实际供应的铅精矿和锌精矿的总量。
- 提供证据表明在此期间嘉能可向中国客户提供的锌精矿和铅精矿的现货合同和长期合同报盘条件（包括与价格相关的条件）是公平、合理的，并且应当在考虑到产品质量、数量、交付期、付款条件、买方信誉和其他任何相关因素的情况下，与当时的国际市场条款一致。

(d) 内部合规

嘉能可将制订培训材料，广泛分发给嘉能可从事向中国客户销售铜精矿、锌精矿和铅精矿的工作人员。该培训材料将列明嘉能可员工在供应承诺下的义务。

3. Supply Commitments

(a) Detailed Work Plan

The Supervision Trustee shall, within 30 business days after it accepts the appointment, submit to MOFCOM a detailed work plan, describing how it intends to carry out the supervision of Glencore's compliance with the requirements under the Supply Commitments.

Although the exact scope and specific terms of the work plan shall be determined by the Supervision Trustee (after consultation with MOFCOM and Glencore), Glencore lists below some key points which it believes shall be included in the work plan (such key points also demonstrate that the work plan is effective and enforceable). The key points include:

(b) Copper Concentrate Supply Commitments

Glencore commits to provide the Supervision Trustee every year with the copper concentrate production budget for the next year made by Glencore in connection with the relevant assets under Glencore's control, so as to enable the Supervision Trustee to determine and quantify the percentage changes in Glencore's Copper Concentrate Production Budget. This will enable the Supervision Trustee to determine whether it is necessary to change the Minimum Volume of copper concentrate with which Glencore must offer to supply Chinese Customers under Long-term Contracts starting from January 1, 2013 in compliance with the Copper Concentrate Supply Commitments.

Glencore commits to, within 45 days after the end of each year in the Supply Commitment Period, provide a report to the Supervision Trustee, which shall:

- specify in detail the total volume of copper concentrate Glencore offered

(*Continued*)

在供应承诺期内每年结束后的45天内，嘉能可将向监督受托人提供一份报告，汇报以下情况:
- 嘉能可内部合规制度的详细情况，以确保嘉能可向中国客户供应时的条款符合供应承诺中的要求；以及
- 确认嘉能可的相关员工在上一年中确已接受关于供应承诺的培训。

for supply to Chinese Customers under Long-term Contracts in the previous year, and the total volume of copper concentrate actually supplied to Chinese Customers under Long-term Contracts;
- include evidence showing Glencore's offer to supply Chinese Customers with copper concentrate under Long-term Contracts in the previous year and the price terms for the copper concentrate actually supplied.

(c) Zinc Concentrate and Lead Concentrate Supply Commitments

Glencore commits to, within 45 days after the end of each year in the Supply Commitment Period, provide a report to the Supervision Trustee, which shall:
- specify in detail the total volumes of lead concentrate and zinc concentrate Glencore offered for supply to Chinese Customers under Long-term Contracts and Spot Contracts in the previous year, and the total volumes of lead concentrate and zinc concentrate actually supplied;
- provide evidence showing that in such period, Glencore's terms (including those in relation to price) of the offer to supply Chinese Customers with zinc concentrate and lead concentrate through Spot Contracts and Long-term Contracts, were fair and reasonable and in accordance with prevailing international market terms after taking into account product quality, volume, delivery period, payment conditions, buyer creditworthiness, and any other relevant circumstances.

(d) Internal Compliance

Glencore will prepare training materials and widely distribute them to the working staff who are engaged in the sale of copper concentrate, zinc concentrate, and lead concentrate to Chinese Customers. Such training

	materials will specify the obligations of Glencore's working staff under the Supply Commitments.
	Within 45 days after the end of each year in the Supply Commitment Period, Glencore will provide the Supervision Trustee with a report on the following: • detailed information about Glencore's internal compliance system, to ensure that its terms for the supply to Chinese Customers comply with the Supply Commitments; and • confirmation that the relevant working staff of Glencore did receive trainings in the previous year in relation to the Supply Commitments.

MOFCOM Announcement [2013] No. 22 Regarding the Conditional Approval of the Acquisition of a 100% Equity Interest in Gavilon Holdings, LLC by Marubeni Corporation

商务部公告2013年第22号 关于附加限制性条件批准丸红公司收购高鸿公司100%股权经营者集中反垄断审查决定的公告

(Published on April 22, 2013)

（2013年4月22日公布）

中华人民共和国商务部（以下简称商务部）收到日本丸红株式会社（以下简称丸红公司）收购美国高鸿控股有限责任公司（Gavilon Holdings, LLC，以下简称高鸿公司）100%股权的经营者集中反垄断申报。经审查，商务部决定附加限制性条件批准此项经营者集中。根据《中华人民共和国反垄断法》（以下简称《反垄断法》）第三十条，现公告如下：

The Ministry of Commerce of the People's Republic of China ("MOFCOM") has received an anti-monopoly notification of a concentration of undertakings regarding the acquisition of a 100% equity interest in Gavilon Holdings, LLC ("Gavilon") by Marubeni Corporation ("Marubeni"). After review, MOFCOM decides to approve this concentration of undertakings under restrictive conditions. This announcement is made as follows in accordance with Article 30 of the Anti-Monopoly Law of the People's Republic of China ("AML").

一、立案和审查程序

2012年6月19日，商务部收到丸红公司收购高鸿公司100%股权的经营者集中反垄断申报。 经审核，商务部认为该申报文件、资料不完备，要求申报方予以补充。

1. Acceptance and Review Process

On June 19, 2012, MOFCOM received a notification of a concentration of undertakings concerning the acquisition of a 100% equity interest in Gavilon by Marubeni.

7月31日，商务部确认经补充的申报文件、资料符合《反垄断法》第二十三条的要求，对该项经营者集中申报予以立案并开始初步审查。8月30日，商务部决定对此项经营者集中实施进一步审查。经进一步审查，商务部认为此项经营者集中对中国大豆进口市场可能具有排除、限制竞争效果。11月28日，经申报方同意，商务部决定延长进一步审查期限，截止时间为2013年1月27日。在上述审查期间，申报方就商务部提出的竞争问题提交了解决方案，经审查认为不能有效解决该案竞争问题。2013年1月25日申报方申请撤回案件并于1月31日重新申报。2月5日，商务部予以立案。3月5日，商务部决定对此项经营者集中实施进一步审查。

审查过程中，商务部征求了相关政府部门、行业协会和相关企业的意见，了解了相关市场界定、市场结构、行业特征、未来发展前景等方面信息，并对申报方提交的文件、资料的真实性、完整性和准确性进行了审核。

Following its review and verifications, MOFCOM believed that the notification materials were incomplete and requested the notifying party to supplement. On July 31, MOFCOM confirmed that the supplemented notification materials satisfied the requirements of Article 23 of the AML, accepted this case for review, and started a preliminary review. On August 30, MOFCOM decided to conduct a further review of the concentration. After this further review, MOFCOM believed that the concentration may have the effect of eliminating and/or restricting competition in the Chinese import market of soybeans. On November 28, with the consent of the notifying party, MOFCOM decided to extend the period of further review to January 27, 2013. During the further review, the notifying party submitted solution proposals to address the competition concerns raised by MOFCOM. After review, MOFCOM believed that they were insufficient to effectively address those competition concerns. On January 25, 2013, the notifying party withdrew the case and resubmitted a notification on January 31. On February 5, the resubmitted notification was accepted by MOFCOM. On March 5, MOFCOM decided to conduct a further review of this concentration of undertakings.

During the review, MOFCOM solicited comments from relevant governmental departments, trade associations, and relevant enterprises, collected information in relation to the market definition, market structure, industrial characteristics, future prospects, etc, and reviewed and verified the authenticity, completeness, and accuracy of the documents and materials submitted by the notifying party.

(*Continued*)

二、竞争分析

商务部按照《反垄断法》及配套规定，对此项经营者集中进行了审查，深入分析了该项经营者集中对市场竞争的影响，认为其在中国大豆进口市场可能具有排除、限制竞争的效果。

(一) 交易概况。

丸红公司在日本注册成立，总部位于日本东京，在东京、名古屋和大阪证券交易所上市。丸红公司是大型综合贸易公司，在全球范围内从事食品原料、食品、纺织品、原材料、纸浆和纸张、化学品、能源、金属和矿产资源以及运输机械的贸易。在中国大宗农产品进口市场，丸红公司2011年和2012年进口量均居首位。丸红公司在中国境内设有24家子公司和分支机构，拥有成熟的分销渠道和健全的物流仓储设施。

高鸿公司在美国注册成立，总部位于美国内布拉斯加州奥马哈市，是一家私人持股公司。高鸿公司是大宗商品管理公司，在全球范围内从事谷物和配料、化肥以及能源产品的采购、存储和加工、运输和物流、推广和经销以及风险管理服务。以存储能力衡量，高鸿公司是目前北美第三大谷物采购、存储和经销公司，其在美国经营140多家谷物装载点及大型谷物存储设施，并拥有经销网络。高鸿公司还从美国境外如巴西、澳大利亚和乌克兰等关键产区采购谷物。高鸿公司在中国境内设有1家分支机构。

2012年5月29日，丸红公司与高鸿公司签署了《股权收购协议》(以下简称《协议》)。根据《协议》，丸红公司将通过Gold Marble 投资公司 (丸红公司为本交易而建立的全资子公司) 收购高鸿公司全部股权。交易完成后，丸红公司将间接持有高鸿公司100%的股权。

2. Competition Analysis

In accordance with the AML and its implementing rules, MOFCOM reviewed this concentration of undertakings, conducted an in-depth analysis of the effect of this concentration on market competition, and held that it may have an adverse effect of eliminating and/or restricting competition on the Chinese import market of soybeans.

(1) Overview of the transaction

Marubeni is incorporated in Japan, headquartered in Tokyo, and listed on the Tokyo, Nagoya, and Osaka stock exchanges. Marubeni is a large general trading company, with worldwide activities in trading of food materials, food products, textiles, materials, pulp and paper, chemicals, energy, metals and mineral resources, and transportation machinery. In the Chinese import market of agricultural commodities, Marubeni ranked first in both 2011 and 2012 by import volume. Marubeni has 24 subsidiaries and branches in China, and owns mature distribution channels and robust logistics and storage facilities.

Gavilon is incorporated in the U.S., headquartered in Omaha, Nebraska (U.S.), and is a privately held company. Gavilon is a commodity management company, offering international origination, storage and handling, transportation and logistics, marketing and distribution and risk management services of grains and ingredients, fertilizers and energy products. Gavilon is currently the third largest trader in North American grain procurement, storage and distribution as measured by storage capacity. It operates over 140 grain loading sites and large grain storage facilities and has a distribution network in the U.S. It also purchases

	from key grain producing countries outside the U.S. such as Brazil, Australia, and Ukraine. Gavilon has one branch in China. On May 29, 2012, Marubeni and Gavilon executed an Equity Interest Purchase Agreement (the "Agreement"), pursuant to which, Marubeni will acquire through Gold Marble Investment, Inc., a wholly owned subsidiary of Marubeni created for the purposes of the transaction, all equity interests in Gavilon. After closing, Marubeni will indirectly hold 100% of all equity interests of Gavilon.
(二) 相关市场。 丸红公司从美国、加拿大、巴西、澳大利亚、印度、乌克兰等主要生产区域的农户（约占20%）或其他贸易商（约占80%）处采购大豆、小麦、玉米、动物油脂等大宗农产品，并销往日本、中国、韩国、中国台湾地区、印度尼西亚、越南、美国、加拿大、墨西哥、中美洲地区、加勒比地区、欧洲经济区等地。在中国，丸红公司进行大豆、大豆产品、玉米、干粗酒糟等大宗农产品贸易。2012年，丸红公司出口到中国的大宗农产品总量约1060万吨，其中大豆1050万吨。 高鸿公司从美国、加拿大和澳大利亚的农户（约占85%）或其他贸易商（约占15%）处采购大豆、玉米、动物油脂等大宗农产品，并销往北美、亚洲、欧洲、拉丁美洲、非洲、加勒比海地区、中东、以及大洋洲。在中国，高鸿公司进行黄玉米、大豆、豆粕以及饲料与食物配料等大宗农产品贸易。2012年，高鸿公司出口到中国的大宗农产品总量约40万吨。 根据双方经营范围、方式及商品特性，需求和供给替代等因素，商务部认为中国大豆、玉米、豆粕以及干粗酒糟的进口市场为相关商品市场。	(2) The Relevant Markets Marubeni originates agricultural commodities such as soybeans, wheat, corn, animal fats from farmers (approximately 20%) or from other traders (approximately 80%) in the main production areas such as the U.S., Canada, Brazil, Australia, India, and Ukraine. It sells the same to Japan, China, South Korea, Taiwan, Indonesia, Vietnam, the U.S., Canada, Mexico, Central America, the Caribbean Area, the European Economic Area, etc. In China, Marubeni engages in the trading of agricultural commodities such as soybeans, soybean products, corn, and Distiller's Dried Grains ("DDGs"). In 2012, Marubeni exported approximately 10.6 million tons of agricultural commodities to China, including 10.5 million tons of soybeans. Gavilon originates agricultural commodities such as soybeans, corn, animal fats from farmers (approximately 85%) or from other traders (approximately 15%) in the U.S., Canada, and Australia, and sells the same to North America, Asia, Europe, Latin America, Africa, the Caribbean Area, the Middle East, and Oceania. In China, Gavilon engages in the trading of

(Continued)

同时，考虑到上述商品的实际贸易情况、消费习惯、运输、关税等因素，相关地域市场为中国，同时考虑了全球范围的因素。	agricultural commodities such as yellow corn, soybeans, soybean meal, and feed and food ingredients. In 2012, Gavilon exported approximately 400,000 tons of agricultural commodities to China. Considering factors such as the scope and mode of business operation of the parties as well as the characteristics of the commodities and the demand and supply substitution, MOFCOM held that the Chinese import markets of soybeans, corn, soybean meal, and DDGs are the relevant product markets. Meanwhile, considering factors such as the actual trade conditions, consumption habits, transportation, tariffs of the above products, the relevant geographic market is China-wide, also taking into consideration the worldwide factors.
(三) 竞争分析。 此项经营者集中涉及的相关商品中，中国是世界最大的大豆进口国，2012年中国大豆进口量占全球大豆贸易总量的60%，占中国国内供应量的80%。丸红公司经营的大豆99%出口到中国市场。高鸿公司在北美大豆采购、仓储、物流方面具有相当的能力。此项经营者集中将使丸红公司在拥有中国大豆进口市场综合优势的基础上整合高鸿公司北美大豆市场的潜在能力，提高丸红公司向中国出口大豆的能力，可能实质性增强其在中国大豆进口市场的控制力，产生排除、限制竞争的效果。 1、 中国大豆进口市场。 2012年，中国进口大豆5838万吨。作为主要出口商，丸红公司向中国出口大豆1050万吨，居第一位。其他出口商，如阿彻丹尼尔斯米德兰公司(ADM)、嘉吉公司、托福国际集团、路易达孚公司、邦吉公司等向中国出口大豆量均远低于丸红公司。与主要竞争对手相比，	(3) Competition Analysis Among the relevant products involved in this concentration, China is the largest import country of soybeans. In 2012, the import volume of soybeans into China accounted for 60% of the total trading volume of soybeans in the world and 80% of the domestic supply within China. 99% of soybeans traded by Marubeni are exported to China. Gavilon has comparatively strong capabilities in soybean origination, storage, and logistics in North America. This concentration will enable Marubeni to integrate Gavilon's potential capabilities in the North American soybean market based on Marubeni's comprehensive preponderance in the Chinese import market of soybeans, improve Marubeni's ability to export soybeans to China, which may substantively increase its ability to control the Chinese soybean import market, giving rise to the effect of eliminating and/or restricting competition.

丸红公司在中国大豆市场的分销能力和客户资源方面也具有一定优势。2012年，高鸿公司在全球的大豆销售量为510万吨，同时高鸿公司在北美大豆采购、仓储、物流领域具有一定规模，其拥有美国商用谷物存储能力的7%，在美国大豆主产区拥有多个采购平台，并在美国西北海岸拥有出口设施。

此项经营者集中完成后，丸红公司将可能利用高鸿公司在北美大豆采购、仓储、物流等方面的能力，扩大其大豆采购来源。同时，丸红公司凭借其在中国市场健全的营销网络和丰富的客户资源，大幅提高对中国的大豆出口，从而进一步强化其在中国大豆进口市场已具有的领先地位，增强其对中国大豆进口市场的控制力。

进入大豆贸易市场需要具备获取大豆资源的渠道以及营销网络，且需具备相当的规模经济条件，才能参与有效的市场竞争，市场进入难度较大。最近5年，全球大豆贸易市场和中国大豆进口市场均没有重要的新市场进入者。此项经营者集中将大幅增加丸红公司掌握的全球大豆资源，提高潜在竞争者进入相关市场的难度。市场进入难以减轻或消除此项经营者集中引起的排除、限制竞争效果。

目前，中国大豆高度依赖进口，国内大豆压榨企业集中度低，生产规模小，议价能力较弱。此项经营者集中可能进一步削弱下游大豆压榨企业的议价能力。

综上，此项经营者集中完成后，丸红公司在中国大豆进口市场的控制力进一步增强，市场进入难度进一步增加，可能具有排除、限制相关市场竞争的效果，最终可能损害下游客户及最终消费者利益。

2、 中国玉米、豆粕、干粗酒糟进口市场。

在中国玉米、豆粕和干粗酒糟进口市场，丸红公司和高鸿公司合并后市场份额分别为6%、4.5%和8.4%，

(i) Chinese import market of soybean. In 2012, China imported 58.38 million tons of soybeans. As a major exporter, Marubeni exported 10.5 million tons of soybeans to China, ranking first among others. The export volumes to China from other traders such as ADM, Cargill, Toepfer International, Louis Dreyfus, and Bunge Limited were far below the export volume from Marubeni. Compared to major competitors, Marubeni has certain advantages in distribution capabilities and client resources in the Chinese soybean market. In 2012, Gavilon's sales of soybeans in the world amounted to 5.1 million tons. At the same time, Gavilon has a certain scale in soybean origination, storage and logistics in North America, and its storage capacity of commercial grains accounts for 7% of the total capacity in the U.S. It owns a number of origination platforms in the U.S. main production areas of soybeans and export facilities in the U.S. North-West coast.

After closing, Marubeni may expand its origination sources of soybeans, using Gavilon's capabilities in soybean origination, storage, and logistics in North America. Meanwhile, benefiting from its sound marketing networks and rich client resources in the Chinese market, Marubeni may substantially increase its export of soybeans to China, further strengthening its established leading position in the Chinese soybean import market and increasing its ability to control the Chinese soybean import market.

The entry into the soybean trading market requires soybean origination channels and marketing networks, and an entrant can participate effectively in market competition only with considerable economy of scale. Therefore it is rather difficult to enter

(*Continued*)

且市场上存在众多强有力的竞争对手，能够对合并后实体形成竞争制约。反垄断审查认为，此项经营者集中难以在中国玉米、豆粕和干粗酒糟进口市场产生排除、限制竞争效果。

into the market. During the past five years, there has been no important new entrant into the global soybean trading market or the Chinese soybean import market. This concentration will significantly increase the worldwide soybean resources under Marubeni's control, and will make it more difficult for potential competitors to enter into the relevant market. Market entries can hardly mitigate or eliminate the effect of eliminating and/or restricting competition resulting from this concentration.

At present, the sourcing of soybeans in China relies heavily on imports. Soybean crushing enterprises in China have a low degree of concentration, small production scale, and weak bargaining power. The concentration may further weaken the bargaining power of downstream soybean crushing enterprises.

In conclusion, after closing, Marubeni's control in the Chinese soybean import market will be further increased, and the market entry will be more difficult. The transaction is likely to have the effect of eliminating and/or restricting competition in the relevant market, harming the interests of downstream customers and ultimate consumers.

(ii) Chinese import markets of corn, soybean meal, and DDGs.

In the Chinese import markets of corn, soybean meal, and DDGs, the combined market shares of Marubeni and Gavilon are 6%, 4.5%, and 8.4%, respectively, and there are many strong competitors in the markets, which can impose competition restraint to the merged entity. After the review, MOFCOM held that it is difficult for the concentration to have the effect of eliminating and/or restricting competition on the Chinese import markets of corn, soybean meal, and DDGs.

三、附加限制性条件的商谈 在审查期间，商务部向申报方指出了此项经营者集中在中国大豆进口市场可能产生的竞争问题，并就如何减少此项经营者集中对竞争的不利影响进行了多轮商谈。经评估，商务部认为，丸红公司于2013年4月17日向商务部提交的救济方案能够减少此项经营者集中对竞争产生的不利影响。	**3. Negotiation of Restrictive Conditions** During the review period, MOFCOM pointed out to the notifying party the likely competition concerns of the concentration on the Chinese import market of soybeans, and held several rounds of negotiations on how to mitigate such adverse competitive effects. After evaluation, MOFCOM held that the remedy proposal Marubeni submitted on April 17, 2013 could mitigate the adverse competitive effects of this concentration of undertakings.
四、审查决定 经审查，商务部认为丸红公司收购高鸿公司100%股权案对中国大豆进口市场可能具有排除、限制竞争效果。根据丸红公司向商务部作出的承诺，商务部决定附加限制性条件批准此项经营者集中。交易双方应当履行如下义务： （一）　此项经营者集中完成后，维持丸红公司和高鸿公司向中国出口和销售大豆业务的分离与独立，包括但不限于以下内容： 1、　本决定生效之日起6个月内，丸红公司应设立两家独立的法人实体，组建两支独立的运营团队负责向中国出口和销售大豆。丸红公司将通过丸红大豆子公司向中国出口和销售大豆。高鸿公司将通过高鸿大豆子公司向中国出口和销售大豆。丸红公司应就上述两家独立实体的设立制定实施方案，在报告监督受托人并经商务部批准后实施，接受本决定项下的监督。 2、　维持丸红大豆子公司与高鸿大豆子公司之间的分离和独立，包括但不限于人事任免、采购、营销、销售、定价等方面。为确保上述独立性，丸红公司和高鸿公司应事先制定保障措施，	**4. Review Decision** After review, MOFCOM held that Marubeni's acquisition of the 100% equity interests in Gavilon may have the effect of eliminating and/or restricting competition in the Chinese import market of soybeans. Pursuant to the commitments Marubeni made to MOFCOM, MOFCOM decides to approve this concentration under restrictive conditions. The parties to the transaction shall perform the following obligations: (1)　After closing, Marubeni and Gavilon shall maintain the separation and independence between their businesses of soybean export and sales to China, including but not limited to: (i)　Within six months after this decision comes into effect, Marubeni shall establish two independent legal entities and two independent operation teams to be responsible for export and sales of soybeans into China. Marubeni shall export and sell soybeans into China through the Marubeni Soybean Subsidiary (MSS). Gavilon shall export and sell soybeans into China through the Gavilon Soybean Subsidiary (GSS).

(Continued)

报告监督受托人并经商务部批准后实施，接受本决定项下的监督。 3、 此项经营者集中完成后，丸红大豆子公司不得从高鸿美国资产(高鸿公司单独控制的位于美国的用于产品采购和出口的资产)采购大豆，除非交易依据公平市场条件进行。若集中完成后，丸红公司位于美国的收购和出口资产将转移并合并至高鸿资产，丸红大豆子公司基于公平合理原则采购大豆的义务将同时扩展适用于这些资产。为确保公平交易原则的实施，丸红公司和高鸿公司应事先制定相应保障措施(包括在丸红大豆子公司和高鸿美国资产之间可能设置的防火墙)，报告监督受托人并经商务部批准后实施，接受本决定项下的监督。 4、 丸红大豆子公司和高鸿大豆子公司之间不得交换竞争性信息。竞争性信息是指任何可能导致丸红大豆子公司和高鸿大豆子公司之间协调彼此经营行为的信息，包括但不限于中国大豆销售价格，与采购或销售商业条款相关的信息、成本信息、目前或潜在客户、客户谈判和客户名单、营销和战略规划等。为确保实现上述目标，丸红公司和高鸿公司应事先制定保障措施，特别是在丸红大豆子公司和高鸿大豆子公司之间设置防火墙，确保双方不会交换竞争性信息。上述措施报告监督受托人并经商务部批准后实施，接受本决定项下的监督。 (二) 根据商务部《关于实施经营者集中资产或业务剥离的暂行规定》，丸红公司应委托独立的监督受托人对丸红公司履行上述义务的情况进行监督。	Marubeni shall make an implementing plan relating to the establishment of the above two entities, report it to the supervision trustee, and submit it to MOFCOM for approval before implementation, which is subject to supervision under this decision. (ii) MSS and GSS shall be kept separate and independent, including but not limited to personnel, purchase, marketing, sales, and pricing. To ensure the independence, Marubeni and Gavilon shall propose safeguard measures in advance, report them to the supervision trustee, and submit them to MOFCOM for approval before implementation, which is subject to supervision under this decision. (iii) After closing, MSS shall not purchase soybeans from Gavilon's U.S. assets (assets located in the U.S., used for origination and export of products and under sole control of Gavilon) unless the transactions are conducted on the basis of fair market conditions. If after completion of the concentration, Marubeni's assets located in the U.S. and used for origination and export of products are transferred and combined with Gavilon's assets, MSS's obligation to purchase soybeans under fair market conditions will extend to such assets. To ensure the implementation of the principle of fair market transaction, Marubeni and Gavilon shall propose safeguard measures in advance (including firewalls between MSS and Gavilon's U.S. assets), report them to the supervision trustee, and submit them to MOFCOM for approval before implementation, which is subject to supervision under this decision.

自本决定实施起的24个月期间内，丸红公司应当每6个月就其遵守上述第（一）项义务的情况向商务部和监督受托人报告。24个月期满后，丸红公司可以向商务部提出解除上述第（一）项义务的申请。该申请应说明本决定项下附加限制性条件的实施情况和解除上述义务的理由并提供相关证据。商务部将依申请并根据市场竞争状况做出是否解除的决定。

为履行上述义务，丸红公司应当在监督受托人确定后10天内提交详细的操作方案并报商务部批准后实施。

商务部有权通过监督受托人或自行监督检查丸红公司履行上述义务的情况。丸红公司未适当履行上述义务，商务部将根据《反垄断法》相关规定作出处理。

(iv) MSS and GSS shall not exchange competitively sensitive information. Competitively sensitive information refers to any information that may lead to coordination of operations between MSS and GSS, including but not limited to sales price of soybeans in China, commercial conditions for purchase or sales, cost, current and potential customers, customer negotiations, customer lists, and sales and market strategies. To ensure the realization of the above goals, Marubeni and Gavilon shall propose safeguard measures in advance, in particular firewalls between MSS and GSS to ensure no exchange of competitively sensitive information. Such measures shall be reported to the supervision trustee and approved by MOFCOM before implementation, which is subject to supervision under this decision.

(2) In accordance with MOFCOM's Interim Provisions on Assets of Business Divestiture during the Implementation of Concentrations of Undertakings, Marubeni shall appoint an independent supervision trustee to supervise Marubeni's compliance with the above obligations.

Marubeni shall report to MOFCOM on its compliance with the obligations under item 1 above every six months during the first 24 months after the implementation of this decision. After 24 months, Marubeni may apply to MOFCOM for a waiver of the obligations in item 1 above. Such application shall explain the implementation of the restrictive conditions under this decision and reasons for a waiver of the above

(Continued)

	obligations and provide related evidence. MOFCOM will decide whether to waive the obligations upon request and based on the market conditions.
	For the purpose of fulfilling the above obligations, Marubeni shall propose a detailed work plan to MOFCOM within ten days after the supervision trustee is appointed, and implement such plan after MOFCOM's approval.
	MOFCOM may supervise and examine Marubeni's performance of its obligations through the supervision trustee or on its own. Should Marubeni fail to properly perform its obligations, MOFCOM will address such issues in accordance with the relevant provisions of the AML.
本公告自发布之日起生效。 中华人民共和国商务部 二〇一三年四月二十二日	This decision shall become effective on the date of its announcement. Ministry of Commerce April 22, 2013

MOFCOM Announcement [2013] No. 58 Regarding the Conditional Approval of the Acquisition of Gambro AB by Baxter International Inc.

商务部公告2013年第58号 关于附加限制性条件批准美国百特国际有限公司收购瑞典金宝公司经营者集中反垄断审查决定的公告

(Published on August 13, 2013)

（2013年8月13日公布）

中华人民共和国商务部收到美国百特国际有限公司（Baxter International Inc.，以下简称百特）收购瑞典金宝公司（Gambro AB，以下简称金宝）的经营者集中反垄断申报。经审查，商务部决定附加限制性条件批准此项经营者集中。根据《中华人民共和国反垄断法》（以下简称《反垄断法》）第三十条，现公告如下：

The Ministry of Commerce of the People's Republic of China ("MOFCOM") has received an anti-monopoly notification of a concentration of undertakings regarding the acquisition of Gambro AB ("Gambro") by Baxter International Inc. ("Baxter"). After review, MOFCOM decides to approve this concentration of undertakings under restrictive conditions. This announcement is made as follows in accordance with Article 30 of the Anti-Monopoly Law of the People's Republic of China ("AML"):

一、立案和审查程序

2012年12月31日，商务部收到百特收购金宝经营者集中反垄断申报。经审核，商务部认为该申报文件、资料不完备，要求申报方予以补充。2013年3月12日，商务部确认经补充的申报文件、资料符合《反垄断法》第二十三条的要求，

1 Acceptance and Review Process
On December 31, 2012, MOFCOM received a notification of a concentration of undertakings concerning the acquisition of Gambro AB by Baxter International Inc. Following its review and verifications, MOFCOM believed that the notification materials were incomplete and requested

(Continued)

对此项经营者集中申报予以立案并开始初步审查。4月10日，商务部决定对此项经营者集中实施进一步审查。经进一步审查，商务部认为，此项经营者集中对持续肾脏替代治疗商品（以下简称CRRT系列商品）中的CRRT监测仪、CRRT透析器和CRRT血路管三种商品市场和血液透析系列商品中的血透透析器市场可能具有排除、限制竞争的效果。7月9日，经申报方同意，商务部决定延长进一步审查期限，截止时间为9月7日。 审查过程中，商务部对申报方提交的文件、资料的真实性、完整性和准确性进行了审核，向政府有关部门、相关行业协会、下游客户广泛征求了意见，了解了相关商品情况、行业特征、市场营销状况，听取了业内关于该交易对市场竞争影响的意见。	the notifying party to supplement. On March 12, 2013, MOFCOM confirmed that the notification materials as supplemented satisfied the requirements of Article 23 of the AML, accepted this case, and started a preliminary review. On April 10, MOFCOM decided to conduct a further review of the concentration. After the further review, MOFCOM believed that the concentration may have the effect of eliminating and/or restricting competition in the markets for three continuous renal replacement therapy ("CRRT") products, namely CRRT monitors, CRRT dialyzers, and CRRT bloodlines, and the market for HD dialyzers, one of the hemodialysis products. On July 9, with the consent of the notifying party, MOFCOM decided to extend the period of further review to September 7. During the review, MOFCOM reviewed and verified the authenticity, completeness, and accuracy of the documents and materials submitted by the notifying party, solicited comments from the relevant government departments, trade associations, and downstream customers, collected information about the relevant products, characteristics of the industry, and the marketing conditions, and heard the industry opinions on the competitive effect of this transaction.
二、竞争分析 商务部按照《反垄断法》及配套规定，对此项经营者集中进行了审查，深入分析了此项经营者集中对市场竞争的影响，认为其在CRRT系列商品市场和血透透析器市场可能具有排除、限制竞争的效果。	**2. Competition Analysis** In accordance with the AML and its ancillary rules, MOFCOM reviewed this concentration, conducted an in-depth analysis of its competitive effect, and held that it may have an effect of eliminating and/or restricting competition on the market for CRRT products and the market for HD dialyzers.

(一) 交易概况 收购方百特于1931年在美国注册成立，是纽约证券交易所的上市公司，主要从事治疗血友病、免疫系统紊乱疾病、传染疾病、肾科疾病、创伤和其他慢性及重症病产品的研发、生产与销售业务。被收购方金宝于1942年在瑞典注册成立，是一家跨国医疗技术公司，主要从事肾脏和肝脏透析、骨髓瘤肾治疗、水处理系统以及其他慢性和重症患者的体外疗法产品的研发、生产与销售业务。通过本次交易，百特将间接收购金宝的全部股权，交易完成后，金宝将成为百特的全资子公司。	**(1) Overview of the transaction** The acquirer Baxter was incorporated in the U.S.A. in 1931 and is listed on the New York Stock Exchange. It mainly develops, manufactures, and markets products that treat hemophilia, immune disorders, infectious diseases, kidney disease, trauma, and other chronic and acute medical conditions. The acquired company Gambro is a global medical technology company incorporated in Sweden in 1942. It mainly develops, manufactures, and markets products and therapies for kidney and liver dialysis, myeloma kidney therapy, related water systems, and other extracorporeal therapies for chronic and acute patients. Through this transaction, Baxter will indirectly acquire all the equity interest in Gambro, and post-transaction, Gambro will become a wholly owned subsidiary of Baxter.
(二) 相关市场 交易双方在CRRT系列商品和血液透析系列商品上存在横向业务重叠。 CRRT系列商品又称床旁血滤设备，通常适用于医院重症监护病房中有生命危险的急性肾脏功能损伤患者，CRRT系列商品包括CRRT监测仪、CRRT透析器、CRRT血路管、CRRT导管、CRRT液剂。 血液透析设备主要用于治疗急性常规肾损伤以及慢性肾病，血液透析系列商品包括血透监测仪、血透透析器、血透血路管、血透导管和血透液剂。商务部考察了CRRT系列商品和血液透析系列商品在价格、治疗侧重点、适用对象等需求方面的因素，同时也考虑了这两类商品的技术特征、商品提供所需知识产权及转产的难易程度等供给方面的因素，	**(2) Relevant Markets** The parties to the transaction have horizontal overlaps in CRRT products and HD products. CRRT products, also known as bedside hemofiltration devices, are normally used in ICUs to treat critical patients with acute kidney injury. CRRT products include CRRT monitors, CRRT dialyzers, CRRT bloodlines, CRRT catheters, and CRRT fluids. Hemodialysis devices are mainly used to treat non-critical acute kidney injury and chronic kidney disease. Hemodialysis products include HD monitors, HD dialyzers, HD bloodlines, HD catheters, and HD fluids. MOFCOM considered demand-side factors such as price, treatment focus, and applicable patients of the CRRT products and HD products and also considered supply-side factors such as technical characteristics, necessary IP rights, and difficulties in production switch

(Continued)

确认CRRT系列商品和血液透析系列商品分别构成独立的系列相关商品市场，其中重点审查了CRRT系列商品中的CRRT监测仪市场、CRRT透析器市场和CRRT血路管市场，以及血透透析器市场。 商务部考察了CRRT系列商品和血透系列商品在关税、运输成本、进出口情况及贸易现状等方面的因素，认为需要从全球范围分析本项交易对市场竞争的影响，同时考察了此交易可能对中国境内市场竞争的影响。	of these two groups of products. MOFCOM held that CRRT products and HD products constitute separate markets. MOFCOM focused its review on the markets for CRRT monitors, CRRT dialyzers, and CRRT bloodlines as well as the market for HD dialyzers. MOFCOM considered factors such as tariffs, transportation costs, import and export and trading conditions in respect of CRRT products and HD products. It believed that a worldwide level analysis is necessary to assess the competitive effect of this transaction, and at the same time, it assessed the likely competitive effect of this transaction on the Chinese market.
(三) 竞争评估 商务部依据相关市场的市场份额、市场集中度、市场控制力、市场进入等因素，对CRRT监测仪、CRRT血路管、CRRT透析器和血透透析器市场可能产生的影响进行了评估。 1、　交易导致CRRT系列商品市场集中度进一步提高。无论是在全球还是中国境内，交易前，CRRT系列商品市场集中度已经很高。在全球CRRT监测仪、CRRT血路管和CRRT透析器市场，交易前市场集中度指数(HHI)分别为3612、3162和2908；交易后HHI指数分别为4410、3798和4108，市场集中度指数增量（△HHI）分别达到798、636和1200。在中国境内CRRT监测仪、CRRT血路管和CRRT透析器市场，交易前HHI指数分别为2738、3702和4506；交易后HHI指数分别为3942、7158和6426，集中度增量（△HHI）分别达到1204、3456和1920。	**(3) Competition Assessment** Based on market shares, level of market concentration, market power, market entry, and other factors, MOFCOM assessed the likely effects of this concentration on the markets for CRRT monitors, CRRT bloodlines, CRRT dialyzers, and HD dialyzers. **(i) The transaction would further raise the level of concentration in the market for CRRT products.** Both at the worldwide and China levels, the pre-transaction market for CRRT products is already highly concentrated. In the global markets for CRRT monitors, CRRT bloodlines, and CRRT dialyzers, the pre-transaction HHIs are 3612, 3162, and 2908, respectively, the post-transaction HHIs are 4410, 3798, and 4108, respectively, and the increases in HHIs are 798, 636, and 1200, respectively. In the Chinese markets for CRRT monitors, CRRT bloodlines, and CRRT dialyzers, the pre-transaction HHIs are 2738, 3702, and 4506, respectively, the post-transaction HHIs are 3942, 7158, and 6426, respectively, and the increases in HHIs are 1204, 3456, and 1920, respectively.

2、 交易使收购方在CRRT系列商品市场拥有支配地位。交易前，集中双方在CRRT系列商品市场互为主要竞争者。2012年，在全球范围内，集中双方在CRRT监测仪市场的合计份额为64%（百特7%、金宝57%），在CRRT血路管市场的合计份额为59%（百特6%、金宝53%），在CRRT透析器市场的合计份额为62%（百特12%、金宝50%）；在中国境内，集中双方在CRRT监测仪市场的合计份额为57%（百特14%、金宝43%），在CRRT血路管市场的合计份额为84%（百特36%、金宝48%），在CRRT透析器市场的合计份额为79%（百特15%、金宝64%）。其他竞争者的市场份额均较小，对市场竞争影响有限。本交易消除了CRRT系列商品市场中的主要竞争者，使百特拥有较强的市场控制力，对市场竞争产生不利影响。

3、 交易增加了中国血透透析器市场企业间相互协调、限制竞争的可能性。2012年，在中国血透透析器市场上，尼普洛株式会社（以下简称尼普洛）的市场份额为26%，金宝为19%，百特为3%。交易前，百特的血透透析器产品由尼普洛代工生产。交易后，百特将拥有金宝既有的血透透析器生产能力和销售网络，与尼普洛一起成为中国血透透析器市场的两个主要竞争者，两者市场份额合计达到48%。百特与尼普洛签署的代工协议中包含生产成本、生产数量等竞争性信息，两者之间代工关系的存续便于双方相互协调，限制市场竞争。

(ii) The transaction would create a dominant position for the acquirer in the market for CRRT products. Before the transaction, the parties are each other's main competitors in the market for CRRT products. In 2012, the parties had a combined global market share of 64% (Baxter 7% and Gambro 57%) in the CRRT monitor market, 59% (Baxter 6% and Gambro 53%) in the CRRT bloodline market, and 62% (Baxter 12% and Gambro 50%) in the CRRT dialyzer market. In China, the parties had a combined market share of 57% (Baxter 14% and Gambro 43%) in the CRRT monitor market, 84% (Baxter 36% and Gambro 48%) in the CRRT bloodline market, and 79% (Baxter 15% and Gambro 64%) in the CRRT dialyzer market. Other competitors all had small market shares with limited competitive influence. This transaction would eliminate a main competitor in the market for CRRT products, creating strong market power for Baxter and resulting in adverse competitive effects.

(iii) The transaction would increase the possibility for HD dialyzer suppliers in China to coordinate and restrict competition. In 2012, in the Chinese HD dialyzer market, Nipro Corporation ("Nipro") had a market share of 26%, Gambro 19%, and Baxter 3%. Before the transaction, Baxter's HD dialyzers were manufactured by Nipro through an OEM agreement. After the transaction, Baxter would acquire Gambro's existing production capacity and distribution network for HD dialyzers, and become a major competitor in the Chinese HD dialyzer market along with Nipro, their combined market share reaching 48%. The OEM agreement between Baxter and Nipro contains competitive information such as production cost and manufacture quantities. The continuation of the OEM relationship

(*Continued*)

	between Baxter and Nipro can facilitate coordination between the two parties and restrict competition.
商务部调查认为，CRRT系列商品和血液透析系列商品市场进入存在一定障碍。首先，进入血透系列商品或CRRT系列商品市场需要较长的时间和较高的成本，包括较高的生产、研发资本投入和构建销售网络。其次，拥有相应的专利和知识产权是进入该市场并保持生存的重要条件。另外，各国对上述商品均有严格的市场准入限制，相关商品需要达到一定的技术质量标准才能获得相应资质。在中国境内从事相关业务需获得国家食品药品监督管理总局批准。	After review, MOFCOM found that there are certain entry barriers in the markets for CRRT products and hemodialysis products. First, it requires a long time and high costs to enter the markets for CRRT products and hemodialysis products, including considerable production and R&D investment as well as establishment of distribution networks. Secondly, it is critical to possess relevant patents and IP rights in order to enter into and survive in these markets. Lastly, every country has set market access restrictions for these products, and qualifications require the relevant products to meet certain technology and quality standards. The approval from China Food and Drug Administration must be obtained before one can engage in the relevant business in China.
三、附加限制性条件的商谈 在初步审查阶段，申报方向商务部表示该项集中可能存在竞争问题，并提交了相应的解决方案。在进一步审查阶段，商务部向申报方指出了此项经营者集中可能具有的排除、限制竞争的效果，并要求申报方根据商务部指出的竞争问题，对其提出的解决方案进行修改完善。经过多轮商谈，2013年6月20日，集中双方向商务部提交了最终解决方案。经评估，商务部认为，该方案能够减少此项经营者集中对竞争产生的不利影响。	**3. Negotiation of Restrictive Conditions** During the preliminary review, the notifying party indicated to MOFCOM that the concentration may raise competition concerns and proposed solutions. During the further review, MOFCOM pointed out to the notifying party the concentration's likely effect of eliminating and/or restricting competition and requested the notifying party to amend and improve its proposal according to the competition concerns raised by MOFCOM. Through several rounds of negotiations, the parties to the concentration submitted the final remedy proposal to MOFCOM on June 20, 2013. After evaluation, MOFCOM believes that the proposal could mitigate the concentration's adverse competitive effects.

四、审查决定

审查认为，百特收购金宝对CRRT系列商品市场和血透系列商品中的血透透析器市场可能产生排除、限制竞争的效果，商务部决定附加限制性条件批准此项经营者集中。百特和金宝应履行如下义务：

（一）百特剥离其全球的CRRT业务，包括确保剥离业务存活性和竞争力所需的有形资产和无形资产。

（二）2016年3月31日前，百特在中国境内终止尼普洛代工生产协议（本决定公布时已经存在的客户合同或其他法律法规项下的供应义务除外）。

（三）限制性条件的监督执行除按照本公告办理外，《百特国际有限公司拟议收购金宝公司交易的救济承诺》（见附件）对百特具有同样法律约束力。百特应根据商务部《关于实施经营者集中资产或业务剥离的暂行规定》的要求，委托监督受托人对其履行本决定项下义务情况进行监督。

百特应在本公告发布之日起每季度结束后的15天内，向商务部书面报告业务剥离义务履行情况；在本公告发布之日起每日历年度结束后45天内，向商务部书面报告尼普洛代工生产协议逐步终止义务履行情况。

为履行上述义务，交易双方应当在监督受托人确定后，尽快提交履行上述义务的详细操作方案，报商务部批准后实施。

本公告自发布之日起生效。

4. Review Decision

After review, MOFCOM found that Baxter's acquisition of Gambro may have the effect of eliminating and/or restricting competition in the market for CRRT products and the market for HD dialyzers. MOFCOM decides to approve this concentration under conditions and requires Baxter and Gambro to fulfill the following obligations:

(1) Baxter shall divest its global CRRT business, including the tangible and intangible assets which are necessary to ensure the viability and competitiveness of the divestment business;

(2) Baxter shall terminate its OEM agreement with Nipro with respect to China by March 31, 2016 (except for customer contracts or other legal or regulatory supply obligations existing at the time of this decision);

(3) The monitoring and implementation of the restrictive conditions shall comply with this announcement, and Baxter is also legally bound by the Remedy Proposal Regarding the Proposed Acquisition of Gambro AB by Baxter International Inc. (attached). Baxter shall, in accordance with MOFCOM's Provisional Provisions on Assets or Business Divestiture during the Implementation of Concentrations of Undertakings, engage a monitoring trustee to supervise the fulfillment of its obligations under this decision.

Within 15 days after the end of each quarter following this announcement, Baxter shall report to MOFCOM in writing on its fulfillment of the divestiture obligation. Within 45 days after the end of each calendar year following this announcement, Baxter

(Continued)

	shall report to MOFCOM in writing on its fulfilment of the obligation to gradually terminate the OEM agreement with Nipro.

For the fulfillment of the above obligations, the parties shall, after the appointment of the monitoring trustee, submit a detailed implementation plan as soon as possible, and implement the plan after MOFCOM's approval.

This decision shall become effective as of the date of its announcement. |
| 中华人民共和国商务部
2013年8月8日 | Ministry of Commerce
August 8, 2013 |
| 附件：百特国际有限公司拟议收购金宝公司交易的救济承诺 | Attachment: Remedy Proposal Regarding the Proposed Acquisition of Gambro AB by Baxter International Inc. |

美国百特国际有限公司拟收购瑞典金宝公司的交易救济承诺方案

Remedy Proposal Regarding the Proposed Acquisition of Gambro AB by Baxter International Inc.

	Content
根据《中华人民共和国反垄断法》、商务部《关于实施经营者集中资产或业务剥离的暂行规定》及其他相关商务部规定，美国百特国际有限公司 (Baxter International Inc.，以下简称百特) 就百特拟收购瑞典金宝公司 (Gambro AB，以下简称金宝) 的交易 ("本交易")，向商务部提议如下救济承诺方案 (以下简称救济方案)。	In accordance with the Anti-Monopoly Law of the PRC, MOF-COM's Interim Provisions on Asset or Business Divesture during the Implementation of Concentrations of Undertakings, and other relevant MOFCOM rules, Baxter International Inc. ("Baxter") proposes this Remedy Proposal (the "Remedy Proposal") in connection with Baxter's proposed acquisition of Gambro AB ("Gambro") (the "Transaction").
第一章 定义	**Section A Definitions**
以下词语在本救济方案中具有以下含义: 关联企业:百特控制的企业。 百特:根据美国特拉华州法律成立的美国百特国际有限公司 (Baxter International Inc.)，其注册地址为 One Baxter Parkway, Deerfield, Illinois 60015, U.S.A. (美国伊利诺伊州迪尔费尔德)。	The following terms shall have the following meaning in this Remedy Proposal: **Affiliated Undertakings**: undertakings controlled by Baxter. **Baxter**: Baxter International Inc. incorporated under the laws of the State of Delaware, with registered office at

(Continued)

第一章 定义	**Section A Definitions**
交割:将剥离业务的法定所有权转让给买方。	One Baxter Parkway, Deerfield, Illinois 60015, U.S.A.
CRRT:持续性肾脏替代治疗(英文为 "Continuous Renal Replacement Therapy")。	**Closing**: the transfer of the legal title of the Divestment Business to the Purchaser.
条件:商务部就百特拟收购金宝的交易公告中附加的限制性条件。	**CRRT**: continuous renal replacement therapy.
决定:商务部就百特拟收购金宝的交易做出的附加限制性条件批准经营者集中的决定。	**Conditions:** Conditions imposed by MOFCOM in its announcement in relation to Baxter's proposed acquisition of Gambro.
剥离业务:第二章定义的百特的CRRT业务。	**Decision:** Decision for Conditional Approval of Concentration of Business Operators promulgated by MOFCOM in relation to Baxter's proposed acquisition of Gambro.
剥离受托人:一个或一个以上独立于交易双方的自然人或法人,经商务部批准由百特委托,并获得百特的排他性剥离受托人授权委托协议。	**Divestment Business:** Baxter's CRRT business as defined in Section B.
剥离受托人委托协议:百特授予剥离受托人向买方出售剥离业务的排他性委托协议。	**Divestiture Trustee:** one or more natural or legal person(s), independent from the Parties, approved by MOFCOM and appointed by Baxter, and who has (have) received from Baxter the exclusive Divestiture Trustee Mandate.
生效日:决定做出之日。	**Divestiture Trustee Mandate:** an exclusive mandate granted by Baxter to the Divestiture Trustee to sell the Divestment Business to the Purchaser.
首个剥离期:百特收购金宝交易的交割日起六个月,经申请,可延长至九个月。	**Effective Date**: the date of adoption of the Decision.
保持业务独立管理人:百特为剥离业务指定的、在监督受托人监督之下管理日常业务的人。	**First Divestiture Period**: the period of six months from the closing of Baxter's acquisition of Gambro, which upon application can be extended to nine months.
主要人员:维持剥离业务存活性和竞争性所必需的人员。	**Hold Separate Manager**: the person appointed by Baxter for the Divestment Business to manage the day-to-day business under the supervision of the Monitoring Trustee.
监督受托人:一个或一个以上独立于交易双方的自然人或法人,经商务部批准并由百特委托,承担监督百特遵守决定规定的条件和义务的职责。	**Key Personnel**: the personnel necessary to maintain the viability and competitiveness of the Divestment Business.
尼普洛:日本尼普洛株式会社(英文名为 "Nipro Corporation"),一家依据日本法律成立的公司。	
尼普洛代工生产协议:由百特医疗用品公司(英文名为 "Baxter Healthcare Corporation")与尼普洛签署的自2013年4月1日起生效的《供应商产成品购买协议》。	

双方:百特和金宝。	**Monitoring Trustee**: one or more natural or legal person(s), independent from the Parties, approved by MOFCOM and appointed by Baxter, and who has (have) the duty to monitor Baxter's compliance with the conditions and obligations attached to the Decision.
人员:剥离业务目前雇佣的所有专属人员。	
买方:根据第四章规定的标准,商务部批准收购剥离业务的实体。	
终止:在中国境内(就本救济承诺方案而言,不包括台湾地区、香港特区和澳门特区),尼普洛代工生产协议在其3年期限到期时终止。	**Nipro**: Nipro Corporation, established under the laws of Japan.
	Nipro OEM Agreement: the Supplier–Produced Finished Goods Purchase Agreement entered into between Baxter Healthcare Corporation and Nipro effective April 1, 2013.
终止日:2016年3月31日。	
受托人:监督受托人和/或剥离受托人。	**Parties**: Baxter and Gambro.
	Personnel: all dedicated personnel currently employed in the Divestment Business.
受托人剥离期:首个剥离期结束后六个月。	
	Purchaser: the entity approved by MOFCOM as acquirer of the Divestment Business in accordance with the criteria set out in Section D.
	Termination: Termination of the Nipro OEM Agreement with respect to China (excluding Taiwan, Hong Kong, and Macao for the purpose of this Remedy Proposal) upon expiry of the three-year term of the Nipro OEM Agreement.
	Termination Date: March 31, 2016.
	Trustee(s): the Monitoring Trustee and/or the Divestiture Trustee.
	Trustee Divestiture Period: the period of six months from the end of the First Divestiture Period.
第二章 剥离业务	**Section B The Divestment Business**
1. 剥离业务为百特全球的CRRT业务。 2. 按照买方选择,剥离业务包括以下部分: (1) 有形资产: 剥离业务使用或持有的所有CRRT产品、零部件、物料、 材料及其他存货,	1. The Divestment Business consists of Baxter's worldwide CRRT business. 2. The Divestment Business includes, at the option of the Purchaser: (1) tangible assets: all CRRT products, parts, supplies, materials, and other inventories to the extent used or held for the

(*Continued*)

第二章 剥离业务	**Section B The Divestment Business**
以及安放在任何客户或其他监测仪用户处的由百特所有的监测仪。 (2) 无形资产： 百特持有的(除下文第三点提及的专利外)专门用于CRRT产品在全球的开发、生产和/或销售的所有知识产权和专有技术，包括： • Accusol、Monosol、Aquarius、Aqualine、Aquamax、Aquaspike、Aquaset、Aquastream和Aquasmart以及Aquadrain、Aqua Plus和Aqua+的商标； • 百特于2009年从爱德华生命科学公司(以下简称爱德华)取得的专利，以及百特在收购爱德华之前持有的专门用于CRRT的专利； • 不可撤销的、永久性的免费许可，在CRRT领域内，使用百特最初设计用于腹膜透析液的、但由于范围宽泛还在液剂和出售液剂的包装袋(也称作容器)方面涵盖Accusol的专利； • 有关百特CRRT业务的版权，包括信息手册和网站内容； • 液剂Accusol、Monosol和乳酸盐的生产专有技术，以及取得相关生产批准的专有技术。该等相关专有技术包含在设计历史文档、技术文档、图纸、产品规格、生产流程描述、验证文件、包装规格和质量管控标准内； • 与更新Accusol配方项目有关的文件，即在开发项目期间产生的所有相关数据。百特还将根据买方的意愿，提供与剥离的Accusol拟议项目的转让有关的所有合理技术援助，以便于买方可以成功的、无延迟地继续拟议产品的开发； (3) 许可、批准和授权： • 转让(如果在法律上不可能，则提供适当的途径使用)百特持有的有关剥离业务的所有当前和未决的CE标志，包括有关剥离业务的当前和未决的CE标志的所有百特可以取得的相关卷宗，并在必要时，	Divestment Business as well as the monitors placed with any customers or other user of the monitors owned by Baxter. (2) intangible assets: all IP rights that are held by Baxter and, except in the case of the patents referred to in the third bullet point below, used exclusively with respect to the development, manufacture, and/or sale of CRRT products worldwide and know-how, including: • the trademarks Accusol, Monosol, Aquarius, Aqualine, Aquamax, Aquaspike, Aquaset, Aquastream, and Aquasmart, as well as Aquadrain, Aqua Plus, and Aqua+; • patents that Baxter acquired from Edwards Lifesciences A.G. ("Edwards") in 2009, and patents that Baxter held before the acquisition of Edwards targeted specifically at CRRT; • an irrevocable, perpetual, and royalty-free license for patents that were originally designed by Baxter for PD solutions, but are formulated broad enough so that they also cover Accusol relating to fluids and bags (also referred to as containers) in which the fluids are sold, for use in the CRRT field; • copyrights related to its CRRT business, covering, *inter alia*, information booklets and website content; • production know-how for the manufacture of the fluids Accusol, Monosol, and lactate as well as know-how associated with obtaining the relevant production approvals. The relevant know-how is embodied in design history files, technical files, drawings, product specifications, manufacturing process descriptions, validation documentation, packaging specifications, and quality control standards;

就任何必要的监管申报和必要的授权，向买方提供合理协助；

- 转让（如果在法律上不可能，则提供适当的途径使用）百特持有的、任何政府机构签发的、对于生产和/或销售剥离业务产品所必须的所有许可、批准及授权，包括当前或未决授权的所有百特可以取得的相关卷宗，并且在必要时，在向买方转让剥离业务的相关许可、批准及授权方面，向买方提供合理协助，就任何必要的监管申报和必要的授权，向买方提供合理协助；

(4) 合同、协议、租约、承诺和谅解：

- 百特将尽最大努力，使买方能与日机装（Nikkiso）达成从日机装购买Aquarius监测仪（及附属产品如零部件）的协议，如无法达成这些安排，百特已准备好与买方签订背靠背供应协议，以保证买方能在合理的成本加成基础上获得该等监测仪；
- 百特将尽最大努力，使买方能与贝尔克公司（Bellco S.r.l.）和明泰科公司（Minntech）达成购买透析器的协议，与Haemotronic公司（Haemotronic S.r.l.）达成购买血路管和附属产品（如废液袋、接合器、注射器等）的协议，与Medical Components公司达成购买导管的协议，以及达成其他关于剥离业务的任何关键的供应协议。如无法达成这些安排，百特已准备好与买方签订背靠背供应协议，以保证买方能在合理的成本加成基础上获得这些产品；
- 百特将转让给买方分销协议或分销协议中有关CRRT的部分。如无法达成这些安排，百特已准备好与买方签订背靠背分销协议，在合理的成本加成基础上为买方分销产品；

(5) 客户、信贷和其他记录：
百特与客户签订的关于剥离业务产品的现有合同（在经过客户同意后转让），

documentation relating to the updated Accusol formulation project, i.e., all relevant data generated during the development project. Baxter will also provide, at the option of the Purchaser, all reasonable technical assistance to the Purchaser in relation to the transfer of the divested Accusol pipeline project for the Purchaser successfully to continue the development of the new pipeline product without delay;

(3) licenses, permits, and authorizations:

- transfer of, or if not legally possible, access to, as appropriate, all current and pending CE marks relating to the Divestment Business held by Baxter, including all relevant dossiers relating to the current or pending CE marks relating to the Divestment Business available to Baxter, and where necessary, reasonable assistance to the Purchaser to make any necessary regulatory filings and obtain necessary authorizations;
- transfer of, or, if not legally possible, access to, as appropriate, all licenses, permits, and authorizations issued by any governmental organization and held by Baxter that are necessary to manufacture and/or sell the products belonging to the Divestment Business, including any relevant dossiers relating to current or pending authorizations available to Baxter and, where necessary, reasonable assistance related to the transfer to the Purchaser of such licenses, permits, and authorizations concerning the Divestment Business, and providing reasonable assistance to the Purchaser to make any necessary regulatory filings and obtain any necessary authorizations;

(*Continued*)

第二章 剥离业务	**Section B The Divestment Business**
以及百特的CRRT客户名单和与CRRT产品有关的客户记录。如果客户不同意这一转让，百特将与买方达成背靠背安排，在合理的成本加成基础上，由买方向百特供货，确保百特可以履行其剩余的义务； (6) 以下人员（包括主要人员）：目前从事剥离业务的人员，包括(i)专属CRRT生产的技师/工程师，(ii)研发/监管人员，和(iii)营销和销售人员。截至2013年4月，这些人员包括亚太区的约30名员工、欧盟和瑞士的17名员工，以及拉丁美洲的4名员工。除非当地法律有禁止规定，百特会确保这些员工转聘至买方。 3. 剥离业务不包括： • 任何研发设施； • 任何生产性资产； • 百特CRRT业务部门的常驻美国的全球主管(一位营销员工) 4. 为了帮助剥离业务顺利过渡，百特承诺，根据买方意愿，在一段过渡期内，安排百特或关联企业提供以下产品或服务： • 百特已准备好按照与买方商定的合理成本加成的基础，按照良好的行业惯例，与买方签订Accusol和Monosol液剂和乳酸盐的委托生产协议； • 百特已准备好根据一个过渡服务协议，按合理报酬向买方提供某些过渡服务。根据买方的选择，该等服务包括(i)人力资源功能(例如人力资源支持、薪水册、养老金管理)；(ii)财务功能(例如银行业务、供应商付款、信贷、增值税、财政、税务、内部审计、法定会计)；(iii)信息技术(例如电子邮件、企业管理软件、服务支持、服务器托管、电信等)；(iv)销售和客户支持功能(例如客户服务支持、	(4) contracts, agreements, leases, commitments, and understandings: • Baxter will use its best efforts to enable the Purchaser to conclude agreements with Nikkiso to purchase from Nikkiso the Aquarius monitor (and ancillary products (e.g., spare parts)). In the event that such arrangements cannot be made, Baxter is prepared to conclude back-to-back supply agreements with the Purchaser to ensure that such monitors will be available to the Purchaser on a reasonable cost-plus basis; • Baxter will use its best efforts to enable the Purchaser to conclude agreements with Bellco S.r.l. and Minntech to purchase dialyzers, with Haemotronic S.r.l. to purchase bloodlines and ancillary products (e.g., drainage bags, adaptors, syringes etc.), and with Medical Components, Inc., to purchase catheters, as well as any and all other key supply agreements relating to the Divestment Business. In the event that such arrangements cannot be made, Baxter is prepared to conclude back-to-back supply agreements with the Purchaser to ensure that such products will be available to the Purchaser on a reasonable cost-plus basis; • transfer of distribution agreements or of the CRRT part of such agreements to the Purchaser. In the event that such arrangements cannot be made, Baxter is prepared to conclude back-to-back distribution agreements with the Purchaser to distribute products for the Purchaser on a reasonable cost-plus basis; (5) customer, credit, and other records: Baxter's existing contracts with customers relating to the products belonging to the Divestment Business with the consent of the customers, and Baxter's CRRT

零部件订货处、客户支持服务帮助台、库存管理等）；以及（v）其他行政功能（例如保险、法律和出口合规、差旅服务等）。

5. 为了实现剥离，百特承诺在首个剥离期内与买方签订出售剥离业务的买卖协议。如百特未能在首个剥离期结束前签订该协议，百特应授予剥离受托人排他性的委托，以在受托人剥离期内出售剥离业务。

customer list and customer records as they relate to CRRT products. In case a customer would not agree to a transfer, a back-to-back arrangement on a reasonable cost-plus basis to be agreed with the Purchaser will be entered into under which the Purchaser supplies Baxter to ensure that Baxter can fulfill its remaining obligations;

(6) the following Personnel including Key Personnel:

Personnel currently working in the Divestment Business, including (i) technicians/engineers dedicated to CRRT production, (ii) R&D/regulatory personnel, and (iii) marketing and sales staff. As of April 2013, these include approximately 30 employees in the Asia-Pacific region, 17 employees in the European Union and Switzerland, and four employees in Latin America. Baxter will ensure that these employees will be transferred to the Purchaser unless prohibited by local laws.

3. The Divestment Business shall not include:
- any R&D facilities;
- any production assets;
- Baxter's CRRT business unit's global director, a marketing person based in the U.S.

4. To facilitate a smooth transition of the Divestment Business, Baxter commits to provide the arrangements for the supply with the following products or services by Baxter or Affiliated Undertakings for a transitional period at the discretion of the Purchaser:
- Baxter is prepared to conclude a contract manufacturing agreement for Accusol and Monosol fluids and lactate with the Purchaser on a reasonable cost-plus basis to be agreed with the Purchaser, and in accordance with good industry practice;

(*Continued*)

第二章 剥离业务	Section B **The Divestment Business**
	• Baxter is prepared to provide certain transitional services to the Purchaser pursuant to a transition services agreement against a reasonable compensation. At the Purchaser's option, such services would cover (i) HR functions (e.g., HR support, payroll, pensions administration); (ii) finance functions (e.g., banking, supplier payments, credit roll, VAT, treasury, tax, internal audit, and statutory accounting); (iii) IT (e.g., email, business management software, helpdesk, server hosting, telecoms etc.); (iv) sales and customer support functions (e.g., customer service support, order desk for spare parts, customer support services helpdesk, stock management etc.); and (v) other administrative functions (e.g., insurance, legal, and export compliance, travel services etc.). 5. To carry out the divestiture, Baxter commits to enter into a sale and purchase agreement with the Purchaser for the sale of the Divestment Business within the First Divestiture Period. If Baxter has not entered into such an agreement at the end of the First Divestiture Period, Baxter shall grant the Divestiture Trustee an exclusive mandate to sell the Divestment Business within the Trustee Divestiture Period.
第三章 相关承诺	Section C **Related Commitments**
维持存活性、可销售性和竞争性 6. 自生效日起直至交割为止，百特应根据良好业务惯例，维持剥离业务的经济存活性、可销售性和竞争性，并尽可能地把剥离业务失去竞争潜质的任何风险降至最低。具体来说，百特承诺： (a) 不自行采取可能对剥离业务的价值、管理或竞争力产生重大不利影响的，	Preservation of viability, marketability, and competitiveness 6. From the Effective Date until Closing, Baxter shall preserve the economic viability, marketability, and competitiveness of the Divestment Business, in accordance with good business practice, and shall minimize as far as possible any risk of loss of competitive potential

或者可能改变剥离业务经营
活动的性质和范围或行业或
商业战略或投资政策的任何
行为；

(b) 按照当前及延续的业务
计划，为剥离业务的发
展提供充足资源；

(c) 采取所有合理措施，包括适
当的激励计划（基于行业惯
例），以鼓励所有主要人员
留在剥离业务内。

双方保持独立的义务

7. 百特承诺，自生效日起至交割为
止，保持剥离业务与其保留业务
的分离，并确保剥离业务的主要
人员——包括保持业务独立管理
人——没有参与任何保留业务，反
之亦然。百特还应确保人员不向剥
离业务以外的任何个人报告。

8. 在交割之前，百特应协助监督受
托人确保剥离业务作为与百特保
留业务分离的一个单独的和可销
售的实体予以管理。百特应任命
在监督受托人监督下的负责管理
剥离业务及保持业务独立管理
人。保持业务独立管理人应独立
地管理剥离业务，并符合业务的
最大利益，以确保其持续经济存
活性、可销售性、竞争性及与双
方所保留业务的独立性。

绝缘防范

9. 百特应落实所有必要措施，以确
保其在生效日后，不会取得有关
剥离业务的任何商业秘密、专有
技术、商业信息或其他任何具有
保密或专有性质的信息。特别
是，应在不损害剥离业务存活性
的前提下，尽可能分离剥离业务
在中心信息技术网络的参与。百
特可取得有关出售剥离业务合理
所需的或法律要求向百特披露的
信息。

10. 相应地，百特应确保在其收
购金宝之后，剥离业务不会
取得有关金宝的CRRT业务的
任何商业秘密、专有技术、

of the Divestment Business. In particular Baxter undertakes:

(a) not to carry out any act upon its own authority that might have a significant adverse impact on the value, management, or competitiveness of the Divestment Business or that might alter the nature and scope of activity, or the industrial or commercial strategy or the investment policy of the Divestment Business;

(b) to make available sufficient resources for the development of the Divestment Business, on the basis and continuation of the existing business plans;

(c) to take all reasonable steps, including appropriate incentive schemes (based on industry practice), to encourage all Key Personnel to remain with the Divestment Business.

Hold-separate obligations of the Parties

7. Baxter commits, from the Effective Date until Closing, to keep the Divestment Business separate from the businesses it is retaining and to ensure that Key Personnel of the Divestment Business—including the Hold Separate Manager—have no involvement in any business retained and vice versa. Baxter shall also ensure that the Personnel do not report to any individual outside the Divestment Business.

8. Until Closing, Baxter shall assist the Monitoring Trustee in ensuring that the Divestment Business is managed as a distinct and saleable entity separate from the businesses retained by Baxter. Baxter shall appoint a Hold Separate Manager who shall be responsible for the management of the Divestment Business, under the supervision

(Continued)

第三章 相关承诺	Section C Related Commitments

商业信息或其他任何具有保密或专有性质的信息。
 	
禁止诱聘条款
 	
11. 百特承诺，在符合常规限制的前提下，在交割后两年内，不诱聘（并促使关联企业不诱聘）与剥离业务一起转让的主要人员。
 	
尽职调查
 	
12. 为了使潜在买方能对剥离业务进行合理尽职调查，在符合常规保密性保护的前提下，根据剥离程序所处的阶段，百特应：
  (a) 向潜在买方提供有关剥离业务的充足信息；
  (b) 向潜在买方提供有关人员的充足信息，允许他们合理接触人员。
 	
报告
 	
13. 百特应在生效日后每个月结束后十天内（或在商务部另行要求的期限内），向商务部和监督受托人书面报告有关剥离业务潜在买方和与该潜在买方谈判的情况。
14. 百特应提供其他商务部或监督受托人要求的任何信息和更新内容。
	of the Monitoring Trustee. The Hold Separate Manager shall manage the Divestment Business independently and in the best interest of the business with a view to ensuring its continued economic viability, marketability, and competitiveness and its independence from the businesses retained by the Parties.
	
	Ring-fencing
	9. Baxter shall implement all necessary measures to ensure that it does not after the Effective Date obtain any business secrets, know-how, commercial information, or any other information of a confidential or proprietary nature relating to the Divestment Business. In particular, the participation of the Divestment Business in a central information technology network shall be severed to the extent possible, without compromising the viability of the Divestment Business. Baxter may obtain information which is reasonably necessary for the divestiture of the Divestment Business or whose disclosure to Baxter is required by law.
	10. Conversely, Baxter shall see to it that, following its acquisition of Gambro, the Divestment Business does not obtain any business secrets, know-how, commercial information, or any other information of a confidential or proprietary nature relating to Gambro's CRRT business.
	
	Non-solicitation clause
	11. Baxter undertakes, subject to customary limitations, not to solicit, and to procure that Affiliated Undertakings do not solicit, the Key Personnel transferred with the Divestment

<table>
<tr>
<td></td>
<td>Business for a period of two years after Closing.

Due diligence

12. In order to enable potential purchasers to carry out a reasonable due diligence of the Divestment Business, Baxter shall, subject to customary confidentiality assurances and dependent on the stage of the divestiture process:

(a) provide to potential purchasers sufficient information as regards the Divestment Business;

(b) provide to potential purchasers sufficient information relating to the Personnel and allow them reasonable access to the Personnel.

Reporting

13. Baxter shall submit written reports on potential purchasers of the Divestment Business and the status of negotiations with such potential purchasers to MOFCOM and the Monitoring Trustee no later than ten days after the end of every month following the Effective Date (or otherwise at MOFCOM's request).

14. Baxter shall provide any and all other information and updates as requested by MOFCOM or the Monitoring Trustee.</td>
</tr>
<tr>
<td>第四章 买方</td>
<td>**Section D The Purchaser**</td>
</tr>
<tr>
<td>15. 为确保有效竞争的迅速恢复，以获得商务部的批准，买方必须符合以下条件：

(a) 买方必须独立于双方；

(b) 买方必须具有财务资源、可靠专长与动机以维持并发展剥离业务，具有活力的、积极的竞争力量，能够与双方及其他竞争者展开竞争；以及</td>
<td>15. In order to ensure the immediate restoration of effective competition, the Purchaser, in order to be approved by MOFCOM, must:

(a) be independent from the Parties;

(b) have the financial resources, proven expertise, and incentive to maintain and develop the Divestment Business as a viable and active competitive force in</td>
</tr>
</table>

(Continued)

第三章 相关承诺	Section C Related Commitments
(c) 根据商务部掌握的信息，买方不会造成明显的竞争问题，特别是买方须合理期待可就对剥离业务的收购获得相关主管机构的所有必要批准(有关买方的上述标准以下称为"买方要求")。 16. 百特与买方之间的买卖协议应以商务部对买方身份和与买方的买卖协议条款的批准为前提条件，并且如果在商务部批准之前就已经达成买卖协议，买卖协议应允许对其条款(包括剥离业务范围)的修改。当百特已与某潜在买方达成买卖协议，百特应向商务部提交该协议。 17. 百特必须能够向商务部证明，并且商务部应核实，买方符合买方要求并且剥离业务将以符合条件的方式出售。如果剥离业务在出售后的存活性和竞争性不受影响(将拟定买方纳入考虑)，商务部可以批准排除某一项或多项资产或者部分人员出售剥离业务。	competition with the Parties and other competitors; (c) neither be likely to create, in the light of the information available to MOFCOM, prima facie competition concerns, and must, in particular, reasonably be expected to obtain all necessary approvals from the relevant regulatory authorities for the acquisition of the Divestment Business (the before-mentioned criteria for the Purchaser, hereafter the "Purchaser Requirements"). 16. The sale and purchase agreement between Baxter and the Purchaser shall be conditional on MOFCOM's approval of the identity of the Purchaser and the terms of the sale and purchase agreement with the Purchaser and, to the extent that it is entered into prior to such MOFCOM approvals, shall allow for modification of its terms (including the scope of the Divestment Business) as may be required by MOFCOM. When Baxter has reached such an agreement with a potential purchaser, it shall submit the agreement to MOFCOM. 17. Baxter must be able to demonstrate to MOFCOM and MOFCOM shall verify that the Purchaser meets the Purchaser Requirements and that the Divestment Business is being sold in a manner consistent with the Conditions. MOFCOM may approve the sale of the Divestment Business without one or more assets or parts of the Personnel, if this does not affect the viability and competitiveness of the Divestment Business after the sale, taking account of the proposed purchaser.

第五章 在中国境内终止尼普洛代工生产协议的承诺	Section E Commitment to Terminate the Nipro OEM Agreement with Respect to China
18. 百特承诺在终止日之前，在中国境内全面终止尼普洛代工生产协议（"尼普洛承诺"），但需要满足现有的客户合同或其它法律或法规项下之供应义务除外。 就该尼普洛承诺而言： 1) "现有的客户合同"指的是在商务部决定公布时已经存在的①百特与百特的第三方经销商之间的，②以及该等第三方经销商与医院客户之间的，关于供应百特血透透析器的合同；并且 2) "法律或法规项下的供应义务"指依据中国法律法规，省级或市级招标的中标方按照中标价供应具体产品的法律义务。 19. 为避免疑义，在终止日后，百特将终止从尼普洛购买用于在中国销售的血透透析器，但需要满足现有的客户合同或其它法律或法规项下之供应义务除外。但是，该承诺并不禁止百特： 1) 继续从尼普洛或其关联方接收，在终止日之前百特根据尼普洛代工生产协议已向尼普洛下订单订购的用于在中国销售的尼普洛产品，直至该订单得以履行，订单应在终止日后尽快履行完毕；及 2) 在中国继续销售在该尼普洛承诺范围内获得的产品，该产品应在终止日后尽快销售完毕。 20. 任何百特在2016年3月之后对尼普洛代工生产协议进行的更新，或未来与尼普洛或其关联方签订的血透透析器供应协议，会明确将中国境内市场排除在该协议的适用范围之外。	18. Baxter commits to entirely terminate the Nipro OEM Agreement with Respect to China no later than the Termination Date (the "Nipro Commitment"), except as needed to satisfy Existing Customer Contracts or other Legal or Regulatory Supply Obligations. For the purposes of this Nipro Commitment: 1) "Existing Customer Contracts" means contracts in China existing at the time of the MOFCOM Decision and that are between (a) Baxter and third party distributors and (b) those third party distributors and hospital customers for the supply of Baxter HD dialyzers; and 2) "Legal or Regulatory Supply Obligations" mean the legal obligation under PRC laws and regulations to supply the specific products at the bidding price by the winning bidders at provincial or city level tenders. 19. For avoidance of doubt, after the Termination Date, Baxter will cease purchasing from Nipro for sale in China any dialyzers used for hemodialysis, except as required to satisfy Existing Customer Contracts or other Legal or Regulatory Supply Obligations. However, this commitment does not prohibit Baxter from: 1) continuing to receive from Nipro or its affiliates deliveries of Nipro products under the Nipro OEM Agreement intended for sale in China for which Baxter placed orders

(Continued)

第五章 在中国境内终止尼普洛代工生产协议的承诺	Section E Commitment to Terminate the Nipro OEM Agreement with Respect to China
	with Nipro pursuant to the Nipro OEM Agreement and before the Termination Date, until its orders are fulfilled (such orders shall be fulfilled as soon as possible after the Termination Date); and 2) continuing to sell in China products obtained within the scope of this Nipro Commitment (such products shall be all sold as soon as possible after the Termination Date). 20. Any renewal by Baxter of the Nipro OEM Agreement beyond March 2016 or future agreement with Nipro or its affiliates for the supply of HD dialyzers specifically will exclude the market in China from its territorial scope.
第六章 受托人	**Section F Trustee**
21. 百特应委任一名监督受托人对条件的实施情况进行监督。如果百特在首个剥离期结束前一个月仍未能签订买卖协议，或者届时如果商务部否决了百特提议的所有潜在买方，百特应委任一名剥离受托人履行条件中规定的剥离受托人职责。剥离受托人的委任应在受托人剥离期开始时生效。 22. 受托人应独立于双方，具备必要的资质履行其委托协议，例如投资银行、顾问或者审计师，且当时不存在以后也不会有利益冲突。受托人由百特支付薪酬，该支付不应妨碍受托人独立和有效地履行其委托协议。	21. Baxter shall appoint a Monitoring Trustee to supervise the implementation of the Conditions. If Baxter has not entered into a sale and purchase agreement one month before the end of the First Divestiture Period or if MOFCOM has rejected all potential purchasers proposed by Baxter up to then, Baxter shall appoint a Divestiture Trustee to carry out the functions specified in the Conditions for a Divestiture Trustee. The appointment of the Divestiture Trustee shall take effect upon the commencement of the Trustee Divestment Period. 22. The Trustee shall be independent of the Parties, possess the necessary qualifications to carry out its mandate, for example as an investment bank or consultant

	or auditor, and shall neither have nor become exposed to a conflict of interest. The Trustee shall be remunerated by Baxter in a way that does not impede the independent and effective fulfillment of its mandate.
第七章 条件的复审/终止	**Section G The Review Clause**
23. 经百特请求并出示合理理由，并且监督受托人提供报告后，商务部可以在适当情况下： (1) 同意延长条件中预定的时限，或 (2) 在特殊情况下，豁免、变更或替换条件中的一项或多项承诺。 24. 如百特请求延长某时限，应至少在该时限届满前一个月向商务部提出请求，并出示合理理由。只有在特殊情况下，百特才有权在任何时限的最后一个月内提出延期请求。	23. MOFCOM may, where appropriate, in response to a request from Baxter showing good cause and accompanied by a report from the Monitoring Trustee: 1) grant an extension of the time periods foreseen in the Conditions, or 2) waive, modify, or substitute, in exceptional circumstances, one or more of the undertakings in these Conditions. 24. Where Baxter seeks an extension of a time period, it shall submit a request to MOFCOM no later than one month before the expiry of that period, showing good cause. Only in exceptional circumstances shall Baxter be entitled to request an extension within the last month of any period.
第八章 条件的实施	**Section H Implementation of the Conditions**
25. 委任监督委托人 百特应委任一名或多名独立的监督委托人。委任监督委托人的程序和条款已在《关于实施经营者集中资产或业务剥离的暂行规定》和本救济方案中列明。监督委托人应负责监督百特遵守条件的情况。 26. 剥离承诺 监督委托人应在其接受委任之日起三十个工作日内，向商务部提交一份详细的工作计划，说明其将如何监督百特遵守条件的要求。	25. Appointment of the Monitoring Trustee Baxter shall appoint one or more independent Monitoring Trustees. The procedure and terms for the appointment of the Monitoring Trustees are set out in the Interim Provisions on Asset or Business Divesture during the Implementation of Concentrations of Undertakings and this Remedy Proposal. The Monitoring Trustee shall be responsible for supervising Baxter's compliance with the Conditions.

(Continued)

第八章 条件的实施	Section H Implementation of the Conditions
工作方案的准确范围和具体条款应经商务部审查批准后执行。	26. Divestiture commitments The Monitoring Trustee shall, within 30 business days after it accepts the appointment, submit to MOFCOM a detailed work plan, describing how it intends to carry out the supervision of Baxter's compliance with the Conditions. The exact scope and specific terms of the work plan shall be implemented after review and approval by MOFCOM.